THE NATIONAL SERVICE SAILOR

THE NATIONAL SERVICE

SAILOR

by

Peter M. Cobbold

Quentin Books Ltd
Wivenhoe, Essex
1993

First published in 1993 by
Quentin Books Limited
10 Brook Street, Wivenhoe,
Essex CO7 9DS

Design, Layout and Typesetting
S. J. Newman, Ipswich, Suffolk

Printed in Great Britain by
BPCC Wheatons Ltd, Exeter

ISBN 0-947614-03-6

With acknowledgement and sincere appreciation
to all those who encouraged me in the
writing of this book.

To Sid Newman who proof-read and desk top edited
the work in a way that I would never have been able.

To Deborah Povey for the Publishers
who read it, re-read it and in spite of
having no previous knowledge of the Navy,
patiently picked her way through the intricacies
of naval jargon to produce a truly satisfying finished product.

To the kind young lady in the
Colchester Library who so skilfully assisted
my first attempts at researching data from the archives.

To the many old sailors who wrote to me during my
abortive attempt to discover the whereabouts of
the *Scharnhorst*'s port nameplate, mentioned
between these pages,
and finally to the Royal Navy,
without whom there would have been
no story!

Peter M. Cobbold

CONTENTS

CONTENTS (contd)

CONTENTS (contd)

Chapter

PREFACE

This is a book about the national serviceman's place in the Royal Navy of the middle 1950s.

At this time, the Navy had seen almost ten years of relative peace except where the odd local war had flared up, such as Korea. The Service had come through the Second World War as a tight invincible unit, albeit with a shortage of men and ships. It had not faltered in its traditional role as Britain's principle line of defence.

During the war years, the Navy had been bolstered with men conscripted by Act of Parliament and every ship, shore establishment and unit had a large contingent of H.O. (Hostilities Only) men. When hostilities finally ceased, the majority of those trained, efficient officers and men needed to be returned to industry and to their wives and families. The Services would have faced a severe manpower shortage, since the work of the Navy, Army and Air Force stretched over many continents and occupied territories, thus the H.O. men needed to be replaced by an alternative manpower supply. This need was fulfilled by the introduction of the newly-titled "national serviceman", called up for service under the National Service Acts of 1948 - 1950, and supplemented with the normal intake of career volunteers.

The Act itself dictated that all young men reaching the age of eighteen, were to present themselves for medical examination and if passed fit, were to serve a minimum of two years (or more if circumstances demanded) in the service of the Crown in the Armed Forces. Often, because "circumstances demanded", many persons served in excess of this period but two years was the criterium set, and the majority did serve just two years.

The training of a rating in the Royal Navy was very expensive and at the end of the day the national serviceman completed his two-year forced engagement and left. Under the terms of the Act, he then served another five years on the emergency reserves, where he may or may not be called upon to return to the Service in moments of need. In reality, few were ever called to put on the uniform again.

Accordingly, the Navy held her national servicemen for too short a period to justify any great investment, and my opinion was that she tended to train them to such a standard that they were unlikely to fall overboard and could be expected not to hamper proceedings too much! Greater emphasis seemed to be placed upon the need to teach a sailor to paint a ship, to assist in its management at sea to a small degree and to ensure that he at least dressed and drilled like a member of the Royal Navy. There were few courses where the national serviceman could learn the fighting skills of his counterpart, the regular enlisted man, and it was only individual ships and some establishments that took any real effort to further educate their intake quota in the art of technical warfare afloat. Accordingly, few national servicemen were persuaded by their two-years experience to consider further engagement.

The Armed Forces of the 1950s, therefore, were manned by a mixture of new career recruits, national servicemen and ex-Second World War veterans. However, in the conflicts that did flare up, such as Korea, Malaya and Kenya, the national serviceman played an equal part alongside the regular serviceman and under those circumstances, was fully trained and equipped for the part. We need to remember, that since the end of the Second World War, a new "cold war" had raged with the Russian bear and Britain was an integral part of NATO's first line of defence. Therefore, each of the Services had needed to stand at a high pitch of readiness.

By 1955 however, staffing levels had recovered from the necessities of the early post-war days and even allowing for current requirements to contain the threat from the east, we were approaching a situation in the Royal Navy, of too many outmoded ships and an excess of men, and the need for the national service intake was beginning to fade.

They became I suspect, a bit of an encumbrance to the Service at the prevailing stage of naval development and the national serviceman was to be the logical dogsbody for the ship and shore establishments. Accordingly he marched up and down, guarding the cook-house coal or picking up leaves from the parade ground as part of the barrack guard, or endured life at sea as a basic seaman until the day came for release. In so doing, he gave away perhaps two of the most formative years of his life and apparently had little to show for it.

National service was already a dying dinosaur and many clapped their hands when the final intake went in in 1959 and the Act was repealed in 1963. It had been in operation for just ten or eleven years and only young men born between the years 1930 and 1939 actually became subject to it. There was no such system for females and they were never called under the National Service Acts.

Traditionally, the Royal Navy of the past "recruited" her crews in times of trouble by the use of the notorious pressgangs and many a national service sailor regarded his enforced two year service as being just a legal extension of the same principle. It rankled to be drawn out of your settled way of life, merely to comply with a law designed to augment a shortage caused by a war which was now becoming more distant with every passing day. I know from first-hand experience that had there been another war in the making, our attitudes would have been entirely more enthusiastic. I shared the often expressed view among my fellow national servicemen, that the Navy ought to have attended to her staffing levels in more constructive ways than by relying on part-timers. The life of a sailor should, and indeed could, have been made much more attractive to the labour force ashore and then there would have been no need for "us" to have been there.

Being hauled into any of the Services as a national serviceman was a rather traumatic experience. One moment a person was enjoying the freedom and sweetness of the carefree world of 1955; these were the early days of rock and roll, the milkbars, the cinema... it was the time that a young man was just finding out about girls! Suddenly, he was hauled into the Army, Navy, or Air Force by Act of Parliament and would then spend the next two years doing a job for which he was barely trained and which would be of little use to him when he had completed his "time" unless he was lucky enough to secure a trade-related task akin to his civilian job.

But although I blandly say that "we apparently had little to show for it", the truth is that in reality, we had. We became temporary members of a select "club" which is the Royal Navy; even today to meet a man wearing the distinctive Navy tie, tells you some basic truths about him without a word being spoken. We saw a bit of the world, we matured into more responsible adults, and our very mode of life taught us to cook and sew, to endure and to be adaptable and resilient. We learned discipline and tolerance for our fellow man. Eighteen men aboard a destroyer, occupying a space twenty-four feet by nine must learn to adapt, as there is no alternative!

I have told it as I found it, the good times and the bad, the hard times and the easy ones and I have aimed for as high a standard of accuracy as possible, given the fact that most of what I relate is drawn from memory and from the diaries that I kept at the time. I have not deliberately tried to be sensational and I hope that it will prove a true reflection of the times and bring back the nostalgic past to many an ex-national service sailor.

This story of what happened to a national serviceman during his two years in the Service cannot be said to be anything unique because it happened to us all and, in effect, I am writing it for us all. I shall mention actual characters by name, except where I think that they might feel embarrassed by my so doing.

For many young men of those far-off days, it was their first excursion out into the real world, their first time away from home and from the influences of their parents. They were pitched into an all male society. I often equated it to playing rugby for the first time... sweaty feet, a team effort, booze, swearing and fags.

All servicemen remember the day that they came out. That wonderful moment when you passed through the gate and boarded the train for home, the final quiet moment when you took off the uniform in the silence of your bedroom and became a civilian again. At the end of the day, although most of it was a waste of time and a very disruptive influence to our careers and working lives, I cannot help but come to the conclusion that it was a time of tremendous character-building and a period in one's life never to be forgotten.

Some it made,
some it failed to impress,
and a few it broke.

CHAPTER
ONE

I was born in the new wing of the Ilford Maternity Hospital at Newbury Park, on the morning of the 27th March 1937. It was Easter Saturday and a bright, cold spring morning. Doctors looked at me and shook their heads. I had jaundice, an obstruction to the liver and a heart defect and was transferred a few days later to the Queen Alexandra Hospital in London's East End for more specialised care. I was christened in the hospital and mother went home without me.

The importance of blood groupings had only just been discovered and after a blood transfusion I began to join the human race. The jaundice went, the liver began to function normally, the heart steadily improved and I went home to Sunnyside Road, Ilford.

Shortly afterwards, Adolf Hitler declared war on the rest of the world and we started six years of privation, fear and disruption.

The war proved to be a very nomadic time for our family. We were bombed out twice and moved into requisitioned property, after living with one of my father's aunts in Odessa Road, Leytonstone. We eventually moved to Marlands Road, in the Clayhall area of Ilford and it was only there that life became in any way what one may consider as being normal.

I started school at Clayhall Infants but after about a year, the evacuation scheme for our area was implemented and children between the ages of five and fifteen were taken from home and billeted with volunteers living in areas away from principle target areas for Hitler's bombs. Together with my elder sister Shirley and younger brother Terry, I boarded a bus for Kings Cross and we were taken north by train to Bradford. I remember that our first night was spent in Bradford Town Hall. We slept on palliasses on the main floor of the hall and looked up to see the ornate minstrel gallery above us. We boys must have presented pathetic sights in our large short trousers, navy-blue raincoats and with our gasmasks slung in cardboard boxes over our shoulders. My sister looked particularly forlorn, in a straight, plain dress and with her hair in bunches. We clung together, but the WVS ladies were very kind and reassuring and we were billeted in three separate homes within a mile or so of each other at Lightcliff near Halifax, comforted in the knowledge that at least we were just up the road from each other.

1

All over war-torn Europe, other children were on the move but many poor souls had more sinister destinations.

After about a year at the house in Lightcliff with the Greenwood family, I was re-billeted with Mr and Mrs Tom Mason in their house "Sunnyvale" on the outskirts of Brighouse. Although I was then some miles from my brother and sister, this time was a very happy one for me. I wonder if the people of today can appreciate the spirit and kindness of the vast majority of those wonderful people who took in us evacuees, with all the miseries of our homesickness and the difficulties of feeding and clothing us in those days of strict rationing and austerity. I think each should have been issued a medal for their service to their country in those awful times.

Eventually, the tide of the war turned. Hitler's bombers no longer came to pay an evening visit to the citizens of London, our troops gained a foothold in France and the great push into the Reich began. The end of the war was clearly in sight and we evacuees were recalled to our parents.

I must admit to leaving my new life in Yorkshire very reluctantly but in early 1945, I arrived home to the bomb-sites and the smoke and grime of the City of London. The London bus took us to a school in Barkingside and I clearly remember the walk home with our mother, whom we were convinced had a heavy head-cold and a very strange accent. We ex-evacuees spoke broad Yorkshire!

I remember VE night and the parties in the street and the speeches on the radio and the need, no longer, to "put that bloomin' light out!" And then there was VJ night and eventually, the return of an uncle from a Japanese POW camp. The worst was past but there were hard days ahead and the world would not be the same again. We were at the start of an uneasy peace.

My father bought me a cycle for Christmas 1947 and I became a cycling addict. I lived for the opportunity to go out on my bike and after completing mother's shopping on a Saturday, I would disappear into the countryside around northeast Ilford where we lived, often getting home just as it became dusk and getting a bash on the ear for being out so long!

I became a pupil of Gearies Secondary Modern School at Gants Hill, Ilford and I served with no particular distinction, although I firmly established myself at the top of the class in English, History and Geography. I will not mention my mathematic results!

Our family moved home once more and we went to live in Hainault, in a large council house in Tudor Crescent, halfway up the hill to Chigwell. I eventually left school at Easter 1953. A friend of the family arranged a job for me as an office boy with a firm of solicitors in Arundel Street, just off the Strand in London. I ran messages, licked stamps, did general office duties and rather contented myself with going into the office on five and a half days a week, for the princely sum of £3 2s 6d and getting as fit as possible doing as much biking as I could. In any case, no-one took you seriously before your term of national service and there was an air of just filling in time until that period was over.

Nevertheless, I did not last very long in my first job. I was sent to the Post Office for a supply of stamps and National Insurance stamps on one occasion and on my way back to the office, I saw a collection of people peering over the embankment into the river. When I joined them, I found that they were watching the efforts of the river police to recover the badly decomposed body of a middle-aged gentleman from the dark waters of the Thames. Such an event was too much for a curious lad as I, and the time ticked by until the recovery was completed with the use of a net and the patrol boat made off in the direction of Westminster pier with its sad catch.

As it was then my lunch hour, I wandered about the Inns of Court and finally returned to the office, some two hours after leaving, to be summoned to the office of the senior partner. He listened to my tale of "The Body in the River" with lessening interest and then gave me a lecture about attention to duty. Just when I thought that I had escaped with a caution, he concluded with the instruction to go and see the wages clerk where I would find my cards and wages awaiting me. I was not impressed and felt very sad at being so treated, however, the friend of the family arranged an interview at the Law Society where there was a vacancy for a junior Audit Clerk. I went for the interview although I had not the slightest idea what an Audit Clerk was, and I was surprised to hear that I had got the job and could start on the following Monday at 9.45 at £3 7s 6d per week!

Auditing, I quickly discovered, was the persistent checking of figures! There were no adding machines or calculators in those days and all such figure-work had to be done in one's head. Figures were my one absolute and utter horror in life; I did not like them nor understand them and so I attended the job for some weeks, hoping that no-one would ask me to add anything up. Eventually they did and my deficiencies became abundantly clear.

The office was run by an ex-Royal Air Force gentleman who had seen service in India and Ceylon. Most of the office staff were ex-servicemen from one branch of the Forces or another and I would listen to their horrific war stories with great fascination. They were a friendly, helpful bunch and I know that I must have strained their tolerance and patience to breaking point at times.

The office manager found some old Law Society ledgers from the mid-nineteenth century, blanked out the totals and set me to recast them and

3

crosscast them to agree and I did this heartbreaking task with their.encouragement, for several months, until I could add up and figures became a familiar part of my working life. The Law Society did however, have one of the early Power-Samas accounting machines and most of our day was spent poring over the reams of paper that spewed from it.

I made friends with another Peter in the office, and through him joined the Comet Cycling Club based in Walthamstow and became very interested in road racing and club runs. I cycled to the City and back each day and two evenings a week would go on a training ride, usually in a thirty-mile loop. Weekends would be spent racing or on club runs.

One afternoon, in the early part of March 1955, I chanced to meet a girl. I had been out on one of my training rides and was climbing the hill on Clayhall Avenue, when my eye fell on a pretty sixteen year-old on her way home from the shops. I was not at all adverse to female company although I favoured that of the cycling fraternity as a rule, but Pat was really an exception and I chatted her up in the street.

I walked her home, although I think she was a little embarrassed by my cycling rig of shorts, little ankle socks and cycling shoes whose steel pedal plates clicked loudly on the pavement as we walked, but I arranged to take her to the pictures that evening and thus began what was to be the start of a quite serious relationship. Even though she did not even possess a bike, we fell deeply in love as only teenage sweethearts can.

Pat's father was an ex-Royal Marine. With national service looming ever nearer, I was interested in his tales of Service life, and besides, theirs was a very happy close-knit family, and their hospitality was warm and trusting.

I gave up two evenings per week to go courting Pat when I ought to have been doing my usual thirty-mile evening training "bash" around the lanes of Ongar, Epping and Brentwood. However, the first racing results of the year compared well with the previous year and in any case, I knew that I would be unlikely to complete a full racing calendar for 1955 because of national service. My first ride of 1955 was a 25-mile time trial in which I returned a presentable 1 hr 6 mins. On a previous occasion I had timed myself on the same course, with an ordinary road machine at 1 hr 4 mins and 6 seconds but somehow I had not been able to "get going" in this race, perhaps due to a late night out at the State cinema at Barkingside where Pat and I stayed as firmly glued together as decency would allow in the back row of the stalls! There was a tendency in those days to "burn the candle at both ends" because the shadow of national service hung over everything one did. Often I felt that it was not worth giving my all to the matter in hand as it really did not matter at the end of the day, an attitude that prevailed and deepened as the spring drew on to a few brief glimpses of the summer to come.

That March saw my eighteenth birthday. I cycled home from work one cold April evening, arriving home at about seven o'clock. I put the bike to bed in the garage and hung up my cape up to dry, together with my cycling shoes. A cooked tea was almost ready. Mother turned from the oven and nodded her head in the direction of the mantlepiece.

"There's a letter for you", she said.

Behind the large walnut and brass clock, leaned a large buff envelope bearing the words "On Her Majesty's Service".

In my heart I knew that it was not just another silly tax form. It was slightly larger and heavier. I opened it on the kitchen table, sitting opposite my nosey younger brother who was pretending to do his homework by reading the questions out loud, hoping that we more knowledgeable ones would call out the answers for him.

As I slit the envelope open, out tumbled a pile of buff-coloured forms, the forms that the chaps in the office kept making reference to. They were from the War Office, instructing me that under the National Service Acts, 1948 - 1950, I was instructed to present my body for inspection by a medical board to determine my eligibility for service in the Armed Forces. Form N.S.6 told me that I had to report to the Board's centre, situated in temporary accommodation on the bombsite to the rear of the George Hotel at Wanstead, on Friday, 15th April.

My heart sank.

I knew that I had to comply since it was a criminal offence not to, and there were few ways of escaping the clutches of the Board. If one were engaged in full-time study at a University or Technical College, one could claim a deferment period until the age of twenty-six, but the moment the conditions of such a deferment were breached, either by ceasing your studies or changing your employment, the "system" would call you in for a medical and you could be drafted into one of the Services. The only other way out was to be found medically unfit but even then, one needed to be in a sorry medical condition to avoid falling into even the lowest group of categories, which ranged down through the alphabet as far as D4! It was no good inventing poor health. There was an efficient cross-check with your doctor's medical records.

The die was cast and I determined to make the best of a bad job. I was given the day off to attend the medical. My office colleagues regaled me with all sorts of foolish advice on how to avoid conscription and many an afternoon was wasted at the Law Society with their tales of people they had known, or had read about, that had escaped the Board's clutches by some devious means or other. It was all highly amusing but of little practical assistance for the moment.

I took the underground from Hainault to Wanstead, crossed the road to the George Hotel and entered the door of the TA Centre, Section B, Medical Department at the appointed time. I was met by an Army Sergeant who ticked my name off a list and directed me to a waiting area consisting of rows of wooden school-type chairs.

Looking about me at the sea of strangers, some smoking in spite of the "No Smoking" signs, some reading the Daily Mirror or the Daily Sketch, I was relieved to see the familiar faces of ex-schoolmates. I was not alone. But I stayed where I was and avoided the smoke from my immediate neighbour's Woodbine.

Suddenly, the Sergeant put on his beret and consulted his wristwatch, "Right," he said. "Sit up straight, put them fags out and keep quiet."

Once this had been done he came to attention, banged his right boot to the wooden floor and crashed off in the direction of a door stencilled "M.O. Private". Here he halted, with another boot-crashing jolt sufficient to rattle the teeth of the occupants of the front row, knocked and went in, leaving the door wide open. I could not see what went on in the office but the noise of his big boots was spine-chilling. "Please, dear Lord," I silently prayed, "don't let me go in the Army!"

The Sergeant returned with further footware symphonics, followed by an officer, a single crown on his shoulder-straps indicating that he was a Major. He carried a short brown leather-bound stick. What did he do with that?, I wondered. I was not enjoying myself. April rain slashed against the windows and drummed noisily on the felted roof.

"Settle down, chaps," said the Major, by way of an opening gambit. Now that the boots had finished beating a tattoo on our brains, we relaxed. The officer began by explaining a bit about the National Service Acts and how we were required by Act of Parliament to present our "corpses delecti" for medical examination and grading. At the use of the word "grading" someone chipped in with "Do you mean like with eggs?" which raised a tense giggle from us, no reaction from the Major but caused the Sergeant's moustache to ripple from left to right. However, the latter merely put his forefinger to his lips in a silent "Sch!"

We were issued with a sheaf of forms to complete, pens and ink were supplied and the next half-hour was taken up in scratching marks on the paper, crossing-out, and sucking the end of the wooden pens. Finally the forms were collected up, but not before the Sergeant had assisted a few slow ones to complete their blot-covered papers.

The real business of the day then began. In alphabetical order we filed along a corridor, visiting a doctor in each of the small cubicles to left and right along the way.

Eyes, ears, nose and throat, chest and abdomen were examined, sounded and pummelled. We were measured and weighed. Feet and legs, arms, hands and fingers were pulled and pushed. The long-dreaded "cough test" was executed. At no time was any remark made by our medical inspectors and we came out at the end of the corridor, passed our specimen flasks to a chap in a white coat, quietly dressed and resumed our seats in the hall.

It wasn't too bad we all agreed, and it had stopped raining. A watery sun shone on a small buddleia bush and the early buds drank in the energy. With luck, I could be out and home by two-thirty and out for a ride on the bike before calling round Pat's in the evening, as I had promised, to tell her how I had got on. But that was not the end of the proceedings. Out came the Sergeant, the Major and another officer with two "pips" on each shoulder.

"Happy to tell you that you are all still alive, chaps!" quipped this Lieutenant. "Now we need to know if your brain works as well as your bodies!"

More sheets of paper were produced and we were put through a sort of mini-exam, consisting of simple intelligence tests and puzzles. Several candidates proved incapable of reading or understanding the questions, let alone writing much of an answer. The three Army men were kept busy whispering advice and keeping a wary eye out for exam cheats.

At one o'clock, we stopped for lunch and were told to return at two-thirty for an interview and our results. Most of the lads, unlit cigarettes at the ready, streamed out of the hut door into the sunlight and turned right towards the smoky Public Bar of the George. I spoke briefly with an ex-school chum, then went for a sobering walk along the Eastern Avenue and stood on the bridge over the river Roding, watching the shallow waters gurgling over concrete blocks thrown into the stream by two small boys. A tepid damp breeze, bearing a promise of finer weather, blew easily from the west and I felt there were better ways of spending my time than horsing about like this. I thought about Pat, we were soon to be parted. Would our love survive in spite of the separation?

Lying in my arms and gazing doe-eyed up at me, she had said that she would wait for ever. So said I, but deep down I knew that two years was a long time in a young life and I felt it was best to live for the moment and see what the future brought. There were lots of girls in the world and foolishly confining yourself to one, lovely as she was, was not a very sensible idea but then, there is little practicality in young love. I resolved to keep in touch as long as I could. There were hard times ahead and I may find comfort in a letter from a loved one. Then again, the relationship could become an encumbrance and I should have to deal with that situation as it arose.

I returned to the TA Centre for Round Two. Our names were called out and one by one, we entered a small office where we were directed to a seat before a table manned by the Major and the Lieutenant. A round pink-faced lady in Army uniform turned over the leaves of a notebook and wrote my name at the head of a fresh page. There followed what I consider a quite amazing interview. The Major led the field.

"Cobbold, isn't it?" he asked.

"Yes sir," I answered.

The stick rapped the palms of the left hand.

"Yer did awfully well in the old intelligence test, yerhs, awfully well. Got any exam results from school or going to night school, what?"

"Yes sir," I replied, "I'm at the Ilford County High night classes in book-keeping and first year German."

"So I see, first class, first class, top-hole," he muttered, turning over the pages of my form which he was obviously reading for the first time. He reminded me of Terry Thomas.

"What's your sport, old boy? I see you're very fit." He rocked back in his chair and poked my form with his stick.

"I'm very keen on cycling and I enjoy swimming, sir." I replied.

"D'yer play football or rugby?" he queried.

"No, sir," I said. Then came a question that I was not expecting.

"Which Service are you applying for Cobbold?" I did not know.

I never suspected one could have any sort of choice in the matter. I thought that the object of the exercise was to hijack us into whichever Service had the most vacancies.

I hesitated, long enough for the Army lady to peer quizzically over the rim of her glasses.

Suddenly I thought of my mother's cousin who had served in the Royal Navy and had risen to the rank of Lieutenant Commander in the early days of the Fleet Air Arm. I found myself saying: "Royal Navy, sir please!"

The two spoke as one.

"Can't be done, old boy!"

"No can do!"

"Never get in!"

The Army lady scratched something out on her pad.

"Second choice?" asked the Major. I did not say what I suspect he wanted to hear. "Royal Air Force, sir," I answered.

He lost interest immediately. He was obviously in the business of recruiting soldiers. I must have been a great disappointment to him and scruffing over my form, he started reading the next. However, the Lieutenant, before passing me on to the Sergeant lamely enquired if I had anyone serving in the Navy at the present. I told him no, but my mother's cousin had been a Lieutenant Commander in the Fleet Air Arm. The Major did not look up from the next victim's form and the Lieutenant merely said, "Really!" I was led out to await further developments in the waiting room.

I tried holding a conversation with a lad from Ilford, whose every other word was an expletive. I finally gave up and resorted to reading the various recruiting posters and TA advertising paraphernalia pinned up about the room until, at long last, the final interviewees trickled back and the Army again took over the stage. The Major, hands clasped behind his back and small brown stick jammed under his left armpit, waggled his neck within his khaki collar.

"Pleased to tell you that you have all passed your medicals at one grade or other, all fit and well. Some of you are colour blind, nothing to worry about... problems with your feet, Harris," indicating a tubby lad in overalls at the back.

"But you are all fine healthy specimens and fully acceptable into service with HM Forces. Well done!"

As if we had anything to do with it! One lad I had noticed, had an awful raspy cough which didn't sound right to me. Even he looked amazed at the result of his medical.

"Well done," said the Major again. "Carry on Mr Phipps," and he retired to the office marked "Private", accompanied by the noise and vibrations of the Sergeant's and Mr Phipps' footwear as they saluted.

Lt. Phipps came forward with a sheaf of papers. The fading sun glinted briefly on his shoulder pips. He cleared his throat to catch our attention.

"The Service to which you will be seconded has been decided as a result of your medical and your aptitude tests," he said. "The following will go into the Royal Navy... Cobbold, P.M. and Knight, A.J."

I could not believe it! So there were places to be had! Even so, I had counted fifty-two candidates attending the medical and only two went to the Navy!

He reeled off a list of names of those going to the Air Force, each person either groaning or grinning broadly as his name was called, and then completed the list with those going to the Army.

Finally he said "You will hear from the War Department when you will be required to report to your units and your travelling expenses for today will be posted on to you."

With a final "Well done" he handed us over to the Sergeant, who said his little bit and ushered us out to a wet, darkening street. It was just after four-thirty and I was to become a sailor.

The Fourth of July dawned and I arose shortly afterwards. What was Independence Day for some had the opposite connotations for me and the other thirty-one young men also in receipt of call-up papers and destined to be part of a New Entry Division for that fateful Tuesday. Fresh from a hot bath and with my last civilian breakfast inside me, I took leave of my bike in the garden shed. How long, I wondered, would it be before I next sprinted up the road in the carefree manner to which I had grown accustomed. I had sais goodbye to Pat in the hallway of her home the night before. When would we next meet?

My suitcase was packed with a few final items, in accordance with the list provided. Basically, one was allowed to bring a raincoat, suit or sports clothes and two changes of shirts and underwear. It did not look much. My office colleagues had had a whip-round and presented me with a travelling bag containing shoe-cleaning equipment and a silver monogrammed hairbrush and comb kit, which I still have today. I was assured that the comb would receive little use as the first thing one parted with, to the naval barber, was one's hair. I dreaded that.

In reality, I had resigned myself to the inevitable and was beginning to be quite proud of the fact that I had been accepted into the Senior Service. At least I would not be spending the next two years marching up and down with a heavy pack on my back and wearing a rough khaki battledress, or else scratching about an airfield, dressed in blue. The naval uniform had a certain air about it... not that I knew anything about the Royal Navy or its history or traditions. My knowledge was confined to having seen *The Cruel Sea* twice and hearing tales of the cousin on my mother's side, the famous Lieutenant Commander, and his life aboard the First World War cruiser *HMS Cumberland*.

Father shook hands, wished me luck and was off to work just before eight o'clock. My two younger brothers, after giving me a good teasing and promising to ride the tyres off my prized bike in my absence, also set out on their daily tasks, one to work and the other to school. Shortly before nine, I drank a final cup of tea and collecting my gear about me, made for the door with a lump in my throat. Then mother started blubbing and that set me off! I had so resolved to go out like a man!

I was only too pleased that there was no-one to see. We dried our eyes at the door "in case the neighbours are looking" as mother put it, and after a final check that I had travel warrant, money, raincoat and suitcase, we walked to the front gate. With a final choked goodbye, I strode purposefully off down the hill, glad when I turned the bend and mother was lost from sight. It only took ten minutes to walk to Hainault tube station, past all the familiar sights and sounds that I knew so well. I finally slumped down in a seat of the Central Line train and the adventure had begun.

The journey to Portsmouth was pretty uneventful. Burdened as I was with suitcase and raincoat, it could hardly be called a pleasure. The luggage essential as it was, was an absolute hindrance. I longed to hurl it from the train window but I had to hang on to it and tolerate its weight and the way it twisted about my legs and got in my way whenever I had need to show my travel warrant, which never seemed to be in the pocket where I thought I had last put it! Eventually, the steam train drew into Portsmouth station. I got out, as did several other young men, each carrying suitcases and raincoats. However, I determined to keep these last few moments of freedom to myself and ducked into a milkbar just outside the station, drank a luke-warm cup of expresso coffee and chased a sorry-looking cheese roll about the thick white plate, until they had all passed by.

My joining instructions stated that I must report to Victoria Barracks, Southsea at 1400 hours. Since my office "military advisers" had previously explained the international clock to me, I saw that I had about half an hour before this deadline was reached and so, quitting the smells of the milkbar and following the directions of a news vendor, I strolled toward the barracks.

The main gate was manned by several sailors, smartly turned out in their blue uniforms, white caps, belts and short gaiters. A gentleman in a navy-blue suit with six gold buttons to the front of his jacket, a further three gold buttons on each sleeve and sporting a white cap with a black shiny peak and a most elaborate badge to the front, paced importantly up and down. He wore rather old-fashioned side whiskers on his ruddy weather-beaten cheeks and he fiddled endlessly with a large silver chain, hanging across the front of his jacket.

This entourage stared curiously at me as I wandered past their hallowed gate, to come to a halt some fifty yards further down the street. It was not yet time to enter their domain for I was early. Punctuality was one of my strong points and so I put my heavy case against the stone wall, folded my raincoat neatly on top and sat on it, enjoying the hot sun on my face and the final precious moments of freedom.

The peace was shattered by the bewhiskered gentleman. He poked his head from the Navy side to the civvy street side.

"What are you, lad?" he roared.

11

It was the first of many thousands of similarly oblique and obscure questions to be rained on me during my time in the Service. I gave the only answer that I felt applied.

"A civilian," I said.

He looked puzzled at this and his whiskers bristled. "Hain't you a noo entry, then?" he asked.

I ignored his appalling diction. "Not yet," I answered.

He was confused, for my answers were every bit as ambiguous as his original question. But, as he felt that he had to say something since the sailors at the gate obviously expected it of him, he puffed himself up, waggled his neck inside its stiff collar somewhat after the fashion of a scratching chicken, and bellowed "Well git orf my bleeding wall then!" with which he clasped his huge hands behind his back and disappeared into the Navy side.

I moved my case six inches or so away from his "bleeding wall" and resumed my seat. The hands of my old Newark watch crept on toward the twelve and the two respectively.

A flurry of young men in gaberdine raincoats and carrying suitcases came hurrying from the direction of the nearby seafront park, stubbing out cigarettes as they came. With a deep breath, I arose and as they scampered past, I gathered up my belongings and tagged reluctantly on the end. A distant clock struck once and then again as we clattered through the black iron gates.

I was in!

CHAPTER
TWO

We lined up in front of the bewhiskered gentleman. He called us to attention and we shuffled upright. He did it again and then again, until we snapped straight at the order but it was clear that by his standards we had a long way to go. He patrolled up and down our line, lecturing us about the Navy and how lucky we were to be accepted into such a fine service, steeped as it was in a tradition of bravery and honour. He assured us that we came in boys and would, if he had aught to do with it, leave as men!

Somebody passed wind at that juncture and this induced him to bellow "Pick up...cases!" We did, but not as snappily as we ought to have, which led to further distress on his behalf and he set to, marching us up and down with the ubiquitous suitcases. The point was soon taken. We lost our giggles and were glad when, after about an hour of trying to get us into step and march together, he dismissed us to a dormitory under the control of an Able Seaman.

We were allocated a bed space and a large aluminium locker and given the time to stow our gear away. This done, we were led to the messhall where we joined a queue of uniformed sailors and ultimately took tea. Supper, we were informed, would be issued in the messhall at 1830 hours and we were left to our own devices. I had a wash and cleaned my shoes. Sitting on our beds, we introduced ourselves to our immediate neighbours. Fags were passed around and all sorts of rumours became rife.

It was all very strange and new, yet I could not feel that there would be any permanency to our incarceration in this place, and at any time I expected to see the double doors at the end of the dormitory open and a uniformed officer appear to tell us that it was all a mistake, that our services would not, after all, be required and that after supper in the huge green and white tiled messhall we could catch the next train back to London. I could have been home by ten, but of course it did not happen. We ate a very good supper and afterwards most of us filtered off to the television room or the NAAFI. I returned to the dormitory, where I was caught by the Able Seaman who got me clearing up the place for "rounds".

At nine o'clock, a very imposing gentleman preceded by a sailor blowing on a silver pipe-like object, swept through the dormitory, together with our friend with the whiskers. He muttered something about it not being good enough, to be reassured by "Whiskers" that we were new entries that very afternoon, with which he pressed on at great speed much to the relief of the Able Seaman who seemed quite upset and frightened by the whole event.

The NAAFI and television room closed at about ten o'clock and one by one, my new shipmates returned to their nests. There was a good deal of banter and some really brilliant repartee as we prepared to settle down for the night. Suddenly the Tannoy loudspeaker system crackled into life and someone played a doleful tune on a bugle. Several of our number leapt to their feet and saluted in an amateurish fashion but as the notes of the bugle echoed away around the large parade ground the lights went out, leaving several chaps stranded, trying to sort themselves out by the faint light of the two red police lamps at either end of the dormitory. A considerable amount of noise ensued, with jokes being told and tales of the various journeys to Portsmouth getting an airing as I lay in my hard bed enjoying it all.

Suddenly, the door flung wide and the lights came on, dazzling us all. It was Whiskers. Apparently, we were supposed to be asleep! If he heard another squeak out of us, he would see that we did a repeat performance of our earlier attempts at drill, only this time we would be in our pyjamas and bare feet.

We lapsed into a respectful silence but once the sound of his huge boots faded into the distant recesses of the building, the few "wags" started up with their jokes and silly noises. One by one, we dropped off the end of this strange regimented world into the realms of sleep. But just before I drifted off, I heard someone's muffled sobs from the other end of the dormitory.

I guessed that the first morning would be full of shocks and I was right. I think that I had only just got used to the squeaks and the echoing "ping" of the wire bedframe of our bunks which, with the hardness of my thin horse-hair palliasse had made sleep very difficult, when some idiot started to blow a demented bugle call over the Tannoy system. I looked at my trusty New-mark. It read six-thirty.

Suddenly the door at the end of the dormitory flung wide and silhouetted against the dawn light in the corridor was a gentleman in naval uniform. It wasn't Whiskers. In point of fact we did not see him again during our stay at the Victoria Barracks. We naturally claimed the credit for his mysterious departure.

This new gentleman was a Petty Officer, and he appeared to be unwell. First, he switched on all the lights, a thing no-one in his right mind would do at that time of the morning. He then treated us to a solid five minutes of wakey, wakey-type rhetoric, recited at the peak of his vocal range, accompanied by brutal kicks at our bedroom furniture! The object of all this was to make us get out of bed in a smart and seamanlike manner. This I did, I did not like to see an adult make such an exhibition of himself over such a trivial matter but there were the one or two who gamely tried sleeping through it all, which only served to induce our tormentor to re-double his insane efforts.

One by one, everyone got out of bed and began to wander aimlessly about, searching blearily for socks and pants and washing gear. I knew where mine were and was down the corridor towards the washroom with the first wave of sleepy bodies. No-one spoke. We merely washed, cleaned our teeth and shaved, perhaps regretting the sleep lost the evening before. Finally, rinsing round the washbasin, we handed over the position to the next in the weary queue that leaned, yawning, about the tiled wall.

I returned to the dormitory to find that one brave, idle soul was back in his bed. I got a two-finger salute for my imitation of the Petty Officer's wakey, wakey routine. I dressed and stripped my bed and reassembled it. I was combing my hair in my locker mirror when in came the Petty Officer again. He slammed the door shut, cutting off the few in the dormitory from the trickle of men returning from the washroom.

"Attention," he roared. As we did not know how to respond to that instruction, we merely shuffled upright where we stood.

"My name is Petty Officer Williams," he growled. He then continued to tell us how slow, lazy and lifeless we were and punctuated this by opening the door and admitting the latecomers from the washroom, haranguing them roundly for being "adrift". They would have to do better, he told them and he would see to that over the course of the next few weeks.

The lad in bed would have been better advised to have remained where he was and gambled on not being seen but he took the opportunity to slide out from under the sheets and drop soundlessly to the deck. This slightest movement caught the Petty Officer's eye. He had already shrieked at us to stand still and stop shuffling about like a shower of schoolgirls and he rounded on his luckless victim with venom. His imitation of Robert Newton's performance as Long John Silver in *Treasure Island* was something to behold!

As we stood to attention at the foot of our beds, he roared and snorted, simpered and stammered, crooned and raved at the offender for a full five minutes, the end result of which was that we had only ten minutes for breakfast and would be required to fall in for extra instruction at 1600 hrs.

It was a bad start to a bad day. Our hair was cut (as everyone said it would be) by the barracks' barber and we emerged from his "caboosh" with nearly bald heads and our ears sticking out. We were taught to "fall in" and to "fall out" and how to march. I quite enjoyed that for the first hour or so but then it became a bit repetitious and boring because we could not get it right first time and had to practise it again and again in the hot sun with no protective "golden locks" to ward off the heat and glare.

We were also subject to a torrent of foul language, which if it had been applied anywhere outside of this brutal establishment, would have been cause for a civil action through the Courts. Clearly, our instructor had little respect for the fact that we were young men, fresh from the more civilised conditions of our hearth and home. Their attitude to us was quite demonic at times, especially should we fail to learn a lesson quickly enough for their liking. They made no allowance for our total lack of nautical experience, glared and swore at us profusely and inflicted all kinds of summary punishments for our inefficiency.

Marching and otherwise moving about seemed to be one of the most important tasks facing a recruit in Her Majesty's Royal Navy and I wondered if my adversion to a life in khaki was proving to be justified! In spite of being quite fit from my cycle training, I was very pleased when a halt was called for dinner.

At 1330 we fell in on the parade ground expecting more of the morning's punishment but along came an officer. He was the first one we had seen and his uniform was neater and more flamboyant than that of the Chief Petty Officer or Petty Officer. He wore a single gold ring around each sleeve of his jacket and a different cap-badge. Petty Officer Williams came to attention, called us to attention, saluted the officer and announced: "New Entry Class, present and correct, sir!" We were stood at ease at the officer's instruction.

"Stand easy, men," said the officer. "I am Sub-lieutenant Taylor, your Divisional Officer." He turned out to be some sort of welcoming agent for the Royal Navy and also the officer in charge of our class, responsible for our training during our four-week stay in HMS Victory, and also for our welfare and well-being.

He gave an address of welcome and repeated the tale told by Whiskers when we had first entered the gate, that indeed we were lucky to be part of such a wonderful organisation as the Navy and that he hoped that we would respond to the highest traditions of the Service and always do our best. If we had any complaints or any requests, we were to address them to him, through the offices of Petty Officer Williams and the Officer of the Day... whoever he may have been. Without waiting to see if we had any views on the subject, he said: "Carry on, P.O.!" turned on his heels and departed. We never saw him again, other than at a distance on the Sunday morning parades.

Just to make our first day an enjoyable one to remember, we were marched off to the medical department for a full medical! Our P.O. marched us to the rear of the main barracks and into a large conservatory which ran alongside the main building. He left us in the charge of a sailor, whose badges indicated that he was a Leading Sick Berth Attendant, since he wore the traditional Red Cross insignia and a large red fouled anchor. We were lined up in twos.

"Right," said the LSBA. "Strip right off and carry your clothes over your left arm." And so we did. The Killick (the nickname given to all Leading rates in the Navy, so called because the anchor on their badge represents a fouled Killick anchor) passed among us with a clipboard taking the names of one or two of our party. He then entered a small door further along the corridor, leaving all thirty-two of us standing in our skins in the afternoon sunshine which streamed in through the glass roof.

Suddenly, a door opened in the corridor and out stepped a Wren. We had heard about them and recognised them instantly! She was greeted with lusty "Hello Darlings!" and various groans of lechery, fortified by our safety in numbers, and uttering a little feminine cry of shy horror, she sprang back into her office. Hardly had her door closed, than another flew open and out came an officer, wearing on his sleeves two gold stripes with red cloth between them.

"What the hell do you shower think you're playing at?" he thundered. We were in trouble again. We explained that we were ordered to strip and await the Medical Officer by a Leading hand. After a few moments of questions and stupid answers, this officer departed having told us to put on our pants and trousers, convinced that the Navy was recruiting more idiots every day. The general concensus was that we had encountered a "pooftah" in the personage of the LSBA, and those whose names he had taken had better watch out for themselves!

Eventually, we were called into various medical departments where we were subjected to being stethoscoped, X-rayed and thumped on our joints with rubber hammers as well as the usual "cough" test. From there we were led into a large gymnasium where we queued to receive an armful of injections. That safely took us up to a little after 1600 and we marched back to our quarters, feeling somewhat jaded. Tea did little to cheer us up but we were pleased to be at what we had imagined was the end of our first day's work... however we had forgotten all about Petty Officer Williams and the extra duty that we had so easily earned by our performance at reveille. At his insistence, we cut short our tea and joined him on the parade ground until supper at 1830. We were lucky that our punishment only lasted two hours, our Petty Officer making allowances for the fact that it was our first day in the Navy!

We sloped off for supper, which proved to be the best meal of the day, with Navy sausages, stewed fried egg, beans and sloppy tomatoes all washed down with cups of hot sticky tea which, we were assured by an old hand, "had something in it" to take away our manly thoughts and longings for the fair sex. Following this repast, most of us retired to the relative peace of our bunks via the luke-warm waters of the tiled bathroom, hoping that our poor old feet and legs would recover their strength for the onslaught of the days yet to come.

Throughout the Royal Navy there exists a tremendous esprit de corps, a fellow feeling that binds all the men into a strange sort of unity. Within an hour of we thirty-two strangers being grouped together in this foreign environment, we chatted amongst ourselves and took the first steps to becoming friends and comrades. It was this common bond which welded us as a unit and whatever happened to one, happened in spirit to us all. It is not a phenomenon peculiar to the Navy. The Army and Royal Air Force enjoy exactly the same rapport and although one tends to cling nostalgically to one's own particular Service, the number of old Soldiers', Sailors' and Airmen's Clubs, not only in Britain but throughout the world, are evidence of this vital element of Service life. I met people on that fateful Fourth of July that I have never forgotten, although I rarely see any of them. We drifted apart upon leaving the Service but a Christmas card and the odd letter keeps us in touch.

There are many more that we do not forget, yet have no idea of where they might be or what they are doing today, over thirty years later. I hope that some of them will read this book and remember the times that I relate.

One tended to have a circle of closer friends, chaps one went ashore with for a night out, chaps with whom one would discuss girlfriends and any personal matters, or one that you would swap a watch with to ensure you kept that important date with the latest heart-throb ashore. Such were my good friends Garth, George and Jim. We bedded down in the same area in the dormitory and in the first few days got to know each other very well.

Garth hailed from Sarratt, near Rickmansworth in Hertfordshire. His father was a local builder and Garth was the only child. He was the original gentle giant. Although not very tall, he was very stocky and strong and possessed an easy-going, humorous nature which was guaranteed to cheer us all up when the going got rough. He could also be very handy with his fists, and we felt safe when he was around!

George was from Dunstable and an only son. He was also the only chap with any naval knowledge whatsoever, being an ex-Leading seaman from the Luton and Dunstable Sea Cadet Corps, and was a mine of information on daily routines and bugle calls. He was a rather shy, amiable lad and I do not think that he enjoyed the limelight too much but since he was the only sailor among us at that stage, he was issued with a small red cloth badge depicting a fouled Killick anchor and made Leading hand of the mess. We were instructed to obey his commands but he only gave those that he had to, and we rebellious characters did as we were told, more out of respect for the nice chap that he was than for the authority demonstrated by the little badge.

Jim came from Northampton and was a tall facsimile of Elvis Presley. He even sang a little like his hero and bore no inhibitions about his talent. The barracks' barber may have ruined his Elvis-style coiffure but not his spirit! Our Jim was a ladies' man and was always to be found with pen and paper and a small pile of penny stamps and envelopes. I suspect that he was sorely missed in the dance halls of Northampton! Another thing that I always remember about Jim was that despite the ill-fitting uniforms with which we were eventually issued, he always managed to appear immaculate and well groomed. I am sure that his smart appearance saved him many a kit muster from the officer inspecting.

Ian from Durham had been working on the railways and his time in the Navy was like a holiday to him, or so he said.

"Three good meals a dee mon, ye canna beat it!" he would say when he heard us bemoaning our fate.

Antony Sebag-Montefiore was different again. I likened him to a brain on legs. His intellect constantly shone out as a ray of sunshine amongst our manure heap of ignorance but not so his dress and style. He always succeeded in looking as though he had just survived a bomb explosion. His were the boots first to dull over, his denim collar always slewed away from its undercollar and rode at a saucy angle, the front of his ill-fitting national service issue uniform, in trying to follow the contours of his short frame, looked for all the world as if he allowed a family of ferrets to reside there.

His family were well represented in the higher echelons of the legal profession and I suspect that "Seabag", as we swiftly dubbed him, had not really tried hard enough to avoid conscription. He once told me that he had been studying for the Bar when national service had come along but that he had seen no reason for opting out of it. I much admired him for this since we peasants, not so well connected, had had little say in the matter. He quickly became part of the team and whenever he collected a kit muster, we often clubbed together to help him lay it out and to supply the missing bits and pieces which were usually in transit to his home for washing!

There were others of course. We met on various ships and under different circumstances and they all get a mention. I hope that they will recognise themselves and smile.

So it was, that no matter what physical discomfort and misery of separation from our loved ones was inflicted upon us, we had the knowledge that we were "shipmates", all in the same boat, and that we would survive because of each other. At the end of a hard day, away from the rigours of our basic training, there was always a true friend with whom to share either a grumble or a laugh over a cigarette or a glass of sticky squash in the NAAFI. This, coupled with the knowledge that we would eventually finish our time and once again become free spirits, kept us going in those early days. The Navy gave us precious little other comfort.

The second day of service in Her Majesty's Royal Navy started as had the first, with the raucous rasp of the bugle, but before our P.O. could leap in on us, we rolled out of bed as the last notes faded. Williams was disappointed. He shot in through the doors, all ready for a right old rave at us but we had all got up! Nothing daunted, he found countless other things to complain of but at least we did not get any dog watch instruction. The P.O.'s right hand man, the skinny Able Seaman, put in an appearance upon our return from the morning washing session and organised us into "watches" and "divisions" and instructed the men comprising the watch as to when they would be on duty and what tasks they were expected to undertake. Each was responsible with his neighbour for the immediate bed spaces and for the tidiness of his locker and bedding.

We were then dispatched to breakfast. I think it is fair to say that the Admiralty did their best to feed us well and provided the raw materials for the job. We had eggs, chips, bacon and sausages in abundance, for Their Lordships knew what a gruelling time we had ahead of us in our task as new entries. There were as many cups of tea as one wanted and you were allowed to take as many slices of bread as you liked, providing that you consumed them and they did not end up in the pig-bin. But somewhere along the way, the eggs seemed to get steamed to rubber and changed in flavour to something tasting and smelling of mildew. The bacon was likewise tainted and so one learned to breakfast on chips, bread and butter, sausages and tea. Sometimes there was a bowl of cornflakes with watery milk to supplement this feast but the catering staff never conquered the problem of the eggs and bacon. Scrambled eggs were a different matter, providing one ignored the pool of oily water that they floated in!

After breakfast we would fall in outside for our day's instruction and the next break would be "Stand Easy" at 0945, after which we would fall in again. At 1140, the bugler sounded "Secure" and then, "Up Spirits!" The daily rum would then be issued to those entitled, ie those over the age of twenty.

We then attended our second meal of the day, which was dinner. Usually not a bad affair. My theory was that the catering improved as the day progressed but I wondered if the rum issue had anything to do with it. An hour or so would be given over to dinner and then it would be time to fall in on the hot concrete outside the block, where we would be quickly shaken out of any post-lunch stupor by the strident voice of Petty Officer Williams.

Tea was taken at 1615 and supper, following at 1830, was another proper cooked meal. Thank goodness that we were given an active itinerary to follow in order to burn up all those calories or we would surely have put on pounds! In all, we had very little to complain of in the organisation of the eating side of our lives.

After breakfast on our second day, however, it was back to the mess where the Able Seaman organised the cleaning up of the messdeck. The cleaning of the windows and scrubbing of the floors was done on a duty watch rota basis and each duty messman took his turn to kneel and scrub the deck, dry it off with a cloth and square the dormitory off for the daily morning rounds. Meanwhile, the non-duty parts of the watch were out playing sailors in the sunshine and the duty messmen would rejoin them at 0945, when the bugle sounded "Stand Easy". This precious quarter of an hour was spent in the NAAFI, quaffing a glass of orange squash and consuming a Wagon Wheel or a similarly sticky confection. I personally preferred their jam-doughnuts!

Jimmy Young's "Unchained Melody" would bring a lump to the throat of the love-lorn and it was often a relief to escape to the outside daily tasks. A little after 0930 on this day, however, we were marched about to the rear of the barracks to a large store bearing the single legend "Slops" in white stencilling. This turned out to be the clothing store and we were thrilled to realise that we were about to be issued with our uniforms!

Up until this stage, we were dressed in our civilian clothes which ranged from the very popular Teddy-boy suits to sports jackets and trousers or even the occasional suit. Now we were to forsake those for the uniform of a sailor and at least we could adopt the anonimity of all looking the same. It was a bit off-putting to be remembered by the P.O. as "You in that 'orrible green shirt, where the bleedin 'ell did that come from, lad?"

However, as we lined up in single file ready to go in, an LSBA hove in sight. Not the LSBA encountered on our earlier expedition I might add! He called out one of our number to report back to the medical department. Off the lad trotted, followed by our admonishments that he should "watch out for the LSBA!" and we saw him no more. He had been discharged to shore as being medically unfit, lucky blighter!

The large door of the Slops department opened and we began to file through. We started at a large counter that wound its way, snake-like, over the floor area of the store. The other side was manned by a mixture of stores ratings and Wrens. Again, we recognised the Wrens! They started issuing clothing and equipment to us, our pile of acquisitions growing larger and larger as we progressed through the store, and I began to be most anxious that I would not be able to carry it all away, and that any item I dropped would be pinched and not returned by some passing wag.

We were asked our hat size, shoe size, waist size and inside leg measurement but scarce any of us knew them. The staff therefore, just peered at us through slitted eyes, guessed the sizes and issued us what they had in stock. Finally I had progressed to the very last of the black linoleum-topped counters to a department where each man was required to draw sufficient wooden marking stencils, and these, when stamped onto an ink-pad, were assembled to spell out his name and number, for it was at this stage that the Navy started to de-personalise us all by addressing us as a number.

Mine was CJ/953009. I was put to work stencilling this number, together with my name, on every item of clothing and equipment issued to me. It was even emblazoned on the inside of the two pairs of boots given us, hammering a metal die to cut the detail into the hard leather. The stamping of our names and numbers was a very precise job. The information had to be correctly applied to certain areas of the material and to nowhere else. Our kit was laid out, following the design demonstrated on a large poster and that, we were told, was the way that it was always to be done.

The issuing of kit also opened up another possible form of torture, for we quickly discovered that we could be ordered a kit muster for any slackness or other misdemeanour and heaven help the man whose gear was deficient in any way!

I here list the items issued to us:-

Caps, black, one.
Caps, white canvas, two.
Boots, black, best, one.
Boots, black, working, one.
Socks, black, woollen, four pairs.
Uniform jacket-top, navy-blue No. 1, one.
Ditto, No. 2 working, one.
Bell bottom trousers, No. 1, one.
Bell bottom trousers, No. 2, one.
Blue jean collars, two.
Black silk kerchief, one.
No. 8 working shirts, blue, two.
No. 8 working trousers, blue, two.
Lanyard, white cord, two.

Seaman's clasp knife with spike, one.
Kitbag, one.
Marking kit, one.
Singlets, woollen, two.
Underpants, woollen, two.
Money-belt, blue canvas, one.
White shirts, blue square-edged to front, two.
Hammock and slings, one.
Hammock palliasse, horse-hair, one.
Sheets, cotton white, two.
Blankets, woollen, two.
Paybook holder, one.
Bootbrush, two.
Bathtowel, one.
Handtowels, two.
Pyjamas, two.
Handkerchief, two.
Sewing kit (housewife).

Having been issued with our uniform and kit, a whole two-hour period was given over to instructing us how to wear it. This period also highlighted any items of kit which did not fit and most of us doubled over to the Slops department to change items too large or too small. P.O. Williams and the Able Seaman bustled amongst us, assisting our attempts to dress for the first time in our No. 1 best uniform. My friend George, being an ex-Sea Cadet, needed no help and stood by giving advice and assistance.

We were issued with a cap tally, a band of black silky material which had to be tied with a fancy bow to the righthand side of the cap. We had seen many sailors wearing these tallies but instead of *"HMS Victory"* resplendent in gold wire, our ones merely read *"HMS"*.

The silk scarf, worn between the tunic and the blue jean collar, had to be folded down from about a three-foot square of silk into a long strip of folds, about two inches wide. The ends were sewn together, using the sewing kit in our "housewives" to form a long black scarf which was worn under the collar and tied together at the front of our chests to form a small bunch and bow. The ends of the black material forming the bow were then neatly dovetailed off with the use of scissors. All this gear had to be humped in one go back to our mess. I think it piled higher than me but I managed it somehow.

With the issue of the uniform came a whole new routine of torture. The uniform must be worn just so and when not being worn, must also be stowed away clean and neat. It must not be lost, stolen, bartered or otherwise disposed of and it frequently had to be brought out for inspection. The dormitory door also carried a poster showing how one's kit must be laid out. Everything needed to be spaced symmetrically, to ensure that the fold in a blanket was correct or that one boot was an exact distance from its neighbour. I thought it was childish in the extreme and hated it. We were marched across the parade ground in our new uniforms after "Stand Easy" and sat in a classroom where P.O. Williams lectured us on the naval tradition perpetuated in the sailors' uniform.

Life in the RN is based on tradition. Some traditions are very old and out of date and quite irrelevant to the modern Navy that they serve but these traditions, old or new, still prevail and are observed most strictly. The practice of saluting the quarterdeck stems from the very early days of shipping, when the quarterdeck housed the Church area and holy relics and a sailor, on stepping aboard, would face aft and touch his forelock in reverence to his Maker. Today, all officers and men still salute the quarterdeck in the same fashion.

Only Commissioned Officers are saluted, but the salute is given with the palm of the hand innermost, that is to say, with the back of the hand toward the recipient, and was originally intended in order that the sailor's dirty hand would not be shown to the officer. A sailor's hands after all, would be pretty grubby with the accumulation of tar pitch and dirt involved in his daily tasks, aggravated by the scarcity of fresh water with which to wash.

The uniform itself is also steeped in tradition and legend. In the early days of the Royal Navy, a sailor would dress himself in almost anything that he lay a palm and needle to. This would include worn out sailcloth or sacking and it was not until the middle of the eighteenth century that any sort of uniformed style of dress came into use. It was said that the Captain of *HMS Blazer* dressed his gig's crew in a sort of uniform with a straw or sennet hat, in order that when he was rowed to visit some dignitary ashore, they would look extra smart in contrast to the usual gaggle of pirates that would row a Captain to port. Hence the modern gentleman's blazer.

The idea became popular and soon Captains of the Fleet pressed the Admiralty for an issue of material with which each sailor could run himself up a standard uniform of warm clothes. The Admiralty also used this clothing issue as a system of payment in kind and claimed that they were embellishing the poor sailor's lot by such a generous gift!

It so happened that the Navy's Purser was sold bolts of dark-blue serge cloth by a chandler in Salop at a very advantageous price. The modern clothing store's slang title of "Slops" is a derivative of Salop and the word "Pusser" comes from Purser.

About this time there was some dissension in the Service from the lower deck concerning pay and conditions and the issue of proper clothing went some way to quelling the matter. Each sailor was issued with enough cloth to make a suit from but since buttons were expensive, the jacket developed into a tube which pulled over the wearer's head and over his body, with just a simple pair of sleeves stitched in.

The sailor of those days had little fresh water for niceties such as washing his hair and he tended to scruff his hair back into a pigtail which he lacquered down with pitch or tar to congeal it together to keep out of his face in a strong wind. Since this tarry mixture soon put an unsightly streak on the back of his smart new jacket, he stitched on a blue collar to prevent this and then later added another light blue cotton collar on top of that, which since it was detachable, could be washed to improve the appearance of his outfit.

The trousers were as smart as the skill of their manufacturer and not many sailors made exemplary tailors. The legs of the trousers tended to be straight, wide-bottomed tubes, which flapped wildly as the wearer walked. They had the advantage that they rolled up easily when the owner needed to get on his knees to holy-stone the ship's wooden decks and being voluminous were easy to drop out of, should the wearer fall over the side!

Later on, tradition instituted the bellbottoms being creased along the side of the leg whilst turned inside-out and then folded and ironed concertina style with seven creases, one for each of the seven seas, or so legend had it. Legend also allowed that the three white strips around the blue jean collar stood for each of Nelson's main victories. However, it was for decoration only since the style was in use well before Nelson's day.

The black silk scarf, worn as previously described, was said to be in mourning for Nelson but it is more likely that since the new Navy uniform incorporated a smart straw hat, the neck was the new lodging-place for the sweat band worn previously about the forehead when the wearer was at action stations amidst the smoke and grime of the early firing pieces.

A lanyard of white cordage was also worn about the neck and tucked down the front of the jumper. In fact, this lanyard could provide a good piece of slow-match for a cannon in an emergency and was a good place to hang a clasp knife discreetly out of sight when ashore in a public place. This same clasp knife was always worn when the owner was up on deck but its use was principally in the course of a sailor's duties.

A dark-blue woollen jumper could be worn under the jacket-top for extra warmth in the winter and a nice "tiddly" white collarless vest, later enjoying the addition of a pretty blue edging in square neck fashion, for the warmer months.

Footwear did not become uniform for some time. Most seamen padded around barefoot or in rope-style sandals but eventually, dark blue socks and black leather shoes were issued to complete the ensemble. The straw pan-ama-style hat went out at the latter end of the First World War and was replaced by the familiar pill-box caps in black serge or white canvas worn by today's sailor. The Navy joined the age of technology in 1956 when they issued white plastic caps in place of the canvas blancoed variety and black caps were discontinued.

At about the same time, officially a long zip could be inserted down the front of the jacket making it much easier to struggle in and out of, but you had to alter your uniform yourself or have this labour-saving device incorporated into any new uniform that you bought from a naval tailor. However, the old tube-style ones were still being issued as uniform in 1961.

Instructed then on our uniforms, when and how to wear them, we were given brown paper and string and told to make up parcels of our civilian clothes, which were then posted off home free of charge. After my parcel had been dispatched, I discovered that I had omitted one of my civilian ties, a black one with a gold and white diagonal stripe, and I took great delight in wearing this tie after working hours, enjoying the feeling of individuality it gave me. For as I pointed out to my shipmates: "I'm a civilian really!"

The days passed by and we began to settle into the Navy way of life.We rose at 0530, washed, cleaned our bed spaces and the dormitory, dressed into whichever rig of the day was promulgated on Daily Orders, breakfasted and fell in on the parade ground at 0730. We would come under some sort of classroom instruction until 0945 when there would be our precious fifteen-minute Stand Easy and then go on with a bit of square-bashing or lecturing.

We lived for when we fell out at 1145 when "Up Spirits" and then "Cooks to the Galley" were piped, and we washed up for dinner. The dining hall was self-service, where one collected a metal tray and joined a queue at a counter manned by the catering section. The food was plopped into shaped indentations in the tray, invariably ran over and amalgamated, but most were too hungry to worry.

The Daily Orders were pinned up on the notice board in the corridor outside our dormitory and we were duty bound to read them before break-fast. These orders gave the "rig of the day" so that we knew what uniform to put on. Sometimes we wore our No. 2 uniform or else our No. 8 working rig of blue working shirt and denim style trousers. No. 1s were usually only worn on Sunday on "divisions", the Navy word for a parade or Church parade.

After 1600, the rig of the day was always "night clothing" which would be No. 2 uniform, without the top blue jean collar. Woe betide anyone caught not in the correct rig of the day!

There was a tendency for people to neglect to read the Daily Orders, they just asked what was happening from other mess mates. I recall once returning early from the washroom, to be asked by someone what the rig of the day was, to which I replied "No. 8s" whereas in fact it was "No. 2s". On my return from breakfast, I found most of my class in No. 8s whereas I was in the correct rig. My joke was not appreciated as they all frantically changed uniform!

I enjoyed a practical joke whether against me or one of my own making. It was easy to spread the latest "buzz", a slang word for rumour, and I was good and convincing at it. It brightened up some grey days and we were all both perpetrators as well as victims of buzzes.

Among my few personal belongings, I chanced to have a small piece of graph paper and it was this that gave me the idea to mark off sufficient squares to represent the number of days in the next two years. We were discussing the subject of national service after supper on the second day of our service and I pointedly said "Never mind, only seven hundred and twenty-eight days to do!" which of course was 365 days x 2, less the two that we had done, a total of seven hundred and thirty in all. It sounded an awful lot of days.

I marked up the sides of the graph in such a way that each square represented one day. It gave me great delight to blot out the first two squares. Throughout my two-year service, no matter what sort of day it had been, I had a moment of satisfaction in blotting out another day from the 730-day calendar. However, leave periods and the one time that I was sick at home, were blotted from the calendar in red. Those I regarded as bonus days!

I also kept a diary which I wrote up regularly every day. Some entries were made in no more than a dozen words, some went on at great length! Beautiful days usually merited quite a lyrical waxing and the rough, cold, wet ones were dismissed in but a few words. Sunny, warm, calm days, were described in brighter vein and reading some of those descriptions, thirty-odd years after the event, the spirit and atmosphere of the day is captured again.

27

CHAPTER
THREE

Friday, the fourth day of our induction dawned. Daily Orders put us in No. 8s and on the parade ground first thing. Later we went to a classroom and took instruction with an officer on ranks and badges and how to salute. Only officers are saluted as they hold a Queen's Commission but as we were now under training, we were to salute all Chief and Petty Officers too.

As the weekend was fast approaching, we asked if we were to be allowed out, either to sample the delights of Portsmouth, or to frantically make a dash for home. Our Divisional P.O. shook his head.

"Leave," he told us, "is a privilege!" We had yet to earn the privilege.

The Navy began to feel more like a prison than before. The prospect of being constantly locked in the barracks crashed our spirits to rock bottom.

Andy Gray, who lived about a mile away from the barracks, telephoned his family and someone passed him goodies through the iron railings. The remainder of us were bereft of any family contact other than writing home, which we did nearly every day. I even sent my love to my two brothers! However, we need not have worried that the Navy was to leave us to pine away over the weekend!

After the usual "wakey, wakey" routine and breakfast on the Saturday morning, we were turned to in our dormitory and the adjacent passageways, bathrooms and "heads", the latter so called because when seated on a ship's lavatory, one's head is clearly seen since the sides of the cubicle are shortened off for the purpose. Don't ask me to quote you the numerous reasons given me for this practice, suffice to say that it is yet another old naval tradition, perpetuated into the space age!

We scrubbed and polished, dusted and cleaned and then changed into our No. 2 uniform to await the Captain's rounds. Just before 1130, the Commanding Officer of the barracks, resplendent in his smart uniform and followed by a cluster of lesser officers including our Divisional Officer, came into our messdeck where we stood to attention at the foot of our bunks. He inspected the deck, the window ledges, the fronts of our aluminium lockers, the windows and even the tops of the doors and the fire buckets and extinguishers but said nothing.

29

Coming to the end of the room, he turned about and began to inspect us, straightening a cap here, awarding a "haircut" there. He even spoke to us socially, although I got the feeling that he was not very interested in our replies. I looked him in the eye and refused to go red. He asked my name and where I came from. What was my favorite sport? When told it was cycling he focused on me and said: "Not much chance of that, I'm afraid", his reply more addressed to his respectful entourage than to me, but at least they all moved on without picking up any fault in my dress or stance. As the door closed on the retreating "brass" and the shrill call of the Bosun's pipe went into other blocks to create fear and trembling there, we were stood at ease.

A little while later, our P.O. came in looking rather flustered to inform us that we had done very well and a re-scrub had not been ordered. Since a re-scrub meant doing all of the cleaning again, we were delighted.

We were free after dinner to get changed into sports rig and could spend the rest of the day playing football, cricket or running on the Navy's sports field. And so we actually did pass through those gates in columns of three, not in the direction of the bars or fleshpots of Portsmouth but to the clipped grass of the fenced-in sports field, which became our substitute prison until 1550, when our P.O. marched us back. We agreed that we would much rather have crashed out on our bunks for the afternoon but as soon as supper was over at 1900, most of us went for a "kip" in the television room, where our sleep was disturbed by the chanting cat-calls over the "Omo" adverts! Thus did Saturday pass into Sunday. Another day was blotted from the calendar.

We eventually learned that our initial training was four weeks in the barracks where, as new recruits, we were to be taught the basic elements of naval life such as parade training, how to wear the uniform, naval routines ashore, firefighting and anti-gas drill. We were also to receive various aptitude tests which seemed to be aimed at determining our general attitude and capabilities, but whether or not these results were ever acted upon is impossible to say.

It was also the best opportunity to overhaul us medically and this was done with great zeal and persistence. When the doctors had done their worst, the dentists had a go. So too did the psychiatrists. I well remember an interview with a person in a white coat, who asked me questions. I did my best to give the most obscure answers, as I had been told what was up by the lad preceding me in the queue! The person in the white coat seemed reluctant to call our interview to an end but time was pressing, and there was by now a queue of other dozy-looking new entries to process, each of whom had had a few moments to think up some really perplexing answers to the most basic of questions.

Heavy rain broke out during our morning parade training session and we were dismissed to the dormitory to dry out a little, smoke a forbidden fag and generally loaf about until "Stand Easy" was piped. Our Able Seaman appeared. He was a very quiet, withdrawn sort of chap, never volunteering any advice or information unless asked. We nicknamed him "Punch" because when he did pop up he did so at unexpected times and always seemed to say "That's the way to do it!" somewhere along the line of his conversation. We were to change into our No. 8s, working shirt and denim style trousers and muster outside after "Stand Easy".

Thus attired, we marched off, swinging our arms in true "new entry" style up to shoulder height, and were bought to a halt outside the barracks cinema. Doris Day topped the bill but we saw little of her other than the rosy-cheeked posters. Once seated in absolute silence, we were shown several instructional films made by the Admiralty's own film units. One was a recruiting style film. Another was on safety precautions with a rifle.

The instructor in the film droned on and we only woke up when the rifle was actually fired and the target was hit in the middle. There followed the usual questions by our instructor and then we were handed over to the AB to march back for lunch. The rain hung in grey, soaking curtains from a very dark sky and we were taken back at the double.

We washed and filed in for dinner in the messhall. I found a small garden slug in my lettuce and put him to the edge of my plate and he kept us amused by trying to get back to feed on my herring in tomato sauce.

A Chief Petty Officer came from the back of the servery and called out: "Any complaints?" This happened every meal-time and no-one ever had the nerve to complain but quite suddenly, perhaps it was the effect of the increasing gloom that had enveloped me over the course of the past few days, or the fact that the slug had got to my herring without my noticing it and I could not therefore finish my lunch, I got to my feet and said: "I have, Chief!"

The Chief, who had already turned to go back into the kitchen, stopped as if pole-axed. A look of great consternation came over his face and he went a bit red as he hurried across through the throng of sailors returning their mess-trays. Every eye was on me.

"Got this slug in my salad" I said weakly. He looked from the slug to me and from me to the slug.

"That, lad" he said, "just goes to prove how fresh and young your greens is!" and he turned and walked away. I sat down to a great roar of laughter from the assembled diners. I never complained again.

We spilled out onto the wet concrete and shuffled into line, shortest in the centre, tallest on the flank. The rain dripped from the brims of our blancoed caps and stained our shirts with wet white streaks. It was back to the cinema. We took our seats quietly and respectfully since our instructor turned out to be a doctor, a Lieutenant, who some days previously had taken one of our number to task for not saluting him. His manner in so doing had been a bit on the hard side, bearing in mind that we were new bodies and not yet used to whom to salute and how one went about the function.

The doctor then proceeded to destroy all our previous opinions of him.

"Good afternoon, gentlemen," he said. There must be a catch here, we thought, as no-one had bidden us a "good afternoon" or "good morning" since we had walked through those gates and we had not yet been referred to as gentlemen!

"Good afternoon, sir," we mumbled in chorus.

"You may smoke," were his next words. "I am going to show you a film made by the Admiralty, concerning the causes and effects of venereal disease."

We sat bolt upright on our hard wooden seats. The projectionist switched out the lights and the traditional white cross in a circle enclosing the count-down figures, appeared on the screen. I counted with the jumpy projector, five, four, three, two, one... The title "Crown Film Unit" came next accompanied by music, out of synchronisation with the picture as usual.

The camera took us into a naval hospital and we followed a doctor on his rounds through the wards. We saw the victims of all sorts of venereal complaints and were treated to diagrams of how the diseases were contracted and the various methods used to treat them. Our doctor stood to one side of the screen, pointing with a long ruler to the various parts and instruments referred to in the commentary. This sickening film came to a conclusion and not before time, in my estimation! The faces of the surrounding audience reflected their horror and disgust at the degrading diseases that man can expose himself to in the name of lust.

When the lights came on the doctor took the stage. He lectured us for some time on what we had seen and said that no matter how shocked and disgusted we were at the present, our time of temptation was yet to come and that, according to Service statistics, there was a possibility of some ten percent of our number winding up with some form of sexually transmitted disease. "Not me," I thought.

He then opened a drawer in the small desk to the side of the stage and produced a cellophane packet containing a condom. These, he said, were issued free of charge to any unmarried rating on going ashore and who may consider themselves at risk from such infection. It was wise, he said, to keep one on one's person at all times... just in case. They were readily available from the Ship's Office or the guardroom on going ashore. No questions would be asked, they were merely taken from a tray when placing your station card in the rack. Never has such a film made more of an impression on a young man. I know that I never forgot it and I am sure from the conversations in the mess that my shipmates felt the same.

I took to carrying a "free issue", as these condoms were called, in the folds of my paybook, "just in case", with embarrassing results, for on one occasion I took out my paybook to show my parents my nice new photograph and a free issue skidded across the kitchen floor! It proved a very good way of warming one's ears on a cold day!

It had been assumed from day one that we were all capable of swimming. I recall being asked on several occasions if I could swim. However, the Navy needed to know how good we were at the aquatic art and accordingly we mustered outside our block dressed in No. 2s carrying a towel and were bussed by lorries to the RN swimming baths in Portsmouth.

Once inside the rather old-fashioned tiled edifice, we were each given a white duck tropical suit and told to change and line up at the deep end, facing the shallows. The Navy fairly bristled with Physical Training Instructors and these baths were no exception. The P.T.I.'s badge of office was crossed Indian clubs, surmounted by a number of stars or a crown, depending on the wearer's standard of efficiency. All P.T.I.s seemed of the same stamp, extremely brisk and tense and always moving at the double. The inevitable P.T.I.'s whistle hung from the lower lip and they enjoyed shrieking it in one's ear.

The nickname for them was "Clubs". They were good sorts really and if one had a good try at everything they were one of the few senior rates to treat us with respect and make us feel part of a team, an essential requirement of a sports instructor in any case.

Dressed in our white uniforms, we resembled a line of penguins as we stood at the deep end. There was the usual high-pitched banter between us and the Chief P.T.I. blew his whistle twice to call us to order. We were a load of fairies, he told us.

Was there anyone who could not swim? he asked. Silence. Was there anyone who could swim but was a poor swimmer? Silence.

"Good!" he said. "Then you will find no difficulty in swimming two lengths of these baths and floating in the deep end on your back for five minutes, starting with a jump or a dive. Stand by, go!"

Loud whistle. I pitched forward in a headlong dive. I liked swimming and could easily swim the prescribed distance, so I decided that I would show off a bit and swim the first length underwater. The canvas uniform dragged me back a bit but I surfaced finally at the shallow end rail to be met by a barrage of shrill whistles.

"Oy! you!" roared one of the P.T.I.s. "Were you told to swim it under water, lad?"

"No, P.O." I mumbled.

"Then start again from the deep end."

And so I did the test twice and thoroughly enjoyed it. But there were those among us that could not complete the course and who clung for life onto the side rails. The P.T.I. staff knelt giving them encouragement and advice but at the end of the session, several had still not completed the test. Dressed once more in our No. 2s, we returned our borrowed gear and lined up at the edge of the baths ready for the lorry ride back. The Chief P.T.I. addressed us.

Two persons, he said, had failed the Navy swimming test, which meant that they could not expect to go to sea in future. However, they were awarded a "re-scrub", the naval term for doing it again, but that would require their attending the baths in their free time to practise. Somehow, I found myself volunteering to assist. The rest of my class-mates called me "Anchor-faced" for offering to help but it was all in good fun. During the week that followed, the three of us hopped into a Navy Bedford personnel carrier (nicknamed a "Tilly") after instruction each day and spent about an hour practising the swimming test. At the end of the week, both candidates passed and I enjoyed a daily swim!

Our first week had been a very hectic one. A great deal of the time was spent in marching and in forming pretty patterns on the parade ground. When not thus employed, we were involved in some sort of induction routine or other, such as medicals, dentistry and interviews. We were even read the Queen's Rules and Regulations and had all sorts of questions answered about our conditions of service. The "dos" and "don'ts" covered under the Articles of QRRs had some very serious punishments in store for any offender. A whole lot of civil rights, which we had previously enjoyed as civilians, were now taken away and we became subject entirely to naval law.

When one bears in mind that we were not volunteers, you may understand our resentment to this enforced authority. It was a resentment which was building up in me. I found my enforced imprisonment in the barracks, the manner in which my superiors gave their orders to me and the pettiness of some of these instructions, coupled with my total inability to protest over some of these matters, very stressful and it was fast leading to me "doing something about it".

I took to wearing my civilian tie more openly, I even went to supper wearing it on one occasion without comment and I dragged my feet and made no real effort to jump to my tormentor's commands, if I thought that I could get away with it. I began to collect a number of small punishments, such as doubling around the parade ground for dumb insolence or for answering back when sworn at. I hated being sworn at, and I always countered any direct cursing with either a quietly muttered "Wash your mouth out!" or by a scowl!

It did not make me popular with my instructors, but at the end of the day it was always "they" who won the conflict and I expended a lot of energy in putting up a solid resistance to the "system" which, in view of its objectives, and proven efficiency in making sailors from civilians in the past, was hardly likely to be reviewed by the powers that be to suit me!

A defaulter, doubling around the parade ground in the hot sun, was a common sight and one which earned a grudging respect and sympathy from those on parade. He had done what they would all like to have the nerve to do in bucking authority.

Cleaning our dormitory and lavatories and passageways was a principal daily labour. Cleaning our kit, boots, belt and gaiters was done in our own time but as we were not yet allowed ashore, there was little else to spend time on. We wrote long letters home and even longer ones to our girlfriends. Several messmates were married, an unusual thing in the mid-1950s for a young man of eighteen. Some chaps were not up to writing but telephoned home instead and there was always a queue outside the phone booth.

Television was a source of entertainment. Many of the TV adverts were funnier than the programmes. We knew them off by heart and enjoyed parodying them. After the day's work, providing that you were not on duty and had no great pile of dhobying to attend to, it was great entertaiment to sit in the smoke-filled TV room and listen to the banter and funny remarks.

Our radio went on at 1600 and was turned off at the control unit at 2100. There were some wonderful rock and roll and "pop" programmes to enjoy. Little Richard, Bill Haley, Jimmy Young, Guy Mitchell, and Brenda Lee were a few of the stars I recall.

We also had the canteen, the ubiquitous NAAFI. We were given a tobacco allowance which enabled us to purchase six hundred duty-free cigarettes per month from the canteen. The cigarettes were dubbed "Blue Liners" because the packet had a blue line running around it, with the initials "RN" on the front. They were reputed to be the sweepings of a famous branded cigarette manufacturer's factory floor and were only available to serving naval personnel. I had never taken to smoking before but at two shillings and fourpence per hundred, I found myself puffing away with the rest.

These simple things were our only real sort of escape, and welcome ones, for we were all homesick. All perhaps, except Ian Body from Lancashire: "Three good meals a dee boy, and a warm bed, ye canna beat it!"

Many shipmates got quite low during the first weeks and the more resilient ones spent quite some time playing "Dutch Uncles" to their misery, listening for hours about their problems.

Our very existence hinged on hope, hope that this time would soon pass, hope that it would not be too long before we got home again and hope that we would soon move out of these barracks and be done with these "big ship routines". The married men suffered more than most I think, for their greater responsibility lay at home with their wives and in at least one case, the new baby. The Chaplain was called anonymously on one occasion to one sufferer but nothing could really be done to ease the situation, although several lads had their family visit them.

Most fathers and mothers missed their sons as much as we missed them and made the journey to Portsmouth to spend a short time in an annex near the main gate with their lad, usually of an evening. Their son would be piped over the Tannoy to report to the main gate and there would be mum and dad! It always seemed to me that the "inmate" was the worse for such a visit and I am glad it did not happen to me.

It is fair to say that we went in the Service in high spirits but then took to feeling pretty low for a while, what with the strict routines and daily tasks but as we got to know each other, a sense of comradeship, a team spirit and our own brand of humour began to permeate our lives and we began to look forward to our first run ashore together.

"God help Pompey," we said, Pompey being the naval slang for Portsmouth.

No provision was made for any advancement or promotion. After some eighteen months as an Ordinary Seaman, so we heard, one took a test to be rated Able Seaman but there was no distinguishing mark or badge, although one's pay increased slightly.

The pay as an Ordinary Seaman was, in July 1955, one pound and ten shillings a week. From this sum, one had to provide some items essential to the upkeep of one's uniform, such as washing powder, boot polish and blanco for the canvas caps and white belt and gaiters, when these were issued for wear. Toothpaste and soaps, razor blades and such also needed to be purchased from this sum.

This pittance was paid fortnightly and one donned one's best uniform, endured an inspection parade and ran the subsequent risk of a kit muster before finally appearing before the Paymaster and a bevy of accompanying officers. One was doubled in by a Chief Petty Officer, who yelled: "Salute the Officer, off cap, name and number!" I always thought these farcical parades a terrible waste of man hours and often got into trouble for saying so, but the Service thought them good for discipline and everyone seemed to enjoy it, apart that is from the national serviceman who had to endure them, secure in the knowledge that his pay was half that of his regular counterpart.

In retrospect, we were worse off financially than in our civilian jobs. Most lads that I spoke to seemed to have been earning an average of somewhere between £4 to £6 per week, from which they would have only their living expenses at home with their parents to settle. Navy pay was therefore marginally a drop in circumstances for the lower paid, and quite a bigger loss for the better paid.

Your keep was free, you were well fed and clothed. Some entertainment was thrown in and there was a good healthy programme of sport, with swimming, cricket and football and all the major games available for those precious free hours. Some sport was compulsory but just as long as you had a go and got suitably muddy, you were considered to be fitting into the run of things. The odd black eye or other minor injury was always a good talking point when Sunday Church parades were inspected by the C.O. of the barracks. Rarely did one collect a kit muster after explaining how one gained such evidence of sporting prowess.

My love of cycling, at this stage, was not pandered to in any way. I did enjoy swimming and climbing ropes and running but the more "teamy" sports such as football or rugby found me running about achieving little.

Rumour had it that after the period of barracks training, we were to be sent for a further ten weeks sea training on a ship, at the conclusion of which we would be officially rated Ordinary Seaman and then returned to our home station to be further distributed throughout the Fleet. No-one advised us officially of the whole scale of this master plan; we merely endured each stage as it happened and accepted our fate as it came.

Victoria Barracks, originally a barracks for the soldiers of the Crimean wars, was therefore a reception centre for national servicemen but in fact, recruits from different parts of the country were placed finally in one of three main assembly stations, depending which was nearer to their home address. These would be known as your "Home Port". There were anomalies and exceptions to the rule, all for no apparent reason. We had lads from Essex, Middlesex, Hertfordshire, Lancashire, Merseyside and one from Lewis in the Western Isles. The lads from the eastern side of the country were eventually based at Chatham in Kent, whilst the remainder found Plymouth or Portsmouth their Home Port. The lad from Stornaway spent some time in

Chatham until he finally persuaded the powers that be that Portsmouth provided the easier access to the routes north for him and he was finally relocated.

Our usual daily rig would be No. 8 working dress. However, one morning our Daily Orders instructed us to dress in our No. 2 uniforms for we were due for a firefighting course at *HMS Phoenix*. It was to be our first proper excursion out of the Victoria Barracks other than to the sports fields and we were overjoyed to escape our prison of the past twelve days. We were further delighted to see that we had a pair of smart Navy Bedford lorries to travel in and we were to be there most of the day because the galley issued each man with a packed lunch! Our excitement knew no bounds.

Our instructor threatened us to be on our very best behaviour but we took little heed to his words. We felt like kids on a Sunday School outing to the seaside and we would not let him put a dampener on our spirits. The Navy owed us a bit of a good time and we were going to enjoy this outing.

In reality, the day proved every bit as arduous as if we had remained in the barracks, because apart from the ride on the lorry to the firefighting school on a site over to the north side of Portsmouth, and the occasional glimpse of a real live female either walking along the road or riding a cycle, we ended up hot and clammy from spraying various combinations of water, foam and gases on all sorts of simulated fires and then had to complete a written exam at the end of it.

All regular sailors were taught a trade or skill in which they were expected to excel. They were sent to various naval schools to acquire their knowledge and there they studied such nautical matters as Gunnery, Asdics, Torpedoes, Signals, Radar and the like. They remained seamen as such but they did these extra jobs after the Service had spent thousands of pounds of taxpayers' money on training them.

But the poor national serviceman did not get the opportunity. The only course open to him was the Shallow Water Diving Course. For Chatham ratings this involved a ten week course at the St Mary's Island Diving School and the successful candidate, if not drowned in the process, won a small Diver's helmet badge worn on the left cuff. He was also paid threepence an hour for every hour submerged and could well expect to spend at least five or six hours per year beneath the surface of the wet stuff, usually in some smelly naval dockyard. There were not many takers!

Our early training had been a blur of new experiences. We even had to learn a new language for many naval things had their own service names. At the centre of it was "Pusser"; that was the overall name for all things belonging to the Navy. The ships would be "Pusser's Ships", one would purchase Slops from "Pusser's Stores" and follow "Pusser's Daily Orders".

Other objects collected their own names in a manner similar to cockney rhyming slang. Shoes were called "crabs". Therefore, one could be said to be wearing "Pusser's crabs", but only if the shoes were purchased from naval stock and not if bought from a naval tailor or civilian shoeshop, in which case they were merely "crabs". Many persons had nicknames for their vocations in life; we quickly learned that a "Crusher" was a severe example of a naval policeman but this system of giving such nicknames was complex because a naval policeman was also known as a "Jaunty". It took some time to fall into the ways of naval language and it proved to be one of the more important aspects of early naval life.

I was surprised to discover that there was a preponderant use of bad language in the Navy. However, as it seemed to be confined to the messdecks and parade grounds and was in frequent use by all ranks, with the notable exception of most officers, and since it rarely came into use in the company of civilians and ladies, it became the norm and very much a part of naval life. It was certainly an excellent way of letting off steam after suffering a "green rub" (a raw deal) and, although I did not revel in swearing, I fell in step with the rest. In reality, swearing became so much a part of everyday life that the actual words bore no real meaning.

It took some time to knock us into shape, but at long last our instructor began to smile - well, almost! The odd flash of Navy humour would brighten our parade training sessions. We did, however, have one utter failure that taxed our Petty Officer most sorely.

New Entry Cook could not march, he had no aptitude for it and his brain could not conform to it. He could only "march" bear-fashion, the right arm in line with the right leg and vice-versa, and no amount of shouting, demonstrating in slow time or cajoling, made the slightest difference. After a very few steps, "Cookie" would relapse into a bear-like shuffle which reduced us all to a staggering rabble. We even tried lashing him between two men who would then march off at a stiff rate in an effort to induce a sense of rythm into his frozen limbs, but we failed. Cookie was reduced to being a pennant holder, he stood at the perimeter of the parade area holding a small staff and pennant and acted as a marker for the limits of the marching areas.

He didn't mind at all. He watched us sweat the hot summer mornings away on our complex marching and counter-marching with a slight smile on his face.

Then came the day when we were marched to a great concrete blockhouse, which was unlocked with several keys to reveal steel doors leading to an armoury and we filed in to be issued a real Lea Enfield .303 rifle and a sling and bayonet, belt and scabbard. We were really a force to be reckoned with now. Fierce pride surged through our young bodies as we were taught to strip and handle this fearsome weapon! However, we never even saw a bullet, for the gun was not for shooting! It was for playing tin soldiers with and we were taught to Slope Arms, Order Arms and Present Arms until the 9lb 3ozs of wood and steel became part of what was beginning to be a concise military machine.

Our next sortie onto the parade ground with our friend Lea Enfield proved to be a very painful one indeed, for the sores that came up on our arms from the injections at the Sick Bay did not go with the exercise of rifle drill and the blue serge of our jackets helped them to go septic. Some of the lads reported sick with nausea but after a very brief period of time spent "hors de combat" in the dormitory, they returned to the parade ground.

On the morning of July 13th, they hanged Ruth Ellis, the mother of two children working as a hostess in a London night club who had stolen a gun and shot and killed her lover. It made me feel gloomy all day. I always felt gloomy on hanging days. It seemed such a bitter waste of life all round and I was naive enough to believe man capable of better things. Surely, the war had taught us more respect for life than this? Compared with some, I considered Mrs Ellis' crime was not as ghastly.

I think the reasons for her execution centred around the fact that she had used a revolver, premeditated the murder by hanging around for some hours outside a club awaiting her victim and neglecting her children to no small degree during her affair with the man involved. She was the last woman hanged in Britain.

I sat moodily in the messhall, taking breakfast. I made comment on the case to the stranger sitting alongside me.

"What did she do?" he asked. "Fiddle the Inland Revenue?" I did not bother explaining but remarked "A bit more than that" and abandoned the subject.

CHAPTER
FOUR

The third weekend of our induction into Her Majesty's Royal Navy approached and we finally received the news that we would be allowed ashore from 1300 until 2359 on the Saturday night. At first, we could not believe it. After all these long days of incarceration we were to be allowed ashore!

There would be no time to get home and back of course, but at least we could escape for a while from the parade ground and the NAAFI and the tiled bathroom and the dormitory and stretch our legs along the promenade at Southsea and have a bag of chips! What luxuries these simple things had become.

We fell in for inspection as libertymen for the very first time. The Regulating Chief Petty Officer addressed us concerning the limits of our leave and then both he and the Officer of the Day walked the ranks, inspecting our uniforms. We were well prepared and there were no faults; in fact, we were commended by the officer, which made the C.P.O. smile!

We burst out of the gates through which we had last entered as civilians. What different people we were by now! The least I can say is that we all felt more "grown-up" than at any previous time of our lives and strangely enough, proud to be ashore in the uniform of the Royal Navy, although we would not have admitted it in as many words! Our class of thirty-two split this way and that as we filtered into the centre of Portsmouth.

Garth, George, Jim, myself and wee "Mac" were the only group together at the head of the town and we had our fill of looking at the shops and eyeing the lasses before we retraced our steps back toward the front at Southsea and the amusements area.

We sat on a bench in the sun on the seafront, watching the world go by. The sea was dotted with sleek, dark grey destroyers, for the American 7th Fleet was in Portsmouth paying the town a courtesy visit. We had heard that London had emptied of prostitutes for the day and that some girls had even come from as far away as Birmingham to pick the Americans clean of their dollars. Yanks streamed past us in a constant tide, each with "adoring" girls dressed in short skirts and seamed stockings hanging on their arms, and we smiled, for we knew that our American cousins were likely to steam off with more than they had bargained for! The Admiralty film on the subject of VD was fresh in our memories!

The sun began to dip into the west beyond the buildings of *HMS Dolphin* and we repaired back to town and had supper in a cafe. Thus revived, we strolled back to the front determined to enjoy every moment of our first taste of freedom. Jim got talking to a girl who was on holiday from Northampton and the remainder of our little patrol sauntered into the Long Bar for a glass of beer before returning to the barracks.

The bar was quite full and occupied entirely by servicemen. The Americans sat at one end while the British tars sat at the other, a factor that we did not pay any attention to at first. We ordered our beers and took a seat in the middle. It was only as we sat down that Garth noticed that we sat in a "separation zone" but by then it was too late to get up and move without our move being obvious.

An American voice sang out from the American end. Something was said about our Queen. I won't repeat it. An English voice replied, insinuating that General Eisenhower was not all that we may have thought.

An empty brown ale bottle sailed through the air in slow motion and burst amidst the tightly packed ranks of the English and the battle was on. Both ends of the bar charged the middle where our innocent party sat and the fists flew. Our table was upended and I was punched out of my seat by a large, beefy-faced Yank.

I stared at him in astonishment.

"I beg your pardon!" I gasped. He stared back in surprise at my reaction. I got to my feet.

"What was that for?" I asked, and before he could reply I hit him as hard as I could on the chin because out of the corner of my eye, I saw Garth, wee Mac and George, slogging away at the circle of crazed Yanks who threatened to engulf us. Back to back, we fought for the exit. However, it was blocked by even more Yanks and Brits, trying to force their way in to join the mêlée and so we leapt over the bar, ran through the kitchens and burst out of the back door into the yard beyond. Straight into the arms of the Naval Patrol!

Only wee Mac escaped and legged it to safety. The remainder were unceremoniously thrown into an RN Patrol Wagon which once full, took off up the street to the Victoria Barracks, *HMS Victory*. We were handed over to the gate staff and locked up in the guardhouse for the night. I was very angry that this matter should have involved us and I upset the regulating staff considerably by my rebellious attitude. Normally, I was a very easy-going sort of person and certainly not one to pick a fight, but having been hyped-up by the events of the evening, it took some time for me to cool down.

The following morning we were awakened early by a grumpy Regulating Petty Officer and marched to a washroom to brighten ourselves up, from where we progressed to a messhall where we had breakfast under escort. At 0900, we attended the Commander's table as defaulters, the first time that such an event had overtaken us. Some of our party however, were old hands at it and told us how to approach the table and make our excuses but I was in no doubt as to how to conduct my defence on this sorry occasion!

The affair was none of our doing and I intended to make that point. I happened to be the first of my group to be called to the table. The Chief Regulating Petty Officer called my name and doubled me to the Commander, who stood looking very fierce and intimidating behind a wooden lectern. I was ordered to remove my cap. My name and number was called out in an unnecessarily loud voice and I was formally charged with being involved, contrary to Queen's Rules and Regulations, in causing an affray by fighting in a public place and causing damages to a bar to the value of £120.

The events of the previous evening were related to the Commander but no mention of the reasons for the fracas were made. The Commander's face reddened and grew more thunderous at every twist of the tale but I faced him as coolly as my quailing heart would allow.

At the culmination of the reading of my list of offences, nine in all as I remember, I was asked if I had anything to say to explain my conduct.

"Yes sir," said I in a bold voice "I came into the bar at the end of my first ever run ashore as a new entry to the Navy and seated myself quietly with my colleagues at a table in the middle of the room, to have a glass of ale before returning to barracks. An American sailor said something about Her Majesty which I have no intention of repeating and a fight broke out which I had neither contributed to nor invited. I was forced, as an innocent bystander to defend myself and to quit the premises with my friends as quickly as possible. This we did by means of the rear exit and were wrongfully arrested by the Shore Patrol and locked up in the barracks. I am not guilty on all charges and ask to be released, sir!"

There was a deathly silence at my eloquence and I began to think that I had overdone it. The Commander asked to hear what it was that was said about Her Majesty but I refused to repeat it. It was apparent to him that I spoke the truth. I was lectured nevertheless on a sailor's conduct ashore but the sting was taken out of the proceedings and acquittal followed acquittal.

We fell in outside in a corridor and the CRPO finally came out to us.

"You were very lucky today, my lads" he told us. "The Commander was in a good mood." I queried to myself what the Commander's current mood and the course of justice had in common but I said nothing. The Jaunty probably considered justice as a privilege in the same way that leave was.

We marched to the main gate and a Tilly took us back to our part of the barracks. We had an interesting half-hour at our gate, explaining why we had not arrived back on board the previous evening.

I was, however, left with the distinct impression that we could easily have been rail-roaded into being guilty had I not spoken up for us all, for my shipmates seemed reluctant to say anything in their defence and were prepared to stand there and accept what Fate, in the shape of the fierce Commander, chose to hand out.

The unexpected proceedings concerned in our first run ashore proved to be the exception rather than the rule and having once been let out, and presumably because we all came back, leave ashore began to be granted almost every evening excepting when one was duty watch.

The hot days of summer pressed on. Our training became more intense and demanding and we were on the go from morning to late afternoon and often into the dog watches as well. The dog watches, we discovered, were the periods 1600 to 1800, known as the First Dog, so called because that is when the "Dog Star" (actually, Sirius) is first sighted in the night sky in the northern hemisphere. The period 1800 to 2000 was called the Last Dog, presumably because at that time of night the Dog Star would hardly be distinguishable from all the others in the heavens.

There was little energy left for patrolling the streets of Portsmouth at the end of a typical day and little money either, for our pay was pitiful to say the least. Some said that our pay was kept low to prevent our being able to afford to go AWOL. If that were the case, then it worked for none of our group actually did so.

I wrote perhaps three letters a week to Pat but did not receive as many back. Looking forward to a letter from home was one of the highlights of the day and we often survived a hard morning in the gym or on the parade ground, full of hope that we would be one of the lucky ones handed a letter by the duty Petty Officer.

The particularly warm summer of 1955, the hot uniform and the unaccustomed exercise, caused many a body to keel over when on parade and the Petty Officer was most put out, rounding on us for being so soft and feeble. Even Cookie with his pennant fell victim and collapsed with an awful clatter on Sunday morning divisions, although he did have the presence of mind to hold his flag up to the last before it tumbled finally over his inert form. It took three hands to carry him off as he was quite a stout fellow.

Another naval joke that was played on us at that time was to try to gas us. We were issued with a Second World War gasmask and chased in single file through a tunnel filled with some sort of irritant gas. We went through first at great speed without the gasmask on, and then again at a more leisurely pace, with the badly-fitting mask in place. I was more thoroughly gassed the second time than the first and spent quite an unhappy hour until the effects wore off.

We were also shown how to combat the effects of mustard gas. Back in the safety of the dormitory, we unanimously decided that Britain would have to lose us as her first line of defence should an enemy attack with chemical warfare, as we firmly avowed to shoot ourselves rather than suffer such a fate. Assuming, of course, that we were ever issued with ammunition in such circumstances!

And so, in the space of just three weeks, the Royal Navy had tried to imprison us, burn us, gas us, de-personalise and demoralise us and wear us out with parade training. Suddenly, just when we thought it would never end, our Divisional Officer told us that the date for our passing-out parade was imminent and we were to prepare ourselves and our uniforms for the great day. We determined to do our very best. There were after all, no other means of escape from this purgatory!

The Royal Marine Band marched us on parade, resplendent in our freshly pressed and immaculate No.1s, our great heavy boots flashing and crashing on the hot concrete parade ground. Our spirits were high and put that extra spring in our step. Our drill was performed with exultation this time, instead of sufferance as before.

The Commodore of the barracks, his decorations and gold lace glittering in the glare of another hot summer day, passed along our stiff, proud ranks, stopping occasionally to say something mediocre to a man here and there. No-one failed to pass muster and we marched past the saluting base with heads high, proud of our class and shipmates. Petty Officer Williams and Sub.-Lt Taylor heaped praise on our sweating brows and we dismissed to tea in fine spirits, having collected official approval to progress to our period of sea training. We were pleased at the prospect of escape from the regimentation of the naval barracks at Portsmouth and what we had come to know as the "big ship routines".

The 27th of July, our date for leaving Victoria Barracks, finally arrived. Lorries arrived at the parade ground and we bade farewell to our green and white dormitory, slung our kitbags and hammocks into one vehicle and ourselves into the other. Had it been but twenty-three days since we started this adventure? Daily Orders had blandly stated that we were off to join the

Fleet training carriers at Portland for ten weeks sea training and another phase of our new life was beginning.

There is something very masculine about uniformed chaps riding in the back of a lorry, or perhaps I had been watching too many newsreels of the Allies' entry into Paris at the end of the last war! However, no nubile young things came to throw flowers at us on our short journey to the station!

Our Divisional Petty Officer had come to see that we actually got to the station; even at this stage there were the odd rebels talking of making a break for it and joining the underground crime syndicates in London rather than continue their enforced national service. He fell us in and gave us a bit of a lecture about behaving ourselves in public as representatives of the Royal Navy. We were to travel to Weymouth, there was to be no getting off the train for any purpose whatsoever ("Did you hear that Cook?") and we would be met at the other end by transport. He turned on his heels and then hesitated, turned back and said:

"Good luck, lads, you have not been a bad bunch, keep it up" and, followed by a volley of "Cheerio P.O." and "See you", disappeared into the crowd of civilian holidaymakers and was soon lost to sight.

We were left in a public place unattended. It was too much for our suppressed spirits. Some vanished into telephone boxes, others sought a quick pint, others nipped behind advertising hoardings where they whispered undying love etcetera, to the bevy of young ladies of Portsmouth whom they had earlier primed about our departure and who had come to see us off. That left but a few of us standing by the piles of kitbags and cases but our escape from reality was shortlived, for the train was then announced. We loaded the gear into a special carriage and climbed aboard. As the clock on the Guildhall chimed ten, the engine belched steam and smoke and we drew out of Portsmouth Central.

Later that afternoon, the train drew into Weymouth station and we put our caps back on and disembarked. A florid-faced Chief Petty Officer and a thin Petty Officer were on the platform to greet us. Under their barked instruction, we loaded our belongings and formed up to march out of the confines of the station to the familiar Navy Bedford lorries outside.

The two vehicles, followed by a Bedford Tilly and occupied by two young Midshipmen and the Chief and Petty Officer, made their way through the town, along the front and down an isthmus to the Portland Naval Base, where we halted at the gate. Our paybooks were sighted and we were studiously counted, finally allowed through and marched to what served as a coaling jetty. There awaited two diesel naval cutters. Anchored in the bay we saw several large warships, including two light Fleet aircraft carriers and a submarine depot ship. We were fallen in in twos as usual. The Chief called out names and those called fell in where directed, the remainder of us merely closing ranks to fill the gaps.

It suddenly dawned on us that we were being separated! We could only stand and stare as half our crew were marched down to one of the cutters and they and their gear set off across the blue water in the direction of the aircraft carriers. They waved at us as they went but we could not reply as we were fell in. The Chief had gone with that party and the thin Petty Officer took station at our front.

"You have been appointed to the aircraft carrier *HMS Ocean* for ten weeks seamanship training," he said, "after which, you will be drafted throughout the Home Fleet on destroyers or frigates. No noise or skylarking, carry on to the boats."

We rattled down the steps into the cutter, being careful not to soil our immaculate uniforms which we had been taught to treat as being more important than life itself. I sat up in the bow just behind a sailor, whose cap-tally bore the legend *"HMS Ocean"* and the powerful boat set off across the glittering waters of the harbour, past several minesweepers and fussy destroyers. A strange white-painted ship, bearing the name *"HMS Shackleton"* was passed to starboard. I later learned she was a Fleet hydrographic research vessel and the only ship currently running on coal in the Navy.

Finally, the enormous bow of the carrier *Ocean* loomed up ahead and we came gently alongside the gangway. We struggled up the great teak and steel ladder, burdened down with the awkward bundles representing our hammocks, kitbags and cases and pitched them down at last on the brow, turning aft as we had been taught, in order to salute the quarterdeck.

Having joined our first ship, we could now call ourselves Sailors! We were shepherded from the top of that impressive gangway, through massive steel passageways which led out into a huge aircraft hangar in the centre of the hull. What looked like a solitary Sea Vampire jet fighter occupied the far end of the hangar.

We were fallen in and our names ticked off a list by a Petty Officer.

"Pay attention!" he shouted, and his voice echoed from the steel bulkheads. "I don't intend to say this all again! You are now in Hawke 232 class and are here to complete ten weeks sea training to be rated Ordinary Seamen. I expect, and want, speed, efficiency and smartness from you at all times. Part of this hangar will be your mess," and he indicated an area boxed off by means of a square of aluminium lockers and containing a mess table and benches, all within the confines of a temporary construction of portable bulkheads. It put

47

me in mind of a rabbit warren; I could imagine us all coming and going like so many bunnies through its single entrance.

Our humble class of sixteen were not the only men under sea training; the carrier was a floating school to several hundred men, both regulars and national sevicemen, every man as "green" as we.

Finally, we were dismissed to stow our gear and find a hammock space before tea. A little while later the Petty Officer reappeared and bellowed at a lad that he caught smoking. The area of the aircraft hangar was strictly out of bounds for smoking and he pointed with great emphasis at the "No Smoking" signs on display at every two yards or so! Smoking was only allowed in the area of the port and starboard sponsons, to be found to the side and just below the edges of the flight deck.

The P.O. seized a passing rating, obviously a ship's crewman judging by the worn condition of his faded No. 8s and instructed him to give us a guided tour of the flight deck, heads and all relevant classrooms and passageways. This lad was none too pleased at his unsolicited task and fairly tore through the route. We were little the wiser as to our geography on our return to the draughty area that was to be our home for the next few months.

Tea was taken in the dining mess, one of the few places that we had committed to memory on the tour. One just walked in, took a mug and filled it at the tea urn took a few slices of bread and a knife and made a jam sandwich from small saucers of jam to be found on the mess table. Supper, and every other meal, was to be a line-up-and-get-it job.

It was a very tired man that returned from the washroom, slung his hammock, ticked of the small black square on the calendar and turned in to sleep that night. It was my first experience of sleeping in a hammock and after a few spring-ups in order to get into the thing, I wrapped myself up in my sheet and blanket and fell asleep in seconds, despite the constant noise and people bumping my hammock as they passed.

Our training started at 0730 the following morning with the bugle hauling us out of our slumbers. We got up at the double as usual - our new P.O. wasn't going to catch us on that one! Breakfast started at 0730 and was served until 0815, so one had to be pretty smart about washing, stowing one's hammock and gear and getting in the queue in good time, for we fell in for divisions at 0830 on the flight deck alongside the Island. Following divisions, we were then dismissed for instruction and doubled away to the hangar.

Our P.O. was already there. He watched a sample of our standard of marching and we did our best on the strange steel surface which felt very slippery and had a degree of movement which led to a feeling of insecurity in our step. The ship was still at anchor in Weymouth Bay but I found myself wondering how it would be to march when she rolled or pitched at sea. The opportunity to find out was soon to come!

From "Stand Easy" onward we were sat in a schoolroom, filling in forms about ourselves and were then issued with a ship's cap-tally bearing the title "*HMS Ocean*" in gold wire. That was to be our best one, for then a second was issued, the lettering in not so impressive gold thread. That was worn with our second-best cap and usually got the most wear.

We were introduced to our new divisional officer, a Sub-lieutenant who told us something of the history of *HMS Ocean*. She was a light fleet carrier. He quoted the tonnage and the horsepower but it is a good thing that he did not ask questions afterward because these facts were immediately forgotten. However, he did mention that *Ocean* was the first aircraft carrier in the world to have a jet aircraft land on her deck. Lt.-Commander Eric M. Brown RNVR, landed a Vampire jet on the flight deck on the 3rd and 4th December 1945 off the Isle of Wight in atrocious weather. I have always been able to remember that fact but had an awful time learning much else about the ship.

Dinner split the day in half and after lunch we had to change into "half blues", that is, bellbottoms and white front, for it was a very hot day and the breeze across the surface of the armoured flight deck was like something blowing off a desert. Our instruction now centred on the aspects of seamanship that we needed to learn for the purpose of our new existence.

We learned bends and hitches, where one struggled to make a knot in a piece of resisting, self-willed rope. We learned signalling with the ship's Yeoman of Signals. Our semaphore resembled lunatic windmills in a gale. Morse was a foreign language to me.

There was "Damage Control", or how to save a ship from sinking. Our ships were doomed to sink, judging by our early attempts on the subject! Later, we were cast adrift in one of the ship's many boats and taught how to row back again in time for supper. We even hoisted a sail in a whaler and tore merrily about the hot sunny bay, giving way to no-one, usually quite out of control and at times quite worried whether we were going to be able to get the thing to go the other way in time for our next meal!

We learned that big ships carried Royal Marines and they invariably had a very good band and from this detachment would be detailed a duty bugler. All orders were announced by means of a bugle call, usually a "G" for a general call but often with a very fancy tune for standard other ones. We soon learned them off by heart.

We mustered for P.T. on the flight deck each morning, come rain or shine, having washed and shaved, shifted in the rig of the day and stowed our hammocks, and were subjected to about twenty minutes of leaping about like idiots under the instruction of the P.T.I., which only succeeded in jarring the brain and hurting the feet. A few minutes would then be spent reading the Daily Orders on our way to breakfast in the canteen.

From breakfast we had to square off the mess in general and then it would be off to instruction until "Stand Easy", usually followed by further instruction until lunch. We fell in at 1330 and followed even more instruction until 1600 and sometimes into the dog watches.

Usually, we were free after 1600 to clean up our gear, do our washing, write our letters or go ashore as we pleased, providing that our watch did not constitute part of the duty watch for that evening. They then let us ashore, something that we had not expected.

Provided we followed our course of instruction diligently throughout the day and were not duty watch, we would be free to join the first libertyboat at 1630 and get the bus from Portland into Weymouth, where we would patrol the sea front or raid the pubs on the promenade, finishing off with a big bag of greasy chips and the last bus back at 2230.

We sang dirty Navy songs on the upper deck, to the amusement of the holidaymakers on the lower one.

One quickly learned the new routines for settling into *Ocean* with the minimum amount of fuss. One evening, my freshly ironed laundry disappeared from the messdeck table and I rounded on my shipmates angrily, believing that they were pulling my leg and had hidden it somewhere. However, it had been snatched away by the Duty Chief who had placed it in the "Scran Bag" and I was obliged to pay a fine on each item in order to retrieve it. The proceeds of the Scran Bag always went to mess social funds or to one of the many Naval charities but it was a cost that I could ill afford in those days and so I quickly learned to stow gear away once it was finished with. We also stowed other people's gear away too, to save them the cost of being caught out by the Scran Bag man.

Our sister ship, *HMS Theseus*, lay some quarter of a mile from us in the bay but the opportunity to call on our ex-mates from the original class at Portsmouth did not occur and the only occasion that I can recall seeing any of them was when we had a Regatta. I was in our whaler team and we pulled against theirs. However we were now rivals, each pulling hard for his own ship and friendship did not come into it any more. They beat us but we managed a friendly wave after the event.

It was the custom for the whole ship's company to parade every morning on the flight deck for divisions. The ship's White Ensign would be hoisted with great pomp and ceremony, each ship following her cue from the senior ship in the harbour.

Sunday divisions were the big event of the week; everyone attended in their very best uniform and the ship's company was inspected by the Captain and his officers. There was the added terror that you may get asked some sort of question or, worse still, be picked up for some misdemeanour of dress and told to lay out that kit again.

For some months, so I had been told, the ship had been paid a daily visit by a large herring gull who sported only one leg. He was a most disagreeable type, totally fearless of man and would hold his ground ferociously when approached, pecking out at anyone who dared to get too close. We nicknamed him "Skipper" and often stowed a morsel for him in the pockets of our No. 8 working shirts, thus encouraging his daily attentions. He would strut in and out amongst us during the parade and peck at the tops of our boots, usually at the precise moment we would be expected to be standing still at attention. Providing you flicked a piece of bread, or what ever you had brought for him, without being noticed by the Parade C.P.O., he normally ate it and hopped off. However, matters came to a head one Sunday morning during divisions, when the Captain and Skipper came face to face on the flank of the first row of Hawk 232.

Our brave Captain stopped, and said: "Ha, I've heard about you, old chap!" and poked the end of his glittering naval sword at the obstructing bird. He ought not to have done that. True to form, Skipper came forward in a most intimidating manner hissing viciously and, taking a firm hold on the end of the scabbard, refused to relinquish his hold. With wings outstretched, he hopped on his one leg and followed our Captain's every effort to dislodge him. Our brave Captain's entourage took shelter behind the bulk of their venerable superior.

The Captain, not expecting such a powerful response from so small a creature, lost his balance momentarily and barged through the second rank of sailors in our division, who trying to discreetly hide their mirth at the circumstances, opened up like the walls of Jericho. Captain, irate seagull and Staff burst through.

It took a very brave P.O. to rush forward to try to distract the bird and thus restore order. Skipper retreated a few yards and shook his head and swore at all and sundry whilst our Captain, a little red from his experience, brushed himself off and glared at his gaggle of officers. Their composure recovered, the inspection continued.

Gentleman as he was, I heard the Captain apologising if he had stomped on anyone's toes in the mêlée. The slow inspection over, the officers took the dais, the Royal Marine Band struck up and we marched past the saluting base by divisions, the by now quite composed Captain taking the salute. The parade over, the Captain addressed the ship's company as he was sometimes wont to do.

"It is said," he quoted, "that the seagull is in reality the soul of a long lost sailor, doomed to roam the winds of the earth until the last tromp. That being the case, I think that I have encountered the soul of none other than Lord Nelson this morning!" and amidst much laughter from officers, NCOs and ourselves, we were dismissed to church.

Church was compulsory for all men under training. All denominations were represented, Catholics, Protestants and Church of Scotland. I happened to be C of E but I had noticed that on my papers which I briefly sighted on a table in the barracks, I was typed in as being C of T. I immediately claimed that it was because I was Church of Turkey and actually got out of going to church on one occasion, a joke that made me feel very disrespectful. Needless to say, the Padre caught up with me and came into the mess to enquire what basis there was in the Church of Turkey, and with red ears I had to explain the joke. He laughed, he had heard it before, but I made sure to attend in future and my papers were subsequently altered.

One evening found me sitting at the messdeck table after supper, penning a letter to Pat. I was having the first of my problems with her: she did not like writing letters. I wrote three long letters to her one and although her letters said the things that I wanted to hear, the period of waiting for them was getting me down for I thought that she might be cooling off. After all, two years is a long time to wait, and although I had known that from the start it was none the easier to live with.

My diligent scribing was interrupted by a chap who came and sat on the bench alongside me. I had seen him about the ship quite a bit; he had failed to pass-out from several classes back and had been on *Ocean* for almost six months. He had a reputation for being a bit of a "skate", a naval term for a no-gooder and I tried to avoid talking to him. A Prince from one of the European families that had sought asylum here in Britain following the threat of Communist insurrection in their own country, he had expected to find a Commission in our Royal Navy to be a right that should be afforded him on the strength of his antecedents. He had soon found that the Service did not work that way. Now he wanted "out", but he was signed on for seven years and the Navy was trying to make a go of his time, for his sake as well as theirs, and were stubbornly hanging on to him in spite of his belligerent attitude.

He was on the bum for fags as usual. Instead of telling him to "piss off" as the majority of my shipmates did, I gave him first one and then a packet of twenty-five Blue Liners, which he promised to return on the next occasion that the canteen was open. He never did, of course.

He wanted to talk, and eventually I abandoned the letter. He began to tell me how hard life was, a very common subject with him. I listened for a while and then countered with a few moans of my own but he wasn't listening and gazed hawklike about the mess, just muttering "yes" and "no" at the right times. I suggested to him that instead of moaning and sulking about all the time as he did, that he buckle to, turn over a new leaf and try to make a go of it.

It was his turn to say "piss off" and he left. However, he returned a few evenings afterward and approaching me rather like a long-lost friend, begged the loan of my raincoat since his own had been stolen, he had a date ashore and it was raining rather hard.

"Poor deluded girl!" I thought, but eventually loaned him the coat, having extracted the most sincere promise that it would be returned as soon as he came back aboard. I saw him no more that evening and a thorough search during "Stand Easy" failed to find him on the following morning. I began to get worried.

Later in the day, I heard that he had gone AWOL and with him went my raincoat. I kept silent about the matter, hoping that he would reappear and return the item before I was called upon to muster my kit, for any missing kit had to be purchased from Slops to make up the deficiency and such a coat retailed at about nine pounds, or nearly two months pay!

The matter was resolved some days later when he returned to the Portland jetty under escort and in handcuffs. Apparently, he had travelled to London on the proceeds of my raincoat pawned in Weymouth but had foolishly confided in a sailor sharing the same train compartment that he was going "on the run", whereupon his companion had produced a pair of handcuffs and arrested him on the spot, since the latter was a member of the regulating branch! My raincoat was recovered from the pawnbrokers and I was given a telling off for having loaned out my gear.

The Service gave up at that point and I heard that our friend was taken ashore to serve a stretch in the "glasshouse" at Portsmouth, from whence he was to be dismissed the service with ignominy.

As August grew to a close, the question of the ship's participation in the annual Navy Day celebrations arose. It was decided to stage a Crossing-the-Line ceremony, a tradition experienced by all sailors when crossing the equator for the first time. The victim was hauled before "King Neptune" to be initiated by his "elves". This was a jolly event, involving the liberal soaping of the candidate's lower face with an enormous shaving brush and then having gallons of foam scraped off with a large wooden razor. Sometimes the victim was shown a huge steel razor-sharp blade but this was switched behind his back for the wooden one! This was followed by a dumping in cold water, when the candidate was then declared to be a proper Deep-Sea Mariner and usually issued with a certificate to that effect.

I was elected to act as a candidate! We practised for some time in the ship's collapsible swimming pool, which would be rigged on the upper deck for the purpose. We worked out quite a good routine. Most of the "actors" were ship's company staff and I was only one of two national servicemen selected.

Navy Days started on the Saturday and the ship's boats were in constant use, bringing civilians to the ship and assisting the female ones up the gangway. The male visitors had to look out for themselves. Since the Crossing-the-Line ceremony was to be the highlight of the Monday's proceedings, I was given other tasks to perform. I was put in charge of a sheeted-off area of the heads, for the use of the lady visitors. It was my first experience of being a lavatory attendant! Initially, all went well; the ladies were all very polite and I was most helpful and obliging and kept up a steady supply of toilet rolls, each delivered at just the right time and not before my "customers" had run out of them. I even collected one shilling and sevenpence in tips.

On the first day, as I stood at the entrance to the toilets officially indicating the correct way in, a rating slid up to me clasping a ten bob note. Could I look the other way, whilst he and his young lady visited my toilets together?

"Not on your life, mate," said I, "hop it!" He went away, but came back a little while later. His girlfriend had a mate. We could all go in together. The spectre of the VD film arose before me but as he was obviously desperate because his young lady had come all the way from Battersea to be with him, I opted for his original offer and took the money.

The pair waited until the coast was clear, scuttled into the "Ladies" and the canvas screen closed behind them. I waited outside with my heart in my mouth until they came out one at a time, about half an hour later. The girl winked broadly at me as she passed.

The second day of my being "Captain of the Heads" passed without incident apart from the fact that the visiting public kept me very busy. When they had at last departed for the shore, it was my task to clean and secure the toilets, in readiness for the final day's visitors on the Bank Holiday Monday. In the course of my duties, I came upon a pair of pale green ladies' knickers, sans elastic at the waist, probably explaining the reason for their summary abandonment.

These I tucked into my pocket and the next that was seen of this feminine item was on divisions on Monday morning, when they were to be seen fluttering in the summer breeze from the jib of the carrier's mobile jumbo deck crane! The hundreds of assembled ratings thought it a great wheeze but the officers appeared quite put out by it all, possibly because they were under constant scrutiny by neighbouring warships, waiting for such an opportunity to engage in humorous banter by means of flags and signal lamps. The impromptu signal was struck from the crane's jib, a task which involved starting the engine and lowering the boom. I could have told them how to accomplish the task in an easier fashion!

I handed over my toilet duty to another and went ashore in the motorboat together with the rest of King Neptune's party to carry out our Crossing-the-Line ceremony on the beach at Weymouth.

Our shaving bench was set up in the shallows at the edge of the beach and as soon as a big enough audience had assembled, one of the officers, acting as MC, addressed the throng of holidaymakers and told them about the naval tradition that they were about to witness. We "victims" were seized one by one by King Neptune's blackamoors, made to sit on the rough shaving stool, covered in great blobs of foam much to the delight of small children in the crowd, then shaved with the fearsome razor and unceremonously tipped backwards into the chill sea. It all went down rather well and our patrons gave generously to the Soldiers, Sailors and Airmen Funds when we went amongst them with our collecting boxes.

We did three performances and just when I thought that we may miss supper altogether, the gear was packed away and we made off in the motor boat which had been busily employed ferrying children about the harbour on jolly trips. In all, it had been a very enjoyable day. An old sailor in the crowd had treated us ratings to a bottle of beer each, we had enjoyed a packed lunch on the beach in the pleasant company of two young ladies from Droitwich and the sun had shone hotly from behind the clouds on more than one occasion.

Upon my return to *Ocean* I found a letter propped up in the mess trap for me from Pat, telling me that she was coming on holiday to Weymouth the next Saturday with her parents and that if I could get ashore, she would be looking for me along the front in the early afternoon. Of course, the week dragged as slowly as time ever did and I was forced to swop watches with a friend, as it would have been my turn for duty watch on the Saturday. But at last, I boarded the ship's libertyboat and we danced off across the sparkling water for my first meeting with Pat in over eight weeks.

It was like something from an American musical film. Through the sea of faces marching toward me along the promenade, I suddenly saw her. I grinned from ear to ear, she burst into tears and we ran into each others arms and hugged and hugged. Her mum and dad stood by sheepishly but then it was handshakes all round and enquiries as to how I was getting on and how I liked it all. Of course I lied and made it sound like the next best thing to sliced bread, but the smell and the soft, warm feel of my dear Pat had wakened a lot of suppressed urges and I would have given anything to have been cycling down a green English lane with Pat and to hell with the Navy! But it was not the thing to whinge about such matters in those days. It was your duty and you jolly well got on with it and did not openly complain.

After coffee with mum and dad, we two sweethearts were left to our own devices and were asked to be sure to meet up at seven o'clock at a certain place along the front. Four precious hours together in the brilliant sunshine was all one could wish for. We found a quiet place behind a hedge in a field overlooking the sea and talked our hearts out. My faith in our relationship was refuelled.

We kissed and cuddled, smoked and chatted and the four hours of heaven sped swiftly by until it was time to return to the promenade and for Pat to go back with her folks to continue their holiday. We were a bit late, but not overtly so, and I had to bid my farewells, promising to let her know when I was coming home on leave. She walked away and I waved her out of sight. I never saw her again. She wrote a few weeks later and called the affair off, largely I suspect because of the waiting.

The ship took part in a Fleet Regatta as August turned to September. At eight stones four pounds, I was not able to put a lot of weight on an oar so I was given a job on the rescue boat, which also doubled as a committee boat for the officials and judges, a best uniform job. I performed the task of bowman, hooking onto the ship with a large boathook, keeping an eye out for the coxwain and bearing off when we let go.

It was an easy task but I was obliged, when not performing my tasks, to remain below deck in the small forward canopy, which led to a bit of a queasy stomach so I was glad when, on one occasion, an officer had to be returned to his ship to start his watch and we lay in the lee of the submarine depot ship *HMS Maidstone* in still water for a while and my stomach made a recovery. Thus I survived the rest of the day's events. I seem to recall that our ship won one or two of the pulling events but the overall result was a poor one for us.

One evening in mid-September George Billington and I were patrolling along the front at Weymouth. It was just getting dark after a very hot, still summer's day and the beach was still occupied by families and couples who were just beginning to think about quitting the sands. Amongst the crowds, George and I saw two girls in bikinis sitting on their towels. My "Dear John" letter still hot in my locker from Pat spurred me on and I coerced George into coming down onto the beach to try to chat up the two girls.

It was obvious, when we got nearer, that these two young ladies were quite a bit younger than we had imagined but we could not turn back as they had seen us coming and were exchanging hurried, shy whispers. We sat on the sands next to them and started our patter, as young men everywhere do, and very soon we were on good terms and completely at our ease. I had settled on the elder of the two.

She told me that her name was Jenny and that she came from Bristol. She and her friend Sue were staying at Jenny's aunt's boarding house in Weymouth for the next week or so. George and I walked them home after quite a few hours chat, buying chips from a shop on the way, and arranged to meet them for the pictures on the following day. Thus started another relationship, doomed as the first but for different reasons this time.

On the following day the girls met us as arranged and after the pictures, because Jenny's aunt had extended an invitation to her boarding house for supper, we returned there. It had been a long time since we had tasted civvy food and the simple fry-up was fantastic. Afterwards the girls walked us back to the landing jetty to catch the libertyboat and for the first time we kissed and cuddled in a bus shelter. It was several days before I could see Jenny again and her greeting had a sense of desperation in it. I deliberately took her to the same field that Pat and I had been, to even though I knew it was being a bit perverse. George was just a bush away, petting with Sue and I kissed and cuddled with Jenny like there was no tomorrow, but I did not want to hurt this sweet seventeen year old with the trauma that I had so recently endured, so kept it all very much under control. Jenny took this for lack of passion on my part and I finally had to explain the saga of Pat to her. This drew us together strangely enough and she promised that she would never let me go.

I carefully stuck to the kiss and cuddle routine. She was too nice to take advantage of, a tame tale by today's standards! Their holiday at an end, the girls returned to Bristol, Jenny to a finishing school and her friend off on her first job. George and I saw them to the station. George was glad to see Sue go for he felt that she was much too young for him at sixteen and he did not write to her. Nor, as it happens, did she write to him, so there were no bones broken there.

Jenny, however, lost no time in writing to me. Her letters were a wonderful tonic and did no end of good in perking me up. I loved writing to her and telling her about our daily events, but in the meantime, George and I were already dating a couple of girls from Stockport! These two ladies were not up to the same standard as our earlier encounters. They were on holiday at a caravan site with the younger one's aunt and uncle and on one occasion when their chaperones were on an outing, leaving the girls to amuse themselves, we were invited back to the caravan. We played a game involving the removal of almost all of our clothing, which led to us tucked up in bed with a girl each and a "free issue" as company.

Having thus started, we spent the rest of their holiday, when we could get ashore, in sexual activities of one sort or another but being very careful not to be foolish about it. They never wrote to us either!

The end of September approached. Suddenly, on the Daily Orders came the news that the ship was to pay a courtesy visit to Penzance. The anchors came up a little after 0800 and we headed out through the breakwater into the Channel. It was a new experience to sit in our classroom feeling the deck rising and falling and having to hold on to the sides of the desk to maintain balance.

We had been assigned a new instructor just a few days previously, a Cornishman, Petty Officer Camper. He was an old sailor from the last war and this was his last job before retiring from the Royal Navy after twenty-two years service. In fact, we were his last class and he was very anxious that we should be the best one aboard. He was such a nice, helpful, patient fellow that we did our very best for him and things went along fine.

A strong westerly drove the Channel into a succession of long grey rollers and dinner was taken with some consternation by some, including me, for I had begun to feel very clammy and weak and was developing a nauseous feeling. Standing in the wind blowing over the flight deck cured the situation but I could hardly do that all afternoon and we were not due to dock until 1800.

The lunch hour soon passed and I attended afternoon instruction, holding on to my gorge by sheer determination. My classmates had paled considerably too, and even P.O. Camper looked a bit "off", but there were one or two who appeared quite unaffected by it all. Then the Tannoy boomed "Hands to stations for entering harbour, special sea dutymen to your stations". P.O. Camper put down his chalk.

"That's enough of points of a compass for one session lads, we shall go to the fo'c'sle and observe how the ship's anchors are laid."

We all trooped forward to the area just below the flight deck, right in the bows of the carrier, where the ship's company ratings were preparing the mighty anchors for lowering. We lined up each side of the pair of anchor chains, known as cables in the Service, and watched how they were got ready and held back by the steam winch's brakes until the final "slips" or retaining clamps would be let off and the whole lot released when so instructed by the officers on the bridge.

The movement up and down with the pitch of the heavy ship as she made her way into Penzance Bay was even more pronounced on the foredeck and

I prayed for the the blasted ship to be still. My prayers were totally ignored and I finally knew that for the first time in my life I was about to be seasick.

"Excuse me, P.O.," I spluttered, stepping out of line, much to the undisguised amusement of the anchor party. One glance at me told P.O. Camper the whole story.

"Through that hatchway," he said, "the heads are on the port side!" With my hand over my mouth in case of accidents, I fled the fo'c'sle. I made the heads and spewed heavily.

Through bleary eyes, I saw another body alongside me also being sick. It was our Petty Officer. He later told us that he had never been sick in his life before being torpedoed in the Mediterranean in 1942 but since then he had been sick every time he went to sea. It was nothing therefore to be ashamed of, but rather something that you did not allow to get the better of you. I was almost always sick thereafter but the test was in one's attitude to it and I always tried to tolerate it and recover, as I usually did fairly quickly.

We returned to the foredeck just in time to join the depleted balance of our class in witnessing the releasing of the anchors, which left the anchoreyes with a great roar of tortured steel and a cloud of red rust, followed by a loud splash and then by a loud clattering and flaying on the "Scotsman", the name for the reinforced deck, as the anchors bit into the bottom of the bay and the mass of the carrier swung round to point to anchor. The thousands of tons of steel came to a rest at last, all pitching and rolling ceased, and we quickly recovered our stomachs in time for supper.

We had anchored some way from the shore and no shore leave was posted up on the ship's company notice board. Looking at the state of the strong westerly swell, there would not have been many takers anyway. We all decided to await calmer waters before forcing a landing at Penzance! I went into the mess hall and had supper. By now, I was feeling quite well and the great ship was hardly moving at all.

There was a film showing in the hangar but I played deck quoits until it got a bit dark and the aircraft landing lights were switched on, when I went below, cleaned my boots and Garth's too, then washed for bed. Reveille came too soon and we tumbled sleepily from our hammocks, filed into the bathrooms and washed and shaved rather like zombies. Daily Orders gave no indication of any matter of note but when I observed the sea through one of the port sponson openings, it looked a little smoother and I contemplated a small run ashore to discover the lie of the land. However, we were surprised to hear just after "Stand Easy" that the carrier was taking immediate passage to Plymouth, nicknamed "Guzz" to us sailor folk. I dreaded the return to sea.

Even though it was now considerably smoother, it still bore terrors from the effects of the day before.

I need not have worried. The ship hardly rolled a foot either way and the coastline to port slipped by easily. Just before tea-time, the lower deck was ordered to be cleared of all but special dutymen - it was they after all that were steering and working the ship - and we fell in in curious ranks in the aircraft hangar to be addressed by the Captain, a most unusual event and something not mentioned in the Daily Orders. "Buzzes" were already rife as to why the ship should have sailed so prematurely from Penzance but it appeared that we were soon to find out why. We were called to attention by the Carrier's Commander as the Captain entered the hangar.

There was a whispered consultation between them when we were stood at ease and our Captain came to the front of the group of officers to address us. We had received secret orders to sail at a moment's notice. It was regretted that at this moment he could not tell us where we were bound, but he would keep us posted on future developments. At present we were on passage to Plymouth, there was to be no shore leave and no mail would be landed at Plymouth, although mail would be received and distributed. Upon our arrival at Plymouth, we were not to communicate with any person ashore on any aspect of this matter. There were loud groans at the news of the cancellation of leave, which were dismissed by the Captain with a wave of his hand.

"Leave will come later" he said, "when our job is done. I want one hundred percent effort from you, particularly from the new influx of national servicemen for sea training, so let us see what you are made of." We dismissed to a buzz of rumour, speculation and some disgruntled remarks, since we had all been in the Navy for over two months now and had yet to get shore leave home. This exercise, or whatever it was, could only further delay matters.

Plymouth and its famous landmark, Drake's Memorial, came into view just as the sun dipped into the cloud bank to the west of us. The gale in the Channel had blown itself out and as the seas were following ones, our passage had been easy. The towering mass of steel that was *HMS Ocean* came slowly to rest alongside the dock, the tugs were slipped and we were fallen out from our places on the flight deck where we lined up, as all sailors do on entering harbour.

This is a tradition dating from the days of constant wars at sea, for when a ship came demonstrating peaceful intentions the fact that her crew were all in sight and could be counted, allowed her to pass unchallenged beneath the guns of the harbour defences. Likewise the tradition of firing a salute when entering or leaving harbour indicated that the guns were unloaded and that no act of aggression was to be expected from the visitor. A returned salute indicated that the good intentions were reciprocated.

Supper was late that evening and our meal was punctuated by the bangs and crashes of heavy equipment being manoeuvred about the flight deck. When I went topsides to discover what was happening, I found the dockyard cranes busy craning aboard all sorts of military vehicles and equipment. In fact, it was a very noisy night for us all as the dockyard "maties" worked non-stop in loading the ship. We awoke in the morning to the sound of the hangar lift descending, covered in lorries, jeeps and trailers which were man-handled into rows with little room in between for us to pass through.

That was the end of our below decks football team for the time being! There were no divisions that morning and no P.T.! Any delusions we may have held about entering into a holiday atmosphere were quickly dispelled when, after mustering in our mess, we were given into the care of senior Leading hand and a dockyard matie and set to work in lashing all of these obstructive vehicles down to ring-bolts, welded into the deck for the purpose. It was our task to make short wire strops, which we used to secure the vehicle to the deck by passing it through the wheels and then chocking them in tight. Heavier vehicles, such as radar or wireless lorries and personnel carriers, were likewise wired down on the flight deck, although I seem to recall that our dear old Sea Vampire fighter remained in situ.

It was obvious that we were going somewhere and that a long sea voyage was intended. Most of the vehicles aboard were in airforce blue and it was with some surprise that I found row upon row of soldiers, carrying their rifles and in-field equipment and steel helmets, streaming over the crest of the gangway. Military policemen appeared from nowhere to shepherd them about the ship and suddenly, space aboard was at a premium.

We worked until supper-time, a staggered affair since there were now several hundred more bodies to feed and water. We were asked by our P.O. to help the "Pongoes", Navy slang for soldiers, wherever possible, which gave us an air of authority and as a result, ensured our closest co-operation. We worked voluntarily on occasions when we need not have, to ensure the comfort of our "passengers" and to show them about the ship.

We sailed within thirty-six hours of first tying up in Plymouth and headed out into the smooth English Channel. We headed due west at first, then south-south west and there were no prizes for guessing that we were bound for the Atlantic, South Atlantic or the Mediterranean, though in my opinion clearly the latter, since the papers had been full of a fresh spate of violence in the Middle East, Cyprus in particular. By evening, the English coast was a mere smoky stain away to our starboard quarter and the western tip of the

Cap la Hague and the distant Channel Islands lay to port. We entered the northern extremities of the Bay of Biscay. A light grey smudge far astern was *Theseus* for she had followed through the same routine, also bound for the same mysterious destination as we.

We were soon to discover that there were good things about this trip and bad things too. Morning divisions were largely abandoned and the ship worked on a more relaxed attitude. Our instruction took in other subjects, such as sentry duty, bayonet drill and even more damage control.

We were instructed in the art of acting as look-outs and stood watches during the daylight hours. With such a large contingent of soldiers and Marines aboard, there was an increase in the number of deck games played and a healthy fixture of deck quoits and hockey matches developed.

One evening, a Petty Officer P.T.I. came into the mess looking for people to take part in a boxing tournament to be held in the hangar.

"You would make a smashing Bantam weight!" he told me and I volunteered. I did quite a bit of training too and took it quite seriously.

The events started after rounds on the Saturday and the eliminating events went on most of the day, the finals being scheduled for the evening in front of the ship's company in the hangar. I was put up against a regular, one of the *Ocean*'s company who was my size and weight and had also never boxed before.

Our three round amateur event started at about 1530 and the ringside was packed with my messmates, who had either come to cheer me on or to see me get a hiding! They were to be disappointed. My opponent only struck out at me on the retreat, with largely ineffectual flailing blows. I chased him about the ring, causing no real damage but winning easily on points.

This took me into the quarter-finals in my weight and I approached the ring with some confidence. My opponent in this instance was a national serviceman, tall and extremely thin with a thick mop of ginger hair. I had seen him before, his mess was not far from mine. We touched gloves and listened to the referee's instructions, then the bell went for round one.

I came out, chin tucked into my gloves and, springing from foot to foot, determined to put on a very professional show for my shipmates. "Ginger" pushed out a left which caught me on the forehead. I counter-punched but he was then out of range. I pushed forward, he poked me back with the straight left and followed it up with an equally straight right which stung a bit. I swung viciously and missed and the remainder of the first round was spent trying to get close enough to even hit my adversary. The bell went. My seconds worked briefly on my reddened forehead and cheekbones and advised me to let the man come to me, get under his jabs and give him what for.

I returned behind the enormous gloves, feeling somewhat angry that I had not yet had the chance to really clout my ginger tormentor and then made a few risky dashes under the long jabs, which struck at me with the speed of a rattlesnake. I sustained a small cut over the right eye in exchange for two or three heavy body-blows and a swift uppercut to Ginger's chin, all of which he did not enjoy but which certainly did nothing to alter his demeanor. I therefore spent the closing seconds of the round dodging the jabs and not scoring anything. The seconds repeated their advice and I went out for the third and final round, determining to heed their instructions.

But Ginger was in for the kill. He had had enough of softening me up and was set to put me on my back. His lively attack at least gave me the opportunity to land a few heavy blows to his slight torso but there was no avoiding that jab and at the end of the round, the referee held up his glove in victory and I retired to my corner for the blood from the eye wound to be treated. Ginger went on to become champion in his class after a very good win over another of my ilk.

Later, we often stopped and spoke when the opportunity arose. Trying to bash the living daylights out of one another seemed a good way to get on conversational terms.

The finals of the boxing tournament in the after part of the hangar, in an atmosphere thick with blue cigarette smoke, the frenzied cries of the audience and the increasing roll and pitch of the ship as she steamed further south into the Bay of Biscay, was akin to a night out in Hades! The benches and chairs stowed away, we made for our hammocks, to awake the following day to a heavy head sea and more seasickness, which fortunately soon passed. There was the constant duty of patrolling the tethered Army and Air Force vehicles ensuring that none broke loose, although whilst I was at lunch, a small jeep did break loose and was flung across the hangar, causing no damage to the ship but considerably denting and rendering its bodywork. It was tied down for later repairs.

I remember standing at one of the starboard sponsons, just beneath the level of the flight deck watching *Theseus* some half a mile astern, pitching and wallowing, throwing tons of grey water over her bows and thinking that our poor ship was doing just as badly.

However, the spell of bad weather passed on during the night and later in the evening we purred along with the merest vibration, heading ever southward. The sun went down on the red cliffs on our port horizon and the Army personnel came out on deck again.

After several hot, sunny days of this pleasant cruising, the ship's company notice board announced: "The ship will dock at 1200 hours at Gibraltar. Notice regarding the entitlement for leave will be promulgated later." A little later, we were assembled in the hangar where long tables had been erected and we were issued with tropical rig of white shorts, long white socks and white canvas shoes. We were obviously bound for hotter climes.

The Portuguese shoreline mingled with that of the Spanish coast and the morning sun made the cliffs burn with a renewed fire. Our first visit to a foreign station was about to become a reality and although no-one would admit it, we were all excited and looking forward to stepping ashore at last.

CHAPTER
FIVE

The estimated time of arrival at Gibraltar was given as 1145 but "Stand Easy" had come and gone and we were still ensconced in the classroom below decks, leaving the rattles and bangs of industry above, as the *Ocean*'s crew prepared the ship for entering harbour. Suddenly, our instructor consulted his watch and we were told to fall in outside in the passageway. We were led up into the island superstructure of the carrier and from there, marched out onto the flight deck. A right turn led us toward the bow and we halted in two ranks, one facing to port and the other to starboard. Gibraltar lay some five miles on the horizon ahead, bathed in the warm pink light of the morning sun and shimmering in a heat haze. The hills of Algeciras, dotted with dark green scrub and stark white stone, formed a contrasting backdrop to the massive Rock, with its distinctive concrete slab to the south side. North Africa shimmered redly on the starboard bow as we approached from the southwest.

We were already in position as "Hands to stations for entering harbour" was piped. We rocked easily on the balls of our feet in the hot September sun, cooled only by a breeze caused by the slipstream coming over the bow. This was one of the most relaxing times that I can recall of those early months in the Service. The huge steel bow gently rose and fell into the clear blue sea and a small cloud of pure white gulls hung motionless above us, matching our speed with the merest dip of the wing. Several hundred yards to port, *Theseus* dipped and rose, her flight deck also crowded with row after row of clean white uniforms.

A sudden rumble vibrated through our feet as the anchor party veered the cable, ready for letting the anchor go in an emergency, and wisps of steam from the mighty capstans blew up over the bow, rapidly evaporating in the balmy air.

The famous Rock, captured by Admiral Rooke and his Royal Marines in a daring night climb which dislodged the Moorish occupiers in 1704, loomed ever larger until it was bigger than the ship, finally dwarfing our minuscule light Fleet carrier into insignificance by the sheer magnificence of its grey-white bulk. We slipped through the northern breakwater into the harbour.

A cannon flashed from the fort ashore and the concussion rippled lazily across the calm water to reverberate against our steel hull. Our own saluting gun crashed a reply and we came to attention at the piping of the "Still". We tied up, starboard side to, on the dockside and the gangways were run ashore.

Whenever early summer blesses us with a still, hot day, when the crickets chirp in the tall grass, the air is alive with the buzz of insects and the sun burns hot on my back, I call it a "Gibraltar day", for that is where I first truly experienced such a relaxed feeling of contentment.

In those days, Gibraltar was an odd mixture of England, North Africa and Spain. The border into Spain at La Linea was open and every morning the causeway was packed with commuters travelling to their work on the Rock from their Spanish homes and then back again in the evening, leaving the Rock to that proud breed of souls, the Gibraltarians. A mixture of Moor, Spaniard and Anglo-Saxon, they lived a secluded life on the island fortress. Their currency was in pounds, they had English-style policemen, there was a Marks and Spencer in the high street and Toby beer in the bars and cafes, but through all these things British, Spanish influences permeated, reflected in the architecture, in the street names and the names of the bars, such as the "Trocadero" and the "Continental". I fell in love with this strange, homely anomaly and have never tired of revisiting its dry dusty streets, its quaint rocky parks and minute beaches.

Garth, George, Jim Baxter and I hurried ashore at the earliest opportunity. It was my first ever trip to foreign parts and I loved the strangeness of it all. We walked around the headland, glad to be free of the steel ships and the dockyard area, swam in Catlan Bay and basked in the sun on the tiny beach. I collected some large glazed seashells, resembling freshwater mussels in shape but with such a range of pink and blue colours that I could not resist picking them up to take home to mother. I wrapped them up with my swimming costume and towel for safe keeping. The freedom and space of even such a small beach was heaven after the crowded quarters of our aircraft carrier. A sudden chill as the afternoon sun crept round to the other side of the Rock got us dressed and we set off on the return journey to the ship.

We went by way of Eastern Beach, the border area to La Linea, back along the high street and past the Governor's residence which was guarded by a handful of British soldiers, pausing long enough to watch the changing of the guard executed in slow time and a joy to watch. We even admitted that we were nowhere as proficient as those soldiers when it came to rifle drill and ceremony. Doubtless they had been at it longer than we but it was magic just the same.

Back at the dockyard and the fuss and bustle of the activity around *Ocean*, further stores and even more trucks and personnel carriers were being loaded, although where we had space for them all seemed a mystery to me. Even the flight deck had some of the heavier vehicles bowsed down with wire strops, having been removed from the hangar deck to allow space for lighter vehicles.

The ship resembled a huge car ferry by now and there was worse to come, for even more soldiers were embarked from heaven knows where and they and their equipment cluttered up every available space on the lower decks and on the gun sponsons. I swear that the old ship sank lower in the water with every passing hour and by now her lifeboat capacity must have been well outstripped. That meant that in the event of a sinking, it would be passengers to the boats first and our contingent would be expected to make our own provision for survival! Little help could be expected from the supply of Cardey rafts provided, for one fell over the side one afternoon and immediately sank! It had rotted away and become quite useless.

The move from Gibraltar was sudden and unexpected. We had had the impression that we would sojourn there for some time, but there was work to do on the High Seas and we slipped our berth almost stealthily on the Sunday afternoon, heading east into the warm, blue Mediterranean. The Rock finally dipped from sight at the setting of the sun and we were again in convoy with *Theseus*, bound for our unknown destination which everyone guessed was Cyprus.

The following morning we were engaged in our usual seamanship instruction in the aircraft hangar. We were cramped for space but the draught from the outside, and the fact that we were not in the direct sunlight, kept us cool. The ship forged ahead at about seventeen knots, a clean easy pace, with hardly any roll or pitch to it. A little after "Stand Easy", we came up to the flight deck for a spell of parade training and the heat of the sun on the steel flight deck burned through our boots, proving most uncomfortable.

"Up spirits" was piped at 1150 and the ship's company ratings and NCOs over the age of twenty fell out for their daily tot of rum. We were not yet old enough to draw ours. However, we lined up to receive a glass of lime juice in the hangar and since we were in tropical climes and subject to dehydration, salt tablets were also issued. I did not consume any more, having sampled the first one. Later in the afternoon, the ship's P.T.I.s got us to rig a canvas swimming pool and this proved very popular. The carriers steamed further eastward and an air of being a passenger on a summer cruise, began to permeate the seamen's messdecks. For the first time we began to enjoy being sailors. It did not last of course.

The next day we were under a blistering sun, relashing several of the upper deck vehicles into new positions which would facilitate their easier dispatch when being moved to shore, hot and uncomfortable work which was given to us in preference to the Army lads, since there was a considerable amount of splicing of short strops to be done.

However, a small bonus came from this. The Commander happened by during one of our "puff and sweat" sessions and as it was almost lunch-time, instructed the ship to be stopped and we were allowed a swim in the cooling waters of the Mediterranean. A safety boat was lowered for our convenience. This was very popular. At one time the sea around the carrier was as thick with swimmers as if she had been hit and was being abandoned and the P.T.I.s and their whistles had quite a job in rounding us all up and getting us back on board.

The following day, the practice was allowed to continue and just before lunch, the ship hove to and the gangways were lowered over the side. Some people walked down the gangways and plunged into the sparkling blue water from these but others leapt from the gun-sponsons, uttering cries of "Geronimo". Several braver souls leapt from the flight deck and seeing this, I suggested to several of my mates that we could do the same. Hand in hand in a line, we ran to the end of the flight deck astern and launched ourselves feet first into space. It was a longer way down than I had thought and we hit the water with a mighty splash.

However, as I began to rise I chanced to open my eyes and to my horror, saw not far off to my right, a grey torpedo shape with a dorsal fin swimming on a parallel course. I broke surface in a panic and almost ran across the surface of the sea toward the safety boat shouting, "Shark, shark!", for I was convinced that that was what I had seen. Of course, everyone thought that I was having a skylark and took several moments to see that I was serious. With that the whistles were blown, the water cleared and we all retired safely aboard. Anxious faces scanned the calm sea then, one by one, a school of playful porpoises surfaced, blowing spray from their blowholes and half the ship collapsed with laughter. I got lost in the crowd lining the side.

Several of the officers plunged into the sea to approach the porpoises but the beautiful creatures kept their distance and when the officers eventually returned to the ship, we got under way again and continued east. Fortunately, hardly anyone seemed aware that it was I who had started this panic but it was the subject of much merriment for the rest of that day.

Later that evening, we passed by several beautiful, wooded islands that rose straight up out of the sea. We passed close enough for me to observe a man on a bicycle pedalling along the shoreline road and I momentarily felt homesick for my bike and the open road.

Our leisure hours were spent watching the sea hiss past from the relative shelter of the side decks beneath the gun sponsons, where the sun could not penetrate to fry us. The atmosphere between decks was stifling.

I had my hair cut in a crew-cut and was left with just over a quarter of an inch of amazed stubble growing upright from my scalp by the time the barber had finished with me.

The Glass Mountain was showing at the ship's cinema and I went to see that again that evening before retiring to my hammock, tired and weary at the end of yet another day.

We entered Grand Harbour, Malta, late on Friday evening. The lights of Valletta shimmered invitingly across the water but a visit was out of the question as orders for libertymen had not been posted on the ship's company notice board and we were forced to wait until the next day. We contented ourselves in leaning on the rails at the side deck spaces, watching the shore lights and calling out to the small boats that came slowly out from the shore, manned by their Maltese owners selling lighters, watches, embroidered tablecloths and lace. As our main shopping could wait until the next day, very little cash changed hands and eventually, the boats pulled for the island and were soon lost in the black mass of the land.

Daily Orders told us that as our stay in Malta was to be a short one, only one run ashore would be possible. I was not free to go, as my watch was duty, so I spent most of the Saturday afternoon bringing provisions and stores aboard from a lighter alongside, whilst most of my colleagues streamed into Valletta on a brilliant, hot day.

The air in the harbour was hot and still and there were few places on the great steel ship where one could find any refuge from the heat. I began to feel glad that I had not made the trip into town, for it was sure to be hotter there and when the first of our libertymen returned with their supply of "rabbits", a slang name for gifts, they confirmed how hot it had been and how cool the carrier was in comparison. I heard tales of the markets and streets of Valletta, of the seedy street of steps known as "the Gut" and of the bars and cafes which lined each side of the street.

We encountered our instructor just after supper and he told us that when our task in the Mediterranean was completed, we should be returning home via Malta and Gibraltar giving plenty of opportunity to get to see the sights again. That made me feel better, so when we slipped out of the harbour with even more troops aboard, I watched the Rocks slip into the western sky and made a mental promise to return.

We returned to the daily routines of instruction and our normal domestic duties, such as keeping the mess in tip-top condition and the constant dhobying sessions, the monotony punctuated by the occasional film-show in the hangar or with organised deck games. We also spent many an hour leaning over the edges of the gun sponsons just smoking and watching the fluorescence in the wake of the ship and shouting excitedly each time a shooting star flashed across the velvet sky. We talked about our lives, where we came from and what we did in civvy street. There were representatives from all sorts of trades and from a few professions, and we really got to know one another's problems, girlfriends, and likes and dislikes. The days passed by easily.

The Mediterranean was a beautiful carpet of blue water, over which we glided effortlessly. It could also be other things. One morning the sky turned to copper, a powerful wind sprang up from the north and in no time at all, the sea was a boiling cauldron of white water, which set a roll on our carrier, threatening to tear the tethered vehicles from the flight deck and cast them into the sea. We set about lashing heavy wire cables from truck to truck but had they started to go over the side; nothing would have stopped them. Even our heavy Jumbo crane went for a walk on its own until an engineer came up from below and put it in gear to stop it moving further. This sudden storm stopped just short of making me sick and soon the sun came out and peace was restored, although I remember having to sweep up sacks full of the desert dust from the not too distant African continent that had blown aboard from the upper atmosphere. Very soon, all that could be seen on the surface of the sea was our wake, which stretched over the horizon astern.

Cyprus announced its presence by a grey-pink smudge in the distant east and some time later, we lined the flight deck once more for entering harbour. Our destination turned out to be Famagusta, on the far eastern side of the island and we actually turned west to enter the harbour where we dropped anchor.

Our arrival appeared to go unnoticed until a launch came out from the shore and some Army officers were piped aboard. A little later, a local boat appeared. It resembled a Venetian gondola, complete with a small fringed canopy beneath which a gentleman sat reading a newspaper. It seemed a great distance to row a craft merely to read a paper and I learned later that when the gentleman was investigated by means of a powerful gunnery telescope, two large holes were cut in the paper and he was, in fact, observing us! Apparently, a bren gun was sent for, rigged up on the end of the flight deck and a short burst of fire aimed into the sea near the spy, whereupon he leapt to his feet, pulled the cord of a hidden outboard motor and streaked off shorewards never to return. I heard the gunfire and raced to the sponsons aft to see what was happening, but sadly missed all the action.

Harbour launches and small tugs towed out a constant supply of small lighters to the port side and the task of loading the military vehicles on to them and transporting them all to shore began. This work continued all night and for most of the following day and what with the gangways full of disembarking troops, it was a very hectic time, leaving us tired, hot and hungry. We worked in shifts, initially eight hours on then four off, but this rate of labour was reduced to four on and then four off.

To our surprise, troops came aboard from the island and the rumour was that we would be embarking them for exchange with other troops in Suez. It was from them that we learned a lot of the troubles affecting the people of Cyprus. The unloading completed, the armed guards were called off the flight deck and we left the harbour under cover of darkness, heading once more out to sea. Our course this time was a more southerly one, which further fuelled the buzz concerning a visit to Egypt. The ship appeared in no hurry. Perhaps we were waiting for *Theseus* to join us, having unloaded her cargo of men and machinery. Eventually, a day or so later, she hove in sight with much flashing of signal lamps and waving of coloured flags, and we set of once more in convoy.

Toward the afternoon, my attention was called to the changing colour of the sea about us. Instead of the usual brilliant sparkling blue Mediterranean, the sea was changing to a thick, soupy beige. We had entered the waters of the Nile.

As yet only a faint, grey stain on the horizon gave a hint where land lay, and so it proved to be, for the Nile carried her precious silt out into the Mediterranean for some eleven miles before it all finally sank from sight and the waters became blue again.

We went to stations for entering harbour and at about 1600, *Ocean* anchored in the harbour at Port Said. Almost immediately, she was surrounded by native boats packed with Arab traders selling all sorts of souvenirs, which were hauled aboard in wicker baskets with much haggling between vendor and purchaser. The after gangway was rigged. Several dignitaries were bought out in the Admiral's barge and aboard crafts of their own. The air was filled with the shrill sound of the Bo'sun's call, and it was better to keep clear of the quarterdeck and the upper flight deck.

Dusk fell early in those climes. The Officer of the Watch and his staff cleared the area of all "bum boats" and their Arab occupants before dark and a full watch was detailed to keep an eye on all access points to the gangways and other boarding points. I took station on one of the gun sponsons watching

71

the traffic on the river, a river as old as time itself, a river steeped in both history and mystery. This was a place to remember and I looked forward to getting ashore and treading the ancient sands for myself.

During the night, there was a bit of a commotion. There were few nights on such a crowded ship when one enjoyed an unbroken rest but in the morning we awoke to be told that the flight deck was out of bounds and that armed guards were patrolling the deck and sponsons. The anchor watch had reported seeing signs of frogmen alongside the carrier and several grenades were said to have been thrown overboard in an attempt to surface them. I spoke to a sailor whom I met returning his .303 rifle to the armoury. He laughed. Had he seen a frogman, he told me, he could have done little about it as he had not been issued with any ammunition! However, boat patrols were maintained during the next twenty-four hours but apparently nothing was seen and eventually the flight deck was patrolled by men armed only with whistles.

The hot day passed on with seamanship instruction. We learned how to throw a heaving-line across the chasm of one of the aircraft lifts, which took some mastering, but we stuck to it until we had managed to complete at least one throw. What it would have been like in a rain-storm or in a gale, I do not care to speculate but at least we learned the principle and with a bit of practice, could expect to master the art. At least no-one fell down into the hangar!

The Imman called the Faithful to pray for the umpteenth time from the distant minarets as we made below for tea and to change into our No. 2 uniform, for there was to be a concert on the upper deck before dark. A number of Arab performers were brought off by boat and the duty watch were busily stacking chairs on the flight deck in the cool air.

A very entertaining evening it was. An Arab lady performed a traditional sort of belly-dance, to the accompaniment of drums beaten with a strange bent stick. A huge dark Arab joined in the dance and the couple flashed and twirled in the mysterious twilight as dancers before them had done for centuries. They finished to tumultuous applause from Captain down to Ordinary Seaman and were obviously pleased with their reception and our appreciation of their talents.

The following act was a wizened little man, dressed in the typical Arab cotton shirt which enveloped him from neck to ankle. He waved his hands above him, uttering strange incantations and then produced a small yellow chick from thin air and then another, and another, and more and more until the deck was running over with the tiny yellow puffballs of life and several of the audience were fully employed in the urgent recovery and placing of these tweeting mites into the confines of a huge wicker basket. Where they all came from was impossible to tell. I have yet to see a more skilled slight of hand than demonstrated by that "Gillie-gillie man".

Next, several members of the crew came on "stage" and did a sketch or sang. One man played "Annie Laurie" on a piece of rubber pipe whilst another made funny comments. The sun sank into an angry red cloud in the west and night fell immediately but the show continued by the light of the deck landing lights and illumination rigged up by the electricians for the purpose.

Finally, the ship's Bluejacket Band played the National Anthem and we all dispersed to supper or the mess, excepting of course, the duty watch and men under punishment, who were employed in returning the chairs to their rightful places.

Until the Saturday, the only rating allowed ashore had been the postman and then he had only been as far as the office housing the military police near the old Governor's residence. He recounted quite a few interesting tales, gleaned from the duty Sergeant at the post but we chose to regard anything that did not fit our impression of the east as being sensationalism.

The Saturday finally dawned. Daily Orders were pinned up and the usually sparse sheet was crammed with information on the times of departures and returns of the libertyboats. Immediately after morning rounds and the general cleaning tasks of the day were completed, we were free to go ashore as and when we pleased. The most convenient libertyboat was at about 1330 and so, after a hurried lunch, we repaired to the heat of the mess to change into the tropical rig for going ashore, a white vest with a blue edged square neck, white shorts, white socks to the knee and white canvas shoes and cap.

White is a very difficult colour to maintain in a kitbag or in a steel locker for it tends to go either cream or turn a nice shade of grey, but special attention had been made to our kit in anticipation of this run ashore and we easily passed muster.

We fell in on the gangway flat in several rows. The Officer of the Day passed along the ranks inspecting our dress but no-one was fallen out of line for any reason. The Master at Arms read the rules for leave. We were to stay in groups of no less than three. There was to be no swearing or public drinking, for we were visitors to a Muslim country.

We were to be polite to all civilians encountered ashore and this rule also applied to the street vendors and market traders, whom we would treat firmly and politely.

73

"In other words," he said, "don't 'it 'em!" We would not enter the Arab quarter of the town, "even if invited by a small boy whose sister is deeply in love with you, having seen you from afar!" It was strictly out of bounds. We would observe the regulations with regard to saluting all officers of any of the Armed Forces encountered ashore. We would await the libertyboat to come offshore in a quiet and civilised manner.

The Officer of the Day said it all again, almost word for word, but added that we were to regard ourselves as ambassadors of our country and would be expected to act accordingly.

"Carry on to the boats, Master," he said finally and we were on our way. Once embarked in the cutter lying alongside, the air closer to the water was remarkably cooler. We said nothing about the increase in smell coming off the brown surface. I had heard somewhere that to fall in the Nile cost a European two weeks in hospital as a matter of course and some dozen injections against the known viruses and considerable prayers from the Padre for the unknown ones! The cutter wallowed towards the nearest jetty and finally came to rest against a pair of slimy sandstone steps. One officer stepped ashore, followed by a Chief and then a Petty Officer. And then us, at great speed and with all the delight of children on a Sunday School outing!

I had teamed up with Garth, George and Jim and somehow, Seabag tagged along. We made off in the general direction of the main street with all its covered bazaars and other shops which sold all sorts of goods. Not that we had much local money; we sought just a cheap memento of Port Said to return with.

At first, all was well. A sea of white-clad sailors swept as a living tide into the main street. Suddenly, we were swallowed and engulfed by a surge of brown Arabs. These street hawkers had been awaiting our arrival in the alleyways and cafés along the street and pounced on us with a howl, jostling and scragging one another for the space to walk in front of us, displaying their wares from a tray slung from a cord about their necks. Cheap watches, lighters and flick knives flashed in the sun. They shouted in our faces to outdo their competitors. The prices tumbled on items as we progressed painfully along the rough road, locked together in our groups, for they tried to isolate us to make a sale easier by intimidation.

A flick knife came within an inch of Seabag's nose and he hurriedly bought it! That was a signal for the other hawkers to redouble their efforts and for a second or so, Seabag disappeared from sight in a crowd of squabbling, gesticulating Egyptians. When we pulled him free his money belt was open and empty and a fingernail broken from having to clutch on tightly to his paybook.

Sweat trickled down our backs as we tried to outpace these street vultures but they skipped lithely ahead of us, thrusting watches and pens and lighters into our faces. They understood English well enough but not the word "No!"

Suddenly, we were alone. The vendors had vanished into the side streets as quickly as they had appeared and we were left in the middle of the thoroughfare with the ordinary local Egyptian people streaming either side, going about their everyday business. Head and shoulders above them loomed the sight of an Egyptian policeman and two military policemen and we were safe for a while. We found it prudent to do our shopping within a safe distance of these representatives of the law.

The harassment of the street vendors had, however, quite unnerved us and we could not concentrate on our purchases, so we left the shade of the bazaars and the side shops and made our way back the way we had come, thoroughly disillusioned with Port Said. The other groups of shipmates we met each had a tale to tell of the horrors of main street, and by now the noise, the heat, the flies and general atmosphere of peril convinced us that we had better call it a day and make our way back to the ship.

The main bunch set off but I decided to give it one last chance and sat down on the seats outside a café with half a dozen other stalwarts. The proprietor came out and took our order for soft drinks and cakes and we sat in some sort of suspended peace, awaiting our refreshments. It did not last long. First one and then another street vendor crept from the shadows of the alleyways and started their bargaining. We could hardly hear ourselves think. After so many months of being cossetted aboard our ship, we seemed to have lost the will to resist these pushy salesmen and in the end began to feel that if we made at least one small purchase, we may be left alone to enjoy the sun and the lemonade. I had a watch thrust toward me.

"You wan' to buy?" enquired its owner.

"How much?" I asked.

"For you, brave English captain, only five pounds". I shook my head.

"Three pounds, as a special gift for your father," I was told. I started to say no, but my wrist was grabbed and the Egyptian inspected my old Newmark watch. It had seen better days and had bounced quite a few miles over rough roads during my cycling expeditions but still ticked away well enough.

"I swap with you, yes?" said the vendor, holding up a gold plated watch of unknown pedigree. The dial was covered in red, blue and green calibrations and it ticked rather wheezily. "My new watch," he said, "your old rusty one and three English pounds?" I did not have three pounds.

"I'll tell you what I'll do," I countered. "I'll give you my old watch and this gold coin," and from my money belt, I fished out a brass three-penny piece.

I did not really set out to cheat this rogue but I had had enough of their picking pockets and shoving to last a lifetime and I wanted to see this Arab curl his lip and leave in disgust. But he did not. He looked at the strange English coin. He looked at Her Majesty's portrait on one side and the emblem of the thrift plant on the other. What could be more English. He bit it.

"Pure eight carat gold," said Garth.

"Not many of those about," added Jim. The man was clearly puzzled and offered the coin to another of his colleagues, who was none the wiser but looked interested.

Suddenly, our friend thought that he was on to a good thing. He almost snatched my old Newmark and the threepenny piece and thrusting the new watch into my open hand, dashed off into the crowd. We drank up, paid our bill and left in the opposite direction, weak with laughter. We were still giggling as we came to the jetty and milled about, passing my new watch from hand to hand, repeating the story to each new listener, until the cutter arrived from the *Ocean* to take us back. An hour and twenty minutes had been spent in the land of the Pharoahs, none of it worthy or enjoyable. And the laugh was on me, for the watch stopped and despite the diligent ministrations of my father, who was a dab hand at watch repairing, and of my younger brother who worked in the trade, it was never to go again.

Later that evening, I paused for a cigarette at the 'midships port gun sponson. It was just coming on to dusk. A solitary bum boat slowly patrolled the glassy water along the ship's side, its Egyptian owner wailing up at the mighty canyon of steel, listing his wares. The Quartermaster, possibly acting on the orders of the Officer of the Day, called on him to clear off but the boatman had spotted a fresh gaggle of possible purchasers at the ship's side and ignored the order. The instruction was given more forcefully and again ignored. The Master at Arms was called and he added his full voice, in no uncertain manner telling the boat owner to clear off. But still the Egyptian ignored all threats and orders, whereupon the saltwater deck hoses were run out and the water turned on.

A great sheet of water was directed toward the frail boat and in a few seconds, despite its master's protestations in English and Arabic, it soon became awash to the gunwhales, and the helmsman frantically backed out of range, much to the amusement of the audience at the rail. I could not bring myself to laugh. It seemed another example of the high-handed Briton abroad to me and I went below in disgust.

Our contingent of Pongoes had long disappeared ashore to the garrison at Port Said and we were surprised to receive another wave of soldiers on board from Suez or Aden. They were all of the same regiment and were going home to the UK, having been replaced by the lot from Cyprus. They were in high spirits, delighted to be going home after a long spell of duty abroad and we could not keep them out of our mess nor away from our teapot, which never seemed to get cold! They were a happy bunch and we got along well with our temporary shipmates.

Ocean sailed from Port Said. I was not sad to be leaving the most uninviting place I could have imagined and I was glad to leave the outfall of the Nile and get out into clean, blue sea at last. Sunburned day melted into clear, starfilled night and many an evening was spent yarning at the gun sponson rails. Every star in the sky was clearly visible and those amongst us that knew the constellations pointed out the well-known clusters of stars to those interested enough to listen. I learned to identify the principal ones and having seen the blue-black velvet heavens so serenely spread out in a blaze of white diamonds, I have been interested in the night sky ever since.

Eventually, land was sighted again. This was Malta and here I longed to get my long-awaited run ashore. We entered Grand Harbour, in company with *Theseus* and at last, I boarded the libertyboat for shore, where I followed the general mêlée for the town centre. Since I had no idea of Malta's geography, I joined a group of shipmates to view the shops and the infamous Gut. Tales of debauchery and similar naughty goings-on had run riot on the *Ocean* following our earlier visit and even allowing for the sailors' penchant for exaggeration, I imagined the Gut to be a very seamy place indeed.

On the face of it, it was just a descending street of cobbled steps with small innocuous bars and gift shops to either side, but following the advice of a shipmate who had paid a certain bar an earlier visit, we entered the dark interior from the oppressive heat of the outside cobbles and took a seat at a table. A swarthy barman put down the glass that he had been polishing and flicked half an inch of ash from a Turkish cigarette.

"What can I get you, Johnnie?" he asked, leaning over the bar to see us better.

"Five Tiger beers," replied our guide. The man opened a cooler and withdrew five green bottles from the mist of the arctic cold within, knocked the tops from the bottles in an easy lifting action and poured out the drinks, delivering them to us on a tray which he wiped lazily with a grubby teacloth. The beer was cold and had a strange continental taste. It was strong too, but a second soon followed the first and loosened us all up.

Thus relaxed, we looked toward our guide for the "entertainment" that he had told us was the speciality of this place. Under considerable pressure to furnish us with information on this entertainment, he approached the bar and whispered earnestly with the proprietor. He returned and resumed his seat but before we could question him further, the proprietor came around the bar. He flipped his soiled teacloth over his shoulder and placing one enormous palm on the glass top to our table, he ground out the sparks from another Turkish cigarette.

"Have you boys gotta English cigarette to sell, yes?" Anxious to keep in his good books, we rooted about our persons and came up with about fifty Blue Liners. He did not offer to pay for them but merely tucked them into the top pocket of his multicoloured shirt. "You buy more beers and I see I get a show on for you," with which he returned behind the bar and opened the bottles for our third order. Our guide nudged his neighbour.

"Now we'll see!" he whispered.

Our drinks duly dispensed and the account settled, the barman disappeared beyond a bead curtain to return a few seconds latter. He said nothing, merely lighting one of our Blue Liners - anything was preferable to the foul stench of the Turkish excuse for a cigarette - and carried on as before, smearing stains around some glasses.

The bar remained deserted but for us and we talked amongst ourselves, no-one really listening to what was being said and keeping half an eye on the bead curtain, from where we had the impression the "entertainment" would emerge.

A quarter of an hour must have passed. The fan in the ceiling groaned round and round, not cooling the air but merely recirculating the same sweaty heat from ceiling to floor and back again. The barman pressed another round of Tiger beers on us and we took it in turns to visit the outside toilet, an edifice that delicacy prevents me from describing in these pages.

Still nothing had happened. I determined to smoke one more fag and call it a day. This was obviously some sort of Maltese con trick and I was determined not be caught by it further. I had just taken my second or third drag when the curtain burst apart to the sudden shrill rattle of a tambourine and there, dressed in a loose fitting Arab kaftan, sprang a young brown girl. We jolted upright in surprise.

Shaking her tambourine, she advanced through the bar towards a small dance area, almost in front of us. She sang some sort of Arabic tribal song in a high-pitched reedlike voice and danced, swinging her hips, rotating her arms and crashing the tambourine like a wild thing. She leapt into the air and ended on the dancefloor in the "splits", swivelling slowly around, slowly enough for all to see that she wore the flimsiest of underwear, pulled well up into her crotch. Our sex-starved eyes grew wider. The barman continued polishing his glasses and scarcely gave the girl a second glance. He had seen it all before.

Tambourine crashing loudly, the slim young thing raced about the floor, giving the occasional flash of lean, brown thigh until the song reached a climax and she stopped suddenly, in a typical ballerina pose. We burst into applause. She arose, smiling and pulling at the fringes of her flowing robe.

"Money," she demanded. "You give me money, I dance more."

The barman leaned over his bar. "Give her money and the more you give, the more interesting she dance." He placed considerable emphasis on the word "interesting" and so we collected together a few handfuls of copper and silver coins and offered them to the girl.

She dashed forward to collect them, stuffing them into an inner pocket in the dress and then extended her slightly dirty hand for more. Someone gave her a pound note and someone else a ten-shilling note and only when it was apparent that there was no more to follow did she hide the cash away and in one swift stroke, slipped out of the arab dress, pulling it over her head. Her young brown body, tiny breasts encased in a sequinned brassière that had never seen a wash and her taut lithe hips and buttocks, clad only in the silken panties that we had earlier glimpsed, twirled seductively as she spun from table to table.

The titillation ceased at that moment for me. I did like a girl to be well-rounded and clean, and this young adventuress was far from that, but most of my shipmates thought differently and the next dance commenced with them on the edges of their seats. The barman sidled up with an unordered round of beers and no-one protested, merely scooping the money out from their pockets and paying up.

"Throw money," urged the barman, "she take it all off and do naughty things for you."

A few coins rattled and chinked across the dance floor and sure enough, off came the bra and then the panties. A cheer rang out as she removed the latter and this brought in more sailors from the street, reinforcing the financial incentive. Our little dancer weaved in and out of her admiring audience, pushing our faces into her hot damp cleavage, sitting on our laps and grabbing wildly at the front of our shorts. Someone took a bite at her bottom as she whisked past and that was the general signal for half of the Royal Navy to grope and grab at her whenever she came in range.

The barman urged us to throw more money; he had been scuttling about the floor, collecting the girl's bounty for her. "She make jig-a-jig in a minute!" he whispered.

The newcomers, whose pockets were better filled, threw more money and suddenly, the girl seized hold of a protesting submariner, hauled him to the centre of the dance floor and tried to divest him of his shorts. There followed a considerable struggle, for the lad wished to retain his crisp, white tropical rig, especially in front of a number of his colleagues. Eventually, the girl gave up and snatching up her cast-off dress, pushed her way through the bar, pausing at the bead curtain to flash her bare bottom at us before finally vanishing into the darkness beyond.

The submariner was roundly castigated for having been the cause of the premature cessation of the afternoon's entertainment and he finally scuttled out red-faced into the street and the sunlight. I finished off my seventh beer and also made to retire. The barman was selling beer to the newcomers as fast as he could snatch it from the cooler and on his rounds delivering it to the customers at their tables, was doing his best to drum up trade for the girl, who awaited anyone prepared to spend three pounds, in the room behind the curtain.

I walked out into the sunshine and counted the cost of the "floor show", more than I could really afford on my poor national serviceman's pay. Further down the street, I met a few messmates and spent a less hectic time in a tour of the market and the shops, where I bought an ornate table runner depicting a stag at bay for mother, and a petrol lighter for father.

The following day, since I was not on duty, I went ashore again, intending this time to see something of Valletta and I had a hot, dusty walk up to a large Catholic Church called, I believe, the Church of the Santa Maria. I went inside and sat in the cool quiet of the beautiful interior, thinking of home and the life that I had left behind, and ruminating on the depths of depravity to which I had become exposed. I could not help but come to the eventual conclusion that, after all, these were mere experiences and not damaging to the soul unless undertaken actively. I felt heartened.

As I sat in quiet thought, a priest approached from the altar but he did not stop to talk to me, although I was his only customer. Perhaps he knew in some way that I was not a Catholic, and he went out of the Church, closing the heavy door behind him. The Church was quiet and private. Privacy was something that had been unknown since the Fourth of July and I suddenly felt quite exhausted and moved to tears by the pressure of events since then, needing those moments of peace to recharge my batteries.

I walked out into the hot sun, feeling much better and a little silly at having given way to my "softer" instincts and resolving to try to toughen up a bit in the future. I was finding it hard being an individualist in this society and the strain had been telling.

Not fancying the long walk back to Valletta, I waited for a few moments at a bus stop and caught a wheezy, rusty single-decker back to town. The fare was threepence. It was the most hair-raising bus ride that I had ever taken and I kept that bus ticket for years in an old wallet. It culminated with the driver aiming the vehicle at the centre of one of the old Roman arches into Valletta, putting his foot on the accelerator and irrespective of who might be approaching the arch from the far side, careering through, with only inches to spare either side of his vehicle! I had shut my eyes and taken a firm grip on the seat in front but there was no vehicle to run into on the other side, even though it was two-way traffic on that piece of busy road. I dismounted from the bus and stepped back quickly, glad to have survived.

A "banyan" was organised, leaving Grand Harbour in the *Ocean*'s boats and landing for a picnic and games on a quiet beach some ten miles to the southeast. We took packed lunches, brewed tea on the beach, swam, played all sorts of games from football to throwing a medicine ball, and it was a very weary crew that returned to the ship at dusk, tanned almost black. Our instruction continued and there were all sorts of posh parades to entertain us, but the sun burned down relentlessly and we began to look forward to the cool of the evening, when we could escape the heat.

It was with relief that Daily Orders gave notice of our imminent departure and we slipped out of Grand Harbour, along with our shadow *Theseus* to the shrill of the bo'sun's pipes. At sea, we all felt the cool breeze denied us ashore and our listlessness vanished as we steamed east on a dead calm sea.

I took no time at all to revert back to our daily routine of instruction and more instruction. I suspect that we had more or less completed the Navy's Part One Seamanship syllabus. Matters were complicated by the number of Pongoes who loafed about at all quarters of the ship. They watched our rifle drill on the flight deck with mock interest and muttered criticisms under their breath until chased off by one of their Corporals to be found some menial task.

They did very little training other than mustering at the boat stations at regular intervals and cleaning their equipment endlessly. They were awfully good at sleeping; one of their favourite places was in the hammock rackings and it was a common sight to see several of them bolt upright with the support of our hammocks, sound asleep! A pair of large black army issue boots would often be seen poking out from the tops of our lockers when we came back to the mess for "Stand Easy", their owner fast asleep and it would take several rattles of the tea fanny to wake him. It worked every time!

The first day in October found us a few miles north of Bizerte and the Tunisian coast but we saw no signs of life and soon tired of looking at the sun-bleached dunes. Soon the coast was lost to sight in a strange, red mist. Our course took a more northerly track and on the following day, land was sighted to port at a great distance. We had no idea what this place might be and no-one bothered to inform us. Occasionally, we had a Tannoy announcement concerning matters of general interest but nothing was mentioned of this red rocky island and we had no charts to consult, nor indeed much idea of our speed and only an approximation of our heading.

However, the mystery of the sun-bleached island was revealed, for the Daily Orders announced that a banyan was to be organised on Sardinia for all interested men not on duty and shortly after the anchors were laid, I piled into a motorboat and headed for the shore in tropical rig and with my towel and "cozzie" under my arm.

We beached the boats on hot white sand and the boats returned for more men. The officers began setting up a cricket fixture against the Chiefs and P.O.s and were soundly licked for their enthusiasm. We "erks" swam in the warm water and lazed after the style of beached seals, cooling down again with a quick sprint back to the clear water. This spot was miles from anywhere and there was nowhere to go to to buy a drink. Tea kitchens were rigged and it was strangely cooling to sip hot tea in the midday sun.

I lay sleepily on my towel, listening to a Lance Corporal from Leeds telling his colleague about a particularly unlikely conquest in Aden, which seemed to have involved not only the girl but her mother, younger sister and an aunt too. All this narrative was punctuated by the most raucous expletives possible, which only served to add to the dubious origins of the tale, when I sighted, a few feet ahead of me, what appeared to be a small, ginger crab approaching.

I idly pulled my eyes into focus and froze. The pedestrian crab was no other than a small scorpion, back arched and claws extended. I stared Death in the eye and it kept coming. I butted in on the amorous Corporal's tale at a most interesting moment and pointed to our visitor.

We leapt from our towels like a bunch of schoolgirls and, watching very carefully where we trod, retreated, keeping the scorpion well in sight. He tramped industriously over my towel, paused at a half-eaten sandwich and then carried on into the shade of a small group of rocks. That spoiled the day for me. I don't like spiders, snakes nor beetles bigger than a quarter of an inch and now I did not like scorpions either.

I spent the next few hours sitting on the prow of a ship's boat until it was time to return to *Ocean*. Scorpions featured in many of my dreams for weeks afterwards!

The now familiar bulk of Gibraltar was there to greet us at last. We entered harbour in traditional style. It was Saturday and as I was duty hand of the mess. I sat in an empty mess for most of the day until my shipmates returned just before midnight, noisy and elated at their various adventures ashore. An illegal brew of tea was "wetted" and they whispered loudly into the small hours.

Sunday started with a heavy shower that steamed thickly on the hot steel of the flight deck. We mustered aft for Church Parade and Sunday divisions as usual, dressed in our immaculate whites. Not one of the inspecting officers spoke to me and I did not collect a kit muster. We retired to the ship's chapel and sang hymns that I knew and it was all very Sunday-ish and enjoyable.

We had dinner and I fell in for libertymen at 13.30. I had no real plans other than a good old walk. The confines of the ship were very restricting and a long walk about the flight deck never had the physical benefit of a short walk on dry land. I intended a walk to the eastern end of the island, a glass of beer and a stroll back in time for supper. I made the short climb out of the dockyard area and turned into the main thoroughfare into the town. A sailor came towards me from a side street.

"Hello, brother," he said. "Are you going anywhere special?"

I admitted that I was not. He asked if I should like to go with him to a meeting.

"What kind of meeting?" I enquired, and was told that it was a religious meeting to be held in a private house not far from the border with La Linea. The organisers served refreshments and were always interested in making new friends.

I truly missed a bit of spiritual comfort in those days. My present life was a lot different from the way that I had been brought up and my soul needed nothing more than to be in harmony with like souls, in order that I could gain some strength of spirit to help ride life as it was. I accepted the kind offer.

The afternoon was accordingly spent in an old house amongst a mixture of Regency and Moorish influences, sitting in an extremely comfortable armchair the like of which I had not seen in months, drinking coffee and then orange squash and largely listening to the confessions of the congregation. If they had witnessed just some of the depravity that I had during my short service, they may well have thought that they had something to confess! I felt their confessions, often punctuated with tears of remorse, trivial in the extreme but they were an amiable, simple group and I quite enjoyed my quiet time under the cool rotating fan in that crowded living room.

I half promised to come again and thanking mine host and the Scots sailor for their invitation, I returned aboard for supper and thought little more of the incident. The Scots nautical evangelist and I were to meet later in my naval career.

When the time came to leave the sunshine of the Mediterranean, our two carriers slipped from the concrete jetty, with its reeking gash bins and wheeling gulls and with the aid of a harbour tug, made out to sea again. Each day became progressively cooler and we returned our tropical kit to Slops and adopted our rig of No. 8s, working shirt and trousers for our seaborne routines.

The Bay of Biscay was kind to us, the sea remained flat calm but the days drew shorter and the air grew colder. We sat in the sponsons after supper, dressed in our night clothing of No. 2 uniform, our second-best serge uniform without the blue jean collar, until a sudden chill would force us to retire to the warmth of the ship's steel labyrinth where, now that it was cooler, we could sleep more soundly.

The coast of Portugal and the western extremes of the French shore slipped easily by to starboard and the bow began a steady pitch as we finally entered the Western Approaches.

The Cornish coast greeted us at last and we were excitedly awaiting our return to the homeland and perhaps, some leave and the chance to contact our families.

Throughout our whole journey and all those months away from the United Kingdom, the Royal Mail had done a wonderful job in ensuring that our mail reached us in very good time. I recall receiving a letter in Malta from Jenny, only three days after posting from Bristol! Our correspondence had managed to bridge that gap of thousands of miles and through the entire period of my service in the Royal Navy, it never ceased to amaze me just how efficient the postal service to the forces abroad could be. A letter, simply addressed to an officer or man, giving his name, rank and number and the name of his ship, "Care of HM Ships afloat, GPO, London" and bearing just a two-and-a-half penny stamp, would find that person wherever he was, whether in the UK, Iceland, Hong Kong or Aden, in as much time as the average city gent took to post off his tailor's cheque.

Our destination turned out to be Plymouth. Customs officials boarded the carriers just outside the harbour and we had a form issued to us, upon which we had to declare our foreign purchases. It listed an allowance which was a duty-free concession and very few persons, a notable exception being Seabag, paid any excess duty.

Leave was given and I went ashore alone to telephone a neighbour at home to ask that a message be given to my parents up the road that I was back in England and that I hoped to be home soon. The sound of Mrs Heath's voice at number sixty-seven brought pangs of homesickness. It was over four and a half months since I had seen home.

Our trip to Cyprus had hardly hit the newspapers at all, although the troubles in that confused land were talking point enough. There was no hero's welcome but we only naively expected one. No-one commented on our suntans in the pubs or the cinemas and we did not talk much of our adventure. To do so was a bit infra dig in those days.

Daily Orders had us leaving harbour for Portland on the Thursday and we heard rumours that we were to go on leave from there. However, the reality of the situation was that we did an examination on seamanship, communications, first aid, firefighting, damage control, parade training, boatwork, and ranks and badges, which we all confidently took on the flight deck in the late afternoon. P.O. Camper's last class did him proud by passing out with flying colours! We were all rated Ordinary Seaman and our Petty Officer had come to his last days as a serving man. We had a whip-round in the mess and bought him a new Ronson gas lighter, an expensive and valued gift in those days, which brought a tear to the Cornishman's eye. He left us late Thursday afternoon to complete his leaving routines with the Navy and to go on demobilisation leave.

We, meanwhile, left harbour under the temporary charge of an Acting Petty Officer and took our final voyage on *Ocean* to Portland, arriving about midday on the Friday. That morning's Daily Orders announced the termination of our training class and we were instructed to pack our gear to go on draft to *HMS Pembroke*, the naval barracks at Chatham on the following Wednesday. Much as we had enjoyed our sojourn out of English waters, the prospect of getting home at last was getting closer and our excitement grew by the minute.

The final departure from the *Ocean* was quite routine. No-one saw us off; we just carried our kitbags, hammocks and suitcases down the familiar gangway, boarded the motorboats and sheered off in the direction of the coaling jetty. It all seemed so matter of fact but I can recall those few moments in time easily. The huge, grey hulk of the ship that had been our home over the last few months slipped astern, all characteristics soon lost in her overall mass. I looked no more and she was gone.

CHAPTER
SIX

We boarded lorries once ashore at the coaling jetty, our kitbags and hammocks occupying one and we the others. Several other classes from the *Theseus* and *Ocean* were also on draft to Royal Naval Barracks and when we boarded the London train we formed the larger contingent of her passengers. Not all were bound for Chatham and we split several ways once in the main terminus of Waterloo but we had the opportunity to see Wee Mac, old Cookie and Andy Gray again, bound for Portsmouth which was to be their home.

The journey was horrendous and took forever. It was dark by the time that we reached Chatham station to be met by the usual convoy of lorries. Since the advent of October brought a change to our uniform dress (the crisp white front was replaced with a dark blue woollen jumper and our white, blancoed caps were replaced by black serge ones), the extra heat had us sweating and looking forward to a meal and a cooling bath. It would be the First of May before we would change back to our summer rig.

HMS Pembroke is what is known in the Service as a "stone frigate", a ship ashore in every sense of the word but including several more comfortable amenities than a traditional frigate. One slept in a real bed, ate in a messhall and only washed up if on messhall duty. The barracks shared the same cul-de-sac as the dockyard gate, their entrances situated at the end of a long descending hill known to all service personnel as the "Khyber Pass", the dockyard entrance being to the left and the barracks to the right. The walls on each side of the Khyber Pass were fifteen to twenty feet high and quite unscalable without the use of a rope.

Our fleet of lorries swept noisily down the Pass and we disembarked, absolutely exhausted, at the barrack gate. We were ushered through and thoroughly counted. It was not unknown for men to seize the opportunity of absconding during an unsupervised draft and the Barrack Guard needed to be absolutely sure that the correct number of bodies on their books tallied with the draft documents. This requirement satisfied, a Killick took us over to the messhall for a late supper. We had been expected and seven dried-up suppers of sausage, eggs and beans, with chips as hard as flints, were served to us from the ovens. We ate what we could and washed the hardness down with several mugs of tea, washed up our own crockery at the P.O. cook's insistence and were led to a dormitory in Nelson block. Seven creaky bunk beds awaited but as there was no bedding – that would have to be drawn on the morrow – we stripped our hammocks and used the sheets and blankets therein.

Although the rest of the dormitory was full of sailors and their kit and beds, most of the "residents" were ashore on the town but a Stoker directed me to the bathroom and I dropped into a hot bath at last. Sliding into bed thus refreshed was heaven and I knew no more until a bugle announced Thursday.

Once again we enjoyed the ritual queue-up-and-wash in a naval bathroom, the chase back to the dormitory, making our beds and tidying up the bed-spaces. We then followed our dormitory colleagues out of Nelson to the messhall, drew eating irons, a knife, fork, spoon and cup and had breakfast. However, the pace was considerably more leisurely after the panic and rush of being a man under training and we had no-one continually badgering us to get a move on or to look lively. We ate, returned our irons and wandered back to the mess.

The inevitable Daily Orders made no reference to us at all but upon our return to the dormitory, we found a typed note pinned to the door: "Ratings arriving on the Draft RNB from *Ocean* are to muster in the rig of the day outside the Regulating Office at 09.00 today." We discovered that the Regulating Office was up at the main gate and we shifted into No. 2s with collars. With our kit stowed under our naked beds for the time being, we doubled down to the main gate, arriving just before a Petty Officer, who turned out to be in temporary charge of us since he had all our names on a clipboard.

We were detailed off for a job within the barracks complex and were told that when dismissed, we should draw bedding and other equipment from Slops and listen carefully to the Tannoy in case our names were called to attend a medical, dentist and the like. Were there any questions? There were!

"What about Leave?" was the main one. The P.O. raised his clipboard to pull our questioning hands down.

"As far as I know, you lads are to get a week's leave from Saturday next and you will not be required for duty watches tonight or Friday night. But your leave will start from Saturday, and Saturday means Saturday and not before. You have a joining routine to follow in the barracks and need to see several offices, so you can't go yet. You also have to be issued a travel warrant and money for your victualling allowance and these things take time." He tipped his cap back and straightened his greying forelock. "Take it easy, get on with your allotted jobs and keep your ears open in case you are called. Saturday is only two days away," he said.

We dismissed to the barrack office, where we collected a station card and filled in another form about ourselves. It was forbidden to walk about the barrack square; everything had to be done on the double, even during "Stand Easy", and we were soon "notified" of this by a large burly Leading hand as we sauntered across the parade ground!

Once out of the barrack office, we were directed to the bedding store and drew sheets and blankets, taking these to the dormitory and returning with our hammocks which were put into store. From there we were sent to the Nelson block office and issued with a proper bed space allocation and a steel locker and a key. The C.P.O. in charge of our block told us about the rules and regulations of the barracks and we managed, by dint of asking lots of questions, to drag this routine out until lunch-time.

After a very reasonable lunch, we went to the clothing store and a cap-tally, bearing the title "*HMS Pembroke*" was issued. Some threw away their "*Ocean*" tallies but I kept mine in my paybook folder.

My task designate was "sweeper" in the snooker room. I was directed there and met up with an Able Seaman, the current sweeper. The word "sweeper", for the uninitiated, meant cleaner and it became my task to assist the AB to daily wash and polish the decks of the corridors adjacent to the snooker room, to sweep and clean the carpet in the room itself and to empty the ash trays, or "spit-kids" as they were otherwise known. There were windows to shine, tables to dust and polish, chairs to stack and restack but we had all day to do it in and once the scrubbing and polishing was done, using a rotary polishing machine, the rest of the work looked fairly straightforward.

My AB was considerably put out to learn that I would be off on leave from the Saturday. He rolled another thin fag and moaned about how he would be expected to manage on his own, but I saw no sense in his argument, since he had been on his own for some weeks previously! The afternoon ticked pleasantly by and somewhere along the way, I made up my mind to go home to Ilford that very evening as I was not on duty. My workmate gave me the best advice on making the journey, reminding me that I must be back on board by 0800 on the following morning.

Neither hell nor high water would have stopped me from going home for that very first time and at 1630, I presented myself for inspection at the main gate libertymen parade. The Officer of the Day passed me by with a searching look but no remark, and I escaped with the first surge of blue uniforms into the street outside.

I ignored the bus stops. Suddenly all I wanted to do was walk and walk and walk and in no time at all I had climbed the Khyber Pass and arrived in the town centre. We had yet to be paid and I only had a few shillings, so like thousands of poor sailors before me, I stood on the town bridge which carried the main London road and offered my thumb in the traditional hitch-hiking way. Several other sailors and Royal Marines were also "thumbing it" and we more or less took the lifts offered in turn. After about half an hour or so, a small van stopped for me. The driver gave his destination as Rotherhithe and I gratefully slid into the old dusty seat alongside him. We fell into pleasant conversation and the air in the van became thick with the smoke from my Blue Liners, a supply of which I had purchased from the canteen that very afternoon.

I left my friend on the north side of the Tunnel and had no difficulty in getting a lift in a battered Standard motor car into Ilford Broadway, from where I caught a bus to Hainault. It had been dark for some time and rain was in the air as I alighted outside the Maypole public house and strode at last along the familiar streets. I turned in at the garden gate through which I had passed, a very different person, four months and eight days before.

My "middle" brother answered my ring to the bell and I stepped into the little hallway to be greeted with great suprise by the rest of the family. The last that they had heard from me was the message from Mrs Heath along the road, for the letter that I had posted a few days before had not yet been delivered, but in no time at all I was out of my boots and sitting at the table enjoying one of mum's roasts.

There was lots to talk about and small presents to distribute but at last the question of when I was to return came up. In truth, I had not given the thought of how I may get back to Chatham from Hainault much consideration but now it became a pressing matter. Father suggested that I go down to the telephone kiosk at the end of the road and ring up the Railway to find the times of the trains and their arrival times in Chatham, but it was raining lightly and I was too weary to bother, "I will go back on my bike," I announced.

And thus a little after four in the morning, dressed in uniform but with my cap and boots in the saddlebag and wearing my long white cycling socks and cycling shoes, refreshed from seeing the family and having had a good night's rest, I pushed my rather dusty cycle up the front garden path and set off down the road to the whine of the dynamo, leaving the rest of the Cobbold family asleep. My hastily planned route was Barkingside, Ilford, East Ham, North Woolwich, through the pedestrian tunnel over to South Woolwich and from there, down the main Rochester Way that is now the M2.

The watery sun broke free of the first black layer of sleepy clouds as I sped into the outskirts of Northfleet, the time a little after six thirty. In spite of my long absence from the saddle, I had settled in amazingly well and my only anxiety was whether or not I had time enough to reach the barrack gate by 0800 for it seemed a long way off and I had not been that way for years.

I flew into Rochester and Strood under the added impetus of the steep slope of Gun Hill and crossed the river Medway bridge into Chatham town. A clock announced that it was 0730 and I was able to ease off at last. I halted at a churchyard just short of the entrance to the Khyber Pass to replace cycling shoes and socks for navy blue socks and my heavy boots, and placing my cap firmly on my head, freewheeled down the Khyber Pass and came to a halt outside the barrack gate. I rummaged in my saddlebag for my identity card. It was eight minutes to eight.

I fell under the gaze of a Chief R.P.O. and he came out of the Regulating Office and stood, rocking backwards and forwards on the studs in his massive boots. I was in trouble.

"Allo, Allo," he smirked, "and what have we here? Could it be little Boy Blue, I wonder?"

"Good morning, Chief," said I, holding out my ID card for his inspection. He ignored it and did a little promenade around me and the bike. He prodded the rear wheel with the end of his pacey stick.

"And what is this 'ere... that can't come into my barracks, you ain't got a "chit" for it, 'ave you?" The idea that I would need permission to bring the bike into barracks just had not occurred to me and I was lost for what to say! I did explain that this was my first leave from Chatham and that since I had seen dozens of cycles going into the dockyard gates, I had assumed that it would be quite in order to bring mine into the barracks. He leapt on the word "assumed".

"Assumed?" he exaggerated. "Assumed? You know what he did, he assumed he'd shit but he'd only farted! Oh no, young feller-me-lad, that won't do at all! No chit, no bike, you've got five minutes to sort it out before you become adrift!"

"How do I get a chit?" I asked, trying hard to control my rising irritation at all things naval. He gazed off into the distance and waved a hand airily.

"You makes a request to proceed ashore in sports rig to the Officer of the Day and First Lieutenant, that's what you do! But you don't come in 'ere with that oily bike until you 'as a chit!" My dam of irritation burst, and throwing my leg over the crossbar, I kicked the pedal up in anger.

"If the bike doesn't come in, then nor do I. I'll take it back home and come back tomorrow!" I growled and turned to go. Just then a Sub-lieutenant appeared, whom I had glimpsed watching the events through the office window.

"Just a moment, lad!" he called, pulling the C.R.P.O. to one side and the two whispered together. I dismounted and awaited the outcome. The Chief withdrew into the interior of the guard room and the "Subby" called me in.

He pointed out that the C.R.P.O. was perfectly correct in his attitude toward my bringing in the bike; after all the Navy could not be responsible for the machine whilst it was there and I had to be aware of this when making any application for the machine to be on the premises. That was why there was a chit system as such for cycles, cars or motorcycles and I should have checked on that before attempting to arrive on my cycle. He was eyeing the bike all over whilst saying all this and then he asked me where I had ridden from that morning and when I told him Ilford, his face took on a kindlier look.

"Do you belong to a club?" he asked and when I told him about the Comet C.C., his face burst into a wide smile. "You would know Arthur Cook, then?" Of course I did, Arthur was President of the Comet Cycling Club at that time and I had been treasurer until I was called up.

It was apparent that I had met a proper cyclist in the shape of this young Sublieutenant and as the C.R.P.O. was not at that time in sight, we exchanged a few pleasantries and I was given permission to leave the bike in the rear of the guardroom until such time as I had a chit to keep it on the premises. The Sub-lieutenant told me that he was a member of the Navy's cycling team and that I could apply to join as there were several inter-service races to be held at Lee-on-Solent soon and good, fit riders were at a premium in the RN. I said that I would join and later that morning I attended the Requestmen and Defaulters table in the gym and received a chit to come in and out of barracks in sports rig and to keep the bike on the premises. I retrieved my bike from the guardroom and it was padlocked in a sports storeroom in the gym.

Saturday morning finally arrived and we were issued with our travel warrants and victualling allowance. At 1230, we fell in at the main gate for leave inspection and the terms of our leave were read out. Two lads from the far reaches of the north had already gone, since they were allowed extra travelling time. I fell in, to the amusement of my colleagues, in my sports rig and was questioned avidly by the Officer of the Day, who thought it all most peculiar and took a great interest in my special cycling shoes. I had to explain the pedal plates to him and show how they gripped the edge of the metal pedals to give pull as well as push when riding and strapped into the toe-clips. This caused a little delay on our being dismissed; I could sense the libertymen's impatience and deliberately procrastinated!

We finally dismissed, my shipmates dashing for the Chatham bus, which then continued to wait another quarter of an hour before taking off! I stood in the guardroom, speaking to the Sub-lieutenant about the Navy cycling team until I saw the bus go and then had great delight in catching it up at its first stop and passing it, ringing my bell derisively!

Leave always passes too quickly and I know that mine did. I went to my cycling club on the Wednesday at Leyton, saw all the old faces, visited my comrades in the office as all national servicemen did in those days, and told "salty tales" all afternoon. I had some lovely rides out in the countryside and resolved that when all this national service lark was over, I would become a wandering cyclist and live in a tent at the edge of a wood somewhere and never be subject to any rules and regulations again, just coming and going on my bike as I pleased. However, I did find time to undermine all these crazy ideas by meeting a very "tasty" young lady at the Ilford Palais but as was almost always the case, she never replied to my letters and I cannot even recall her name now!

I returned to Chatham, using the return half of my travel warrant and in uniform, which I had taken home anyway in the saddlebag. I had discovered that the quickest route was from home to Barking station, where I would catch the 0545 train to Tilbury, then across the ferry, sprint up the hill to Gravesend station and onto the Chatham train. A bus outside Chatham station ran straight to the dockyard gates and I would arrive aboard at 0750.

My first journey back to Chatham is worthy of mention. I jumped onto the train at Gravesend and sat alongside a Leading Stoker whilst opposite us sat three brand new Wrens. They shyly answered our small talk questions as to why they had joined and what they were doing in the Wrens. They did not seem too sure of what they were expecting from the Service. The Leading Stoker leaned back and yawned.

"When you gets all our washing and ironing and mending of socks to do", he drawled, "then you will know what it's all about!"

That was the beginning of a big leg-pull that continued until the train drew into Chatham and at the end of the journey those poor girls were furious at what they had apparently let themselves in for. They believed every word of the Killick's story and were most disillusioned! We bust ourselves laughing at our prank, a little heartless though it was.

I was returned to my task as snooker room sweeper under the control of the Able Seaman. He was alternately a happy soul and a manic depressive, and I had to carefully assess his mood each morning before starting work. He put the majority of the daily tasks onto me and I was always busy whilst he usually perched somewhere, rolling a "tickler". I was for ever picking up his dog-ends and he had an annoying habit of disappearing at various times during the day without giving me the slightest hint of his whereabouts. I had to cover up for him and say that he was in the heads if asked.

Our immediate superior was a Petty Officer. He only seemed to come out of the P.O.s' mess just before morning rounds each day and then usually once more, late in the afternoon. You could set your watch by him; he did not catch us off guard and it was usually just after his last daily visit that the AB would clear off for the rest of the day and I would see him in his going ashore rig, making for the main gate and leave.

I used every opportunity that I could to go home. I had quickly brought the bike back to barracks and spent many evenings cycling furiously along the Kentish lanes during the weekdays and cycling home at weekends. We had only one weekend of duty in four to endure. Of the remaining three, two were granted as short weekend leaves, that is to say Saturday lunch-time to 0800 on Monday morning and the other as a "Friday while" as we called it, from 1600 on Friday afternoon until the Monday morning.

The work in the snooker room, boring as it was, was no real strain and I sometimes spent a few hours each day playing snooker or trying out trick shots. It helped to pass the time. I had joined the Navy cycling team but as there were only four members in the Depot we could not all get together to train or plan any racing. In fact, I did not meet the Sub-lieutenant again. I had only one training session where myself and another chap had a Wednesday afternoon off and went for a sixty-mile ride around the Isle of Sheppey and back. He was married and wanted to get home, so we had to be back by 1600. It was all a damp squib and the Service did not appear very keen on the sport.

Then, one morning, just after Rounds during my third week in *Pembroke*, I heard my name called over the Tannoy, along with Garth's, George's and Seabag's, instructing us to muster at the Draft Office. I thrust the duster that I wielded into my startled AB's hand and dashed off across the parade ground to join a small queue. I was there before Garth. He arrived puffing; he had not heard the first "pipe" and had to rush somewhat, having caught the second calling of his name. I could not resist a bit of a leg-pull.

"Bad news," I moaned, looking very dejected.

"What's up, then?" he asked, mopping his brow.

"Bloody China Station, isn't it!"

"What?"

"You, me and George," I said with a straight face. "Hong Kong, gash barge posting on the Yellow River until May 1957." A gash barge is a rubbish barge, usually loaded in foreign ports by local labour and always considered a very smelly, humble job.

We stood in the queue with downcast shoulders, bemoaning our fate until Garth was called to the table. I watched him in conversation with the Drafting C.P.O. and whilst the "Drafty" concentrated on something that he was writing on his form, Garth took the opportunity to look over his shoulder at George and I and to shake his fist at me! My leg-pull had been rumbled but we did laugh about it later. Garth was dismissed from the drafting table and said "See you later" as he passed by on his way back to his allotted task. I then took his place at the table. The Chief took out my ship's papers.

"Cobbold?" he asked without looking up.

"Yes, Chief," I replied.

"You are on *Savage* as from 12th November. That gives you just a week to let your part of ship working party know and to pack your gear. Here are your discharge papers from barracks, and you will be told where to join the ship in due course. She's not long come out of the London Graving Dock after having a new set of bows fitted following a collision off Christiansand, Norway, with a timber carrier. I hope you are a good swimmer," he quipped, "it seems like you may need to be!" I accepted a sheaf of papers from him and raised my eyes ruefully as I passed George on my way out back to the snooker room.

My AB was missing as usual and so I had no-one to discuss the latest development with until I met up with Garth and George in the messhall at tea-time, where we sat shuffling the papers that we had been given. I then learned that Garth was also going to *Savage* but George had received a draft to the frigate HMS *Tyrian* and so we were once more further decimated. The original class of thirty-two looked as if it was now down to just Garth and I. We felt a bit crestfallen at having received a draft so early in our period in the barracks. It had been warm and comfortable and we had a predictable pattern of leave. The food was good, they had a cinema and a bar and even if one was on duty watch, you could always slip into the bar for a quick "half" and a chat to break the monotony. But here were our instructions sending us off to sea again.

"Let's go ashore and drown our sorrows," suggested Garth, but George was duty watch and unable to find a subsitute to stand in for him and so, after supper, Garth and I walked into Chatham for a pint. For someone who previously to being called up had hardly ever been in a pub, let alone drunk as much as a pint of beer, I was becoming quite a sot! We wandered into a pub in the high street called The Duchess. It was quite crowded and we had to stand at the bar with our first drink. We had not been there long when the barman bought us up another pint each.

"Compliments of those gentlemen down the other end," he said and we looked through the blue haze of cigarette smoke to see two tall, rather well dressed civvies grinning back at us. We raised our glasses in salute. It was not uncommon in those days for ex-matelots to buy serving men a drink for old times' sake and we thought nothing of it until the two chaps came down the bar to talk to us.

It was immediately obvious that we had made the acquaintance of a pair of raging homosexuals, who nauseatingly fawned and crowed at us. I could not wait to get away from them and made sure to acquit my indebtedness to them by buying a round in reply but the strange couple would not take a hint and in any case, Garth seemed quite easy in their company. They both went out to the toilet.

"What are you doing, mate!" I asked Garth, "they're a pair of "poofs" and they're twice the size of us, let's hop it before they come back!" Perhaps Garth was paying me back for the earlier leg-pull.

"We'll be alright, leave it to me!" he said and at that moment, the pair returned and ordered another round of drinks. The taller of the two was gazing into my eyes and telling me what a pretty face I had! I could feel the sweat trickling down my back and I nearly leapt out of my skin when he took a grip on my knee with his strong fingers. The pub was too crowded for a quick getaway and in any case, I could not run out on Garth, who chatted away quite happily with the other man.

The barman finally rang a brass bell. "Time, gentlemen, please!" and we still had not got rid of our tormentors. At this they asked if we would like to come back to their place for a meal and a nightcap. So that's what they called it! To my horror, Garth readily agreed and we spilled out onto the cold night pavement, we two sailors in the middle, an escort on either side. By now I was really getting frightened and having difficulty in hiding the fact but Garth was smiling and chatting away in his usual fashion as the two "pooftahs" kept trying to hold our hands and touch our bottoms at the slightest excuse.

As we turned a corner, a large public convenience stood before us, isolated on an island of grass and shrubs at the side of the road.

"I must go in there, Pete," said Garth, looking at me rather piercingly. I guessed that the toilet must be closed at that time of night and there would be no entrance to be had at the turnstile.

"So must I," I added and we broke away from the two men who saw us rush into the circular steel doorway, where we clicked the entrance turnstile vigorously. As we had thought, the toilet was shut but we were able to reach to the inner turnstile through the metal bars. Through a slight gap in the welded doorway, I saw our two companions stroll to the exit side of the toilet, where they stopped in conversation. Keeping the building between them and ourselves, we retreated silently backwards down the street and along several side roads before breaking into a fast dash to the far end of the high street, where we caught a taxi back to *Pembroke*.

The dormitory, at that time of night, was in darkness and full of the noises of sleeping men but Garth insisted on waking up George and telling him, in a loud whisper, of the encounter with the two homosexuals and of my terror. It was a funny incident, considering that it was principly designed to pay me back for my prank earlier in the day, and the two of them collapsed into hysterical laughter muffled by their pillows, tears running down their faces. Their suppressed mirth aroused several sleeping neighbours and the air was blue with threats from them to "pack it in", but a fit of giggles had set in and Garth and George had great trouble in controlling themselves.

By now, I too was bubbling full of laughter and we dare not look at one another for fear of an outburst of giggles, so we tucked down in bed, trying to suppress the noise. Silence reigned for about half a minute. A sleeper further along the dormitory chose this moment to add his few words of condemnation to the situation and when all had died down, he suddenly said in a very loud voice: "Bloody pissy-arsed bastards!" and we were off again, rolling uncontrollably in our squeaky, badly sprung beds, crying with laughter into the pillows.

Laughter is infectious and eventually several of our shipmates were laughing too, although they had no idea what all the mirth was about. It took nearly a quarter of an hour for the noise and bursts of giggles to die down and for silence to return to the dormitory. Of course, in the light of early morning, the incident hardly raised a smile and the end result of our evening ashore was that I was quite afraid to walk the streets of Chatham for many days to come and always caught the bus up to town in plenty of company, keeping well clear of pubs and cinemas when alone.

Our final week in barracks came to a close all too quickly. We followed our leaving routine, returning bedding to the store and doing the rounds of the medical department, the dentist and the Pay Office. Garth and I were told that *Savage* was currently based at Weymouth and that we had to travel by train back to London and on to Weymouth again, whereas George's new ship, *Tyrian*, was in the dockyard. We helped him across the dockyard with his kit and saw him onto the gangway, where we solemnly shook hands and promised to drop him a line when we reached our new draft and to look out for him whenever we were in Chatham.

The following morning, we fell in at the Draft Office to collect our travel warrants and to join our transport to Chatham station. To our suprise we met Seabag, also on draft to *Savage* and boarded a Tilly for Chatham, ascending the Khyber Pass and leaving behind our thoughts of leave at home and "Friday whiles" with every turn of the wheel.

Once on the London train, the conversation turned to doing a "bunk" and having a few days off in the "Smoke" but we knew it was not to be. *HMS Savage* lay alongside the coaling jetty at Portland and we were conveyed there by the ubiquitous Bedford. She was all that one imagined a destroyer to be, long and slim, with a low freeboard, so low in parts that she almost seemed awash. I remember the smell of raw fuel oil as I came aboard and saluted the quarterdeck.

We were met by the ship's Coxswain, a C.P.O. He welcomed us aboard and asked our names, relieved us of our draft documents and ticked us off from a clipboard. It was evident then that we had been expected and any thoughts of flight for a few days off in the bright lights of the city would therefore have met with considerable retribution!

A seaman conducted us forward to the starboard messdeck and we were introduced to the other sixteen crewmen already there. The mess complement was eighteen, so we learned afterward, and we three swelled this number to nineteen. This situation was corrected the following day when a man left on a drafting to training school and we were glad to be able to spread ourselves out a little, for room was at a premium in the fo'c'sle. Eighteen men ate, slept, sat and lived (stowing their gear in lockers which formed the seating arrangement) in an area about sixteen feet by twelve aft and tapering to a mere seven feet where the mess abutted the cable locker and the paintshop bulkhead!

HMS Savage was built in 1942/3 from funds collected by the people of Burton-on-Trent and the surrounding area during Navy Week. Launched in late September 1942 by Hawthorn Leslie and completed in early June the following year, *Savage* remained very much the same from the time of her original building. She retained the rather old-fashioned forward tripod mast and later refits had mainly let her stay original, at a time when Second World War ships were being refitted to serve the more modern Navy of the 1960s and 1970s and at a time when all sorts of up-to-date naval architectural ideas were being added to these lovely old ships.

She was a class of destroyer on her own, being an "S" Class Emergency War Design destroyer and a prototype for the Battle Class later to be built in numbers. She was also the first destroyer to be equipped with an effective anti-aircraft defence system and her main armament was the smaller 4.5 inch gun in place of the usual 4.7 inch fitted to frigates and destroyers at that time.

She was fast and her bows were specially designed to deflect bow-spray and to thus improve bridge vision in a seaway. Most of her sea-going employment was experimental; she was fitted with small windows under her after hull, through which the action of the propellors could be observed and in this respect, was unique.

I learned that, during the war, *Savage* had been involved in various clandestine operations, including the landing of British agents on the Norwegian occupied coast and hunting German U-Boats in the Atlantic and the North Sea. She had taken part in the notorious Russian convoy runs but her lasting fame must be her participation in sinking the German battle-cruiser, *Scharnhorst* on Boxing Day 1943, when she had fired torpedoes at the battered hulk, scoring at least three hits in spite of spirited German resistance and was instrumental, along with *HMS Saumarez*, in dealing the death blows to the enemy ship.

During the time that I was aboard *Savage* she sported a large port-side nameplate, inscribed *"Scharnhorst"* in heavy German script, which I was led to believe was fished from the water after the engagement, along with thirty-six survivors. Each letter stood clear of the red-painted wooden board, surmounted in German silver and I was later to spend many hours during my service aboard this lovely old ship in the polishing and care of this trophy. It disappeared after the paying-off, or de-commissioning of the ship, and despite exhaustive enquiries on my part, has not yet come to light.

We stowed our hammocks in the rackings and were allotted a locker in which to store our clothing and personal items. The Leading hand of the mess was Leading Seaman Wiltshire, who was in charge of our conduct in the mess and also for our general welfare. Life aboard *Savage* was very different from anything previously experienced. We quickly learned that it was very primitive too. There was no messhall where one queued up for meals. All meals were prepared from supplies purchased by the mess caterer and paid for from an allowance paid to the ship's office monthly by the Admiralty.

The actual victuals came from the ship's refrigerator store, or in the case of perishables such as bread and vegetables, from various lockers aboard. These supplies were controlled by a system of naval ratings all supervised by a civilian canteen manager. He was also responsible for the purchase of foodstuffs ashore. Meat, vegetables, tinned stuffs, bread and butter, were all drawn at certain times from these stores and a system of chits would be issued to account for them. These basic materials would be brought up to the mess and the food would be prepared by the duty "cook of the mess".

We all took it in turns to perform the duties of cook of the mess and it was certainly my first introduction to the art of preparing a menu and gaining some culinary skills. The cook of the mess would, apart from preparing the meals on three occasions each day, also be required to scrub the messdeck, the mess table and the wooden forms which supplemented the lockers as seating arrangements. He would also wash up the crockery, which would then be stowed in an open-ended mess "trap" and generally spend some time in preparing the menu for the day and arranging the collection of stores for the mess. It was a very responsible job and one's shipmates were never short of criticism for any errors or culinary failures! However, it was not as bad as it sounds, as initially one would get a lot of help from the senior members of the mess and each morning a hand or two would be detailed from the working parties on deck to assist in the task of cleaning the mess.

We sat around the messdeck table, a pine collapsible steel framed edifice, with a white surface that we were to spend many an hour preserving with the aid of a scrubbing brush and a bar of Pusser's "Hard" (soap), and were introduced to the routines of our new environment. Our Blue Liner cigarettes were most popular but we found that when these cigarettes ran out, we would be able to purchase up to six hundred duty-free replacements a month of almost any brand of civilian cigarette from the canteen manager at about five shillings per hundred.

The canteen, a large steel "office" situated in the forward port passage, opened regularly several times a day and at "Stand Easy" both morning and afternoon. It sold all the items one needed, from soap to boot-laces and from sweets to jars of jam. Stationery, stamps, washing powder, boot polish, even gifts for one's loved ones, could be obtained from this veritable Aladdin's cave and the canteen manager was a good-hearted, friendly sort, who although not a serviceman and employed by NAAFI, joined in many of our sports and events just like one of the lads. We were allocated a watch and for the first time, expected to take a part as a "part-of-ship" seaman.

The mess comprised men of all ages, a new phenomenon, since previously we had all been the same age and outlook. Accordingly, our new shipmates were a varied crew, including one or two "old timers", ex-wartime veterans who wore medals on Sunday divisions. There were short-service ratings, usually serving somewhere between the second or third year of their seven-year engagement, one other national serviceman shortly due to finish his time and two "three-badge" Able Seamen, that is to say, men wearing three good conduct badges. Since one good conduct badge was issued for every four years of "undetected crime", these men had served at least twelve years!

Here I must pay credit to this happy band of pilgrims. From the very first, they did their best to make us welcome and to help us absorb the new life that was to be ours for the next year or so and, in spite of our differences in age, temperament and relative experience, we lived together in almost total harmony in the cramped, hot, smoky atmosphere of the *Savage*'s starboard mess. This was a fact of even greater wonder, when you also consider that just the other side of the barbette of the twin four-inch turret above us on the fo'c'sle, another eighteen men lived parallel in exactly the same size accommodation and under the same cramped conditions!

As evening approached we shifted into night clothing immediately after a supper of sausages, chips and beans, washed down with cups of hot sticky tea, sweetened with condensed milk, as fresh milk had such a short shelf life. I wrote to Jenny and gave my new address, and started a letter to my parents but part of the way through, I was side-tracked into a game of "uckers" which, in turn, was interrupted by the Duty P.O. and the Officer of the Day on their evening rounds. I found a place to sling my hammock in the starboard passage, not far from a musty-smelling bread locker and repaired to the bathroom with a shower in mind.

The bathroom was a steel compartment, just forward of the ship's office, the last compartment before one stepped onto the upper deck amidships. I slid the heavy door open to find the bathroom crammed with men, either washing at one of the six basins, doing their dhobying in a galvanised bucket on the teak deck grating, or queueing up, dressed only in a towel, awaiting their turn to stand under the one luke-warm shower! I returned to the mess and smoked another cigarette and tried again later but even so, there was always a full house in the bathroom, even in the early hours of the morning, a situation which never really altered during my stay on *Savage* and was always a source of irritation to me.

CHAPTER
SEVEN

We were awakened at 0730, to the shrill call of the Bo'sun's Pipe played by the Bo'sun's Mate over the Tannoy. Each man had his own patter when calling the Hands and some quaint little expressions and rhymes came in to play, which we found quite refreshing after the starchy "wakey, wakeys" of the barracks and *Ocean*.

I was dismayed, however, to discover that there was no provision for breakfast! Apparently, the first meal of the day would be dinner at midday! Since I was new, I raised no comment but it was very hard to try to start the day without any form of sustenance. I was able to buy a Waggon Wheel at the canteen at "Stand Easy" and thus survived. I was later advised that there would be no objection to my making myself a piece of toast on the mess electric fire and this became one of my little routines, although I often wound up as a "toast service" for the rest of the mess, which could be very time consuming.

We fell in on the upper deck to be detailed off for our first day's tasks, conspicuous in our new, bright blue No. 8s against our shipmate's faded ones. I was put to work scrubbing paintwork on the quarterdeck and I reported to the "buffer's store" to draw a bucket, scrubber, a shot of "Teepol" and a bar of the eternal Pusser's Hard.

When "Stand Easy" was piped, we all trooped back to the mess, where the cook of the mess had prepared a huge "fanny" of thick brown tea and I consumed my Waggon Wheel during general conversation with my new messmates. During this period, the ship's postman came in, called out several names and distributed the daily mail. There was nothing for me and I hardly expected there would be, as my mail would need to be redirected from *Ocean* and RNB. "Out pipes" squawked on the Tannoy. Slowly and reluctantly everyone got to their feet,gulping down the last of the tea and stubbing out half-smoked fags.

We new bodies reported to the ship's office where we were issued with a mess number and a station card with details of which watch we were in and were then detailed off for part-of-ship for our daily tasks. We fell in again on the upper deck but there was to be no more paint-scrubbing, for the next pipe was "Hands to stations for leaving harbour, special sea duty-men, fall in!"

and we were put to work in letting go the ropes and wires that secured us to the side of the grimy coaling jetty. It was all accomplished with great aplomb and little fuss, and the ship's screws thrust her astern from her berth and then away across the calm waters of the bay toward the opening in the breakwater of Portland harbour, toward the as yet unseen English Channel beyond.

I was busily engaged in coiling a great obdurate wire rope, sticky and reeking of tar, onto a large storage spool welded onto the side of the after superstructure that I had recently scrubbed clean. Suddenly the deck beneath me lurched in a most unfamiliar fashion as *Savage* cleared the shelter of the breakwater and made out into the rough water of a grey, windy Channel. I had to clutch onto all sorts of articles of rigging to keep my balance. My shiny boots were sloshed with seawater blowing in over the side, and my newly blancoed cap was very nearly snatched away. I made my way to the lee side and clung to the rail, staring in horror at the violence of the sea. But I was not given long to ruminate, for along came my Quarterdeck Petty Officer and he soon found me some work to do.

With my gorge rising, I went about the upper deck, checking lashings and assisting in bowsing in the ship's motor boat with her gripes but my face became whiter and more pale by the minute and my legs turned to rubber, much to the amusement of any onlooker who chanced by. And so it was, after about an hour of the rolling, pitching fairground of my first ride out in one of Her Majesty's destroyers, that I ran to the lee rail and dispatched my tea and Waggon Wheel to Davy Jones' Locker!

Savage ploughed her way onward into a westerly gale until just before dusk, when she came about and steamed slowly back the way she had come until the light at the head of Portland Bill came in sight and we turned to port, back safely inside the breakwater. The coaling jetty was occupied by a small collier and as there were no other available spaces we moored alongside her, putting great rope fender-mats between our own and the other ship's side. I had begun to recover from my queasy stomach since *Savage* first executed her turn up-channel and the reduced motion of the following wind and sea was not as violent. I was able to repair to the messdeck and tea, not having treated myself to dinner! A piece of toast brought back a bit of colour to my face.

Nobody made a direct remark to me about my sickness, although all had seen me sitting weakly with my head in my hands beside the 'midships torpedo tubes but several remarks were made in a pointed fashion.

"I hear that we are in for a hard blow tomorrow, Hookey," and "Did you hear that a gale is forecast for tomorrow, Spike?". I had to laugh and let them see that I enjoyed a joke against myself.

The Postie came into the mess just before supper and my first letter from Jenny arrived. I read it over and over again and instead of going ashore with the others, decided to write an answer, get some dhobying done and get an early night, for a day at sea, especially the one that I had just endured, had left me very weary. I vaguely recall the libertymen coming back from their run ashore some time after 2300, for they made a pot of tea and there was a considerable amount of talking and general noise going on, with cups of tea being passed around and the smell of fresh toast, but I quickly dropped off again.

Suddenly, we were awakened by the sound of an alarm bell and the ship's Tannoy system crackled into life. "Do you hear that! Clear lower deck, hands to stations for leaving harbour! Special sea dutymen, close up!" The deck beneath my hammock was crowded with swearing men, all frantically pulling on their clothes and I swung out of my hammock to join them. The lights came on and I saw that it was just after 0230 in the morning when a Petty Officer appeared at the door to the mess, urging us to get a move on.

The ship was pitching and rolling and groaning in an alarming way and, half asleep, and still adjusting our clothing, we spilled out onto the upper deck. The cause of all the trouble was then obvious. The wind had risen since nightfall and *Savage* had rolled and bumped against her companion collier in such a fashion that the rope fenders had sprung the plates of the weaker ship, a widening hole had appeared in her side and we were dragging her up and down with our weight, allowing the sea to flood into her empty hold. There was nothing for it but to quit her side and we were sent to our part of ship to haul in our securing warps and put to sea.

The bow was let go, followed by the springs and we manoeuvred on our sternline to enable us to leave the collier's side more easily but the weight of the ship came onto the wire too quickly and it smoked and parted with an awful crack. The inboard end flailed the side of the hull; fortunately no-one was close enough to be struck but it taught me a respect for the viciousness of a loaded wire that I never forgot. Once clear of the collier, our powerful engines reversed us out into the bay, but here the surface was a boiling foam and there was nothing for it but to put to sea to ride out the storm. For the rest of that night and for the whole of the following day, we steamed up and down the Channel, climbing the grey, wet, mountains of water, living in our constantly wet clothes and surviving on cups of tea and biscuits.

I was sick at first but to my surprise, the awful feeling diminished and I was sent to do a trick on the ship's wheel in the wheelhouse beneath the bridge, where I joined two other lads in taking turns to hold the ship to a course and to alter the telegraphs controlling the engine revolutions.

The flats outside the heads and the ship's office became crowded with pale-faced sailors, some being sick, dashing through the throng to make for the heads amidst the gibes of their shipmates. The upper deck and the messdecks were not the best places to be at that time. I was considerably cheered to see that at least I was not the only one being sick! Some thirty hours after having left the jetty, we returned to find the collier gone and no more was ever heard of what had happened to her following the episode.

The following afternoon, we sailed for Chatham and, later the next morning, steamed quietly up the river Medway past Gillingham and into the dockyard that Garth, Seabag and I had left just a few days previously.

Our reception period in *HMS Victory* had introduced us to the Navy and had taught us the basics of naval disciplines and the rudiments of marching and ceremonial drill. *Ocean* had instilled in us the very basic lessons of seamanship in a rather restricted way, but life in our new destroyer was life as it was at sea and there were many tasks new to us to be learned. The environment was rougher and cruder than I could have imagined and instead of roughing it with the rest of my mates and settling down to try to see the brighter side of it all, I kicked for some time against it.

The "system" could not allow me to win, of course, and I had a spell of constantly being put in the "rattle", a naval term for being on a charge.

I had tried hard to preserve my independence, finding some of the orders that I was given seemingly pointless or ridiculous, and I was wont to argue, which as any Service person will tell you, is the right way to get labelled a trouble maker and a "skate".

I never wilfully disobeyed but I did argue the merits of an instruction and in no time at all, I began to make regular appearances at the Officer of the Day's table as a defaulter, collating a small list of minor offences on the record book. I refused to see the point of view that I must blindly do as I was told. After all, I was not a willing party to this national service lark and time was passing, with the things in life dearest to me being neglected. The next eighteen-odd months seemed an eternity and my optimism was fast fading.

Matters came to a head one Tuesday afternoon. I was part of the duty watch but as we were in the dockyard, we were not required on deck for any sort of sea duty and only fell in for rounds or as required. I was sitting in the mess drinking a hot cup of tea following a very cold arduous day working on deck, when a pipe was made for the duty watch to muster at the gangway. When I arrived there, I was not in a very good mood and furthermore, when I was given the task of unloading fifty-six pound bags of potatoes from a lorry and stowing them in their locker, my humour and temperament gave way completely.

"That's it!" I shouted, casting the crippling bag of potatoes on to the iron deck in front of the First Lieutenant, "That's my whack for the day!" and stomped off in a very angry mood back to the mess. I returned to my unfinished cup of tea. The Tannoy boomed "Ordinary Seaman Cobbold, report to the gangway". I remained seated and the Leading hand of the mess, realising that something was up, calmly said "You had better answer that, lad," and returned to his letter.

"Sorry, Hookey," I answered, "I've had enough for today. I didn't join this outfit to hump potatoes, in fact, I didn't join this outfit at all, I was press-ganged and I'm blowed if it is going to turn me into a slave. It is time that national service was abolished. It's a bloody cheek!" The Killick looked over the top of the letter again.

"Perhaps you should take that up with Duncan Sandys," he muttered. Duncan Sandys was Defence Minister at the time.

My messmates were a kindly lot who truly did not wish to see a member of their mess get into trouble and several tried to gently persuade me to return to the upper deck and finish my detail before authority forced me in a less pleasant way, but I was too obdurate.

Suddenly, the ship's Coxswain appeared at the door and came towards me. He told me not to be so silly and to return to my duties before the First Lieutenant had me arrested and charged with refusal to obey an order and at last I realised that I must give in and comply. I did so without further mishap but I had put myself in the limelight and it turned out later that I was watched closely. As a result, I was picked up for several minor matters that, ordinarily, I may have got away with, and it was the beginning of a short run of petty misdemeanours and sundry punishments, which led to greater resentment on my part and determination on the part of the "system" to ensure that I toed the line.

It seemed that *Savage* had hardly moored alongside at Chatham and we had started getting used to the dockyard routines, before she slipped again and was off down the river, where she picked up a buoy at Sheerness. From there, she made daily forages out into the North Sea and Thames Estuary. Each passing day seemed to bring a new experience. We were taught how to steer the ship, how to act as a lookout on the sponsons beneath the open bridge, how to secure the ship for sea, and how to act as cook of the mess.

Sea watches took over from the usual harbour routines. They ran as follows:–

Morning Watch 0400 to 0800
Forenoon Watch 0800 to 1200 noon

107

Afternoon Watch 1200 to 1600
First Dog Watch 1600 to 1800
Last Dog Watch 1800 to 2000
Evening Watch 2000 to Midnight
Middle Watch Midnight to 0400.

I was detailed off as Bo'sun's Mate one morning and I waited in dread for the time to make my first Pipe with the Bo'sun's call. My first effort was achieved by making the general call, a metallic sound somewhat like the call of an owl, through my front teeth. "Terwhit, terwhoo," it went, "Able Seaman Gregory lay aft to Requestmen and Defaulters in the Tiller Flat." It sounded quite good and I got away with that one but the next at "Stand Easy" was done under the eye of the First Lieutenant, who leapt on me like a ton of bricks!

"What on earth are you playing at, lad?" he thundered. "Petty Officer White, you have given us a BM who can't play the call! Get me a replacement and send this lad to the Tiller Flat to practise until he can play!" I spent the next few hours down among the steering gear which clanked and wheezed hydraulically, until suddenly I got the knack of the infernal silver pipe and gradually began to play it with some skill. Which was just as well, for I was Bo'sun's Mate again the following day!

Domestically, we progressed in the art of washing, drying our clothes and ironing the items, eventually becoming quite skilful. It was a lesson that stuck. After filling a galvanised bucket with our soiled clothes and hot water, sometimes boosted with a shot of scalding steam from the boiler room, we would slop in the soap powder and stir with a stick until the water was cool enough to allow us to pummel the clothes by hand. All of this was be accomplished in the steamy heat of the crowded bathroom, where we laboured wearing nothing but a towel and frequently nothing but a smile! The soap-suds foamed over the edge of the bucket, to drain off through the teak grating covering the steel deck and the condensation rained on us from above.

When the washing and rinsing was completed, we repaired to the air-lock leading to the boiler room and spread our clothes out on the steel railings of the upper walkways to dry in the stifling heat. It took about seven minutes for a batch of dhobying to dry and we would return, collect our washing, take it back to the mess and then complete our oblutions in the bathroom. Often, if we only had a few items to wash, we would oblige a shipmate and do some of his for him, especially if he drew a "tot", for the next time he drew his ration he may well remember the favour and call one over for "Sippers" as a reward!

To our great delight the news was posted up in Daily Orders that the ship was to return to Chatham. We set off in the final week of November, when the weather had turned muggy, misty and damp. We came into Sheerness and picked up a mooring buoy upstream of Garrison Point. Because of the heavy mist, which developed into a fog, it was decided not to land libertymen but a ration of cans of beer were available from the canteen Manager at a special duty-free rate, as the ship was moored offshore. I bought my ration of two cans, selling one to a chap in the mess who was building an illict store of booze on the side. The Leading hand of the mess got to hear of it and it all had to be consumed pretty quickly to prevent the privilege being withdrawn throughout the ship.

A light westerly breeze cleared the fog early on the following morning and shortly after 1000, we cast off from the buoy and slowly steamed up the Medway and finally into the basin of Chatham Docks. Our bathroom was locked and the heads cleaned and likewise closed, for regulations dictated that when a ship was alongside in the dockyard, the crew would use the shore facilities. Thus, for every call of nature or a wash or dhobying session, we would go ashore to the washrooms alongside. As these were primitive, draughty establishments and certainly no place to linger, we found it a better idea to walk into the barracks complex of *HMS Pembroke* and avail ourselves of the luxury facilities there, where real hot water and proper baths were to be found.

Our stay in Chatham was of short duration but so too was our move out of the dockyard, for we took a mooring slightly downstream opposite the jetty at Gillingham. I was given the job of bowman to the ship's motorboat and was on duty on the first evening at the mooring. The officers had a cocktail party and we were pretty actively engaged in bringing off their guests from the Gillingham Pier. The officers were like so many penguins in their mess kits and the ladies were suitably attired in long evening gowns.

The Officer of the Day came down to speak with Leading seaman Chapman, who was the motor boat's Coxswain, and pointed out that the guests looked like remaining aboard after the last libertyboat trip at 2355. Would we mind staying on duty a little longer? Hookey said: "Of course we would not mind..." but we did, especially our motor boat engineer, who sat amidships tendering to the Dorman diesel and the functions of the gearbox. He was quite put out but careful not to express his dissent in front of the officer.

Following our final run ashore for libertymen, we took up station in the flat outside the Officer's Pantry and had not been there long before the First Lieutenant popped his head through the hatch.

"It's kind of you lads to volunteer to stay on duty and to see our ladies safely ashore. Would you care for a drink?" Suddenly, we all felt better about staying up late! Hookey had a rum, Soapy a tot of whisky.
I was asked what I would like.

"A beer would be fine, sir," I said. Jimmy the One, the First Lieutenant, coughed into the back of his hand.

"Would you not prefer a brandy or a rum, it's a little on the chill side tonight, you know?" But I stuck to the beer and he eventually withdrew to see to our order. Hookey jabbed me in the ribs.

"Twit," he said, "you should have gone for the brandy, the beer is twice the cost of the spirit, that's what the Jimmy was hinting at!" I went a bit red at that. A steward passed the drinks out of the hatch and I got my beer but it was another lesson learned.

The ladies finally mustered, for all the world a group of giggling feminine geese, at the Officers' gangway and their husbands or escorts helped them precariously down the teak steps and into the boat. The Officer of the Day came to see them safely ashore and onto the pier and from there into their transport. It was almost 3am before we secured the motor boat to the boat's boom aft and retired to our hammocks.

After a short thrash about in the Thames Estuary, mostly in the dark and engaged in an exercise that entailed the ship to be thoroughly blacked out and for everyone to wait hours at Action Stations, we returned to Chatham for another short spell in the dockyard. I managed one trip home on the first weekend, when I got out on the bike on a very cold and frosty Sunday morning. Weekend leave was always a hurried affair.

Cash was always a very scarce commodity and we had to conserve what we could, so most of us hitch-hiked to London. I tried a different route and would walk though Rochester and Strood to thumb a lift from the top of Gun Hill and my travelling time was often shorter than going to the city by train and coming back to Ilford by Tube. There were a lot of ex-servicemen driving all sorts of lorries and vans at that time who were glad to repay the lifts that they had enjoyed in the past, so hitch-hiking was usually no problem and was a quick and easy way for the penniless to get home. I usually arrived home at about 1900 on the Friday night and set off back to Chatham at 0445 on the Monday morning. I was always asked the same question upon entering the front door:

"Oh, it's Peter! When are you going back?"

I think it was Able Seaman Ray Bean who introduced me to the Junior Fleet Club and no tale of the Navy of the 'fifties would be complete without a mention of this establishment. The Junior Fleet Club was housed in a tall, old-fashioned Victorian building flanking the busy high street between Chatham and Rochester. Established for the express use of junior naval rates under the age of twenty, it was a real home from home, run by a civilian religious organisation interested in the welfare of naval youngsters ashore. It offered a hot drink after the cinemas had closed, a warm civilian bed together with the use of a television room or a snooker room, a bath if needed and a hot cooked breakfast first thing in the morning, just before one returned to one's ship or the barracks. All for the princely sum of two shillings.

It was a respite from the stress of living aboard a crowded ship, the people who ran it were friendly without being fanatical over their beliefs, easy to talk to and always ready to listen and offer good advice if it were sought. Some evenings, if I was short of cash and could not be bothered to face the hassle of hitch-hiking home, I would go to the Junior Fleet Club and after supper, would join the Manager and his crew in the kitchens to give a hand with the washing up and enjoy some very interesting conversations, returning to the ship in the morning feeling fully refreshed.

Early in December 1955 saw us crossing a cold, miserable North Sea to the northern naval home port of the Royal Netherlands Navy, Den Helder. We were instructed to be on our best behaviour and several games of football and table tennis were arranged with the Dutch Navy. Most were pretty familiar with the Dutch and their tall, elegant cruisers and we held considerable respect for their standard of seamanship. They liked us too and we felt that ordering us to be on our best behaviour was not really necessary. Just as soon as I could, I dressed in my No. 1s and hurried ashore to sample the delights of Den Helder.

It was all too quiet for me but eventually, I forsook the coffee bar and the juke box blasting out Elvis Presley non-stop and wandered into a bar near the waterfront. I stepped into the bright lights of the bar from the wet street, to be greeted by an enormous Dutch seaman, obviously "well in his cups!" as Shakespeare would say. He spoke no English and I no Dutch, but from his manner I could see that he held our Royal Navy in high regard and so I accepted his insistence to join him in a beer. We conversed in broken German for some time. I bought a round, he bought a round and the evening drew on to a very convivial conclusion where, after much handshaking and "English gutes froind", we exchanged caps and went on our merry ways.

I approached the *Savage*'s port gangway feeling that I had done my bit for Anglo-Dutch relationships and was looking forward to a crafty piece of toast scorched on the mess electric fire, a swig of tea and good old kip in my hammock. However, it was not to be, for in attendance on the gangway, stood

111

the Chief Jaunty. His eyes grew wider at the sight of my new headgear, which bore the legend "Konigkliegts Marine".

"And what's all this, then?" he asked, rocking back on his heels. "What Navy are you in, lad?" I began to explain. Placing his hands behind his back and bringing his ear almost down to the level of my chin, he listened patiently. When I had done, he slowly straightened up.

"That ain't not good enough!" he said. "You ain't not allowed to board one of Her Majesty's Ships out of the rig of the day, without the express permission of the Hossifer of the Day hor' the Commanding Officer hisself. Hi suggest that you get off down that there road, find that gentleman with what you exchanged 'ats with and bleedin' well change em back again, and be quick abaht it!" He started to go red and his eyes began to grow even bigger, so I decided not to argue but to "get off down the road", although the prospect of finding my Dutch colleague was highly remote by now and I had no idea which ship I might find him on.

It was the early hours of another wet, cold morning and as I walked rather aimlessly toward the lights of Den Helder, a taxi hove in sight and drew up alongside me. It contained the First Lieutenant, who inquired where I was bound for and even though I was most reluctant to drop anyone in it, I recounted the tale of the hat-swapping incident and the reluctance of the gangway staff to allow me aboard. He agreed that they were quite right in principle and that I was out of the rig of the day, but instead of wandering about Den Helder at that time of night, I should return with him in the taxi and face the music.

I got in the car and we drew up alongside the Officer's Gangway. True to naval tradition, the Quartermaster was on the look out for officers returning and hastened aft to salute the officer aboard, it being the silent hours. This drew the Chief Jaunty out onto the upper deck, straightening his cuffs as he went, which enabled me to slip around the blind side of the taxi, along the shadows of the dockside and up the unattended forward gangway. I nipped quietly forward to the messdeck, ducked under the hammocks of my snoring shipmates and grabbed the first cap that I came across, slipped back aft again and waited patiently at the ratings' gangway to be booked aboard.

The gangway staff took some time to appear from receiving the First Lieutenant from shore and I am quite sure that he held them back purposely to allow me time to retrieve a cap and thus avoid the wrath of the Jaunty. Neither of us ever referred to the incident again, but I made sure to always stand extra straight and smart when giving the First Lieutenant his morning salute! As for the Jaunty, he was quite convinced that I had managed to recover my cap as instructed but I was careful to keep my Dutch trophy safely stowed away in my locker.

We returned at last to our home port of Chatham for Christmas leave and I was suprised to discover that I was to be allocated first leave, which meant that I would be home for Christmas. I drew my travel warrant and pay from the ship's office and went off on my first proper leave since joining up nearly six months before. It was heaven to be able to wear civvy clothes and go out on my bike and get a lie-in on a weekday but the time fairly flew and it seemed that in no time, I was back on the train heading for Chatham.

The New Year was seen in aboard *Savage* with a tot and a lot of noise and I studiously marked off a lot of little squares on my graph. I was a little over a quarter of the way through my service. The Christmas and New Year leave periods were over and the January of 1956 began to get colder and colder. Spirits aboard were generally low after any protracted period of leave and this particular time was no exception. It seemed such a long time to the next spell of leave at Easter. To cheer up my workmates when we fell in on the quarterdeck for work morning and afternoon, I was in the habit of picking up a Tannoy microphone housed there in a little locker and making some flippant address to my assembled mates. This microphone was in a rather exposed position and as it was always full of dried salt from the sea and wind, was virtually unusable. On one particular afternoon, I did this again. I picked up the mike, burped loudly into it and said:

"Do you hear that, this your Captain speaking...!"

To my infinite horror, I heard my words echoing around me and my workmates fell about laughing. At some time during the forenoon an electrician had repaired the instrument and it was working perfectly! I did the only thing that I could. I fled back to the mess and then wandered back to the quarterdeck, looking as though I knew nothing of the incident and the P.O. sent down from the bridge to investigate the matter finally gave up the task, and giving all and sundry a ticking off about interfering with vital communications equipment, returned to his perch on the bridge.

Sailing orders were finally posted up but as no destination was given, all sorts of "buzzes" began to circulate. Some said that we were en route for the Atlantic as a back-up ship for scientists crossing into the Polar regions but I scotched that one by pointing out that it was already too late to get into that part of the world, since the ice-fields were all established.

Speculation went wild when the ship went into dry-dock and the torpedo tubes aft were removed and a strange hut in steel was erected in their place. It measured some 12 x 18 feet and was immediately christened the "Fish and Chip Shop" because of the short chimney and masses of small bore piping that emulated from within. It was evidently some sort of naval secret. Even we sleuths of the fo'ard messdeck could find no information on its origins or purposes. Gangs of dockyard workers clambered over it, under it and through it, displaying untypical enthusiasm over their labours.

Holes were drilled in the ship's sides below the waterline and strange pipes led back to the weird building. Extra stores were brought aboard, we largely providing the physical labour. There were many large crates and quite a lot of extra victuals, so the Boy seamen's messdeck aft was cleared of its junior rates and they were moved in with us. I started a "buzz" that we were taking a party of Wrens to sea on a fact-finding course and indeed, this was borne to be true when six sets of bedding came aboard. This information was gleaned by me, so I said, from a conversation that I had overheard between the Captain and Jimmy the One. No-one ever seemed to notice that this alleged conversation grew longer and longer each time it was repeated!

"The ship will single up and proceed to sea at 0845 on Monday, 11th January." Again, there was no hint of our destination, or of how long we would be away. Some ratings needed to know. There were wives or girl-friends to organise, social events to cancel and the messdeck was in some degree of panic. My "buzz" about the passengers being Wrens was pushed to the end of the agenda. At the last moment and just before the final hawsers were cast ashore, a Pusser's van pulled up abreast the officer's gangway and six civilians emerged and disappeared into the wardroom, leaving the duty hands to stow their luggage in the Boys' messdeck. When my "buzz" was revealed for what it was, an enormous hoax, I was roundly castigated.

We slipped and passed through the lock gates of the dockyard out onto the cleaner waters of the river Medway and past the Bullnose and the Gillingham Pier, where wives and sweethearts always congregated to wave their loved ones off to sea. Downstream, passing the strange signal towers and their weird semaphore arms that once formed the basis of Jackie Fisher's naval communications system from the First War, we sailed onward, leaving *HMS Wildfire* at Sheerness to starboard. We sailed out into the Thames Estuary, leaving astern Garrison Point and the sandbanks of that busy waterway and thus into the void of the open sea.

Late afternoon saw us round the North Foreland and head into a heavy swell up the Channel, steering due west. I soon fell victim to my old friend seasickness and the next night and most of the following day was spent feeling quite unwell, although I still had to muster for my watches and to work part-of-ship as required. I tried not to let it get me down and dosed myself up with toast and Oxo drinks, which I found were the only things I could swallow and hold on to during such weather. My shipmates enjoyed ribbing me, especially as I had ribbed them over the expected visit of the Wrens but eventually I got better and found my sea-legs as they one by one began to succumb to the "mal-de-mer".

Land was sighted to port, which the navigator said was France and the weather worsened to the degree that there was talk of putting into Brest. The mysterious civvies had not been seen since the morning following our sailing, although one was sighted briefly in the process of spewing heavily over the windward side, an act he would be hardly likely to repeat again, as the gale returned his ejected breakfast as fast as he rejected it! It made a mess of the front of his grey suit. This proved our widely held belief that these strangers were not seamen at all and this only heightened our curiosity as to their part in these wet, cold, rough proceedings.

We rounded the French coast and the lighthouse at Brest slipped ever so slowly astern. The sea, although not as rough, now resembled a series of enormous wet, grey mountains of water and we were alternately lost in the troughs and exposed on the crests, where we could see the miserable world of cold water stretching as far as the eye would allow. Great sheets of spray were blown from the tops of the waves and the upper deck was awash for most of the day. Lifelines were rigged and the upper deck was pronounced out of bounds.

When not on watch, human life migrated from the onetime warmth and comfort of the messdecks to the cold, draughty passageways leading to the upper decks. Here, the heads were convenient for the sick and the fresh air helped survival, for we had ceased to live but merely to survive, only just capable of performing our watches and of heading on into further misery. Meal-times were abandoned, the forward galley was out of commission and we ate chunks of bread, washed down with tea. Only one man of eighteen in my mess reported for dinner and supper on the fourth day and the messdeck was abandoned to the five inches of water that had leaked in from the deficient seals in the ship's port-holes, or scuttles, and in which swilled a mixture of socks, discarded cigarettes and other items best not identified.

It had been my practice, now that I had my sea-legs and was feeling much better than my shipmates, to pass among them, asking how they felt and could I get them anything? Like this portion of green bacon that I carried in the pocket of my No. 8 working shirt, for instance? I was performing this Christian function, when I failed to see the First Lieutenant, impervious to the weather as usual, standing behind me as I waved my bacon at a prospective victim.

"Just the chap!" he said. "I've got a very important job for you, my son!" I was sent to the Buffer's Store, where all the mops and scrubbers and cleaning cloths were kept.

"As you are the only man on his feet, you will have to be the duty cook to scrub out your mess today!" And for the next few hours, I fought both gravity, my stomach, the stench and the grey tide of flood water in our mess until at last, I had mopped it dry and tidied away and secured the mess for sea. The First Lieutenant came down to inspect my work and we stood each clasping a stanchion to keep our feet, amidst the roar and vibration as the ships bow crashed into the next wave.

"Well done, young man," he said. "We shall have to see about an extra weekend for you when we get back to Chatham".

Some time during the night, the ship made course for home, leaving the Bay of Biscay and her gigantic seas behind, and returned up the Channel in a snowstorm to arrive at Chatham after twelve days in some of the worst weather that the old ship had seen in recent years. The object of all this misery had been to try out the "Fish and Chip Shop", which in fact was a large air compressor, whose object was to remove the sound and vibration from the effect of the ship's screws underwater by pumping air though the ship's sides, thus confusing any homing torpedo or acoustic mine launched at the vessel. The Bay of Biscay had been chosen as a proving ground because of the vast depths encountered and the ability of the Asdics people to chase a good echo under those conditions.

We did not stay long before slipping down the Medway again and out into the estuary and after a fast run up channel, the ship kept a northerly course with the British coast remaining on our starboard side. I recall being told that a sudden glare of lights to starboard was Blackpool and in the early hours of the morning we sighted land again to the east, this time the coast of Northumberland. Apparently our destination was to be the Clyde, possibly Greenock or Rothsay but as evening drew on in the short winter days, the ship slowed somewhat, just as the unmistakeable hump of the Isle of Arran was sighted ahead. The watery sun rose to a cold calm sea and a large flock of gulls followed us into the estuary of the river.

I happened to be below, working as cook of the mess and when next I came up on deck, we were approaching an anchorage in a quiet, tree-lined Loch. This was Loch Goil. Even in the cold winter weather it was a beautiful place to be and I never tired of watching the small burn on the northwestern side of the hills as it spewed white water down the hillside into the basin of the still, cold Loch. I marvelled at the isolation of the place, whose inhabitants would flock to their gates to see the weekly bus that wound a tortuous route around the purple hills and down into the head of the loch, where it would stop outside the Hotel-cum-Post Office before grinding slowly on to disappear between a cleft in the rock. Apart from the odd fisherman and his small boat and the sheep high on the slopes in early spring, the village of a few small cottages would appear deserted but for the smoke that twined lazily from the chimneys into the frosty air.

The atrocious weather experienced out in the Bay of Biscay had forstalled any of the planned experiments and the "Boffins" emerged from the Boy's mess, piled into the ship's motorboat and, once landed ashore, filed into their Tilly and drove away. However, it was not the end of the project and at various times for some time afterwards, they would arrive at the head of the Loch to be picked up in the ship's motorboat and we would put to sea for days on end, steaming on endless slow courses and then back again whilst they sat in their "Fish and Chip Shop" poring over their instruments.

We spent weeks of tearing up and down the measured mile off the Isle of Arran, testing the equipment. The Boffins even took a house on the banks of the Loch and could monitor the ship's progress from the house itself. These were halcyon days as far as we were concerned, for the Loch was such a beautiful place. At the end of a day's patrol we would anchor in the cold, still waters and fish for our supper (all of which helped to keep our mess bills down) and we fed well on the whiting, codling and mackerel caught there.

I had adapted to the Navy way of life by now, to such an extent that I could hardly recognise myself as the "mother's boy" that had sat on the suitcase outside the barrack gate over six months previously. I smoked, I drank liberally given the chance, and my language was that of my companions on board, although I never swore ashore no matter whose company I was in. I was a sceptic, never believing what I was first told, having rapidly lost faith in man in general with the exception of my friends and immediate colleagues. I bore little allegiance to the Service as a whole, regarding myself as a temporary addition to the Navy and never really losing my feeling of individuality. Had we been on a war footing, I dare say my attitude would have been quite the opposite, but there seemed to me to be little need for national servicemen and a general disrespect for our status. There were, however, good days and bad and I began to forget the bad ones and look forward to the good times.

When the ship steamed up the Clyde and came alongside the Prince Regent Pier in the Greenock Dockyard, going ashore was made easier and more flexible by not having to await the times of libertyboats, as we were able to wander ashore at almost any time after the first few shore-leave musters.

One evening, I wandered ashore with a colleague, whom I refer to as "Jack", and headed for a dance-hall which, we were told, was injecting a bit of life into the local atmosphere. My friend's real name is left out as what follows might cause unnecessary embarrassment to him. Once there, we paid our entrance fee and emerged into the bright lights of the interior, to find that there was no bar and that it was to be a "dry" night indeed, for there was no re-exit concession to enable one to pop up the road to the pub for a "wet" and return to the dance. Nevertheless, we determined to make the best of it.

This Scottish entertainment proved rather lively, the house lights were dimmed and we took the opportunity to ask several young ladies to dance, getting no refusals since there were few local lads to provide partners, the rest being in the pub up the road! For a while we had the pick of the field. Most of the few local boys there seemed well under the influence anyway and quite incapable of dancing; the reason for their intoxicated condition became clear to me when I chanced into the gents' to answer a call of nature. I was accosted by a large Scot who thrust a bottle of whisky at me and demanded half-a-crown. I do not particularly like whisky but I did not like the looks of the man either and so with a hearty "Cheers, mate!" I handed over my money and took a swig of the drink. It was watered down as I suspected it might be and after I had taken my share, the bottle was replaced into its hiding place in the toilet cistern to await the next customer.

I returned to a traditional Scots reel and "Jack" and I were assisted in its execution by a slight, pale girl and her shorter, rather grubby companion. "Jack" was quick to escape at the earliest opportunity from the latter and returned to chat with a tall dark girl, with strong Scottish legs and seamed black stockings. The pale girl was very shy and spoke with a very heavy accent which was difficult to follow. Her name was Anne.

I bought a couple of orange squashes from the staff at the pine trestle table at the end of the hall and we chatted about this and that. She broke off occasionally to join in some sort of hilarious "in" joke with some other girls at the next table, which I found rather irritating but there was no-one else remotely attractive enough to divert my interest, for "Jack" had purloined the only good-looking girl in the hall. They twisted the night away, fused together during the slow ones and from the looks and winks that I exchanged with him, "Jack" seemed well away. It did not suprise me to hear him whisper that I would have to return to *Savage* alone that night as he was promised "all night in"!

He disappeared with the sexy black-rigged girl just before the evening's celebrations drew to a close with the playing of the National Anthem and I helped Anne to recover her coat from the cloakroom, offering to take her

118

home. She declined the offer several times but at last accepted and we stepped out into the cold night air, where we were met by the drunks from the adjacent pub, who were there to collect their wives and girlfriends. As Anne and I set off down the wet street together, I marvelled at the Scot's ability to send his girl to a dance whilst he did his own thing in the pub!

Anne twice tried to avoid me taking her to her door. Ordinarily, I would have taken the hint and returned to the ship but it had been a bit of a boring night out anyway and I did not want to return too early, in case my shipmates realised just how poor a run ashore it had been. So I politely insisted that I see her to her door. This turned out to be the main gate of a sanitorium for sufferers from tuberculosis. I kissed her quietly on the cheek, saw her to the large oak door and wandered wetly back to my hammock on *Savage*, where I slung my hammock, washed, cleaned my teeth and lay smoking a last cigarette in the darkness. Then I heard someone approaching quietly. It was "Jack". He had seen that I was still awake and came over to my hammock.

"I thought you were all night in, Jack," I whispered.

"So did I!" he whispered back. "Can you keep a secret?"

"Of course," I answered, sliding out of my hammock and padding in bare feet over to a quieter corner where we would not disturb the sleeping members of our mess. There the tale unfolded. "Jack" had been petting pretty heavily with the girl at the dance and as the evening drew on, had invited her outside for something a little less public but she had refused. Later, she suddenly asked if he would see her home and spend the night with her? "Jack" had agreed like a shot and he wasted no time in calling a taxi and hastening her to her home. Once inside, there followed some torrid groping and fondling on the settee and the girl had slipped into the bedroom, to "change into something more comfortable". She returned in a short, black negligee which did little to hide her firm bosom and the black stocking tops, but as she rejoined "Jack" on the settee, she began to cry. The reason, she finally admitted, was that she was not a "she" at all, but a pretty good look-alike! I had to agree with "Jack", she had fooled me! After a cup of coffee, "Jack" had refused the "kind offer" of the bed and walked on back to the ship, soaked to the skin and not a little annoyed. It explained the joke being shared by the girls in the dance hall but we couldn't face going there again to share it with them! From Greenock, we sailed to Largs and then to Campbeltown.

Largs in the winter was a very dull spot, I found, and I went for a walk along the front in a biting wind and determined to stay aboard until we sailed. Campbeltown appeared at first to be little better but a football match had been arranged with a local team and I had volunteered to play. The game was held, to our suprise, on a pitch which sloped from port to starboard and which had great holes in its rough grassy surface.

The local team knew every lump and bump and were quite used to the "list" on their pitch, so it was hardly suprising when they beat us easily. We accepted the defeat with wry grins and were quite sorry when our challenge to a rowing race for the Sunday could not go ahead, as there was only one cutter available to race with.

In those days, there were a number of submarines in at Campbeltown. They lay like so many black whales alongside the pier and their crews, dressed in white seamen's jumpers, were busily loading stores and parts, opening hatches and ports that one never knew existed in those great steel hulls. *HMS Adamant* at Rothesay was their usual mother ship. If the weather blew up along this exposed coast, they would all put to sea from Campeltown and leave the jetty empty. They were usually safe in most gales, excepting those from an easterly direction.

I went ashore alone on a Tuesday late afternoon. I needed some odds and ends and I usually sent a postcard home to my parents at each different port visited. It was bright but cold and I was nearly broke as usual, so I returned in time for supper. But the boredom of the mess and the fact that I was already dressed for shore leave, dragged me out of the warmth of the messdeck, down the brow and off up the steep main street.

I had enough money for a pint of mild and a few emergency pounds as well and I wandered into a bar, which I believe was called the Honeypot. It was bright and warm within and I took a seat at the bar and ordered my first half-pint. There were two or three other sailors seated at tables, and I assumed they were submariners, as I had never seen them before. The barstools were otherwise all taken and I idly observed my neighbours in the long mirror facing us. My attention was drawn to a young lady sitting at the opposite end to me and as I looked at her, our eyes met. I smiled but she looked away. She looked at me again and once more, I caught her gaze and smiled. This time she smiled back and then shyly directed her eyes back to the red drink in her goblet. I saw that she was quite a bit older than I but she had a pretty, pale face and was slim, although dressed a little on the old-fashioned side.

Our eyes met again and this time I smiled and indicated my packet of cigarettes. She hesitated for a second, then nodded and with my heart going fifteen to the dozen, I swung off my stool and went down the bar toward her. She swung her thin legs to pivot toward me to give me room at the bar and her long blond hair fell over her shy smile. "Hi!" I said, trying to seem cool and aloof and I offered her a cigarette. It seemed the right time to order up my second half and to offer my new friend a drink too, and in a short while we relaxed into small talk.

Her name was Jean and she lived locally. I expect she was about twenty-eight or so. She asked about my ship and where I had been and what I thought of the Navy. I gave as lighthearted a reply to each of these questions as possible and managed to get her laughing. She drank red wine mixed with cider and was not adverse to a shot of malt whisky, which she drank in the traditional Scots way, straight down and followed by a half of beer.

My emergency pounds came into play. I matched her drink for drink but of course, my drinks were not as potent. When she began to show signs of getting well and truly "plastered", I was still in control. She bought her share, to be honest, and seemed very pleased with my company. Women rarely went into Scottish pubs, she told me; only "naughty" women did! I made no comment at that statement for it seemed obvious that she was not a "naughty" woman. It came to closing time and I helped her on with her coat.

"You'll be seeing me home?" she asked in her soft Scots lilt.

"It will be my pleasure!" said I and taking her arm, we clung together up the cold street, battling against the raw wind that froze our hands and feet. I held her hand in the pocket of my raincoat for warmth.

"You're a cheeky, bonny lad, so you are!" she told me. I had been thinking along the same lines! She came to a halt outside a block of flats, high up in the town.

"I live here," she said. "Thank you for a lovely evening, I have enjoyed your company. Any time you are in Campbeltown do look for me in the bar, I'm usually there on two nights of the week."

I had enjoyed the sophistication of an evening with an older woman. She had laughed at my jokes, had been interested in my tales and had told me a lot about her own life, at least, that which she wished me to know. I had no great regrets at it ending there and then; she was in charge and it had been fun.

"I'll look out for you," I said. "Thank you also for a very nice evening." I bought her cold hand to my lips and brushed it briefly. "Mind you don't get cold now," I said, and turned to go but she suddenly gripped my arm.

"Is that the best you can do?" she asked, with a shy downward smile and her blond hair flew across her face like a golden cloud. I could do better, and I proved it by cradling her slight frame in my arms and administering a long, loving "back-bender" from which she finally drew away, her eyes slightly wider and not as glazed as before.

"Let's go in from this cold," she whispered. "We'll have to be quiet as my mother will not be abed yet," and we hurried up the approach to the flats and

121

out of the cold night air as we stepped into the foyer. We mounted the steps to the first floor and she opened the door with a key. My heartbeats filled my ears and I was sure that the noise was enough to wake the whole block up. Jean looked about the living-room and then waved me in. I shut the door soundlessly behind me.

"Mother is at her bed," Jean whispered, indicating a curtained-off space in the wall, and we tip-toed past into the bedroom. She sat me on the bed after I had taken off my raincoat. "Would you like coffee?" she asked quietly and when I nodded assent, she hung her coat on the door and slipped through to the kitchen where I heard the sounds of tap and kettle.

My boots were killing me. I could tolerate them no longer and slipped them quietly to the floor, looking about the room whilst massaging some warmth back into my toes. Jean had a distinct lack of wardrobe space, for dresses, jumpers, coats and underwear were either hanging from hooks on the walls or were in neat, freshly ironed piles on the chair and other furniture. A fire burned dully in the fireplace, overhung by a long mirror into which brightly coloured postcards were stuck. The mantlepiece was likewise covered with bric-a-brac and standing at the far end was a large silver coloured frame with a photograph of Jean and a tall, muscular sailor. It was a black and white photograph but the sailor looked like a redhead to me. He had a long white scar stretching from the corner of his mouth to his left ear. The couple's eyes followed me about the room as I left the bed and offered my cold feet to the dying fire.

Jean returned with the coffee. She put her cup on the only space left on the crowded mantlepiece and reaching behind her, unfastened the back of her dress. Seeing this, I put my cup down and with shaking hands assisted her efforts. Nothing was said as I quietly undressed her, pausing only long enough to allow her to remove my clothes too. Once down to her knickers and brassière, she slipped into the bed but with modesty thrown to the wind by now, I dropped my underpants and socks at the foot of the bed and slipped in with her.

"You canna stay," she whispered hoarsely, "in case mother wakes up, so we have to be quick!" I nodded in the light of the fire and slipping her brassière straps from her shoulders, struggled briefly with the catch and tossed the flimsy article to the floor to be followed swiftly by her panties. We were not quick. The coffee was cold and the fire just a ruddy glow when we kissed finally and I dressed in the dark. She put on a white silk wrap with an ornate Chinese dragon on the back and saw me quietly to the door. We arranged to meet again the following night at the same bar at eight and I stepped out into the cold and made my way on feathery feet and with my young heart singing, back to the steel interior of *Savage*.

To my relief there were no sailing orders for the following day but at about 1100hrs I was called to my part of ship to assist in rafting a submarine alongside on our mooring. To my horror, the sailor that handed me the steel hawser to secure the submarine's stern was a beefy, ginger-haired tough-guy, with a scar that stretched from the corner of his mouth to his left ear. I did not keep my evening date and I never saw Jean again.

CHAPTER
EIGHT

The instructions were finally pinned up on the notice board. We were to sail for our home port, Chatham. Letters were hastily scribed to loved ones giving our Estimated Time of Arrival. Some sailors even wrote two letters, each with a different ETA; in those days, many sailors divided their affections between more than one lady! We slipped our mooring at the jetty at Campbeltown soon after the postman came back from shore on his final run and I was glad to go, knowing that I need not expect a visit from the scarred submariner in the photograph at Jean's!

We headed west in the gathering dusk of a late March afternoon. I had the First Dog watch which also meant that I would be on duty during the Middle Watch, midnight to 0400, and we were pressed hard to secure the ship for heavy weather on our journey down the Clyde to the open sea.

The Isle of Arran was a great black shape to starboard at suppertime but apart from the occasional shore-light, the night was particularly black and a short, vicious sea set our bows roaring into the waves. The wind was rising and the glass falling. The Coxwain and the Boatswain twice went round the upper deck ensuring that all was lashed and secured and then declared the upper deck out of bounds. Any movements aft would have to be via the catwalks, which were single-way steel bridges between the ship's superstructures.

I turned in soon after supper and the next I knew was being called for the Middle Watch at 2355. I swung out of my hammock and clung to a nearby stanchion in order to dress, for *Savage* was pitching and rolling in a crazy, corkscrew motion. I came up to the port passage for watch muster and waited to be detailed off with my next four hours of duty. My shipmates looked green by the light of the red police lamp and I was hoping that I would be lucky enough to be allotted a job in the open air, which was at least some defence against the seasickness with which I was always dogged. I was lucky, I was to be Bo'sun's Mate, a job that put me on the ship's bridge in the open air where I was to act as messenger and general dogsbody for the Officer of the Watch. I was quite pleased with that. One could retreat into one's duffle-coat collar and concentrate on keeping warm, helping to keep an eye out with the lookouts manning the port and starboard wings of the old ship's open bridge.

One could listen to the officers' conversations, not from personal interest of course, but for some gem of information in which the lower deck delighted during these moments of a black, wet night.

We thudded out into the North Atlantic. There were few other ships to report and even fewer lights in the direction of the distant coast to port. Apart from the occasional radar report or slight adjustment to our course, the cold night progressed in a welter of snowshowers and the constant dip and roar of the bows in the iron black sea. A little after 0200, the Officer of the Watch, Lieutenant Martin, lowered his binoculars and without turning, called: "Bo'sun's Mate!"

"Aye, Aye, sir!" I replied and stepped up to the upper bridge grating.

"Time for a mug of kye, lay aft to the after galley and brew up, lad!"

"Aye, Aye, sir!" said I, glad of the excuse to quit the cold of the bridge and I slid down the ladder at the back of the bridge and made my way to the after superstructure, which bore "X" gun, whose shrapnel shield overhung "Y" gun. I entered the after flat, poked my tongue out at Able Seaman Roberts, the lifebuoy sentry, and slipped into the warmth of the officers' galley.

I soon filled the electric urn and switched it on, whilst I cut up the large blocks of rough cocoa using my sailor's knife. I filled five mugs with the scalding hot greasy liquid, turned off the urn and the galley light, and balancing the five mugs in my fingers, made my way forward, up the ladders, along the catwalk and forward on to the vertical ladder leading to the bridge.

The ship had changed course a few degrees since I had left the bridge and had a more pronounced pitch than before. Careful not to spill any of the hot cocoa during my ascent, I started up the ladder and was delighted to reach the top not having lost any. As I rebalanced myself from my climb, I heard the Watch Petty Officer sing out "Duck!"

"Duck?" I thought. "What on earth are duck doing out here in this weather and at this time of night?" and as I thus ruminated, twin gouts of water crashed all over me and into the precious mugs of kye from the ships hawse-pipes, for as the ship hit the glassy surface of the next big wave, her bows were cutting under, forcing up two great columns of green water up the anchor chain eyes. The bridge staff saw my plight and gales of laughter mingled with the sleet and rain as I upended the half-empty mugs and made my way aft for another session with the urn.

A ship in commission is never still, and most certainly never a silent place. Below decks, the living accommodation is permeated with the roar of exhaust fans, ventilators, generators and refrigeration units, the growl of the turbines and the noises of the gear-room, shafts and steering gear. On a small ship such as a destroyer, all this noise is deafening to the stage of being one cacophany of sound, which after a while, combined with the movement and activity, leaves one deafened and exhausted. Even at night there can be no respite, for it is essentially a twenty-four hour thing and part of the lifeblood of the ship. Sleeping is never difficult; it is the sleep of the physically drained, but one could equate it to sleeping on a fairground generator!

We slept in the traditional hammocks, constructed of a rectangle of stout canvas with eyelets at each end from which sprang the hammock lashings. The internal shape of the hammock was preserved by a six-foot by two-foot-six horse hair palliasse and we would make our bed simply by suspending this device between two hooks welded on the bulkhead for the purpose and by making a cocoon of a sheet and blanket or two. The shape of the hammock was preserved further and made to be a little airier by the addition of two wooden stretchers at the head and feet of the sleeper. These were usually carved from a broomhandle and were often very ornate items. The prospective user climbed into this arrangement by grasping an overhead pipe or other deck-head fitting and merely leapt up into it! I cannot tell you just how it was done, you needed to do it and you did! Even with a fair amount of alcoholic refreshment on board, one seldom missed but I have heard of quite serious injuries being incurred by people that did not get it right.

The hammock was a very comfortable bed indeed. It absorbed the movements fore and aft and rolled with the motion of the ship. It was the only respite from the effects of seasickness, however, as soon as one's feet hit the deck in the morning! I also never heard of anybody falling out of his hammock, at least, under his own volition!

We were taught to secure our hammocks after use by lashing them up sausage-style with no less than seven marlin hitches, after which they would be placed upright in a hammock rack, a steel pen made specially to contain them. They were then free to be used by the ship's Damage Control Party in their efforts to shore up any holes in the ships side, should one occur! They rarely stayed clean for long but the advantage was that they could easily be scrubbed clean and dried in a few moments in the extreme heat of the ships boiler-room.

The *Savage* was again alongside at Chatham. We lived aboard but used shoreline toilet facilities and ate dinner, tea and supper in *HMS Pembroke*. Considerable work went on in the boiler room and the gear room, which caused us seamen little concern as it was not our department. We were, however, severely put out by the vast numbers of dockyard maties who appeared at all hours of the day on our messdecks where they grouped about their teapot and generally loafed until either a man in a bowler hat dispersed them, or they caught a glimpse of our First Lieutenant on the prowl. They feared Jimmy the One more than anyone and abandoned all human dignity in their efforts to flee from his approach. It was comical to watch.

The dockyard workers of those times were descendants of those industrious men of the late thirties and early forties who kept our ships in good repair and fighting trim during the war with Hitler. Their sons came into the trade and each man was usually a pretty skilled workman. But of late, there were few ships to work on and because the Unions flooded each job with an excess of men in an effort to justify manning levels, I think the heart was taken out of the men. They shuffled about in groups, their eyes betraying their boredom and even when they were called upon to work, it took a great effort to wind up the energy to get going again.

Our minor refit dragged on somewhat. I heard the Captain and Navigating Officer complaining among themselves on one occasion. They were impatient to get to sea, whereas we preferred the comforts of RNB for just a bit longer. There was, after all, no real need to go ashore when alongside in the dockyard. If one was not duty watch, one could stroll into the barracks in "night-clothing" and play snooker, drink cheap beer in the ratings' bar or visit the very excellent cinema for a shilling. Or else one could dash ashore at 1600 on the first wave of libertymen to catch the 1622 to London Bridge and all points west for a great night out in London, returning to the Union Jack Club at Waterloo where one arranged an early morning call to catch the milk train from London Bridge, which got you back to your ship before 0800 the following morning.

It was during this period of refit that I suddenly and most mysteriously became ill. It started with a strange feeling of unreality, where life went on about me but I was insulated from it all. I became shaky and pale and finally physically sick. I reported sick to the Sick Bay on the Tuesday afternoon and can vaguely recall being stripped and examined by the doctor before passing out completely. I awoke, tucked up in a white cot bed in the early evening of Thursday. I was in the Royal Naval Hospital at Gillingham. Feeling awfully weak, I peered about a gradually brightening room and an SBA came over to me, drew the curtains about my bed and I was examined by a doctor. There was obviously something wrong but he could find no immediate answer to the problem. I was told that I would be kept in for seven days observation with blood tests and x-rays being scheduled for the following day.

I slept like a dead thing and had great difficulty waking up at 0530 for a wash and tea before falling asleep again and missing breakfast! I was wheeled off for my examinations but come tea-time on the Friday, I began to feel perfectly well again and soon got up for a heavenly bath and went about the ward in a dressing gown talking to other patients and helping the SBAs in their meal duties.

Each day the naval doctor did his rounds but seven days observation I had got and seven days I had to do, despite my request to be allowed to return to the ship. I was getting fed up at playing unpaid SBA, dishing out meals to the bedridden from the dinner trolley and polishing floors, helping to make beds and running up and down with bed-pans.

However, on the Tuesday morning just after doctors' rounds, the almoner, a Queen Alexandra Nursing Officer, told me to report to her office where she gave me a complimentary ticket for the local cinema. I was free to go outside after lunch, as my uniform had been brought up from the ship, ready for my release from hospital on the following Friday. I had to be back at the hospital by supper at 1830 but an SBA told me that no-one strictly adhered to the time, just so long as I was tucked up in bed by midnight and was discreet about it.

Rain beat a fitful tattoo in the puddles on the pavement and my shipmates had neglected to bring my Burberry with them. The air was crystal clear in the rain after the smells of the hospital as I hurried to the cinema in the high street. I presented my ticket at the paybox, it was threaded onto a string to one side and I was directed towards an usherette at the double doors leading to the stalls.

She was a short slight girl, with her hair piled up in a beehive, but when she turned towards me, my eyes were drawn instantly to her massive bosom! She really appeared to be out of proportion with those huge boobs and tiny waist and hips. My eyes, unaccustomed to viewing such luxuries, lingered too long on the tight front of her white blouse and she saw my stare, when I would rather she had not.

"Hospital?" she asked with a slight smile.

"Er, yes," said I, switching my gaze and breaking the spell. The smile widened.

"Doesn't look much wrong with you, dear!" and she reached for her torch on a shelf by the door. The bust moved up gracefully and wobbled gently on the way down. I tried not to notice but I did.

"Doctors think I had a virus," I mumbled, colouring up, "but I'm alright now."

"Good for you, dear," she said, her skirts swirling in a flash of rainbow petticoats. "Follow me, I'll put you in the back row today as there aren't many in."

The light of the black and white picture on the screen sparkled through the blond whisps of the beehive and I followed close behind her, drinking in her perfume. I suppose she was in her early thirties. I was so mesmerised that at nineteen, I wasn't counting!

129

She found me a seat on the edge of the row and I watched her torch disappear toward the front of the stalls. Heaven knows what the film was about, I could not take my eyes off her. I tracked her every move about the stalls, hoping that she would notice me watching her and dreading that she might return to the foyer and be lost from sight. To my dismay, she barged through the swing-doors into the foyer and I was forced to reluctantly return to the film. However, just as the film ground to a finish, she reappeared with an illuminated tray of assorted ice-creams and confection resting on that beautiful bosom. A spotlight picked her out and the audience were encouraged, by means of a crackly public address system, to buy their ices from "our sales staff, now in attendance throughout the cinema."

I could not help worrying about what the effect of cold ice creams might have on those warm, quivering globes. Since I had no money with me, I could not avail myself of a purchase from the lady of my dreams, with perhaps an excuse to view the signs of an early frostbite on her cleavage. I remained in my seat until the twenty-odd patrons had bought their ices or lollies and had returned to their seats to consume them, and the object of my fancies, without the aid of the spotlights to light her way, began to retire to the rear of the stalls. However, instead of making straight for the double doors, she detoured along the front of the house and came up the steps towards me. She came so close that her skirt brushed my knee. She smiled by the light of the illuminated tray and as she passed she dropped something in my lap. It was a choc-ice. I turned my head to whisper "Cheers" but she did not look back.

The news film came to an end and *Tweetie Pie* took over the the screen. I was momentarily distracted and took my eye off the swing-doors. Suddenly, there she was, sliding along the row of empty seats to my left, to drop heavily into the creaking seat next to me. "God," she gasped, "my bloody legs are dropping off today! Got a fag, love?" Of course I had. I opened my pack of Blue Liners, she shook one free and my hand trembled ever so slightly as I lit it with my old petrol lighter.

She drew in the blue smoke, stretched in the seat and exhaled into the stream of projected light from above.

"I needed that," she said.

"Thanks for the choc-ice," I whispered, nervously tucking a cigarette into the corner of my mouth in the way that I'd seen Humphrey Bogart do it. "That's all right," she smiled, "what's your name, dear?" The cartoon, the dim light of the cinema, the sparse audience, all were forgotten; they were just a back drop as we whispered in the dark together. Her name, she told me, was Carol, she lived in Chatham and was separated from her husband. She was thirty-two. Perhaps knowing her age had something to do with it but I found myself acting cool and sophisticated and saying the most subtle, witty things.

I don't know who made the first move, it happened so naturally but suddenly we were kissing. Our mouths squashed gently, almost shyly together and we just melted into a warm, scented deep embrace. She groaned and slipped deeper into the crutch of my left arm and my right hand slid gently around her tiny waist. I could feel her enormous breasts crushing under my chin and she seemed to be pressing them up to meet me. We broke apart briefly while I kissed her exposed neck which drove her to seek my lips again. Her seat creaked loudly as she sank even lower with me in hot pursuit. We both came up for air. There was a look of faint surprise in those blue eyes.

"Wow," she gasped.

"Wow yourself," I smiled in reply. She grasped the back of my neck.

"Again," she whispered. Once more we sank down into those red plush seats, our lips and tongues meshed together. She caught my right hand and clamped it to her bosom and at the same time her hand landed in my lap. And so we fondled, kissed and whispered, our eyes blazing crazily in the dark, until suddenly she took a cue from the distant smoky film.

"I've got to go, Pete," she croaked.

"Must you?" I groaned. She refastened the buttons on her blouse and ran her fingers along the straps to replace any excess boob which had escaped either by accident or design.

"Yes," she kissed my mouth quickly. "Can you meet me after work, half-past ten outside?"

"Sure," I replied. She dodged back along the row, pulling at her dishevelled clothing and with several strands of blond hair streaming awry. When I passed through the foyer on my way out, she looked as calm and as tidy as when I had first laid eyes on her, except her freshly painted mouth looked puffy and red. Our eyes met briefly and an electric shock thrilled through me.

I stepped out into the wet street. It had stopped raining but the sky was black and grey, the heavier clouds driven before a chill damp wind. It was only early evening and I had several hours to kill before meeting Carol. My heart leapt at the thought of her name. I jumped over puddles, splashed with the gaudy lights of the cinema and made my way back towards the hospital. I had six emergency pound notes concealed in the back of an old wallet and tonight was destined to be just such an emergency. My new sweetheart might fancy a meal or a drink before we went back to her place... I forced myself to think no further!

Supper was being served as I swept past the Porter's Lodge and into the stifling heat of the hospital corridors. Pressing the six pound notes into the

131

back of my paybook, I retraced my steps towards the reception area and the Porter's Lodge. It was necessary to slip out without him seeing me. I smoked several cigarettes and he showed no signs of leaving his post. Worse still, he had spotted me sitting on a visitors' bench and looked curiously at me several times.

The clock showed 8.10 and I began to get a bit anxious. I stubbed out another cigarette and wandered off to the toilets to think out the situation. I was beginning to look a bit conspicuous in my uniform and carrying my cap. I had no idea of the hospital geography but made up my mind to do a quick reconnoitre and seek a way out, perhaps to the rear of the building. I set off down the maze of corridors heading north and my instincts served me right, for I soon found myself in an outer corridor with several doors leading outside somewhere. I saw the sky and some stars briefly through a pane of clear glass.

Two of the doors were secured but the third opened easily into a small courtyard. A Humber and an old Austin Big Six were backed on to one wall and a path led around the side of the building, illuminated by the lights of the wards. I walked boldly along this path and quickly found my way out into the street once more.

I had succeeded and had found a way back into the hospital which, with luck, I might use without being detected. Always assuming of course that I would be back that night! My imagination was working overtime; I was hoping against hope that I would well be tucked up in a certain warm usherette's bed for that night and hang the consequences!

After a coffee in a milk bar, I approached the cinema with weak knees and my heart pounding. The garish glare of the lights hurt my eyes as I entered the foyer, empty but for a tall soldier in huge boots who stood, hands in pockets, staring up at a poster of coming attractions. The paybox was deserted, muffled music issued from behind the swing doors. I draped myself against a wall and lit yet another cigarette, ignoring the soldier. The music reached a crescendo and faded and the familiar strains of the National Anthem rang out. The doors burst open and a number of Teddy-boys dashed down the steps and out onto the street. The Anthem died and a commissionaire opened the swing-doors and locked them back to allow several people to stream out.

The foyer was full of people but I could not see my Carol. The last few patrons trickled out into the dark street and there was still no sign of her. Had she stood me up, I wondered? Idly, I realised that the soldier was still there and was eyeing me curiously. I paid no attention. The commissionaire released the bolts noisily on the double doors and disappeared into the stalls.

The doors creaked and one side opened and out came my Carol. She started down the stairs towards me with a smile. I started toward her, my young heart pounding with excitement in my temple, a grin spreading from ear to ear. Then she saw the soldier, who had been partly obscured from view by a potted palm. He too had began to move toward the stairs in greeting. Carol stopped with a sort of whimper. The soldier looked at me and I looked at him with increasing horror. He had "Husband" written all over his brutal features.

"What the hell's going on here then?" he thundered, glaring at me. He turned towards my blonde angel, "Are you at it again then?" Carol tripped sideways down the stairs towards him, setting up a tidal wave of vibration across the front of the tight white blouse, glimpsed briefly beneath her unsecured ocelot coat. She was obviously thinking quickly but her story was betrayed by her strawberry-flushed cheeks.

"Come on now, Ted," she spluttered. "Pete's a friend of Angela's and I said I would pass on a message from him if he met me outside this evening." Numbly, I nodded assent but my eyes were as guilty as hell. The soldier was not deceived. With a growl he pushed Carol's hand away, hard enough to send her sprawling backward on the stairs in a flurry of petticoats and black stocking tops. His lips curved viciously and all six feet four of him moved heavily towards me. My eight stone four also moved, but at twice his speed, as I made for the exit. In spite of his bulk he had the advantage with the angle to the door and he knew it. His great fists curled up like club hammers ready to beat me to a pulp but my greater speed and nimbleness accelerated me through the door and his first blow flayed the air behind me. He was in hot pursuit however, and my path was hindered by several patrons standing on the pavement outside and by a large black car parked in the kerb along with several motorcycles. But I slipped swiftly past the startled audience and with Carol's shrill "Ted, Ted, stop!" ringing in my ears, I vaulted clear over the pillion of a motorbike without touching any part of it and raced off up the street.

The crash of big boots and the stream of foul threats faded as I sped away and I chanced a glance astern to see Ted skidding to a halt in the middle of the street and Carol clacking towards him in her high heels, silhouetted against the brilliant lights of the cinema. I put a few extra yards between us and stood getting my breath back in the lee of a small van from where I could watch the couple.

Carol hung on Ted's arm looking up at him, her hair bobbing furiously as she shook her head in blatant denial. He pushed her a few times, glared up the street in my direction once and then spun Carol on her high heels and the pair walked off in the other direction. I lit my last cigarette, crumpled the packet into a ball and tossed it into a waste-bin. My uniform clung stickily to my body, damp from the drizzle and the heat of my effort. The evening's events had taught me several salient lessons and over the course of the next few days, I would go through them mentally and see what was to be learned.

Some women, I decided, can be worse than some men in their affairs. More care should be taken with these types; the signs are easy to read and it is better to give them a wide berth at the outset. They are also certainly a health hazard; I had smoked the better part of twenty-five cigarettes during the course of that day and it was apparent one needed to be sound of wind and limb to be sure of making a quick exit should it prove essential! It was all a bit of a dangerous game and with so many unattached girls about, not worth the candle. I resolved never to tangle with a married party again, a resolution easier made than kept.

The ward Night Sister caught me on my way up to the ward but seemed more upset about my damp clothes than my flagrant breach of the rules. I was urged to shower and turn in quickly, whilst my uniform disappeared for drying. I drifted off to an exhausted sleep, safe in the knowledge that above all else I was most certainly fit and well with no signs of any return of my mysterious virus.

I returned once more to *Savage* and again we sailed for the western coast of Scotland. We arrived on a cold March morning, a thick hoar frost covering all the metal parts of the ship with a white coat. However, instead of arriving at our quiet Loch Goil, we anchored off Rothesay, Isle of Bute, and gazed ashore to the rows of grey granite houses and hotels which lined the front. A few of my shipmates had been there before and were discussing the few merits of the town. Apparently, it was not exactly a good run ashore from the sailor's point of view; ladies were in short supply and drink could only be had in the hotels, whose atmospheres left a lot to be desired.

A large ferry steamed past later that afternoon and we waved furiously at a group of young ladies, wrapped up against the intense cold but nonetheless enjoying the winter sun on the after sun deck. They studiously ignored us. I enquired where the ferry was bound, to be told that it was making for the mainland and a place called Wemyss Bay, which was only an hour or so from Glasgow. My ears pricked up, for my sister and her husband lived near the Paisley Road area of Glasgow and as the weekend was coming up, I decided to telephone them and ask if I may call on them. This I did that very evening from a telephone box in Rothesay.

The following morning I put in a request, through my Divisional Officer, to see the First Lieutenant for weekend leave. To my surprise, my request was granted. It was, however, pointed out that my travel arrangements were to be such that I would be sure to be back aboard ship by 0800 on the Monday morning, ready for a trial cruise. I enquired at the ferry operator's office in Rothesay and discovered that the last ferry on the Sunday night was at 2100 from Wemyss Bay and I knew that our libertyboats ran their last sortie at 2359, so I was confident that I would make it in time.

I was the only man falling in for inspection for libertymen. I was inspected by the Coxswain who told me that I was horrible, scruffy and unseamanlike but he said all this with a twinkle in his eye and taking my station card, waved me ashore. He was a good sort really. It was only a short walk from the landing jetty to the Rothesay Dock and the ferry was alongside. I bought my ticket and sat in the saloon, smoking quietly and watching my fellow passengers come and go until the saloon lights flickered brighter as the engines started and with a bump and a jolt, the ferry left for the mainland. She rolled and pitched into the darkness. I read an abandoned newspaper and a little later the shorelights of Forward Point came winking through the port windows.

Eventually, the ferry nudged alongside the quay at Wemyss Bay and I joined the first wave of passengers to the gangway ashore and stepped out of the lights of the landing stage into the blackness of the night. A large gas lamp hissed and flickered in the wind and sleet, creaking rustily from its single hook above the entrance to the quay. I saw a bus stop on the northbound side of the road and read the timetable for buses to Glasgow. The rising wind, heavy with sleet and cold rain, plucked at my small brown suitcase, my bellbottoms flapped wildly and I tilted my chin into my raincoat collar in order that my cap should not blow away. I was quite alone by now; the people from the ferry had simply melted into the darkness and the only moving thing in sight was the wildly pitching gas light. The cold wind cut my face and I warmed my hands in my raincoat pockets, balancing the case between my legs.

Around the curve in the road wheezed a coach. Its orange headlamps did little to dispel the darkness and the destination plate, reading "Glasgow", seemed brighter than the headlights but I rattled gratefully aboard into the heat of the cosy, leather interior with its quaint chromium-plated coach lights and carpeted aisle. The driver took my money, punched a ticket from a clipboard of tickets and I bumped to the rear of the coach, aware of the curious gaze of my fellow passengers.

The clutch came up with a jolt and we lurched off, first gear whining off to second and then crashing into top until all that could be seen through the side windows was absolute darkness. We appeared to be travelling at perhaps thirty-five miles an hour down a black tunnel. Looking forward up the aisle through the driver's double windows, all one could see was the sudden reflection of an overhanging tree in the feeble headlights or the occasional road sign and I squeaked back into the leather seat and lit a cigarette. I remember stubbing out the cigarette on the stubbing plate on the back of the seat in front and then I must have dozed off, for the next I knew the bus lurched suddenly and I awoke to see the lights of a strange granite town.

I frantically searched for a name for this town on shop fronts or hoardings but I saw none. However, as my watch told me that a mere twenty minutes had elapsed since I had boarded the bus, I doubted that these lights were Glaswegian. So it proved, for the bright lights thinned out and we pitched headlong again into further blackness. I edged across my seat and asked an elderly gentleman, wearing a tweed coat and tam-o'-shanter, how far we were from Glasgow. As I spoke, the driver crashed down to second and the coach was filled with the roar of the engine and the whine of the gearbox and drive shaft. I deciphered little from the heavy accent of my companion's reply but I nodded wisely and smiled as if I had understood, not wishing to appear too foolish. I need not have worried too much, for the darkened clouds to the northeast took on an orange tinge, and we shortly came to the outskirts of a large community. Several small clues pointed to it being Glasgow.

Suddenly, we came upon tramcars and cobbled streets which were increasingly thronged with people, bustling hither and thither. The coach made several stops and I was on the edge of my seat, for I did not have any idea which may be mine, but finally at one stop, the driver rose from his seat and said something which included the words "Paisley Road Toll", at which I mustered my raincoat and suitcase and battled into the wet street, thanking the driver on my way out. The coach pulled wearily away, leaving me in an envelope of blue exhaust smoke. I put on my Burberry and took stock of my surroundings. I had no idea which way to go to begin my search for Middlesex Street where my sister lived.

I surveyed the sea of approaching faces. None seemed friendly but a paperboy gazed curiously at my uniform and so I asked him for Middlesex Street. Following his instructions, I very quickly found the street and climbed the stairs of the tenement building. My knock on the door was answered by my new brother-in-law whom I had not yet met, since my sister had married in Scotland and our side of the family had been unable to travel north for the event. Findlay worked in the Govan shipyard and his handshake matched his employment. I was ushered into their cosy flat to meet my sister, Shirley and my new niece, Mary. Thus began a most convivial weekend.

After supper, Findlay insisted on taking me off for a visit to "the wee hoose for a dram". My Scots was improving, for I understood what he said first time, without the need to ask him to repeat it! Leaving the warmth of the flat, we rattled down the worn limestone stairs to the street and hurried some distance across the Paisley Road with its brightly lit trams and the cold wind and snow flurries, into the glass and mahogany reflections of a pub. It was full of men, some the worse for drink, who broke off their conversations as Findlay and I made for the bar, and stared curiously at me. I felt most conspicuous in my uniform. I need not, however, have felt at all apprehensive, for as soon as Findlay had introduced me as his new brother-in-law "from the Sooth", I quickly had a sea of hands to shake and was treated like a long-lost friend.

Suddenly, the crowd around me claimed nautical antecedents far outstripping my poor experiences and as the night wore on, my ear was full of the exploits of my new acquaintances, most of whom appeared to have served at least a century in the engine room of some tramp steamer or battleship, and had been in service in the most obscure places ever heard of. Some tales in fact remained unfinished, for several lost their tenacious grip on the edge of the battered, wet bar and either pitched headlong down into the sawdust or slid gracefully down in mid oration.

It was impossible to compete with their generosity; as fast as I bought a drink for them they responded roundly and quite a supply of "wee drams" piled up before me. I tried several times to share them out for I knew that I could never swallow them. I was saved by the landlord calling "Time" and suddenly, the milling mass at the bar swallowed every unattended drink in sight and, as one, made for the exit.

The street outside was bitterly cold after the thick atmosphere of the "Hoose" and Findlay and I stood aimlessly in four inches of snow, finding further items to discuss with our new-found friends. I was invited to dinner at no fewer than five homes for the following day and I was hard pressed to find tactful excuses for refusing but promised each would-be host that I would come and see them on my next visit. Another bout of back-slapping over, the group began to disperse and Findlay and I entered the lights and bustle of the Paisley Road, he with his left arm draped over my shoulder for support. I am not too sure who supported whom!

We were stopped once or twice by minor collisions with revellers travelling in the opposite direction and by a lamp post which wandered out in front of us, but eventually came to the edge of the pavement opposite Middlesex Street. Findlay had travelled this way before and, I suspect, under similar circumstances and his previous method of crossing the slippery, cobbled street had been to aim himself at an angle of ninety degrees to the kerb and make a dash for it. One glance either way up and down the Paisley Road told me that this method would not work on this occasion for there were trams approaching in opposite directions, quite apart from a number of cars and motorcycles. But Findlay took aim and launched us with great resolution. I clutched frantically at his coat tails. A big Austin Sixteen swerved and slewed sideways on the slushy cobbles, hooted and roared on and Findlay was pulled back onto the kerb. He glared after the retreating car with unfocussed eyes and muttered: "See you'se..."

We tried again. It looked reasonably clear. Clinging to each other for all the world like a pair of fat ladies on a seaside outing, we passed astern of a two-stroke motorcycle and a cyle bearing no lights and staggered to the centre of the road. Where the tram came from, I do not know. But there it was, as big and as brilliantly lit as the front at Blackpool and with its bell clanging a strident warning. Somehow, we stumbled over the tramlines and lurched on out of its angry path. I felt the heat of the motor and smelt the acrid smell of brake pads as the tram clipped behind us.

My attention was next taken by an elderly couple swathed in tweeds, plus-fours and tammies, astride an equally elderly tandem. Collision was inevitable, when to his everlasting credit, the gentleman driver committed cycling "hara-kiri" by tucking the front wheel under the machine and cyclists and cycle slid across the snow, to come to a bone-jarring crash against a horse-trough. Findlay said: "See you'se..." again, weakly. The couple picked themselves up. It was immediately obvious that they had also been celebrating and it was they who apologised to us!

I half expected to be asked to dinner again... With no apparent damage to either bodies or cycle, they swiftly remounted the machine and wobbled off to the whine of dynamo and the crunch of lost gearing, leaving Findlay and I safely on the homeward side of the busy road. Findlay could not find his door key and when my sister let us in, I was blamed for Findlay's drunken condition and Findlay, in turn, blamed for mine. However, we were soon forgiven and after a late supper, I was put to bed on the settee, to dream of an ever-widening Paisley Road and hordes of speeding trams.

The following morning came far too quickly and after breakfast, we stepped out onto a deserted street for a Sunday morning stroll about the local sights. The snow was gone and a wet, mild breeze picked up from the west, but I was pleased enough to return to the cosiness of the small flat for a delicious Sunday roast. The precious hours of freedom ticked quickly by and I had at last to return to the ship. Shirley, Findlay and little Mary in her pram accompanied me to the bus station. The sun's blood-red edge sank behind a bank of coal-black clouds for all the world as solid as the granite mountains beneath them and the cold westerly breeze had taken a more northerly slant. There was shortly more snow to come.

I boarded the bus and took a back seat so I could wave farewell to my hosts to the last. They were quickly lost from sight in the brilliance of a backdrop of city lights and I settled back, enjoying the darkening view of hills and crags, until the blackness of the night and the increasing snow-flurries made trying to see out of the window a hypnotic puzzle.

Wemyss Bay announced its presence with a reflective road sign. I moved to the front of the bus as it came to a halt, stepped out into the dark and caught my breath at the colder edge to the air. The bus exhaust blew warmly across the front of my bellbottoms as it fought for second gear and I watched its tail-light as it gathered speed into the distance. The gas lamp spluttered above the entrance to the ferry quay. As I crossed the street toward it, I saw a notice, written in chalk. It read, "Due to extreme weather conditions, all ferry sailings are cancelled until further notice." I said "Er!", simply because there was nothing else to say and no-one to hear if I had. The street was deserted and even the houses stared back with black empty eyes. It was as if I was the last man alive in that cold, empty land and I suddenly felt afraid. I stood at the ferry entrance, thinking of what to do. The best plan seemed to return to Glasgow but the last bus had long gone.

I'll thumb a lift, I thought. It was getting colder as I set off on the road towards Glasgow, keeping a keen eye on the road behind for lights of a vehicle. My case seemed heavier at every step and once out of the village, there was little shelter to be had, so I kept moving, switching the cursed case from hand to hand.

My sharp ears heard a vehicle coming and I turned to face that direction, knowing that my white face would easily be seen. I raised my thumb in the traditional manner but the car crossed the road in the effort to avoid stopping and was soon lost to sight over the next hill. Ruefully, I picked up my case and carried on and about half a mile further on, another car passed with the same haste as the earlier one. This time I muttered a curse under my breath about mean Scots! Suddenly, I saw a street light ahead and then a road sign reading "Inverkip," and further along the deserted main street was a police station.

By now, thoroughly cold and tired, I went in. I told my tale to the young constable who manned the station desk. He said "Oh dear" a few times and then asked me to wait where I was, disappearing through a door at the back of the tiny office. I put down my case and stood straightening out my bent frozen fingers. He returned with a police officer and I repeated my adventure. He could not have been more helpful; I was seated in front of a blazing fire

139

with a hot cup of tea whilst the police officer made a few phone calls, the result of which being that I was given a cell for the night whilst further enquires would be made to ensure that I got back to Rothesay in the morning.

How many "prisoners", I wondered, spent such a night in the cells at Inverkip with the great steel door wide open! I slept the sleep of the dead and at 5 o'clock the following morning, I was awakened with a cup of tea followed by a hot bacon sandwich. The station officer came in with a bit of news. The ferries remained cancelled but a boat carrying papers and mail would be leaving Gourock at 0700 for Rothesay and he would see that I got to it. After my wash, I finished my tea and sandwich and bade farewell to my benefactors. I have been a staunch supporter of our wonderful policemen ever since!

The station officer went out into the dark road with me and in a few moments a car came along, heading in the direction of Gourock. He stopped it and asked the driver to take me to Gourock and he agreed. I jumped in, thanking my policeman friend for his kindness and off we sped into the grey shadows of dawn. My new chauffeur was late for work so we made very good time in the old Morris Ten, and he dropped me in sight of the quay, just as a watery sun broke free of the black clouds in the east.

I easily found the paper boat, an elderly MFV, tied up at the jetty and knocked respectfully on the port side of the wheelhouse. The skipper appeared and was expecting me. He showed me aft to a hold which was converted into a messdeck where an iron stove roared merrily, giving off little puffs of smoke. But if I had thought of loafing away in this cosy "caboosh" until the boat made Rothesay, I was sadly wrong. The skipper consulted his watch. "Leave your gear down here, lad," he said, "and then come topsides and give the Mate a hand". I was put to work scrubbing the decks. Just to prove that I was no free-loader I removed my shoes and socks, rolled up my "belles" and did it in my bare feet!

We cast off and headed down towards Forward Point into a short vicious sea. I quickly dispensed with the hose I'd been using, as we were shipping a good supply of green water over the bows at regular intervals! I was aware of the watching eyes on the bridge but had the job done and the gear stowed away smartly. I knocked on the lee side of the wheelhouse for further instructions.

"Can yer mak a wee brew, lad?" I was asked. I confirmed that I could and was soon clinging on for dear life in the tiny galley making four big mugs of tea, which I safely delivered to the wheelhouse for the skipper, mate and engineer. I apparently passed muster at this stage for I was not asked to do anything more and in truth we were all hard put keeping our feet in the wildly tossing boat. The skipper turned his pipe upside down and poked his head through the lee window, studying weather conditions on the more open waters beyond Forward Point through his binoculars. Apart from a brief glimpse of Greenock to port, I had no idea of our position but from Forward Point we steered southwest towards a dark lump of land which was Bute.

We were the only vessel on those cold, rough waters that blew fitfully in from the North Atlantic. In spite of the smash of water against the front of the wheelhouse and the constant need to hold on tight to something, the crew chatted amongst themselves in their heavy accents, largely ignoring me. I tried breaking the ice by passing around my cigarettes and taking an interest in our course and position, but this was a very dour crew indeed and I felt that it would take me some years to be privy to their company. I collected up the mugs and dished them up in the tiny galley and then returned to the stifling heat of the wheelhouse.

It was by now well past eight o'clock and I was "adrift" and getting a bit anxious. If *Savage* had sailed, I would have to ask to be put off on *Barfleur*, the only other ship in Rothesay at the time, other than the submarine depot ship *Adamant* but what if *Barfleur* had sailed too? I need not have worried for as the black mass of land crept closer I saw two lean grey shapes in the harbour and at long last we pounded into quieter waters and headed towards D27. *Savage* was still at anchor.

Retrieving my case from a corner of the hot messroom, I made myself ready with the bowline to starboard. The MFV nudged expertly alongside *Savage* under the watchful eye of Lt.-Commander Gilbert, and thanking my gallant skipper for the trip, I sprang to the destroyer's side and climbed over the guard rail. My crewmates chivvied me about my mode of transport but I passed it off as being my private yacht; in truth I was more concerned at my inevitable confrontation with the Coxswain over my late arrival. I reported to the ship's officer for the return of my station card. This, of course, was refused and I was formally charged by the Officer of the Day as being adrift and referred to the First Lieutenant's Defaulters.

Our sea trial was cancelled, possibly due to the bad weather. Defaulters was held in the after passageway, just forward of "Y" gun. I doubled in from the snowstorms outside and doffed my cap at the First Lieutenant's Defaulters table. The charge was read out. It went on in naval rhetoric for some time but the overall effect was that I was some two hours adrift. Of course, I had to plead guilty since I most obviously was late. The First Lieutenant asked me if I had anything to say and I gave him a resumé of the events from leaving my sister's home at Glasgow until joining ship at Rothesay. He listened, elbows on the desk and fingertips together.

"It seems," he said when I had concluded, "that you made every effort to get back aboard in time. You certainly can't be blamed for the weather. You handled the situation very well under the circumstances but be careful in future... case dismissed!" I joined up with a working party on the upper deck for the rest of the day, my adventure at a happy conclusion. Which was just as well, for we were treated to several days of blinding snow, driven by stormy northeasterlies which would have been no weather to spend tramping around the limits of Wemyss Bay awaiting a ferry!

There follows an incident of which I am not particularly proud, but since it happened as a result of being in the Service and as such being exposed to the temptations of Service life, it must get a mention. March 27th was my nineteenth birthday. We were alongside at Portland. The postman bought me cards from girlfriends and home and even the weather was kind, wet and a little chill but without great mountains of waves to roll over on our daily tasks out in the Channel. Since it was my birthday, my messmates offered me several "wets" of rum, even though I was too young to draw my official ration. An issue in those days was made to any rating over the age of twenty years who had not elected to declare himself an abstainer. Threepence per day was given in lieu should one not wish to take the tot but most people took the spirit if only to use it as a bargaining asset, for although it was not allowed for a man to dispose of his tot by any other means other than to drink it or throw it away, it was often used to trade for someone to stand your harbour watch if you had a date ashore, or to get some urgent ironing done.

The issue was one part rum, fresh from the West Indies, and one part water. Originally, the issue was of pure rum but way back in the eighteenth century, old Admiral Vernon saw the effect that drunkenness was having on the poor sailor of the day and instructed that all future issues would be watered half and half, ensuring that the drink would not keep and thus preventing sailors saving up the rum to go on one drunken binge. It was then called "grog", a nickname actually applied to the grogham material of the coat worn by the Admiral himself, earning him the nickname of "old grog".

"Up Spirits!" was piped and I mustered in my mess for my first taste of rum. The Leading hand of the mess was responsible for the doling out of the rum and it was always a very serious affair. Exactly the right amount was ladelled out of a special container and if a tiny drop was spilled back into the container, the recipient would immediately ask for a re-scrub and the whole measure would have to be redrawn to his satisfaction. I remember more than one occasion when serious rows brewed up over mismanagement of the rum issue.

I was offered several "sippers" and "gulpers" and knocked them straight back, for that was the only way that I could endure the awful taste! Almost everyone in the mess insisted upon my having a sip or a gulp of their issue. The unaccustomed libation went straight to the brain where it paralysed all logical thinking and reduced my eyes to pools of senseless blood. I could stand, I could hear, but I was "not"! When hands were fallen in for work after lunch, my body refused to follow them and I slept heavily on the lockers in the mess.

As it was my birthday, my absence was ignored and I was not charged; in fact the ship's SBA checked me once, ensuring that I was not completely "blotto", since I sat up and answered when questioned as to my condition but later in the afternoon, none other than our First Lieutenant came into the mess. I stood up and stood swaying to attention.

"You are not drunk, are you Cobbold?" he asked.

"No sir!" I replied, and he took a look into the paintshop forward and left me alone without another glance.

We rounded the breakwater into Portland harbour a little after 1530 and I went for a wash to bring myself to. As the hands were dismissed at 1600, I had made a fanny of tea for the mess and was feeling a little shaky but not nearly as bad as before. I was ribbed mercilessly and then someone suggested "the hair of the dog" and I got dressed and went ashore for a night out with the boys. It was disastrous.

We went from pub to pub in Weymouth. I sobered up and then drank to the stage where I was drunk again and sobered up again. I do not know to this day how much I drank but I vaguely remember the bus ride back to Portland and getting off the bus. Someone in the group remembered that I had not yet been "bumped" and the next I knew, my feet were whisked from under me and I was heavily bashed eighteen times on the hard pavement outside a recreation ground. On the nineteenth bump, my colleagues' enthusiasm overcame their intoxicated sense of control. They all released me at the same time and I flew gracefully over the railings and into a bush in the adjacent recreation ground. Assuming that I would be over the railings in a trice since they had seen me pick myself up, they hurried on down to the tea-bar that used to be open until midnight at the entrance to the dockyard gates, leaving me to catch them up.

Try as I might, I could not scale the railings without my bellbottoms becoming speared on the spikes and bringing me to the ground with more bumps than I could cope with and so I retired to the gates of the park, to try my luck there. It was whilst I thus piddled about that a lady hove in sight. She stopped upon spotting me and seeing that my efforts to climb the gate were of no avail, she offered to call out the park keeper who lived in the cottage alongside the park. He arrived, wearing a greatcoat over his pyjamas, in no good frame of mind about being thus called out, my birthday or not, and delivered me into the care of the good lady, who took my arm and said that we should get some hot coffee down me before my present state got me into even more trouble. I do not remember a lot of what happened; all I wanted to do was sleep.

I awoke a little after seven the following morning in the heat of a double bed which I can only describe as a pit, with the back view of my lady benefactor dressed only in long pink drawers with elastic to the knee, cooking bacon over a single burner in the corner of the grubbiest, dingiest room that I have ever had the misfortune to enter. We had obviously shared the same bed together. Heaven knows what had gone on! Her first question to me was "What's your name, sweetheart?"

My every instinct was to flee and I dragged on my crumpled clothes, avoided the bacon and egg "surprise" and clattered down the street to the dockyard and on to the safety of the ship. I spent several anxious days expecting the onset of some horrible infection but nothing happened and I was able to breathe easily once more.

April began to get into its stride. The weather, our constant preoccupation, gave flashes of being kind, with the odd sunny afternoon when we would enjoy a glassy sea, a little warmth on our faces and the tranquillity of a blue sky and wheeling white gulls. The beauty of the granite houses along the Clyde took on new colour and the brown and grey hills adopted a slight tinge of green as the tiny new leaves of life began their struggle to mature into leafy blossom. In just a few weeks, the hills below the treeline would be a mass of green to the edge of the Loch and their hilltops would be capped with dots of feeding sheep. The snow had long disappeared from the top of the Isle of Arran and the wind no longer froze one's face with an icy blast. It was wonderful to feel the warmth of the sun again, even though it was not consistent. We often encountered snow showers when but a few miles distant, the sun shone red on a mountain range. Spring was coming to the north in that wonderful, clean fresh way only experienced in Scotland.

A further visit was made to Greenock but I hardly made for shore, having plenty to occupy me on board. My letters from Jenny became fewer and fewer. I considered the likelihood of our meeting again to be highly remote and I was really only writing to her in the hope of receiving a good mailbag. Even when I was on leave it was not possible to travel to Bristol to see her; I had little money, and nowhere to stay had I got there, even though she had several times offered to put me up at her parents' home. She came from a wealthy, internationally-known family and I did not feel that her parents would do much to encourage her association with me. I eventually wrote to her to end the association and having done so, felt better about it.

With the coming of spring I was free to look about once more in a serious frame of mind and seek a more permanent basis for my love-life, perhaps someone that I could come home to once this national service was over. A girl in every port was not a bad thing mind you and like all my shipmates, I was out to enjoy myself during this period of release from parental control.

A chap in my mess got himself into quite a stew whilst in Greenock. He met a tall, slim, pretty Scots girl at a dance and she fell as heavily for David as he did for her. When our instructions to return to Sheerness by way of Portsmouth finally came, he was quite distraught, as we were sailing the very next day and he was on duty on our last night in Greenock. Of course, I stood in as a "sub" for him, we exchanged duties and he rushed ashore at the earliest possible moment returning on the last libertyboat.

He was not much of a letter writer and feared the new love would lose interest quickly. Many hours were spent in counselling and encouraging him to not be so despondent but in the event, we need not have worried so much, for his very first letter delivered to him when we called into Portsmouth, gave him the news that the girl was pregnant. To our suprise, David immediately lost interest in her! He told me that he could not face the responsibility of a child and did not want to write to or see anything of his sweetheart of the past few weeks ever again. We abandoned him to his fate at this stage. Clearly he had responsibilities and was not the first sailor to receive such a letter and who would have to seek a solution in the best way that he could but there was little anyone else could do to help either party. The subject remained in limbo for a while, with David not replying to the letters, which became more urgent and distressed each time.

Our stay in Portsmouth was of short duration and had something to do with those ubiquitous boffins again. However, a finger from the past caught up with me one evening as I sat in the mess after supper and it was an event that I still remember with regret to this day. The sailor that I had met in Gibraltar whilst aboard *Ocean* and who had conveyed me to the weird religious meeting at the villa , suddenly came into the mess. Cap in hand he smiled at our sea of upturned faces. We had very few visitors and usually they were old "oppos" from other ships renewing acquaintances but it was obvious that he was not expecting to know anyone.

I was not so sure who he was at first, so I did not get up to greet him. However, when he started to talk about the Bible, Jesus, the Devil, our sinful way of life, and his hope for our final salvation, I at last recognised him and stood to say "hello". By then the one or two "hard" types had begun to give a bit of a barracking to our friend's well-meaning intentions but having found an ally, he called upon me to bear witness, recounting the circumstances of our earlier meeting. To my everlasting shame, "I denied him thrice" and he finally took his leave of us, promising to include us in his prayers.

We headed out of Portsmouth toward the Nab Towers and the open Channel on our return trip to Chatham, during which another highly memorable incident occurred. The cook of the mess had prepared a large pot of stew for dinner, a "pot-mess" in Navy terms. The stew contained meat, usually beef, mixed fresh vegetables and seasoning, baked beans and dumplings and was a much welcomed dinner indeed on a cold day.

I had been detained in securing some loose lashings to the motor boat cover this particular lunchtime and had only just come away from the upper deck. I repaired to the washroom to remove the grime from my hands for dinner, balancing myself against the washbasin to keep my feet as *Savage* rolled and pitched. Above the noise of sea and engines, fans and vibrations, I heard the sound of someone retching. Quietly, I rolled the washroom door back on its runner, in time to see our duty cook of the day, Able Seaman "Robbie" Roberts with the large fanny of pot-mess in one hand balancing himself wearily against the passageway bulkhead. Before I could call some ribald remark, he retched again and to my horror, spewed heavily into the hot fanny of stew. Aghast, I slid the door back shut and I heard his stumbling progress past the washroom and on up to the mess. When I returned to the mess, the Leading hand was ladelling out great chunks of pot-mess to a sea of gannet-hungry faces. I could not tell them that "Robbie" had been sick in it.

He lay in a pale heap on the cushions. I refused my dinner that day, feigning "mal de mer" but I could not suppress a grin to see them tucking in and complimenting the sickly cook on his expertise. Not a drop of stew remained in the fanny and a volunteer set to washing up all the crockery since Robbie was still too sick to complete the task. The rest of my messmates, their bellies distended from their over indulgence, sat idly smoking or reading letters, highly satisfied with their dinner!

I met Robbie one day in 1960 quite by accident outside Gamages in London. We went to a pub to talk over old times and I told him of the fact that I knew of his secret sick in the mess lunch. It was the first time that I had ever told anyone about the incident in all those years and Robbie was convulsed over it! As he said, he was too ill to do anything about his seasickness and as he did not have the strength to go through all the work in arranging an alternative dinner for us all, he had decided to let the matter lie.

CHAPTER
NINE

T he weather eased as we rounded North Foreland and began our run up the Thames Estuary. The buoys and landmarks of this complex stretch of water were becoming quite familiar by now and I could hazard a pretty good guess at how far out of Sheerness we were.

We were delayed somewhat on this particular trip by having to rendezvous with an RFA, a Royal Fleet Auxiliary vessel, for the purpose of refuelling. Usually, this task was completed in the dockyard, where it was merely a case of running the fuel-oil pipes aboard and banning smoking for some hours whilst the ship was bunkered with fuel. But occasionally, the powers-that-be thought it a good wheeze to get us to do it the hard way and we would meet the RFA somewhere out to sea.

We would both steam a parallel course, maintaining the same speed exactly, our decks would be prepared to receive the fuel lines and a thin line would be shot from our ship to the deck of the RFA, using a .303 Lee Enfield rifle equipped with a special adaptor, known as a Costin Gunline. We workhorses of the seaman branch would then be called upon to haul in the thin line to carry across a heavier cable and often a heavier one after that and finally, the fuel lines themselves, which would be connected to our tanks to replenish our bunkers with the black, sticky, tarry oil which, when melted, would fire our boilers.

This would be an opportunity too good to miss for the bright boys of the wardroom, who would find all sorts of evolutions for us to carry out whilst captive alongside and steaming at ten knots or so with our RFA. For example, a "jack-stay transfer" would be rigged up. This was a device for transferring personnel from vessel to vessel, and was basically a chair that was hauled across from ship to ship. A highlight of the proceedings would sometimes be provided by a large wave which would oblige and rear itself up between the ships whilst the transfer was in progress, soaking the rider. A great cheer would go up from the crews of both ships and most people, including the wet transferee, regarded the matter as funny.

The jack-stay transfer system was widely in use before the advent of the helicopter and was in great demand for the transfer of the sick to a ship with better facilities, the exchange of documents, stores and ammunition, mail and personnel that had to leave their ship urgently when miles from land.

On this occasion, having received our supply of fuel, to our surprise, *Savage* bore away to the north, skirting the shoals and familiar waters of the Thames and building up speed as she went. The longer nights were fading and it became dark a little before 2100. The scene on the messdecks was one of bewilderment and misery for most had expected to arrive at Chatham, or at the least tie to a buoy in Sheerness from whence they would be free to jump a trot-boat to Gillingham for overnight leave. As every hour passed, the likelihood of doing just that became more and more remote and the rumours and "buzzes" began to circulate. One of the evening watchmen popped his head into the mess on his way to the heads.

"We're on our way to help search for the crew of one of the Grimsby fishing fleet which has sunk off the Dogger Bank!" he informed us. I sat in the light and warmth of the smoky messdeck feeling very sorry for those brave souls, who by now would be cold and frightened and pitching in their small survival dinghy in a coal-black North Sea, not knowing whether they would be found or even if anyone was yet aware of their plight.

That tale was later discovered to be nothing but another "buzz" when the same person later met an off-duty member of the mess and scotched the tale as being the wind-up that it was by adding that the trawler had not actually sunk but was merely awash and the crew were trying to sail it back to Grimsby using the tan mizzen sail and being towed by two large cod that had volunteered from the fish-hold! Another "buzz" was that the Royal Yacht had fouled one of her propellers but her diver was completely out of white gloves at the time and so would not be able to go down to clear the obstruction and that's where we came in. We threw things at the teller of that tale!

Just a little before 2200, the reason for our protracted journey out into the wilds of the North Sea was announced over the Tannoy. The voice of the First Lieutenant interrupted my sleep, for I had decided not to sling my hammock and had just dropped off for forty winks on the lockers. "Do you hear that," he said, "we have a report that an RAF Hawker Hunter pilot has bailed out over the sea somewhere off Cromer. We are proceeding to assist the Air Sea Rescue vessels and the RNLI in that area. Hands will be called to Action Stations in thirty minutes time and extra lookouts will be posted. I suggest that everyone gets a hot drink before turning to, it could be a long cold night. I shall keep you advised. That is all!"

There was a queue at the galley for hot water for tea and kye and several rounds of toast were made on the messdeck electric fires. Everyone got dressed in their warmest clothes and put a supply of cigarettes in their pockets. The grumbling about not having got into harbour immediately ceased. No-one uttered a word of complaint about the disruption to their routine and comfort and we all went to Action Stations, determined to find this poor flier if we possibly could.

I was detailed as First Lieutenant's Runner, my task being to run about the ship with messages and see to any requirements on the bridge. I also commandeered a pair of binoculars and discreetly moved about the bridge, searching here and there, always careful to both keep out of the way and to be close at hand if required. Harwich appeared as a glow in the northwestern sky to port and the sea was dotted with the lights of many small vessels, all apparently sweeping northwards having patrolled as far south as the entrance to the rivers Colne and Blackwater.

By now we were in radio contact with an Air Sea Rescue launch of the RAF and the cruiser *HMS Jamaica*. I overheard several conversations and on one occasion, *Jamaica* asked us to illuminate a radar target with star-shell and with a dull "bang". Y-gun's crew obliged. The brilliant flare lit up the black water for miles and the target turned out to be a harbour launch, also engaged in the search but with an obscured overtaking light and no radio. We closed him and the Navigating Officer spoke to him through a loud-hailer to acquaint us with the latest search situation. He knew no more than us.

From the conversations on the bridge, I deduced that the pilot of the plane had radioed a May Day call at about 1930 hrs, since when, nothing had been heard of him and he had failed to make his destination. Our search continued until just before one in the morning, when we were stood down from Action Stations and the normal Middle Watchmen took over the situation. I turned in, leaving my clothes where I could easily get to them and slept fitfully until the hands were called at 0730.

I came out onto the upper deck from the washroom, to see the East Whittaker buoy slipping slowly astern on a hazy, calm sea as we headed south having abandoned the fruitless search to the local authorities. We arrived at Sheerness and passed Garrison Point a little after nine and made off up the river to Chatham. True to form, we heard no more of the plight of the Hawker's pilot for no-one bothered to acquaint we minions of the lower deck with either the good news of his safe return or the sad news of his loss, and after a few days most of us forgot the subject.

Thirty-three years later, I chanced to recount this tale to a fellow member of the Wivenhoe Sailing Club, who I knew had experience of the RAF Air Sea Rescue service, and had been based at Harwich for several years. He clearly remembered the incident and was able to tell me that the poor pilot had actually May Dayed at Cromer but had bailed out of his sick aircraft at

Shoeburyness. He had landed in the dark on the outer limits of the artillery range and had spent the larger part of the hours of darkness blundering around, trying to be rescued! I was glad to hear that the chap had survived after all.

Once more, we came into Chatham for a few days. The aerials on the mast came in for a bit of treatment on this occasion and we were fitfully employed in swinging from wooden platforms called stages, which were arranged over the sides of the ship's hull in order that we sailors could paint the ship with a nice new coat of grey paint. It was a sticky, dirty job and the water was always waiting for a body to fall into it. Should one be so unlucky, the water was so polluted that it meant an immediate twenty-four hours in the naval hospital and a considerable number of injections in the sick bay, so we made sure to keep our lashings on the stages tight and to check our hand-hold at all times. Whilst paint ship was in operation, there was generally a more relaxed atmosphere about the ship and providing things did not get too out of hand, our NCOs and officers turned a blind eye to any slight excesses. There was a tendency to rib the person sitting wielding the paintbrush on the stage and there were many exchanges of good humour during these periods.

It came about that I was on the upper deck, employed in painting of the steel sides of the after superstructure. Quite honestly, I was making a poor job of the task. I was new to painting and had more paint on the deck and over my hands than successfully appeared on the metal. The First Lieutenant, Lieutenant Commander Gilbert, stopped in his ever critical rounds to show me how the job should be done properly.

"This is the way that you do it, son," he said as he demonstrated how to charge the paintbrush with just the right amount of paint and how to apply it to the surface without leaving unsightly brushstrokes and runs. His reference to my being his "son" was overheard by my shipmates and I was given a right wigging about it during "Stand Easy". It was, however, a title that seemed to stick with me in particular, for on any occasion that Jimmy the One spoke to me on an informal matter, he always called me "my son". Very saucily one day, I replied, "Yes dad!" and he laughed, not seeming at all affronted and it became a bit of a habit and a small joke in the mess. Later in my time aboard *Savage*, it led to a very funny incident which I will relate further on.

The reason for sprucing up the jaded paintwork and making the old ship look spic and span was that we were to retire to Sheerness after the weekend and, following a number of sea trials in the area of the Estuary and the North Sea, were to suffer an inspection by the Commander-in-Chief the Nore. The painting progressed relentlessly but there always seemed more to do than time to do it in. I was to go home on leave on the Thursday evening, knowing that I had a long weekend leave to look forward to, which put me in a very cheerful frame of mind and I set about my painting tasks with added zeal.

I sang loudly at my task and perhaps it was this that attracted the attention of the Jimmy, for he came along the deck to inspect my work and was not very impressed. He pointed out several blemishes in my work and suddenly, my mood went from elation to frustration. It seemed that no matter what I did or how I approached it, I was doomed to failure.

"Sod it!" I said, my cheeks colouring in anger and I literally threw the paintbrush into the painting tin. We stared at one another for a second or two, the First Lieutenant realising that I was on the edge of an outburst from which it would be unlikely that I would hold back. He had already seen me in action over the potato-loading incident.

"Well," he said finally, "You must realise that painting is an art. It took me many years to learn it and my First Lieutenant was always taking me to task over bad workmanship until I finally got it right. I was a seaman, just as you, and I had to learn these lessons." He handed me back my sticky paintbrush. "Clean this out, return it to the paintshop and draw a one-inch brush. Use that until you get the knack of painting and then you can go back to a large one. That's the way that I learned," and he walked slowly away along the deck. Confrontation was avoided. I would have been the loser in any case and I had to learn painting the hard way.

My good temper quickly returned and I smilingly waved my one inch brush at him when I next saw him and he remarked on a slight improvement in my work. I respected his attitude over this incident as many officers would have challenged my hot response to their authority and I would have wound up on a charge. I took a liking to the First Lieutenant from that day on and always did my very best to appear smart and seamanlike, something I would have considered only a few weeks previously as going soft! In truth, although I would never have admitted it, I was developing a pride and interest in the Navy and for the first time was beginning to enjoy myself. I began to make an effort in all that I did and to enjoy doing a job well and putting a bit of extra effort into things. So much for the rebel, vowing that the Service would not change him!

We fell in for long weekend leave and were inspected at the brow by the Coxswain. The limits of our leave were read out as they always were, the Officer of the Day, an Australian Gunnery Officer, inspected us again and we were dismissed. Clattering down the gangway, we sped on the wings of freedom toward the dockyard gate but we had not yet escaped completely. The dockyard police were on the lookout for tobacco smugglers and many of us were selected from the mass approaching the exits and made to turn out our cases and pockets in the police office in case we had more than our ration of duty-free cigarettes. Anyone caught smuggling in those days would be taken back to their ship and charged. That meant the loss of their leave period, punishment by the ship and confiscation of the tobacco. Her Majesty's Customs were constantly threatening to withdraw the duty-free concession to HM ships because of the lost revenue caused by the flood of tobacco that escaped over the dockyard wall one way or another. Woe betide anyone caught red-handed!

I finally passed through the gate into the Khyber Pass and freedom. Since I had been delayed during my search by the dockyard police, I had missed the first bus to Chatham but another had just arrived at the terminus and I made toward it through the thinning crowd of homeward-bound sailors. Suddenly, I became aware that someone was looking at me and I glanced up to see a young lady staring at me from across the road. I recognised her instantly. It was Fiona, the pretty young Scots girl that had become involved with the fellow in my mess. I stopped and allowed her to catch me up. Although we had met but once, she remembered my name and we shook hands.

I asked, in feigned surprise, what she was doing here, knowing full well the story of her pregnancy and David's totally negative response. We stood at the roadside and she told me the story. Of course, I pretended that I knew nothing about the situation. Apparently, she had not yet told her parents of her plight but had just packed a few things and come to Chatham to speak to David, since she had no reply to her letters. Her attitude was not one of an avenging, wronged woman and I found myself feeling quite sorry for her.

She was living in digs at a pub in Gillingham, where she had taken a job as a barmaid for the time being but she felt sure that David would take care of her once she had time to talk things over with him. Could I go back to the ship and ask David to come out and speak to her? I knew she would ask that question and I knew that I would have to help out. I pointed out that David was duty watch for the weekend and that he would not be able to come ashore but might be able to speak to her through the gate and perhaps make some arrangement to discuss the situation on a later date. And so, I returned back through the dockyard gate and aboard *Savage*.

David was lounging about the mess. My shipmates were amazed to see me return of course and their curiosity was evident but I got David away from their prying ears and gave him the bad news. He turned pale and said "Shit!" and I had the feeling that he had almost been expecting this development. We stood in an embarrassed silence for a moment or two; he did not want to speak to his girl at all but it had to be done.

"Could you say that I have gone to somewhere on draft?" he asked weakly.

"No."

"Could you say that I am married?"

"No."

"I suppose I shall have to face the music," he said at length. "Could you say that I can't get ashore just now and I'll meet her after the weekend somewhere?"

"Yes," I said. "Might be a good idea to do just that. It'll give you time to sort out what you are going to say." I returned through the dockyard gate and delivered the message. Fiona thanked me very much for my time and sympathy and the bus carried me away to the station, leaving her looking somewhat lost at the terminus. The matter remained on my mind over the weekend and although it was not any of my business really, I felt quite concerned for the couple.

I went to a dance at the Ilford Palais with my younger brother on the Saturday night, having spent the larger part of the day patrolling Ilford High Street in drainpipe trousers and sorbo-soled shoes. It was not a very eventful exercise. April days were living up to their reputation and I fought high winds and constant showers in the lanes and byways of Essex. I cycled to Potter Street, near Harlow, on the Sunday morning and had refreshments at the Cyclist's Rest café, returning for dinner in the early afternoon. I sat in the lounge watching the television whilst outside the rain beat fitfully on the window pane. The water coursed down in great tears, driven by the wind and I thought of Fiona and David.

I returned from leave to find that we had orders to sail for Sheerness, where we would be carrying out the long dreaded inspection by the C.-in-C. the Nore. He came aboard off Sheerness in true Nelson style. A launch came alongside whilst we were still under way and he climbed our boarding ladder with great energy in spite of his age and elevated position. Obviously, this C.-in-C. was a bit of a stickler and so it turned out, for he had the Electrical Department making toast at the cross-trees of the tripod mast, the Gunnery Department handing, loading and discharging their guns entirely by hand and us seamen rigging a towing line capable of pulling the dear old *Vanguard* across the Channel! He quite wore us out, which I suspect was the object of the exercise.

As we returned to Sheerness at the completion of these evolutions, the Admiral fell us all in on the quarterdeck and gave a bit of a well-done-lads speech. Better than a you-can-do-better lecture, I think. Our Admiral remembered *Savage* from his service days in the last war and regarded her with some affection by the tone of his address. All of this pleased the officers and NCOs no end and when our Captain called for three rousing cheers in true naval style, they cheered as lustily as we did. It was another day when I had to honestly admit that I had enjoyed myself!

The Admiral safely ashore and ourselves snuggly secured to a buoy at the entrance to Stansgate creek on the Medway, I was at last able to speak to David about Fiona. Reluctantly, he had decided on marriage to save the girl's honour. I applauded his sacrifice but doubted the wisdom of it under those circumstances and many hours were spent in discussion over the matter. I was even pressed into being Best Man at the forthcoming nuptials but before anything could be bought to fruition, a letter came for David from Fiona, advising him that Nature had taken a hand and that the forthcoming "sprog" was not to be. David treated the news with no little relief and my role as Best Man was postponed indefinitely. However, even this latest letter received no reply from him and as far as I know, the couple never met again. I often saw Fiona in the pub if I chanced by and we passed the time of day. She seemed happy enough with her life down south and perhaps she met a nice chap and settled down happily ever after.

Each day, there was an improvement in the weather and with it, my spirits. Our period of inspections over, we settled down to a training-up routine. This was a testing time for a beginner to destroyer life such as I, for each day found us up to some new trick or other. The principal benefit was that because we did not stray too far from Chatham or Sheerness, leave began to settle into a regular pattern and I was able to get home on a fairly steady basis. Everyone assured me that it would not last and all sorts of "buzzes" were rife.

Going on leave from Sheerness was an interesting event. There were two ways to go. One could get ashore by boat to the Coaling jetty, an ancient hulk from the Napoleonic wars of the early 1800s, which since it was rigged with a steam crane, was used as a floating coal bunker for the Navy's few coal-fired ships, doubling as a pontoon for landing personnel to the shore by means of a brow. From there, one went to Sheerness station and caught a train to Sittingbourne and from thence to London, in all a pretty long process. Or else one could use the "trot-boats", the Naval Motor Fleet Vessels which also were relics of a war, in fact the 1939-45 one, in which they had performed all sorts of harbour patrol duties and Boom Defence tasks. Now they were relegated to ferrying personnel and supplies to the many Royal Navy ships in the various ports. Built in Scotland and smelling strongly of Scots pine, pitch and tar, sporting powerful diesel engines and with their brasswork and topsides sparkling in the sunlight, they were a delight to behold.

Our own particular fleet of MFVs would take it in turns to call from ship to ship in the Medway complex during leave times and would ferry us from Sheerness up to the pier at Gillingham, or into the dockyard. The trip took about an hour in all and was a most wonderful way of seeing the beauties of the river early in the morning. It also took an hour off our working day on the return journey because our leave expired at 0800 at the trot-boat's point of embarkation and the hour spent cruising down the river was an hour off the tasks of the day. The interior of these lovely old seventy-five foot craft was wooden, varnished and polished and very cosy. A wood stove would roar away in the after saloon in the winter and of course, everyone would be on the upper deck in the summer. I always got off the trot-boat reluctantly!

I remember my first opportunity to play with one of the guns on the *Savage*, when I was seconded to the gunner's party. Garth was already a full-time member of the gun crews and it was a good chance to spend a day together. However, being somewhat slight of build and not awfully physically strong, I was given the task of merely receiving one of the unprimed shells from the next man back in a train leading from the magazine to the gun mounting. I handed the shell to the expert, who put it in a tray and twiddled the nose-cone to set the distance at which it would explode from the barrel once having been fired. We put to sea and were given basic training for our task and dressed in the statutory gun crew rig of steel helmet and antiflash gear. Our faces were smeared with vaseline to prevent flash burns.

We finally came to the firing range area off Shoeburyness. A harbour launch, towing a large wooden raft which served as a target, could be seen in the far distance. Lots of orders were shouted and repeated and I gave my first shell to the gunner for priming. He did his twiddly bit, the shell was stuffed up the gun barrel and a brass cordite case shoved in behind it. The breech was slammed shut and twisted up to lock.

One chap shouted: "Gun ready," another: "Gun aimed," and the P.O. in charge of the gun shouted: "Shoot!" The powerful gun went off with what I can only describe as a heavy "bang", the shock waves seeming to pass right through one's chest. The gun recoiled and the crew opened the breach swiftly and a stinking cloud of burnt cordite blew back at us. It all happened very quickly and as it was my first time, it was a bit of a shock to the system. I gasped and swung round to receive the next shell from the man immediately behind me in the chain.

It was "Jack", or rather had been "Jack"! At the first concussion he had abandoned his role in the proceedings and fled aft! Everyone burst out laughing of course but the Gunnery P.O. was not amused! I dashed over to the top of the hatch leading to the magazine and took "Jack's" shell for him,

155

handed it to the gun layer and continued to do so until someone got "Jack" back into line. Of course, he was alright after the first few rounds were fired off.

The standard of shooting was good on *Savage* I recall, both fairly accurate and a steady rate of fire. The twin turret on the fo'c'sle was never fired. I was told it was because it was budged from its mountings in the North Sea on one occasion whilst escorting one of the Russian convoys and the wiring was unreliable. Nevertheless, it was dutifully cleaned, regularly trained about and looked very menacing. I suppose it was only us that knew it could not fire! I expect it was retained for its psychological advantages.

May warmed slowly into June and the good weather continued, the odd day helping us toward a reasonable suntan. Our expeditions into the Thames Estuary continued, the ship was further painted and spruced up and some of the rigging renewed, old ropes and wires being discarded for new ones. The pace of life was a little more relaxed; after one's duty watch, you were free to lie about the upper parts of the superstructure in the sun and, providing that you did not clutter up the place and were unobtrusive, no-one bothered you.

Daily Orders bought another bonus during the first week of June: the ship was to pay a courtesy visit to the seaside town of Southend! We were to be the guests of the town for a whole week. The mess went crazy at the news! It was an ideal spot from which to get to London, much easier than from Chatham or Sheerness, it was the beginning of the holiday season and what with all the seaside attractions of the seafront, this was promising to be one of our best runs ashore ever! Our uniforms were brushed and cleaned and the boiler room crammed with our white fronts and collars, steaming from an extra careful wash.

We slipped the buoy at Sheerness and steamed slowly across the estuary for the short distance to the end of the longest pier in the world, where we dropped anchor at the tide-edge and the first of our libertyboats bobbed across the waves, dropping a batch of fun-seeking sailors on the steps at the pierhead. I was on duty watch and had an anchor watch, which put me on the bridge with the Officer of the Day. We took constant bearings on the hotels and buildings ashore to make certain that the ship was not dragging her anchor in the strong tide of the ebbing river.

Through powerful binoculars, I watched my colleagues walk the mile-long pier to the entrance of the amusement arcade at the head, from where they were lost from sight. All we could see of them from then on was the occasional white cap amongst the hundreds of holiday makers along the seafront. I eagerly awaited the next day and an opportunity to get ashore.

I was bowman of the last libertyboat, bringing off the libertymen at 2345. The tide was flooding and almost at high water and we motored alongside the pier and picked them up at the top, or landward end. All but a few had returned; some had dashed off home to London or wherever, and would be returning on the 0800 boat the following morning, but one or two (so I later learned) had met up with some young ladies from a holiday camp and were spending the night in a chalet, where a party was in full swing.

The normal day's work had to be done and the day dragged slowly by. A heavy shower obliged and we left the upper deck a little earlier than usual, giving me time to get dressed into my No. 1s in a more leisurely fashion than normal. I went ashore with Garth. The walk to the end of the pier was denied us - we were given the free use of the pier trains and rode to the shore in great style. Once away from the pier, we turned right and slowly patrolled the front, visiting all the amusement arcades one after the other.

It was not long before we picked up with two girls from Battersea and we continued our tour with them, winding up in a fish and chip shop as darkness fell. The girls were on a day trip and as their train left just before 2300 we saw them off with a quick kiss and cuddle on the platform, having exchanged names and addresses. Nothing more was ever heard of either party.

We retraced our steps to the shore end of the pier where we had to pick up the boat since as high water was approaching, there was now sufficient water for her to get in. We encountered a band of Teddy-boys on our return journey from the station and perhaps they thought that two matelots on their own would prove an easy target. They strung out across our path to intimidate us into stopping but we kept coming and merely pushed through their ranks. They swore roundly at us but we made no reply and continued a steady pace along the road, their threats and foul language becoming fainter at every step.

Once aboard the boat, we relaxed again and decided that we had enjoyed our run ashore, all things considered. We will do it again, was the general consensus. And so we did. Several very enjoyable evenings were spent in The Ship along the front near the Kursaal and one memorable expedition to the beach after dark with two girls from Stoke Newington involved some heavy petting, washed down by a couple of bags of chips!

The week passed by, the ship played the usual games with local football and cricket teams and I seem to recall that the Mayor and other civic dignitaries came to dinner on board with the officers. The ship was open to visitors and as part of the motor boat's crew, I was constantly in the boat, ferrying people out to the *Savage*. It was a good opportunity to chat up any particularly desirable female but I had no memorable success that I can recall.

It was also nice to hold a female hand as you assisted her up the steps to the pier!

As Thursday evening approached we were all short of money. There was just enough in the kitty to have a few drinks and some chips on the front again and that would have to be our last foray ashore, on what had been an immensely popular visit. Garth, Jim and I decided that we would make for the Kursaal as we had not yet paid that place a visit. This we did after a few beers in The Ship where an old sailor treated us to several glasses of ale. It was pretty crowded inside the Kursaal and after the usual patrol to get the lie of the land, we retired to the "Spanish Bar" for another drink.

I drank more than enough, to be truthful. We came out of the bar and suddenly, I was alone. My companions were swallowed up in the throng and feeling just a little the worse for wear, I wandered about on my own, knowing that they would be looking for me. It would not be too long before we rediscovered each other.

I came to a halt outside the "Water Shoot". This was an amusement ride, where you paid to be hurtled down a wet slope in a sledge-like contraption which pitched headlong into an artificial pond at the bottom. The riders screamed their heads off and got wet into the bargain. I watched this performance for a little while before I became aware that a lady and a small boy were standing alongside me.

"What a funny way to enjoy yourself!" I said to the blonde woman who held the child's hand.

"Yes," she replied and in no time at all, we fell into conversation and began a tour of the amusements together. It seemed a natural thing to do at the time.

Little David was nine years old and, like all small boys in those days, he was fascinated by my uniform and the Navy. I took him on a couple of rides since his Mum, Grace, did not like fast whirly things and would not ride on anything more hectic than the dodg'ems!

The evening came to an end and we found ourselves back at the entrance to the Kursaal, where Grace shyly offered me her hand and thanked me for the pleasant evening. It was past David's bedtime and she had to go. I readily accepted that and said what a pleasure it had been, adding: "I'm just going for some fish and chips and I shall be going back on board."

She hesitated. She crouched down to the small boy. "Do you fancy some chips, David?" she asked. What small boy ever said no to chips, and she asked if I would care to be her guest for fish and chips at her house.

"Our local fish shop" she said, "fry the best fish and chips in Southend. Please come," she insisted. "It's the least we can do to thank you for your kindness." I readily accepted. It would have been churlish to have done

NATIONAL SERVICE ACTS

MINISTRY OF LABOUR AND NATIONAL SERVICE

HIGHSTONE AVENUE,
CAMBRIDGE PARK,
WANSTEAD, E.11.

5 APR '55 ....(Date)

Registration No. *183 39245.*

> MR. *P. M. Cobbold,*
> *61 Tudor Crescent,*
> *Barkingside*
> *Essex*

DEAR SIR,

I have to inform you that in accordance with the National Service Acts you are required to submit yourself to medical examination by a medical board at *8.30* a.m. on *Fri*-day, **15 APR 1955**, at the Medical Board Centre, 46, EASTERN AVENUE, WANSTEAD, E.11 (OPP. WANSTEAD TUBE STATION).

If you wear glasses, you should bring them with you to the Medical Board.

On reporting for medical examination you should present this form and your Certificate of Registration (N.S.2 or N.S.62) to the clerk in charge of the waiting room.

*A Travelling Warrant for your return journey is enclosed. Before starting your journey you must exchange the warrant for a ticket at the booking office named on the warrant. You should take special care of the return half of the ticket as in the event of loss you will be required to obtain a fresh ticket at normal fare at your own expense.

*If you reside more than six miles from the Medical Board Centre and travel by omnibus or tram your fare will be paid at the Centre. (N.B. Reimbursement of fares is restricted to the cost of the cheapest means of travel.)

Any subsistence allowances which may become payable to you in accordance with the scale overleaf will be paid to you on application when you attend at the Medical Board Centre.

Immediately on receipt of this notice, you should inform your employer of the date and time at which you are required to attend for medical examination.

If you are called up you will receive a further notification giving you at least 14 days' notice, unless you have requested a shorter period of notice. You should accordingly not voluntarily give up your employment because you are required to attend for medical examination.

Your attention is directed to the Notes printed on the back of this Notice.

Yours faithfully,

N.S.6

Delete if not applicable.

PERCY C. GRAHAM
Manager. (P.T.O.)

The piece of paper that started it all...

April 1955 - my last race as a civilian

C.-in-C.'s Inspection, Gibraltar. Left to right front: Garth, me, "Seabag", "Burl" Ives, Jim Baxter; second row: "David" (just visible), "Knokker" White, Jim Boucher

Savage alongside Gibraltar dockyard: ship's comany on parade

Savage at sea

Savage leaves Gibraltar

Gibraltar. Left to right: Leading seaman Chapman, Ray Bean and me

Obdurate at Harwich, 1956

The author tries gardening

otherwise; I wanted the night to continue and I really did not care if the last libertyboat left without me. I was prepared to sleep on the beach if need be.

We walked away from the candy floss, the ice cream parlours and the noise and music of the amusements and into the dark of the quieter back streets of old Southend. Grace told me a little about herself and her life on that walk to the fish shop and then on to her home. She had been widowed seven years previously. She was thirty-one to my tender nineteen but the age gap did not seem to matter as we walked and talked. She slipped her hand into mine and my heart leapt. David skipped on ahead and did not seem to notice but I felt her hand leave mine abruptly when he came running back.

We stood a short while in the fish shop in the brighter lights and I had the few seconds whilst she placed the order, to really look at her for the first time. She was a pretty woman, a little tired-looking but with a shy, ready smile. I gathered that she was very lonely and had made some bad decisions when it came to men in the past but she had taken to me and I was very happy about it, whatever the outcome or whatever her motives. Her earlier life had been on the stage in the West End where she was in several shows as a dancer. It was there that she had met and married her husband. Her present life was rather different. Although she owned her elderly terraced home, she had to supplement her widow's pension by working in a factory and some offices as a cleaner.

Her little two-up two-down house was warm and cosy and covered in cats of all sizes, ages and pedigrees. En masse they rose to greet her and she handed the fish and chips to me, whilst she bent to pet and speak to each one. That done, she laughed and retrieved the hot parcel from me and went into the kitchen for cutlery and plates, whilst David set about laying the table.

Some of the cats milled about my feet, purring and looking up at me in an inquisitive way. I stroked and spoke to those that would tolerate it and determined to make friends with the remainder at a later date. The clock on the mantlepiece showed 10.40 and I think it was slow. We ate noisily, talking and finding small things to laugh at. I told David some tall stories about the Navy during the last war and after his meal of chips and sausages, his eyes grew sleepier. Grace rose and started to clear the table and I helped where I could. We passed closely outside the entrance to the kitchen, she suddenly clasped my hand just for a very brief touching second and set my silly heart pounding again.

With David washed and put to bed, I sat on a fireside chair with a small motherless kitten, who licked my hand each time it came within range, while Grace tidied up, talking all the time. According to the clock, the libertyboat was on its way back to the *Savage* without me. I gave Grace a cigarette and she poured a glass of red wine and taking the sleepy kitten from my lap, replaced it with an ash tray.

We continued chatting but she never seemed to get within range, for my every impulse was to kiss her and see what happened. Suddenly, she looked at the clock as if for the first time.

"Good lord!" she gasped. "Is that the time!"

"It's slow, actually," I replied. "I think it's nearer midnight".

"Grief, what time do you have to be back aboard your ship?" She looked genuinely alarmed. "Don't you get into trouble or something if you are not back on time?"

"It's too late now," I told her. "The last boat went ages ago. I can't get back until eight o'clock tomorrow morning now but I have leave until then, so I won't be in any trouble."

"Thank goodness for that," was her reply. "I'll make you up a bed on the settee if you like and set the clock for you." I would have settled for that. In fact, I was beginning to feel a bit foolish about the whole proceedings and was thinking that I was reading too much into the situation. Yet there were those fleeting moments of touching each other's hands. What did they mean?

A large, rather old-fashioned piano stood to one side of the living room and we fell into conversation about it. I admitted to being able to play anything with my right hand, whereas the left would not cope with even the simplest of movements on the keyboard.

"I must show you how," said Grace and pulled me up from my chair towards the piano. "It's a bit late to hold a party," she laughed, "but one or two won't wake the neighbours!" and she broke into a medley of songs from the currently popular London show *Carousel*. I joined in where I knew the words and we ended up singing "One Enchanted Evening" from one of the shows that Grace had been in. It was the closing words that broke the spell: "never let him go". She looked up from the keys, the suggestion of a tear in her blue eyes.

Suddenly, she flung her left arm around my hips and squeezed me to her earnestly. "I'll try not to," she whispered. I knelt down to face her and swivelled the piano stool toward me, pulled her pale face to mine and kissed her as gently and with as much real feeling as there was in me. The blood whistled in my ears and I did not want to break the spell but she turned away at last, full I think, of self-doubt and confusion. I took the intitative and kissed her and kissed her until the dam burst and she kissed me more and more without reserve. Tears ran down her face and I felt so sorry and protective towards her all of a sudden. The earlier lecherous thoughts that I freely admit to, were washed away by this new feeling of compassion.

We undressed, washed and slipped into bed together. We clung together all night long in the cosiness of her pink bedroom, whispering and crying in a tenderness that only happens a few times in one's life. The sun lit up the room just after 3am and I think we did sleep in each other's arms for a short while.

A little after six o'clock, we got up and I dressed while Grace made breakfast. She had to go to her work and I had to return to the ship. We talked quietly so as not to waken David, and I promised to come back again the following evening, just as soon as I could get ashore. We walked along the sunlit street in the crisp cool air of an early summer's day. Our paths divided at last and I walked on down to the pier, full of a mixture of excitement and confused thoughts. The libertyboat came alongside *Savage* with the gentlest of bumps and brought me back to reality. I said nothing of where I had spent the night and I think my shipmates assumed that I had gone "up the line".

I have always liked Fridays. It has always been my favourite day. In civvy street it meant pay-day. In the Service it was an opener for weekend leave. Friday had a slightly more relaxed atmosphere as people began winding down for the weekend. Having had their fill of the delights of Southend, my shipmates seemed to plump for a trip home and were busily employed in their toilet and in sprucing up their uniforms. The 1615 libertyboat was full and I had to await the return of the first boat from the pier before I was free of the ship. The journey seemed to take ages. The boat dropped us at the end of the pier and we waited nearly fifteen minutes before the little train pulled away on the long journey to the other end of the pier. I stopped at a shop and bought some sweets for David, chocolates and flowers for Grace and rounded the corner to her road a little after five thirty.

My "home-coming" was an emotional affair. Mother and son were both pleased to see me and in no time at all, I was seated in the armchair, with David leaning on its arm and the small kitten once more on my lap. Grace made tea and kept kissing me whenever she passed, providing that David was not looking. I felt happy, secure and wanted in a more intense manner than ever before in my short life.

Grace told me that she had a friend with a small motor car and that if I liked, we could go out for a picnic the following day. I told her that I had to be aboard as I was on duty on Saturday and Sunday. A cloud crossed her face at my words. My next weekend leave was the weekend afterward and was to be a long one, as by then we would have returned to Chatham. I would love to come down and spend it with her and David then, I told her and she immediately brightened up.

"I could collect you from the dockyard in the car on the Friday evening, couldn't I?" she asked. Even then I began to look forward to that weekend.

It turned out that David had a prearranged visit to a school-mate's house further along the road, where he was going to watch the television. After dropping him there and being introduced with great pride by my new love to David's friend's parents, we had the evening to ourselves. Grace had it all planned. We went first to a small pub on the outskirts of town, where we met a workmate and her husband. They invited us to their home a little later on and we had a meal, after which her friend drove us back to pick up David in the little Morris Minor that was ours to borrow the following weekend.

It had been a wonderful evening, filled with all sorts of new strange feelings for me. It added to my confusion. We cuddled and whispered in the warmth of the soft bed and made the craziest of promises to each other; it was too beautiful to end. I did not want to go back to the ship in the morning but we both knew that I must.

She had taken David to the end of the pier to watch us sail away from our visit to Southend. I could just make out their forms in the small crowd on the pier head and my heart reached out to them as we cruised slowly out to sea. She wrote me a letter on the Saturday and I received it on docking at Chatham on the Monday afternoon. It was full of wonderful, romantic, silly things. She said time and time again how much she loved me and how she never wanted to be parted. She wrote of a future, when I had finished my term in the Navy and could come home to her and David to the little pink-bedroomed house in the little quiet tree-lined street, where she could become Mrs Cobbold and we could live happily together for always. It was the sort of thing that cut me to the core for it was, in a way, what I wanted, and I replied in a similar vein and believed every word that I wrote. I told no-one of my new love.

I still received letters from another girl but could not bring myself to reply with any enthusiasm and eventually wrote saying that I was getting engaged elsewhere. That excuse extracted no reply!

Garth eventually noticed a change in me; I was more serious and thoughtful and found that I could not be drawn into the swing of life in the mess as usual and, as he was my best friend, I finally told him about Grace and David. We spent many long hours in discussion on the subject, even to the extent that other messmates noticed us always whispering together and we were jokingly accused of being a pair of "poofs!"

I nipped ashore into the barracks on the Thursday evening and telephoned Grace's workmate to confirm that I would be home on the Friday as arranged and on the Friday morning, another lovely letter came for me from my sweetheart, which made my pulse race. It was with great excitement that I began dressing into my No.1 uniform to go ashore. Silently I prayed that the little Morris Minor would be outside the dockyard gate as my love said it would be. I trembled slightly as I lined up for inspection and listened to the Chief read out our conditions of leave. The word "Dismiss!" never sounded more wonderful and I was in the first wave of men to swell toward the dockyard gate.

She stood by the pale green door of the car, her pretty pale blue flower-decked dress fluttering in the breeze. Her blonde hair blew across her face and she tossed it back impatiently as her blue eyes eagerly scanned the approaching tide of navy blue uniforms. Then, abandoning the car, she dashed the few steps toward me and ran into my arms. Everyone was looking and I was suddenly aware of being embarrassed. In the few seconds of our pent up embrace, I heard a passing sailor say: "I wish my mother met me like that!" and although I did not realise it at the time, it started a small voice nagging inside me.

David was on the back seat of the car, grinning from ear to ear. I tickled his chin with affection.

"Doesn't your Mummy look pretty today, David?" I asked. Grace blushed a little.

"I turned out my wardrobe during the week and kitted myself out from top to bottom with new things." I raised my eyes with an exaggerated look at the word "bottom"; she took my meaning and we laughed.

The Morris made hard work of the climb up the Khyber Pass and I listened to the story of the rather hectic journey that they had had from Southend, for the old engine had an awful misfire at times. We struggled through the evening traffic at Strood and Rochester until I could stand it no longer. Grace stopped the car at the layby at the top of Gun Hill and I traced the fault to a badly fitting plug lead and tightened it up using her nail scissors and tweezers. This gave the old engine a new lease of life and we roared along the A2 toward the Gravesend ferry.

"See how clever uncle Peter is, David?" said Grace as the car purred swiftly along. It was apparent that I could do little wrong in that young man's eyes. Grace was trying to bring herself round to telling David about the feelings between us; she had said earlier that she was worried about how he may feel over it.

Once over the ferry and on the Essex side, the journey neared its end. We stopped at a little pub near Orsett and enjoyed a welcome shandy, David having lemonade and crisps. We sat together on a wooden bench in the bright sunlight, our eyes filled with love and happiness. We had the whole weekend to be together.

163

The shadows were just beginning to lengthen as we pulled up outside the house. I unloaded my case, said "hello" to all the cats and, while Grace made dinner, tinkered about with the Morris's engine with David looking on. After supper, we played on the piano, Grace playing very confidently and almost entirely by ear. David was put to bed, as he kept falling asleep on the settee and we returned to the parlour, having tucked him in.

I pulled her slim waist toward me. "You look absolutely beautiful," I whispered and kissed her neck.

"Thank you, darling," she said between kisses. "You make me come alive. I've thrown out all my old clothes and bought new so that I can be as young as you are!" The words pulled that string again.

We made sandwiches in the kitchen in readiness for the picnic on the following day, chatting about where we might go. We had agreed on a visit to Thaxted and I told Grace about the old Guildhall there, which I had visited many times. All the while we kissed and fondled. There were now no barriers between us, no shy moments nor embarrassments. Grace showed me the new underwear that she had bought specially, she said, to please me.

"I've even got a stunning new nightie but you will have to wait for that!" she giggled.

Saturday dawned and we began loading the car soon after breakfast. The skies looked a bit threatening but as we drove away from the coast the sun came out, the clouds thinned to fluffy white balls and then it became quite hot. We toured the sights of the Guildhall and climbed the hill to the old church beyond. It was strangely cold and quiet inside the old building and we walked about in silence, looking at the plaques that told of locals long gone and read the church notices.

At the altar, she took my hand. "I wish we could be here today to be married", she whispered. I thought at the time that it was the most wonderful thing that anyone had ever said to me and I was very touched. It was a wonderful day. We ate lunch in a quiet field near Halstead and I let David score several goals in an improvised football match, while Grace cheered from the goal-line.

It had to end, as all wonderful days do and we motored slowly back to the house where we arrived in pouring rain, dashing backward and forwards to the car to unload everything indoors. My uniform had got quite damp. It was taken off to dry and I sat in the armchair, wearing Grace's raincoat with a towel around my legs, much to David's amusement. Not having any civilian clothes with me had been a real nuisance and I determined to go home and bring a few things back to Southend to wear when I was at "home". We lay in the peace and security of the pink bedroom with the rain beating furiously against the window panes and whispered about the day's events and how happy we were.

Saturday turned into Sunday. The rain of the previous day seemed set to stay and the walk about the front was abandoned. While Grace made the Sunday roast, I played with David and his small train set on the floor until dinner, by which time the sun made another appearance and set the streets steaming in the pale light. We dressed and had our walk, ending up at Chalkwell with David unable to walk back and me giving him a piggy-back some of the way. We then caught a bus for the remainder of the journey. Grace had to return her friend's car, and she took David with her, leaving me to press my uniform ready for the trip back to Chatham. As her friend needed the car very early in the morning, it had been agreed that I would make my way back by rail.

She came back alone, however, from delivering the vehicle. "I've left David at Evelyn's for tonight," she explained. "I want you alone to myself, my love!" We went upstairs for her to get changed, as I had offered to take her out for a drink before supper and we ended up in the warmth of that beautiful, scented bedroom until the sun disappeared from the patterns on the wallpaper.

We made ourselves get up and get washed and dressed and we arrived at her favourite haunt at about nine o'clock. I was introduced to most of the folk in the pub and it was a very sociable, happy evening. Grace played the piano and we all joined in on a sing-song. I could not help reflecting that pubs and sing-songs were not really my scene but it all seemed so right at the time and I felt easy about it. Here I was at nineteen, sleeping with a woman, singing and dancing in a pub and drinking more alcohol than I had ever drunk in my life. This would never have happened in civvy street; I would never have been able to arrange a night away from home, let alone a whole weekend!

We walked slowly home in the dark of a muggy evening, the pavements wet and dank. Slightly the worse for drink, Grace hung onto my arm and looked up at me with tear-filled eyes. She knew that tomorrow I would be gone and I shared the same feeling of desolation, even though I knew that I would be back on the next weekend. Now I understood the misery that overcame many married men in the Service, when they had to return to their ship after leave and left behind their loved ones.

The new nightie lay discarded on the bedroom floor in a flurry of black nylon as I tiptoed out to the bathroom when first light crept through the pink curtains. I washed and shaved silently and put on my bellbottoms and white front. She lay on her stomach in the bed when I came in for my shoes but she was not asleep. The pillow under her face was wet and her face lined with tears. I sat on the edge of the bed and pulled her toward me and she clung hard and close to me, the tears coursing soundlessly onto my shoulder. I had a lump in my throat too.

"Saturday," I croaked. "I'll write to you as soon as I get back and I will be here at Saturday lunchtime." She stared back through a watery haze at me. Her sad eyes bore into mine.

"I don't think that I will ever see you again." Silence froze the pink room.

"Why do you say that, sweetheart?" I asked. "You know that I love you. I'm only going back because I have to!"

She broke away and drew the bedclothes up over her breasts. "You are so young and sweet, you will soon forget me. Old Grace, you will call me, and you will be off with some other young thing and forget me!" She whispered this in a tired, sad way and slowly wiped her eyes on the sheets. "Still," she said, with a flash of false brightness, "I'll see you to the door and send you off with all my love."

I had a ship to catch and this was not the time to spend in words of comfort. So I followed her to the front door, feeling very confused by this change of atmosphere and, kissing her gently on the cheek, passed through the open door which she shut behind me immediately. I stood there for a few seconds, my mind in a whirl of confused thoughts and then I turned off up the street that I had so happily walked down the previous Friday.

A lorry driver gave me a lift from Southend into Tilbury and I caught my usual train back to Chatham. It was a sadder trip back than I ever imagined. I really did not know what to think. Had Grace been using me? Was her love for me just play-acting? What had she meant by all those lovely sweet words and actions of the past few nights; was it really just a thrill and had she had enough of me?

Her reference to our relative ages was a point that had pulled that sore cord again. She had told me that she was thirty-one but during our conversations over the weekend, I had already been able to add five or six years to that. I did not blame her for her small deception and it really did not matter at the time, but I knew now that it was beginning to matter since she made so much of it. Very sadly, I made the decision to let the affair die as it was. It had been, without doubt, the most passionate and intense love affair I could have dreamed of and I realised, even at my tender age, that it was better to let go then than to suffer worse in the future.

The Royal Marines and certain detachments of the Army, aided to no little degree by ships of the Royal Navy, decided to attack Colonel Nasser's Egypt at this particular time. The historical battle for Suez was launched. There had been something going on for weeks, and of course, we knew nothing about the reason for the undercurrent of naval activity until we were ordered down to the Sheerness end of the Medway, and placed on short order to steam out to sea if and when required.

Chatham emptied of anything that floated, could reasonably steam and be expected to keep station, and for a few days it seemed as if we thrashed about like chickens without heads, our eyes always on the Russian and American responses to our aggressive action. Sir Anthony Eden was to resign over the débâcle that followed and fortunately, the "war" was quickly over and we retired with our feathers ruffled.

The weekend approached. Feeling thoroughly miserable, I had decided to go home and seek solace there, perhaps getting in a few miles on the bike. Thursday's last post bought me a letter bearing a Southend postmark. I saw it in the mess-trap, and there I let it remain until I had sorted out how I felt about opening it. It was there at supper and one of my shipmates saw it and pointed out the fact that it had been there since 1500.

"Don't you read your mail any more?" he asked, and I took it down, stuffed it into my locker and thought some more about it. It was common practice if one did not wish to answer a lady's letters, for whatever reason, to write "ON DRAFT TO HONG KONG" on it and shove it in the nearest postbox ashore. Usually, after this had been done a few times, the lady no longer wrote. I considered that option for a while and then opened the letter. It was written on blue vellum.

"I am so sorry," it said. "Please come on Saturday. I miss you as if the world had ended and so does David and Smutts." Smutts was one of the cats. "I can't explain my despair in this letter. Please give me the chance to explain but I shall understand if you do not come. I have been very silly."

I cringed inwardly as I read it. It had not been my intention to make her crawl like that and I now wished that I had taken the sting out of the situation by writing and asking why she had acted so desperately after so much had passed between us. I allowed my heart to soar once again and siezing paper and pen, replied in three words: "See you Saturday."

Leave had to be taken from Sheerness, via the trot-boat to Gillingham, and as a result it took ages to get across to the Essex side. It was nearly four in the afternoon that I turned into the street of limes. It was hot and oppressive and my heart was going like a steam-hammer. I hated a quarrel with anyone and just wanted this matter to be forgotten as quickly as possible and not referred to again.

The door opened before I had raised the knocker and there she stood. She wore a thin, cornflower blue dress with a square neck and lace at the sleeves, her face was rather heavily made-up and her blonde hair swept back in a chignon. Her eyes, wide and blue, searched my face for any signs of recrimination, but I was determined to bury the hatchet and not to spoil the occasion. I dropped my case on the mat and swept her off her feet, telling her how much I had missed her and how sorry I was for the sadness of our last weekend. She just hugged me to her, whispering: "Darling, darling, I'm so sorry, it's my fault...!" Once in the living room, we kissed and made up.

It was hard, however, to get her off the subject. She kept saying how she destroyed all that she touched and how lucky she was to have this second chance. She was clearly neurotic on the matter and it took some time to calm her down, which I did by asking where David was. On hearing that he was at his friend's house watching television, I demanded a cup of tea, a kiss and an end to the miseries of the past. Grace put on the kettle, talking all the time about the troubles in the Mediterranean and of how she had worried about where I might be when she read of it.

With a swirl of blue petticoats, she paraded the new dress she had bought the week earlier and when I told her how pretty she looked, her eyes gleamed like a wild thing and she whispered that she wanted me to make love to her there and then. I suddenly realised that I did not really want to. Something had changed which for all the world I could not alter, and suddenly I took the stage as an actor, saying sweet things that I now realised were becoming only words to save an embarrassment. We stripped each other in the pink bedroom and made love until the skies darkened and a summer thunderstorm thrashed the street outside with hot rain.

Later, David returned from his friend's house and some of the atmosphere returned, but it was occasionally spoiled by Grace whispering another apology whenever she passed close by, and I determined to talk to her about it later when we were alone. Her neurosis was all too evident. The matter should have been forgotten long ago.

David and I went for fish and chips at the local shop and he introduced me as his uncle Peter to the proprietor. The slightest lift in the man's eyebrows at my assumed title did not escape my notice and the little string in my stomach was tweaked again. I found myself embarrassed at the title, where last week I would have been flattered.

After a warm relaxing bath, we slipped into bed in the small hours and she twined herself around me, my resolve to bring up the subject faded. It would only have magnified our problem and so I took the easy way out and said nothing, hoping that later the cloud would pass and we could return to the wonderful relationship that we had had before. Grace woke me with a cup of tea and a kiss a little after nine the next morning, and standing before my sleepy eyes, clad in only a thin silk dressing gown and with the morning light behind her revealing her every curve, she told me how much she loved me and how much she needed me. She had a way of making an unexpectedly heart-warming statement. To someone of my tender years, they were words never heard before and I drew her hungrily back to bed.

After lunch, we defied a few showers and spent some time in a local park, playing football with David. We had tea in a small café along the front and as the evening drew on, we walked aimlessly about the amusements, Grace hanging on my arm and David hiding behind machines and the like, trying to scare us into believing he was lost. We eventually went back to the house and the resident cats, who sat on the piano whilst Grace played and David slept on the settee. She even had a good command of classical music and I thoroughly enjoyed listening to her. Later we bathed together and returned to the mystery of the pink bedroom. At a little after five-thirty, I slipped out from under the sheets and dressed quietly in the bathroom. I met her on the her way out of the kitchen. "Breakfast," she whispered, "will be ready for sir in just five minutes," and she floated past with no trace of the histrionics of the previous weekend.

I left the house, looking forward to my early return in two weeks time. It was not to be, for upon my arrival aboard *Savage* I heard that the ship was under orders to sail on the afternoon ebb. Our destination was Norway.

Chapter Nine

CHAPTER
TEN

It was with mixed feelings that I read the ship's company notice board, telling of our intended voyage. Few members of the mess had been there and although our precise destination in Norway was not promulgated at that time, we all hoped that we would get the chance to visit Oslo, which, some said, would be a good run ashore. I wondered how Grace was going to react to this news and whether we would have a repeat of the earlier trauma.

I was on duty the next weekend in any case, and would not be able to get to Southend because of the length of time it took to travel across Kent into Essex and east along the river. I had planned a quick trip for the following Thursday night, as a chap in the Electricians' mess lived at Eastwood, only a few miles from Grace's house and I was sure to be able to scrounge a lift on his motorcycle. The news of our sailing altered all that and I determined that evening to write to Grace and tell her of our sailing instructions. I would sound as optimistic as possible but as I had no idea of how long we should be away, I would promise to keep writing and to let her know the moment something concrete was decided about our movements.

I was not the only one suffering with the problem of where we would all be and for how long. The married men of the mess in particular needed to be aware of our location in order that they could keep their families advised, but the notice on the board simply stated that we were going to Norway and that was all.

The morning was spent preparing the ship for sea. It was hard work. Stores were loaded from lorries and the deck covered with dirty, smelly fuelling lines. The Buffer's store, where all the cleaning utensils were stored, seemed to have a never ending queue outside, with hands drawing scrubbers and cloths, brass polish and cotton-waste, Teepol and soda crystals. Things had to be battened down for sea; although the weather forecast promised a fair passage, we nevertheless had to be prepared.

With the ship's motorboat safely griped aboard, *Savage* turned her bows once more to the open estuary and Southend was a shimmering blur to the northwest come "Secure" at the end of the normal day's work at 1600hrs. I had the evening watch to keep. Life was still quite busy in finishing off the odds and ends that needed to be done and I was glad to leave the bridge,

171

relieved of my duty as Bo'sun's Mate, at 2200. The sun was a red stain over the coast of Norfolk to port as I went below for a wash and bed. It had been a long day but I still had my moment of relish ticking off another square on the graph pinned up inside my locker.

One of the last tasks performed before the end of my watch had been the darkening of the ship. She steamed through the night, showing no navigation or deck lights; smoking was forbidden on the upper deck and one was careless with a light at one's peril for "Darken Ship" was an order strictly enforced. The watch on deck found the look-outs doubled and the radar watchkeepers reporting the slightest spot on their screens. It was obvious that there was more to our trip than a "showing the flag" exercise and when Action Stations were called at 0840, I, for one, was not too surprised.

I closed up to the bridge as First Lieutenant's Runner and as he was elsewhere, reported to the Officer of the Watch. I was temporarily assigned to the starboard wing of the bridge as a back up to the look-outs. We scanned the horizon and the water between in constant sweeps, with no idea what we may be on the look-out for but determined to report it if we saw it! My two look-out numbers had binoculars but I searched with the naked eye. My eyesight has always been acute and suddenly, a feather of spray at about a mile distant caught my attention. Staring hard at the spot, I saw it again.

"Bridge, starboard look-out!" I yelled. "Submarine periscope, starboard three-five, range approximate two thousand yards!" My two compatriots swung their glasses to the bearing given and both called "Repeat!" indicating that they too had seen the object. Highly excited, we awaited some enthusiastic response from the officers on the bridge. The Officer of the Watch studied the area through his binoculars, lowered them and said, dryly, "Very good."

I should have known perhaps that the submarine had been detected some time earlier by the ship's Asdic unit and that the staff on the bridge would already have been aware of the boat's presence, but as our duty Chief paused on his way below later and congratulated us on our zeal, we did not feel our effort wasted. Quite what the submarine was doing there and who she was, remained another of those unfinished stories that I was by now quite getting used to.

Gun crews stood down a little before lunch and then after "Out Pipes" and the beginning of the afternoon's work, the upper deck was cleared and we had a little gunnery practice. What we shot at and why, or whether or not we hit anything, remains a mystery. It sounded very good at the time and I quite liked the smell of cordite.

We had chips, fried onions and sausage toad for supper. The sea was very calm and the only means of telling that we were actually under way was a very gentle vibration which hummed softly through the hull. If only every day were like this, I thought, one could almost begin to like it!

I slipped into my hammock at about 2145, just after the Officer of the Watch's evening rounds and was just about to drop off to sleep when the Tannoy, situated not far from my berth, spat out a cloud of dust, usually the first indication that it was about to say something. The First Lieutenant's voice came over the air.

"Do you hear that?" he said. "The ship will come alongside in harbour at Christiansand at 1300 hours tomorrow. We shall be alongside for seven days on a courtesy visit. Leave will be granted to non-duty members of the watch in the usual fashion. I am asking all members of the ship's company to set a good example during this visit and behave correctly at all times. That is all!"

So it was to be Christiansand after all. There followed much discussion on the messdeck. However, the true destination was still a matter of speculation, for there are two Christiansands in Norway and although they sound the same phonetically, they are spelled differently. There is Christiansand, located on the southern tip of the Norwegian coast of the Skagerrak and there is Kristiansund, just below the Arctic circle in the Norwegian Sea.

It turned out that the nearer of the two was to be our destination and the following day, dressed in our No. 2 uniform, we manned the side for our entry into the quaint little harbour of Christiansand, where we tied up alongside the cobblestone jetty which seemed to jut out straight from the small town that formed a base to the pine-covered mountains. The scenery was like something out of Walt Disney; the rocky hills glistened grey in the afternoon sun and the pine forests at their base were worn as a collar to their grandeur. The sun beat down on the glassy waters of the small harbour and the ripples of the water reflected high up the sleek greyness of our hull in oscillating patterns of light.

We could not wait to get ashore to see it all; it was something quite different to the heat and flies of the Mediterranean ports or the sparseness of the Scottish Lochs and we needed to walk among the pines and to see the views to experience it at first hand.

Once the ship was properly secured, we set to sprucing her up ready for the visitors which we were given to expect the following day. The upper decks were scrubbed to perfection, the brass-work on the bridge burned golden in the sunlight and all manner of ornate naval artifacts came out on display, from the beautiful wooden lifebelt stand, with its pure white lifebelt bearing the legend *"HMS Savage"*, to the white gangway ropes and their elaborate turks-head ropework.

Our arrival was greeted by a small brass band, which hampered our tying up rituals a little as it played suitably nautical music at the very spot that we were about to moor. The local equivalent of the Mayor and several Norwegian Naval and Army Officers stood stiffly to attention as the band played first our, and then their, National Anthem. It was quite the most sincere welcome that I had ever seen and I suddenly felt a bit proud to be British and part of this scenario. Our smart little destroyer wore the Norwegian Flag at her masthead, where it hung limp in the hot afternoon air.

We were mustered outside the ship's office by our Divisional Officer, just before "Secure, hands to tea!" was to be piped. The usual sports fixtures were being organised with local clubs and organisations, and volunteers to participate in these events were to put their names on the lists on the ship's company notice board. In view of the remoteness of our location and the very fine weather, it had been decided to try a different work programme. We would turn to at 0630 and secure at 1300hrs, the rest of the afternoon being free to go ashore as one pleased, providing one was not part of the duty watch. Those on duty would be acting as guides to any visitors and would also entertain our Norwegian friends at tea-time.

Our daily rig was to be half-blues, a white front and bellbottoms and white cap, although permission would be granted for anyone to proceed ashore in sports rig if they were taking part in any of the organised events. It sounded like a holiday and I had never known the Navy to show such a benevolent face!

That evening, the ship was visited by several officers of the various Armed Forces, including, so we heard, officers from the Resistance in the days of the Nazi occupation. *Savage* had been fitfully employed in the landing of agents on the coast of Norway during the war and these old soldiers and sailors were once more aboard her, re-living their experiences. It was pretty late when they left the gangway and tottered off noisily over the cobbles.

The following day dawned as hot and airless as the previous one. We fell in for our early day's work, which seemed to pass very swiftly. A whole crowd of us lined up for liberty at 1400 and at last put our feet on Norwegian soil. We walked from the jetty and straight into the small town, with its shops on either side of the main street.

From what I recall, there was little to see, other than the beautifully kept houses and the shops. There were no pubs as such; one could drink in the restaurant or in the hotel and there was a large off-licence where alcohol was available to persons of a sober nature. I remember being accosted by a very drunk Norwegian who, in broken English, asked me to go into the off-licence to purchase a bottle of brandy for him and I did so. He crossed the road and disappeared into the forest, clutching his bottle.

The main street ended at a rather narrow but tidy road which led into the foothills of the pine forest and we walked along this road for some way until we reached the last of the cluster of lovely little houses on either side, each with its own national flag fluttering in the front garden. Whether these flags were flown in our honour or whether the Norwegians always flew them, I am not sure. I rather suspect the latter. Through the trees we spied the sun reflecting on water and quickly found ourselves at the edge of a large fjord. The water looked cool, clean and inviting but since no-one had his costume with him, we sat on the large flat rocks at the water's edge, smoking and chatting.

The afternoon turned into early evening and we rose to return to the ship for supper at 1830. On our way back to the road, we heard the sound of laughter and feminine giggling and went off the path back to the fjord's edge to see what was going on. Some six to eight girls swam naked in the blue water, their clothes stacked neatly on the sun-baked rocks. Where once my eyes may have come out on stalks at such a sight, I found myself strangely amused by the scene. We called out and whistled at the girls and they waved back. Having compared notes on relative sizes of the young ladies' feminine attributes, my companions and I continued our journey back to the ship, where we had supper.

I had to change into sports rig and attend an indoor games match, held in a hall in the town. I had volunteered for several cricket matches and football tournaments against the locals and some Norwegian Navy men, to be held at various dates over the forthcoming week and was quite looking forward to them. I was becoming institutionalised! The Service was beginning to weave its magic spell over me - I was enjoying the life!

After work the following day, a Friday if my memory serves me well, Garth and I set off for the fjord, taking our swimming gear with us this time. The shops in the town closed at lunch-time and the great flat rocks at the water's edge were already adorned by a dozen or more local girls and boys, all stark naked and splashing about in the cold waters. The fact that we kept our costumes on seemed to be a matter of some amusement but apart from our typically English reserve we did not wish to be caught by one of our superiors, who may not have approved. We were sorry when they all put on their clothes again and trooped off back to the shops, for we had just begun a game with a ball which had our eyes popping when a certain well-endowed lady and her equally robust friend joined in! They promised to return later in the day and said that they would be organising themselves into a team to

175

continue the game. As we relaxed on the hot rocks, smoking and chatting, we were joined by several other shipmates, who donned their costumes and awaited the return of the young ladies with their ball.

Across the fjord could be seen a building which we were sure was some sort of beer-bar. The direct route, of course, was across the water and the distance looked a little daunting at about a mile or so. Half-jokingly, I suggested that some of us swim across for a beer and a chap in my mess said, "Come on then!" Tucking some money into a pocket in the side of my costume, I shouted, "OK, then!" and plunged in. A heavy splash told me that Allan was with me and the two of us, jeered on by our colleagues, set off across the still surface.

The further out from the side we swam, the colder the water seemed but we puffed and chatted as we went and the opposite bank drew closer and closer. We could see that several people were standing on the rocky edge outside the beer-bar, closely watching our progress. Then Allan gave a groan and stopped swimming. "Bloody cramp, Pete!" he moaned. We trod water for a moment or two and I became aware for the first time just how tired and stiff my own legs were becoming, "Come on, fattie," I joked. "We're nearly there. Last one ashore buys the beer!" But all of a sudden it was not funny any more. I tried to get Allan to lie along the surface of the water, where the sun made the water a little warmer and his cramp could be eased, but he was a big chap and most of him insisted on staying submerged. We splashed on, a little slower this time, swimming first on our backs and then with a powerful side-stroke. Our colleagues on the shore behind us stood watching our plight from the rocks but there was nothing they could do as we were now more than halfway across.

Glancing towards the far bank, we saw the attempts of an elderly gentleman and a small girl to launch a small varnished dinghy. I told Allan and saw the relief on his face; the effort of towing his numb legs behind him was gradually draining even his robust strength. The dinghy came up to us, pulled by the elderly man. He spoke no English but it was evident that we were being given a right royal telling-off in Norwegian! As Allan was too heavy to haul from the water, the pair of us hung on to a small ratty piece of rope that dangled over the stern as our rescuer pulled slowly for the safety of the shore, some five hundred yards distant. It was heaven to bang my frozen knee on a rock and to haul myself like a seal on to the fierce heat of a sundrenched slab.

Quite a crowd of Norwegians were milling about the water's edge and one took me rather roughly by the shoulder.

"You are English, no?" he asked and when I confirmed the fact, he said: "Five people have been drowned over the past years doing what you try to do today! Tell your friends how dangerous this water is and not to try do it again!"

We thanked our rescuers through this interpreter and were hustled into the building, which was in fact a beer-bar, and given a small glass of brown spirit, which may have been brandy. Their point about the dangers of our exploit made, the Norwegians became very amicable, but by then we were feeling a bit silly about the whole episode and after asking the way back to the other side of the fjord, thanked them profusely and set off on the best part of a three-mile walk to rejoin our companions on the far side of the water. Bearing in mind that we had no shoes on our feet, it was a most uncomfortable walk indeed, even though we did walk on the grass or pine needles at the forest edge most of the time and avoided the gravel road. We arrived back at the side of the fjord nearest to Christiansand and rejoined our colleagues in time for the arrival of the shop girls.

Whilst Allan and I sat exhausted on the rocks, smoking and recovering, several of our shipmates played an ad-hoc game of water polo in the fjord with the girls, several of whom had remembered to bring their swimming togs. We were briefly compensated by the busty girl, who came to talk to us at the waterside wearing nothing at all, though it was difficult to remain casual during the conversation!

A coach had been laid on for a visit to Oslo but it was too expensive for me, so I stood in for a messmate on his part of duty watch and wrote to Grace and David, telling them about our adventures so far in Norway. I teasingly made play of the fact that the local girls liked to swim in their skins, but as soon as I posted the letter I regretted it in case Grace had another of her jealous turns. This was the case, for her reply made further references to our difference in ages and repeated her fears that I would soon tire of her affections. I vowed to be more diplomatic in future and replied, telling her how she left these girls standing both physically and aesthetically.

Sunday started with a church service on the quay, which many of the townsfolk attended. Our Captain took the service, since we had no padre aboard and the lesson was read by our Jimmy and responded to by a Norwegian priest. The congregation wore their Sunday best, men in their best suits and the ladies and younger girls, several of whom we recognised from the bathing party of the day before, in pretty, flowing, summery dresses. The sun shone down on the sparkling water and the green of the pine trees on the mountainside, punctuated by the grey of the massive cliffs above us, made a beautiful backdrop to the proceedings.

After the service, several people came aboard to be entertained by the officers and we repaired to dinner. Otherwise Sunday in Norway did not promote much in the way of social activity and I sat in the sun on the quarterdeck, quietly fishing. I caught several garfish.

I fell into conversation with a Norwegian couple and notwithstanding their English and my pidgin German, passed a pleasant half hour before they bade me "Auf wiedersehen" and returned to their home. I looked up to see the Jimmy grinning at me from the "X" Gun position, where he had heard the conversation between us. "Be sure to clear up that mess," he said, referring to the fishing bait lying about the deck. It had been another lovely day and the weather showed no sign of deterioration.

We sailed on the Wednesday forenoon. The shops in the town closed for the staff to come and see us off and the jetty was crowded with well-wishers. Norway had been a most beautiful country to visit and I promised myself that one day I would go back to those still, green forests, the quiet, clear waters of the fjords and the friendliness of a simple, kindly people. Our Daily Orders stated our destination as Sheerness and we headed out into a calm North Sea, quickly falling into our sea-keeping routine again.

When one considers how many different personalities are cooped up in a ship as small as a destroyer, it is a wonder that there are so few quarrels and fights, even though people used to rub one another up the wrong way in various minor ways and tempers sometimes flared. Strict rules governing our behaviour below decks imposed severe penalties on brawlers or bullies, but it was largely the common sense of the men and the guiding light of the mess Leading hand that defused all of these small altercations before they became more serious.

A quarrel could arise for the simplest of reasons: one's relief may regularly fail to turn up on time and leave you out on the deck for an extra five minutes, someone may jump the canteen queue or shift your dhobying to a cooler position. A hundred small irritations could cause a fracas. There were also, of course, clashes of personalities. The two parties involved may then be separated, sometimes into different messes.

Savage carried two lower deck cooks and one of them was billetted in our mess. This particular body and I clashed almost from the word go. I usually tried to get on with everyone and avoid those I could not, and I had spent a lot of time and patience trying to keep out of Chef's way. For his part, he enjoyed barracking me, his favourite expression when addressing me being: "Oi, you bigheaded little **** !" My tolerance to this practice began to grow a bit thin since this address was always made with venom.

The coastline of Norway had hardly dipped astern and I was leaving the upper deck for a cup of tea on the messdeck when, as I passed the stable door of the ship's galley, the cook made a wild slap at the back of my head. It was not the first time that he had done this and I was getting used to ducking swiftly every time I passed his domain. On this occasion, I reacted as quickly and he not only missed me completely but hit his hand on the door to the galley. The pain bought a curse to his lips and he abandoned his post to chase me up the deck to extract his revenge but I was too fast for him.

I was just about fed up with his attitude and took delight on this occasion to aggravate his temper by mimicking his Yorkshire accent and running rings round him. However, things came to a head just after supper, when he returned to the mess after his spell of duty in the galley. I did not notice his return as I was writing a letter home when suddenly, the paper was ripped from beneath my pen and screwed up in a ball. In language of the foulest nature, he threatened me with total extermination.

I quietly pointed out that his injured hand had been of his own making, knowing that my quiet control and dictatorial manner would further annoy him. "Unlike you," I calmly said, "I will be able to rewrite my letter in just a few moments and so you can't bother me by your bad behaviour. You should learn to grow up!" You could have heard a pin drop in the mess. Our Leading hand did not even look up from his book but I knew that he was watching developments closely.

Cookie's eyes were balls of red hate in a palid taunt mask. He wanted to screw me up into a ball and throw me away as he had done my letter but he knew that our Leading hand would not put up with that in his mess. "I'll see to you later!" he hissed. Without looking up from his book, Leading seaman Wiltshire broke in.

"You will do nothing of the sort, Chef," he said, "and you will curb your cheeky tongue, Cobbie. I want no more of this!" Cookie opened his mouth to say more but thought better of it and slunk off to the other end of the mess. I returned to my letter but I knew that this would not be the end of the matter.

The storm broke at tea-time the following day. The Chef had twice crept up behind me during the day and tried booting me up the backside; one kick had made a glancing contact and the other I had sensed coming at the last second and had avoided altogether. Cookie was enjoying terrorising me with this brand of guerilla warfare and as he was twice my size and twice as ugly, there was little I could do about it. He would continue sniping and knocking bits off me until he tired of the practice.

I returned to the mess for tea, desperately thinking of ways to put paid to my tormentor's control over the situation. I sat at the table, poured out a mug of tea and reached for a cigarette. I saw him swinging in his hammock at the end of the mess, leering viciously at me.

I suddenly realised that he was playing right into my hands, for he was fully dressed in the clothes that he had been wearing in the galley, including his galley boots, great big, uncleaned, outsized objects that shone with a dull layer of grease over them. He also wore his galley apron, which had not seen the dhoby bucket in weeks. A cigarette hung loosely from his stained, unwashed hands and the dirt under his fingernails could have grown carrots. The mess was full of men and our Leading hand was drying his hands on his towel. It was a mess rule that we washed up on every occasion that we left the upper deck, meal times or not and I knew that Hookey was pretty hot on the subject. I stood up and looked at the Chef lounging in his grotty hammock with the most exaggerated look of disgust that I could muster.

"Really, Hookey!" I said. "Do we have to put up with that?" and I pointed at the Chef. The leer fell from his face. He shuffled his greasy boots to the far side of the hammock, out of sight. Our Leading seaman put down his towel. Amid encouraging agreement from my messmates, he moved across to the occupant of the grey hammock.

"Just what do you think you are doing, coming into the mess in that state?" he demanded. "You know the mess rules about cleanliness and you dare to lounge about in your pit in your filthy working clothes and with those disgusting boots on!"

"I'm off duty," stuttered the redfaced Chef.

"He needs a bloody good scrub, if you ask me!" I said, and it was said so quietly that hardly anyone noticed but first one, and then another took up the theme. The mess rose to its feet.

Hookey turned on his heel and picked up his book, and the tide of men swept the luckless Chef from his hammock, scattering bedding right, left and centre and, impervious to his cries, bore him away to the shower compartment in the washroom, whilst I, determined to get my pound of flesh, hurried on to the Buffer's store for a deck-scrubber.

When I pushed my way into the noisy, crowded washroom, the naked Chef was entering the cold shower assisted by several brawny bath attendants who snatched the broom from me and applied it with a vigorous scrubbing action to his pale skinny frame. I thought it prudent to make myself scarce at that point and, grinning from ear to ear, returned to my cup of tea in the mess. Leading seaman Wiltshire looked over the top of his book at me and I diplomatically curbed a smile.

"Let me know if you have any more trouble with our grubby friend, Cobby," he said.

"I will," I replied and nothing further was ever said about the subject between us. The duty P.O. broke up the bathing party and the members of the mess returned in dribs and drabs. A fresh fanny of tea was brewed and a little later on, Chef, by now attired in fresh clean galley rig, entered the mess briefly for his fags and then returned to the galley to get the range ready for supper. We studiously avoided each other and about a week later, Chef went on draft into RNB, never to return. No-one saw him off.

The day we picked up a buoy at Sheerness was a particularly warm day and we lounged about the mess, no-one really interested in going ashore because of the oppressive heat. We had rigged the air scoops to the five scuttles in our mess but even that did little to relieve the stickiness. I wrote a letter to Grace on the cooler air of the upper deck and only came below as it became too dark to write. *The Goon Show* had been on earlier but I had forgotten and had missed it. I did a reasonable imitation of most of the Goon characters, much to Grace's delight, and she was forever asking to hear "Neddy Seagoon" or "Bluebottle", and we often held whole conversations in "Goon-talk". I had even joined her at the piano on one of our visits to the pub and had sung a whole song in a "Goon-voice". The audience must have thought us quite mad!

Grace said that listening to *The Goon Show* would be our way of keeping in touch in a romantic way and missing the show, as I had, made me feel that I had let her down. Lots of chaps in the mess had a favourite song that they felt linked them with their loved one. They knew that their wife or girlfriend would be thinking of them when it was played on the radio and they thought of them in return.

Our Leading seaman returned to the mess at "Stand Easy" on the following morning with the news of another sailing. We would be going to Gibraltar and the Mediterranean after our two weeks summer leave. I wrote to Grace with the news, and said that plans must be made for summer leave over the next weekend. I was shortly due a long weekend and we could discuss it then. Secretly, I was a little worried about what I could tell my parents. I could hardly say nothing at all and pretend that I had no leave because one had to give the address where you were spending your leave to the naval authorities in case of an emergency recall. I wanted to spend my leave at Grace's but I owed allegiance to home. It was a perplexing time as I had never encounted such a situation before.

I chatted to Garth about it and he came up with a solution. Why not tell my folks that I had a week's leave, and one I could share with Grace and the other I could spend at home? That was what I determined to do. After all, neither my folks nor Grace knew exactly how much leave I was to get.

We cruised out into the North Sea and spent some time in dropping depth charges and spoiling the ecology for all sorts of marine life, somewhere north of the Dogger Bank. One afternoon, after a particularly violent explosion, the surface of the water was covered with many species of dead fish and the ship's boat was lowered to bring them in for the cooking pot. Included in this sad collection was a small black porpoise and he was hauled aboard by the Petty Officers, hung by the tail in our shower compartment and cut up for steaks. This had the effect of lining the shower and its teak grating with a thick coating of greasy blood, which took several hard scrubbing sessions to remove. The steaks proved too oily for anyone to eat and at the finish, the remains of the poor porpoise were thrown over the side, to the delight of the usual flock of following gulls. The other fresh fish tasted as fish from a shop can never be, sweet, clean and nourishing with the added bonus of keeping our mess bills down!

I ticked off my small square on the graph and turned in for the night. The graph was now over half-full and in just over a month's time, I would be able to mark off two weeks of "days" in red as they would be our summer leave.

The sun rose a little before 0400hrs and I had the morning watch to keep. I came up on deck to relieve the middlewatchman just as the increasing light was chasing away the shadows to herald another day. The fiery red rim of the rising orb played hide and seek behind some low, iron black clouds before shaking itself free to light the steel grey sea ahead of us. A green flashing light marked the eastern edge of the shore navigation system and we cruised at a slow eight knots or so towards a black mass of land that had, as yet, no definition or identity. A solitary idle gull flapped heavily overhead and then as daylight broke the hold of darkness at last, he was joined in his patrol by others, and finally by so many that the original one was lost in the crowd of wheeling birds. The distant shore warmed to the beginning of another day and we knew that we were in home waters again.

It was Thursday and there was only the journey to our port to complete before Friday came and I could hurry once more to the peace and warmth of the little house in Southend. My task was that of port look-out on this occasion and just before 0730 I reported several small ships away on the port bow. These turned out to be part of the Grimsby or Hull fishing fleet. They were a lovely sight, their hulls glistening with clean, fresh paint. The older ones were still coal-burners and had a wreath of brown smoke issuing from their quaint, vertical funnels, the hot, wet smell of steam strangely attractive as we cruised slowly past them on the side away from their nets. Their small tan mizzen sails held their bows to windward as they slowly took in their nets, filled with gleaming silver fish. We were kept busy dipping our ensign in response to their salute and they finally passed away into the hazy distance astern. I was never to see such a wonderful sight again, for the fleet as such soon became a thing of the past.

We reached Chatham a little before supper and I telephoned Grace's friend Evelyn to give her the message that we were back from Norway and that I would be home at about seven o'clock on the Friday. She was a pleasant lady and wished me luck, saying that she would pass on the message.

Friday started as a typical dockyard day. The dockyard maties filtered in through the dockyard gate at 0730 and headed straight for their first cup of tea, usually on board one of the ships in port. The sound of their heavy boots scraping and banging on our immaculate green-painted decks made us wince. They had proper work to do in the area of the "Fish and Chip Shop" but there was no sign of progress apart from the tangled mass of their welding equipment which cluttered up the deck, and no sign of the workers at all. A cloud of blue cigarette smoke issuing from the Boy's messdeck gave their location away and they finally turned-to some half hour after we did. Most of the day was spent in avoiding them and their tackle and clearing up after them, so I was glad when they all mysteriously disappeared at a little after three in the afternoon.

I scrounged a lift on Sparker's motorbike as far as Eastwood and resolved never to ask again. My friend drove the machine flat out all the time, taking all sorts of risks in navigating through the traffic in Rochester and Strood and more than once I resolved to get off the infernal thing at the next set of traffic lights but lacked the moral decision to do so when the opportunity came.

I did the gentlemanly thing and thanked him very much for the lift when I finally disembarked in Southend. I even offered to pay something to the cost of the journey but the offer was refused and he roared off in a cloud of smoke and spray. It had started to rain ever so slightly, too lightly to put on my Burberry, yet enough to make me feel damp and hot by the time that I came to the door of Grace's house. She had been sitting in the upstairs bedroom window and I saw her jump up, her face beaming in delight. I later learned that she had been there since eight o'clock in the morning and it was almost six-thirty when I finally put down my Pusser's suitcase in the hallway.

She threw herself in tears into my arms and relapsed into the uncontrollable performances of our earlier partings and meetings, which left me drained and disappointed. I never wanted our partings to be such an unhappy affair and I felt awfully guilty about making anyone suffer so much. I could not understand why Grace could not learn to take the rough with the smooth, to enjoy our times together and look forward to the next time that we could be together. David was not at home and I had to put up with about an hour of tears, smothering kisses and bear-like hugs until she began, as I spoke gently to her, to calm down.

I talked at last about our trip to Christiansand and of our little adventures there, tactfully not mentioning the naked girls in the fjord. She had already asked me several times if there was anyone else and I found it a bore convincing her that there was not. As she had been sitting at the window for most of the day, there was no meal prepared and so I sternly told her to calm down and wash her face whilst I went to the fish and chip shop for an evening meal. The manager in the shop gave me an old fashioned look as he took my order. He evidently remembered me.

She had changed into a very pretty skirt and blouse and had put on some make-up on my return and the atmosphere brightened somewhat. She produced a bottle of wine that she had won in a raffle somewhere and although I thought it pretty foul stuff, it helped to ease the tension.

Even the cats, the lights of her life, appeared to have had a rough day with her and they were glad to fall on the scraps left over from the meal. I fed them in the kitchen while Grace went upstairs to do her hair, as we had planned a walk along the seafront before picking David up on the return journey.

A gust of wind lashed the kitchen window with rain and so I went upstairs to tell Grace that it was wet outside. She was in the process of changing yet again, out of the skirt and blouse which she said she would save for a dance that she was intending to take me to on the Saturday night. Standing there in a new underwear set of blue nylon panties and matching brassière, she set my heart pounding in my ears and we cuddled on the bed for some minutes before I forced myself to get her to dress in clothes more suitable for the wet weather outside. I lay on the top of the bed watching her as she put on a pair of slacks, a red shirt and a sleeveless jumper and we talked easily, the trauma of the past tense hours lifting as we did so.

I told her about my week's leave: did she want me to spend it with her? "Of course I do, baby!" she said, her eyes wide in surprise that I could even think otherwise. "You know that I love you and want you with me more than anything in the world." The opportunity to talk to her sensibly had come.

"Then you must stop worrying me with your groundless doubts and tears every time that I have to come and go," I said and I took her hand and kissed her face gently. "It's beginning to hurt me and make me think that we hurt one another more than we should for our love to be healthy. I never stop worrying about how you're feeling when I'm away from you and I'm afraid of what will happen next."

We sat on the bed, with the rain beating against the window in fitful gusts and for the second time since we had met, she promised to take life as it came, to live for the times when I would get home and learn to live with our separations. This was a problem that I had heard of in the mess many times.

The rain stopped us going for the walk but I was happy that we had sorted out the problem between us and we kissed and laughed about my journey on the motorbike to Southend, then hurried down the road for a little drink in the pub before collecting David from Evelyn's. It had been a long hard day and I was absolutely exhausted. I bathed and slipped into bed and was asleep in seconds, vaguely aware of Grace slipping in alongside me. She cuddled up to me and we slept like children until the grey light of Saturday crept into the room.

I took David for an early walk along the promenade and gave him a geography lesson on the various places that I had seen. He was a most enquiring lad and was always interested in learning more. We bought a morning paper and wandered home for breakfast, greeted by the smell of fried bacon and coffee as we opened the front door. Sunlight flooded the kitchen, although the sky still promised rain. Grace kept leaning on me and touching my knees under the table as we talked. I felt very wanted and happy... if only I could stay there, find a job and become a father and husband all in one.

The morning was spent shopping in Southend. We had coffee in a small teashop in the high street and then just looked in the windows of the more expensive shops until David became too bored with it all and we made for home.

I was glad to get my uniform off; it was so conspicuous and uncomfortable. Since we were going to the dance it would require another press and the seven horizontal creases in the trousers were difficult to maintain, even though I had liberally coated the inside of each one with a backing of soap to make the creases crisper. I had bought a fresh white front with me and I pressed that too. Grace laughed at me as I stood at the ironing board in my white pants and navy blue socks and I chased her out of the kitchen.

With young David safely deposited at Evelyn's again, we set off under an umbrella to the hall where the dance was to be held. Grace introduced me to all the girls that worked with her and after a few drinks the evening progressed rather well. Grace knew all of the classical dance steps, whereas I could only manage a waltz, but to my amusement she had little command of the rock and roll steps and when a "twist" caught us on the floor together, she was quite lost and just stood there wriggling on the spot. One of her workmates pushed between us and I "twisted" with her. It would have been most ungallant to have broken off the dance and so I saw it through to the end, and then returned to join Grace who had returned to the table. Her face said it all; she was jealous. She refused to smile or to really talk and my heart sank. I found myself relapsing into a sort of stupor where I just sat with everything going on about me but feeling very detached, observing every little detail yet not being part of it. Our eyes met; hers were slightly moist and mine, I know, were angry.

"Let's go!" I said and rose. Suddenly she looked afraid.

"Am I being silly again?" she whispered.

"As usual," was all I could reply. I turned and made for the cloakroom where I collected my Burberry and cap. Grace followed me but was waylaid by a colleague and I waited on the steps outside for her.

We walked in silence along the wet pavements, a white moon scudding through the black and silver clouds and the wind lashing the trees, making the leaves chatter. I think she started apologising from the bottom of the steps leading from the hall until she put the key in her front door and all the while I coldly said nothing. I think I knew then that this affair was not for me, despite all the other lovely things about it. I could not handle the intenseness and I silently made up my mind to get through the Sunday and then call it a day. I even began to think how I should tell her.

The living room clock showed ten thirty and the cats milled hungrily about our feet. I was glad of something useful to do and, having put the kettle on, I saw to feeding them. She hovered in the doorway in her new skirt and blouse, silent tears on her face, quietly whispering again how silly and sorry she was for spoiling our evening. Several times she said: "When I saw you dancing with June, I knew that I could not expect to hold you," and instead of arguing her out of the assumption, I just found that there was nothing that I could say.

I made the tea. She sat in the armchair nearest the fireplace and I quietly handed her a cup. She shook her head in refusal and so I placed it on the mantelpiece.

"Shall I collect David?" I asked.

"No," she answered. "It will look funny if you turn up on your own." She refused a cigarette. The clock ticked noisily. A kitten jumped up onto my lap as I sat at the table and I stroked it and drank my tea. Hers was nearly cold by the time she reached to drink it; she only took one sip before taking my cup and hers to the kitchen and I heard her empty it down the sink. It irritated me.

"Would you prefer to collect David tomorrow?" I asked, knowing that the arrangement was that he was to be collected that evening.

"No," she replied. "Would you come with me and get him?"

186

As strangers, we walked the short way to Evelyn's house only to find that the lad was sound asleep in bed, since he had dropped off earlier in the evening and was too tired to be walked home anyway. Evelyn made us coffee and we spoke brightly about the evening's events at the dance, leaving out the quarrel.

We took our leave a little before midnight, promising to call for David before breakfast. Grace took my arm as we splashed back through a curtain of more persistent rain and I arrived home, tired, damp and quite fed up. She ran a bath for me and then sat on the edge of it, talking about the problem, with me replying that the solution lay with her and that she must take life as it came.

"I have never yet said anything to you that I did not honestly mean," I told her. "You must believe in me as I must in you". She agreed that this made sense and the matter seemed resolved and once more, I determined to try to put the events of the miserable evening behind us and throw my heart into the situation again.

Sunday seemed like a honeymoon all over again. We had early morning coffee and rose late and as I hurried along the warm, damp street, I felt guilty that I was so late in collecting David from Evelyn. She did not mind but I took David away from under her feet and we walked back home and played cricket in the small back garden.

After dinner, we took the walk that we had been forced to postpone the previous day and went all the way along the front, from the pier to Chalkwell and back. I had intended leaving Southend on the Sunday evening, bearing in mind that I would be back on leave soon and that the journey first thing on a Monday morning was very much at the mercy of the transport system, possibly making a shaky start to the week. A by now very contrite Grace offered to pop up and pack my bag after tea. She was really making an effort.

"Would you prefer I stayed until the morning?" I asked. She melted weakly onto my lap and David or no David looking on, kissed me full on the mouth. David said, "Ooo!" and we all laughed. The old feelings were back, we were a family again.

Evelyn and Ted called in a little later as Grace was cutting sandwiches for tea. Ted had a problem with his car; it would start easily enough but would not run for more than a few seconds. I went down the street with him, stripped the carburettor and succeeded in curing the fault. They stayed for tea and it was nearly dark when they left. My week's leave was discussed; we were offered the use of the car and in return, I promised to do a complete service on it. Grace said that she would give me a hand with it and I said that she would look very sexy bending over a motor bonnet. This remark led to speculative and suggestive talk about what sort of poses one could get into and what sort of "bits and pieces would be exposed under such conditions", as Grace put it!

After seeing Ted and Evelyn off at the door, David was bathed and put to bed. Grace continued the theme of our earlier conversation by changing into a short skirt and tight yellow jumper and demonstrating her skill as a motor mechanic, using the settee as a car bonnet and revealing most of her underwear in the process. This led to a crazy love-making session on the floor of the living room, which progressed to the bedroom.

She brought me up a cup of tea at 5.30 and spoke happily in whispers, so as not to arouse David, and after many hugs and kisses, I left the house and journeyed back to Chatham. I arrived in good time to find that I was detailed cook of the mess for the next twenty-four hours. As was usual for a Monday, dinner consisted of corned beef and potatoes. This seemed to be an unwritten law in the Service. Had a spaceman landed on earth on a Monday and been invited to dinner on one of Her Majesty's ships, whether at sea or in port, he would have been regaled with corned beef hash!

I was kept busy scrubbing the mess, the decks and our two collapsible tables until they fairly gleamed and then I went to the galley to collect the potatoes. When the ritual of "tot-time" was over and all those eligible had swallowed their tot, I dished up dinner on the fresh clean plates from the mess-trap and buttered bread for those that wanted it. Following the washing-up, I was free once more to tidy up the mess, put the eating irons and plates away and enjoy a cigarette before we all fell in on the upper deck for work.

Most of the rest of the afternoon was gainfully employed in wielding a chipping hammer and bashing lumps of rust from various parts of the superstructure. Providing one made enough noise on the matter and always contrived to look busy, there was little interference in the task and you were free to sing or whistle as you wanted and to immerse yourself in your own private thoughts.

I returned my hammer and wire brush to the Buffer's store, just as "Secure" was piped, washed up in the bathroom and repaired to the mess to "wet" the tea. Those not in the duty watch were struggling into their uniforms prior to dashing ashore, either to go "up the line" or to meet the latest heart-throb ashore. I poured out their tea for them and we all engaged in merry banter and comic remarks.

The mess seemed strangely empty when they had gone. I counted up those that would be in for supper, added two as usual and began preparing the evening meal. I must admit that we ate pretty well. Our active lives demanded a good varied diet and we did not suffer any shortages that I can remember. Supper eaten, I washed up once more and tidied the mess up for Rounds at 2100, standing to attention and presenting the mess for the inspection of the Officer of the Day and the duty Chief or P.O.

My duty period of being cook of the mess ended after washing up on the following day and after rounds, I was able to sit and write a long passionate letter to Grace. There were only ten days to the beginning of summer leave and I really looked forward to it. I also wrote home and told my parents of a week's leave coming up. As we would be in Chatham that week, I made up my mind to go home and to bring back some "civvies" with me to go to Southend with.

I hurried ashore on the Wednesday evening with this purpose in mind and since I was, as usual, extremely short of cash, took my place in the queue of hitch-hikers on the bridge in Chatham. My turn came as a red Triumph TR2 pulled up for me and a youngish ginger-haired chap asked where I was bound for. When I said the Ilford area but anywhere near to London would do fine, he asked me in, as he was going to Chelsea. He crashed the car into gear and I was flung back into the small leather seat as we shot from the kerb and roared most impressively through Rochester and Strood. Inwardly, I was congratulating myself in aquiring such an inspiring lift until some miles along the A2, when it became apparent to me that my driver was quite definitely homosexual! Most of the journey was taken in avoiding his inuendoes and outright advances and I was very relieved when he finally gave up and dropped me at the entrance to the Rotherhithe Tunnel, where I politely refused his "goodnight kiss"!

It never ceased to amaze me how many people imagined the Navy to be full of homosexuals, for apart from a few isolated cases, each of which I have taken pains to mention in these pages because they were relevant to the tale at the time, it was in fact an unusual phenomenon in the Navy of the 1950s.

I arrived home to Tudor Crescent, much to the suprise of the family. Although I wrote frequently, coming home on the spur of the moment was always a surprise. Mother would say such things as: "I had a feeling that you would be home yesterday and I put an extra chop in the oven for you!", although what prompted these premonitions of my home-comings, I have no idea. She was invariably wrong in her assumptions and on the occasions that I did arrive on the doorstep unexpectedly, she was always caught out and would bustle about the oven, preparing a meal for me.

I do not think that my parents missed me much. We were never a very affectionate family and neither parent seemed to be able to cope with outbursts of warmth and love. My home-comings were no more exciting than if

I had been away a mere few days rather than months, but I was not aware of any feeling of neglect, as we had all learned to live happily enough with each other's individual attitude to life. My earlier experiences in Yorkshire as an evacuee had made me a naturally more demonstrative person and I would have loved a kiss and cuddle from either of them but it was not the modus operandi in our house. Instead I reacted by serving my mum's and dad's needs in any way that I was able.

I had a bath and a lovely sleep, having packed the items of civvy clothes that I needed to take away with me. The wretched alarm clock woke me early as usual and my long journey back to the ship at Chatham began.

We were not allowed civvy clothes when going ashore from either ships or barracks in those days. We were sailors and had to dress accordingly when ashore, but many chaps would slip into the toilets at the top of the Khyber Pass and change into their civvies there. A wander about the town seemed all the sweeter when dressed as a free civilian and I delighted in a trip to the pictures during the week, where I sat and watched a black and white film starring Ronald Shiner, dressed in the luxury of my black trousers, dog-tooth jacket and black shirt.

Grace and I exchanged several letters over this period. Nowhere in her letters to me could I detect any trace of the jealous streak that had been so upsetting to us both and as summer leave drew ever nearer, I grew more and more excited about it. I would draw up one plan for our days out, only to replace it with another more exciting one the day after.

My friend, the electrician, offered me the use of a tent with which to take my little family camping and I wrote to Grace about the idea. She seemed delighted and what with the availability of Evelyn's little Morris, it began to seem that we would get away for an actual holiday somewhere. I began searching a map of Norfolk and Suffolk for good camping sites.

The day that we were to go on leave finally arrived. Half the ship's company would be staying behind to man the ship during our absence but those going on leave permeated the atmosphere of the ship with the exuberance of their joy at the prospect of an escape home to their families for the next two weeks.

The hours passed by on leaden feet until we attended our pay parade, where we drew our victualling allowance and several weeks' pay. I had never held so much money of my own before and it seemed that our holiday away in the tent would be an extravagant affair, but I was sensible enough to realise that I should pay my mother for the week at home and so I put that cash away in another pocket. Grace was to collect me in the car outside the gate at midday and as I was borrowing his tent, I offered Sparks a lift to Eastwood, so he could save his travel warrant for another time. We were finally allowed to leave the upper deck at the finish of our morning's work and the messdeck became a hive of activity, with men streaming in from the crowded bathroom and frantically pulling on jumpers and other pieces of uniform. I took my time about it, seeing no rush in getting ready as the first libertyboat for summer leave would not be until 1345.

Ablutions completed, we sat impatiently smoking and awaiting the pipe for libertymen to fall in. It took an age to materialise but when it did, we snatched up our cases, bid our duty messmates farewell and made for the sunshine of the upper deck. I swear that the Officer of the Day took longer than usual to inspect our excited ranks but at last the order was given: "Turning For'ard, Dismiss!" and we swept as a living tide of navy blue down the gangway and across the dusty plain of the dockyard toward the gate.

I glimpsed the little Morris through the sea of bobbing caps and pointed it out to Sparks. She was there. She stepped out of the car as we burst though the dockyard gates, collecting a wolf whistle as her skirts blew across her nylon-clad legs and she blushed momentarily at the perpetrator. Totally ignoring my companion, she ran into my arms and kissed me full on the lips.

Someone called: "Put her down, Cobbie, you don't know where she's been!" Another more genteel soul said: "Not in the street, lad!" and we broke apart laughing.

Sparks shifted shyly from foot to foot and I made haste to introduce him to Grace. David was not with her; he had gone to visit her mother in Westcliff for a few days and was due back on the Sunday. We all piled thankfully into the car and spread our luggage around the back seat. Steering carefully through the crowd of homebound sailors, we drew away from the dockyard and began the ascent of the Khyber Pass. Fortunately, I had primed Sparks about not letting on that we had more than a week's leave, which was just as well, for Grace enquired of him just what he was doing during the next week!

The traffic through Rochester and Strood was as chaotic as I had ever seen it but we could not have cared less. However, we were grateful when we finally broke free of the town by way of the Medway bridge and sped along the London road. We chatted almost hysterically as we dashed along. Grace kept giving me ravenous looks and calling me "Baby" and "Sweetheart" and I winked at Sparks as he sat grinning on the back seat.

It was a very happy party that arrived safely in Eastwood and piling the borrowed tent and some equipment into the boot, we said our farewells to Sparks and his family and drove the final few miles to Grace's home. On the journey down, we had arranged that we would drive to Kent on the following Monday, set up camp somewhere near Whitstable and then "play it by ear",

191

depending on the weather. The house seemed quite empty without David somehow. We unloaded the car, put the gear in the spare bedroom and Grace ran me a bath. I was so glad to get out of the confines of my sailor uniform and into my civvies.

The next two days until David was to return seemed like one long honeymoon. I had heard chaps in the mess talking about how they reacted upon being reunited with their wives after being apart for even a short while and that was how it was with us. The time sped by with us always touching, kissing and love-making. There was not a cloud on our horizons and it seemed that at last, all would be well.

David came home on the Sunday. It was quite embarrassing, for Grace had assured me that he would not be back much before tea-time and suddenly, there he was on the doorstep, escorted by Grace's mother at a little after ten in the morning. They rang the doorbell and Grace, clad only in the wispiest black French knickers, peered out of the bedroom window to see who was at the door. The doorbell rang twice more before either of us was decent and could answer it and when we did, Grace's flushed face gave us away.

I had not met her mother or father and the introduction was not under the sort of circumstances that I would have chosen. We shook hands in an embarrassed way and I managed to pass off the matter of the unanswered doorbell by saying that we had been in the garden, looking after the cats. I do not think the tale was believed.

Mother came into the sitting room and Grace made a pot of tea, whilst I briefly escaped into the garden with David, in order to regain my composure. As I came to re-enter the back door, I heard mother's voice raised in condemnation.

"Pull yourself together woman," she said. "He's a mere boy compared to you! You should be ashamed of yourself; what your father will say on the matter, I don't dare to imagine!" I froze in my tracks. Grace answered very slowly and calmly.

"Mum," she said softly, "I don't care how old I am or how young he is, he loves me and I love him. No matter what anyone says, neither of us will take any notice of them. You should give him a chance, you'll find him a wonderful man, very mature for his age, very caring and a good friend to David. Please don't make a scene, mum."

There was the sound of a teacup being replaced onto a saucer and I entered the room just as mother snatched up her handbag and made for the doorway into the hall. She fixed me with a withering stare.

"You may think that because you are a sailor that you know it all, young man," she hissed, "but my advice to you is to find a girl nearer your own age and leave my daughter, who is after all old enough to be your mother, to find a man nearer hers!" I advanced to answer her. I wanted to say that we were together because we loved each other and that we needed one another but the angry woman had ears for neither of us and she slammed the door, the sound reverberating through the little house which, moments before, had been filled with happiness and peace, leaving Grace in tears clutching on to me and David wide-eyed at the kitchen door.

It seemed that I was fated to enter into the same dreadful atmosphere every time I set foot in that little house in Southend and as I held on to Grace and tried to calm her down in the confines of the tiny hallway, I again silently made up my mind that I would call it a day. No matter what my feelings were for Grace, I had to admit to myself that there were several truths in what her mother had said.

I determined to spend the rest of the week in reassessing the situation and if matters did not improve, I would talk to Grace and end the affair. It would not be an easy task. I had a genuine affection for her and for David but she was a lot older than me and I found it difficult to imagine how life with her would be. I could hardly imagine continuing my cycling interest and then there was her rather strong jealous nature to contend with.

A very miserable evening and night were to pass before dawn on the Monday. It broke to a windy but dry day with blue sky and ragged white clouds. We rose early, Grace weary and dispirited and I determined to try to make something of what I guessed would be our last time together. We loaded the car and I checked the engine and tyres while Grace saw to putting out the cats' food where a neighbour could tend to the animals during our four-day absence.

We drew away from the kerbside and headed along the A13 to the ferry at Woolwich and entered the Kent countryside. The atmosphere in the car was strained and reserved and I tried hard to lift our flagging spirits, with little effect. It was mid-afternoon before we arrived in the Whitstable area. We had no difficulty in finding a suitable campsite facing the sea and protected from the wind by the lee afforded by some large flattened oaks.

After putting up the tent, I started a fire, assisted by David who was perhaps the only cheerful party among us. Grace set out the interior of the tent and sat thoughtfully in the sun, gazing out to sea until I dished up supper. A mosquito landed in her soup and I said that it was because it knew how good it was. This extracted a smile from her.

"Come on sweetheart," I whispered, hugging her shoulders. "Life is but a bowl of cherries; all we have to do is spit out the pips!" She laughed at this

and the spell was broken. After a while, she became once more the Grace that
I had first known.

CHAPTER
ELEVEN

We all slept reasonably well in our beds made of tucked-up blankets. We resembled three sausages in a pan as we awoke the following day and this description set David giggling. During the night, I had felt Grace sobbing quietly and I had put my arm out from under my makeshift sleeping bag to cuddle her until she went to sleep again but as the sun rose and warmed the outside of the tent, she cheered up and she and David went off to the washrooms together in fine spirits, leaving me to organise the fire and breakfast. Most of that day was spent on the beach in the sunshine. We came away at last and walked into Whitstable, where we made a few purchases and looked out a reasonable restaurant for an evening meal in case the weather decided to take a turn for the worse. My training as cook of the mess came in very useful as I helped Grace cook the supper. David wandered off some way in his efforts to get a paper kite airborne and we were left alone to talk.

Grace made little reference to the altercation with her mother at first but I knew that it was a matter of paramount importance to her. I felt that it had to come out in the open and be thoroughly discussed if there was to be any sort of future for us. She was very upset at her mother's attitude and felt that she was old enough to be in charge of her own life and the way that she wished to run it. I had to agree that she was right. She became a little tearful and I steered her into the tent away from the eyes of any passer-by and consoled her with a soft word and a kiss, which we both wanted to take further but were prevented from by the return of David and a damaged kite.

After supper and the washing up out of the way, we listened to the radio and wrote cards to friends, saying what a good time we were having. Needless to say, I was unable to write home to say what a good time I was having in Whitstable when it was generally believed that I was at sea! One thing the Navy had done for me was to release me from the apron strings of my mother and I found this new freedom to do almost as I pleased very stimulating.

The following two days were as pleasant as the first. We swam in the sea at Whitstable, loafed about the beach and played cricket on the sand. We ate well in our little camp and enjoyed the outdoor life. David's constant demands on my time prevented any intimate moments between Grace and I but it did not matter as we were all having such a good time.

It rained quite heavily during the night on the Wednesday and we awoke to a wet, dismal campsite. Breakfast was suddenly a marathon task instead of the casual event of the previous days and the rain broke out again in sheets of warm water which permeated all regions of the tent and our clothing. We all took it in good part, however; after all, we had had a good share of the sun.

David had made friends with a little Welsh lad who was staying in a caravan some distance away and after helping with the chores, we let him slip away to see his friend for an hour, having decided that this would be a good day to visit Margate in the car. No sooner had he left when we fell into each other's arms and the hour sped by until we were nearly "caught" by David's punctual return!

The showers had given way to warm sunshine and we parked in a side street and walked onto the front at Margate dressed in shorts and tee-shirts. David had an enduring love of the typical gaming machines that sprang up in such places. We had great trouble prising him away from the penny arcades and it was during one of these occasions, when I had gone into an arcade to bring him to heel, that another event occurred which, on reflection I suppose, brought the affair between Grace and I to a finish. I called to David to come back out into the street and to walk with us but I don't know whether he did not hear or chose not to. I slipped my arm from Grace's waist and went in after him.

Momentarily blinded by the darkness, having come out of the brilliant sunshine, I was not aware that I was walking straight toward a young girl of about nineteen or twenty until we had collided, my shoulder striking the side of her face. She recoiled with a gasp and of course, I stopped immediately to apologise for my speed and carelessness. I had unconsciously taken her arm to show my genuine concern, when Grace appeared on the scene. Her face turned the blackness of thunder clouds, she glared at the girl and at me and turning on her heel, rushed out of the amusement hall. The young lady looked at me in amazement and I merely shrugged my shoulders.

"If you are sure that you're alright," I told her, "I had better go and see what's biting madame!" She nodded and I grabbed David's hand and hurried out into the sunshine. Grace sat on the seawall, tears running down her face. It was an all too familiar sight and it moved me not at all. In fact, I found it boring and annoying all at the same time.

The next hour or so were spent once more explaining and trying to look as inconspicuous as possible, for Grace was not short of dramatic skill in drawing attention to her supposed plight and we must have provided a free sideshow for passers-by. I finally gave up and throwing my hands in the air in frustration, simply walked away from mother and son and took to the long sandy beach, where I sat alone with a cigarette for something like an hour, staring out to sea with all the thoughts in the world rushing unanswered through my brain. David suddenly appeared at my shoulder.

"Mum says, are you coming back now?" he asked. I looked at him sadly; he had a lot to cope with for a lad of such tender years. I ruffled his hair.

"This will teach you to do as you are told in future, young man," I said and I rose and walked back to the promenade where Grace stood, red-eyed staring up the street. She did not look at me but slipped her arm into mine and said quietly, "Sorry."

A strong westerly wind had begun to blow, heralding the approach of evening rain. The small sailing boats out at sea dipped over to their gun-whales and some took in a reef. We sat in the car with a flask of tea, watching them in almost perpetual silence broken only by my conversations with David. I could feel her looking at me but I felt entitled to sulk and would not return her gaze.

The rain fell suddenly in big spots on the roof where the heat of the metal immediately evaporated them but eventually there became too many drop-lets and they cooled the roof and ran down the windows in great rivulets. I suggested that we return to the tent and we drove back through a thunder-storm that I found strangely in tune with my mood. The soft grass of the site quickly turned to a quagmire and we cooked supper at the entrance to the tent. David sat with Grace on an airbed reading a storybook out loud, while I fried eggs over the fire.

Grace kept trying to talk to me and eventually I decided to make the best of the remaining few days of my holiday with her and try to be a little more cheerful, even though I had by now resolved to end our association. I handed her a plate.

"I hope this is to madam's liking," I said, mockingly.

"It looks lovely," she replied, choosing to ignore my obvious sarcasm. The mood was broken however and after supper, it was my turn to lie on the airbed whilst she and David washed the dishes and normal conversation once more flowed. The rain beat remorselessly on the canvas and was on occasions punctuated by a flash of white lightning, followed by an earth-shaking peal of thunder. David slept like a log through the whole thing but Grace tensed every time the thunder boomed. We slipped our blankets to make one large cover over the pair of us.

Saturday morning finally dawned, windy, wet and uncomfortable. We dressed in our raincoats to visit the washrooms and toilets and everywhere the floors and tiles ran with water. We had planned to leave at lunch-time anyway and so after bacon and eggs for breakfast, we washed up and started packing everything away, stowing things into the boot of the car between rainbursts. As luck would have it, a little after ten o'clock the rain gave way to a brief burst of sunshine with sufficient warmth to set things steaming and we took advantage of the opportunity to strike the tent, folding it up over a park bench to prevent it getting muddy on the grass. With that safely stowed in the boot, we started up and left for home.

It was wonderful to relax in a hot bath. With David out on an errand at the shops, I had expected another "talk-in" from Grace but she seemed to be doing her best to put the incident behind her by avoiding the subject. I ran her bath and went into the bedroom to sort out my uniform, which I intended to wear on the following day as if I were returning to the ship. I felt emotionally drained and really wanted to go then. Grace returned from her bath, wrapped in a large white towel.

"Let's go to the pub tonight," she suggested. "Last night out before you go back to the ship." She dressed in black tight-fitting ski-pants with a white lacy blouse, set off by a blue chiffon scarf that I had bought her on an earlier shopping spree.

"Tomorrow I must service the car before it goes back to Ted and Evelyn," I said, "so we mustn't get back late. What shall we do with David?"

"He'll be alright on his own, providing we don't leave it too late," she replied and went to tell David of our plans.

The pub was full of the same old faces. I found myself mentally standing back and studying their tired faces and listening to their small talk. They were always delighted to see Grace but from several glances they gave her when she was not facing them, I could not help but think that she was not particularly regarded as a friend, rather more as an object of scandal. I was glad when the evening came to a close. Grace had declined to entertain on the piano and the pianist that took her place was both a poor player and a very heavy smoker, pouring a constant stream of heavy blue smoke into the air.

I washed and slipped into bed, tired and rather sad. It was dark and windy outside and the shadows of the leaves of the plane trees threw patterns on the pink curtains at the windows. The bright pink curtains looked ash grey in the poor light. I heard the light in the bathroom click off and the bedroom door opened silently. I saw Grace's shadowy figure crossing the room. "A treat for you, darling," she whispered and, dressed only in suspender belt and stockings, slipped into bed beside me. I defy any man to tell his lover that this is to be their last night together under those circumstances, and that which I had so resolutely determined to say was left unsaid.

She wandered about the house in an ecstatic mood all the next morning and David helped in the oil-change and servicing of the car. Evelyn came along in the afternoon to collect it and there had been hardly any time to tell Grace that I would no longer return. I will admit to being cowardly about broaching the matter and the lack of opportunity made it easier for me.

I slipped into the bedroom in the late afternoon, took off my civvy clothes, dressed quietly into my uniform and packed my bag.

"Doesn't uncle Peter look handsome, David?" she said as I entered the living room. "You always look very smart, darling. When will we see you again?" I found myself saying that as soon as we returned from Gibraltar, I would telephone Evelyn and let her know.

"Thank you for such a wonderful holiday, sweetheart," she said, folding her arms over my neck. "I have a little gift for you as a surprise from Dave and me," and she reached under her skirt and took a little blue packet from the top of her stocking. "With our love," she said, handing it to me. She had this disarming habit of making me feel a crab by such simple, sincere actions and this was no exception. I unwrapped the small parcel before their dancing eyes, revealing a silver-plated cigarette case inscribed "To Peter, our love always". It bought tears to my eyes. "*Now tell the girl that you are not seeing her again*!" said my conscience. Yet I left the little house in the quiet side street in Southend with a lump in my throat and an ache in my heart and I did not return. I believed it to be the best thing to do.

I arrived at my parents' home a little before ten o'clock, tired and a little depressed. After a hot bath, a small snack and a bit of a chat, I retired to the privacy of my small bedroom and lay for hours thinking and speculating on Grace and life in general. I tried the rather cavalier approach that it had been a good affair apart from the rough spots and that we had both had something out of it. It had been one continuous honeymoon with lots of love-making and affection; it had been filled with dreams and exciting plans for the future and, to a degree, that had been good in itself. Yet I had to admit that at the end of it all I would have found such a life an awful bore, with a ready-made son and an ageing wife with a jealousy complex.

The sun shone hotly on the Sunday and I left the house before six to cycle to the start of a race at Bishops Stortford, some thirty miles away, arriving long after the event was over but still in time to savour the atmosphere of the cycling fraternity, who still sat yarning on the hot grass outside the club's hut on the edge of Stansted airfield. There were old friends to chat to about my strange new life and we all returned along the Epping Road in a large group of forty-odd riders. Most of the time was spent in laughing about one another's antics and it cheered me out of my depression. I arrived home at the end of my sixty-mile foray happier than I had felt for a few days and ready for my evening meal.

How a week of free time can speed by as quickly as did that one, I do not know but in no time at all it seemed, I was back in the bedroom, struggling into the uniform to return to *Savage*.

Monday morning proceeded at funeral pace and with just about as much enthusiasm. At lunch-time it was the turn of the second watch for leave to get changed into their No. 1s and go off on their two weeks. We chewed our corned beef hash thoughtfully.

A letter from Grace awaited me in the mess-trap and I waited until after dinner to open and read it, seated in a coil of towing line on the after gun superstructure. It was quite a happy letter, telling me how much she loved me and had enjoyed our time together. For just the briefest of moments, I considered not writing the intended letter but in all honesty, I knew that it would have been merely prolonging the inevitable. I started my letter later that evening. After several attempts, I think I got it about right. I said how I felt and tried to explain what I felt at the present were my needs in life. I slipped it sadly into the postbox on board. I received a reply about a week later. She said that she understood but still loved me and if I ever changed my mind, she would wait for me to call. It made me feel even more of a creep but at least I could now feel that the affair was over.

I was duty watch one afternoon and *Savage* still lay in Chatham dockyard awaiting the return of the remainder of the crew from their leave. Just after "Stand Easy" a draft of new MEs, engine room personnel, came aboard from RNB. I passed by their kitbags and hammocks, which were piled up at the gangway awaiting their return from a briefing with the Engineering Officer before being taken below to their mess. The name on one caught my eye; "P. Hepworth" it read.

I had known a Peter Hepworth at school and for some strange reason, hung about to see if it was he. To my amazement, it was! We had a good old chinwag before being chased off the deck by the duty Chief. Our tasks on the ship did not, however, bring us into frequent contact in the normal course of the day's events but it was nice to see a familiar face and have someone to travel "up the line" with, as we only lived a few miles apart.

With summer leave finally at an end, *Savage* slipped out of the dockyard, the dockyard maties watching our departure wistfully as I am sure that they found her a happy ship both to work on and to loaf about on, as was their wont.

With a full complement of crew, since everyone had returned from leave as instructed and none had gone "absent without leave" as often happened, we cruised slowly down the Medway. Daily Orders merely said: "*Savage* will take passage to Gibraltar...". We closed up on our sea watches and the coasts of Kent and Essex faded away like phantom shadows. We sailed closer to the French shore on our way down channel, with only the merest glimpse of the white cliffs of Dover and then later, the Isle of Wight. The sea remained fairly calm as we rounded the French coast and entered the Bay of Biscay, notorious for great long sea swells and violent storms, but neither of these two hazards were encountered and we made good time to Gibraltar.

The Portuguese shore shone pink in the late afternoon sunshine and at last the grey mass of the Rock appeared far ahead and we gathered on the fo'c'sle to see our destination grow ever larger. The ship moored alongside in the dockyard, opposite some disgusting foul-smelling gash bins where all the refuse of the visiting ships was dumped and since the hot August sunshine had had some time to work its magic on them, one could almost chew the smell. Playing a saltwater hose on them to cool them off seemed only to accelerate the rotting process and the following day, they reeked even stronger. It was a brave man who approached them!

It was lovely to go ashore in the cool of the evening to escape the smell and activity of the dockyard and to be on dry land again. Several of us went into Main Street, where we looked into the shops and saw the English-style policeman who patrolled his beat there.

Our wanderings found us not far from the border area at La Linea where one could cross into Spain. We watched the comings and goings at the Customs area, and then found an interesting little street to investigate. It brought us to a small café bearing the legend "Smokey Joe's" and since it was several hours since we had last eaten, we decided to go in and give the local "wop food", as it was called, a try. To our suprise, the meal was excellent. We dined close to busting and then finished our repast off with one or two glasses of Toby ale, an ale nowhere like as feeble and watery as we were used to in the bars and pubs of Chatham, even though it bore the same name. I recall my share of the bill being just four shillings and sevenpence and we were so pleased at our evening out that we decided that we would pay the café another visit at a later date. However, try as we might, we were never able to find the little back street and never got into "Smokey Joe's" again!

Having arrived in Gibraltar, we were naturally interested to know just what we were intended to do there but no information was forthcoming. We entered into our second or third day of inactivity whilst the ship merely leaned against the dockyard wall. The ship was painted and cleaned as usual and then suddenly, we were told that the C.-in- C. Mediterranean was to visit us and inspect the ship's company. I could have thought of better ways to play in the sun than standing on the dockside awaiting the arrival of this august Admiral, a most taxing way of spending a Saturday morning.

The sun burned down furiously and we stood in our severe ranks, hot uncomfortable and anxious to get the whole thing over and done with. Twice we were dismissed to the ship, which formed a backdrop to our sufferings as she lay alongside behind us at the quay. The Admiral had been delayed and there was the opportunity for a quick cigarette but no tea, as the messdecks had been scrubbed clean and there would have been no time for the dishing up to have been done.

We assembled yet again and this time, a large black Buick swept up in a cloud of dust onto the perimeter of the dockside. The First Lieutenant's sword switched up to the attention. His heavy voice echoed back from the Rock. "Ship's Company, atten...tion!" Our stiff legs came reluctantly to life. The shrill whistle of the Bo'sun's Calls burst out from the Piping Party that I had so narrowly escaped being a part of, it having been decided that I was too short to participate. I don't know why, for the Admiral was not much taller than I. Out of the corner of my eye, I saw our Captain salute and then step forward to shake hands with the C.-in-C. I wondered what they would say to one another at such formal moments. The Admiral seemed pleased enough with it, whatever it was, and he then stepped forward to take the salute of the Guard Commander, this part being played by our Sub-Lt. Timmins.

The Guard came to attention, presented arms with their trusty .303 Lee Enfields and Timmins looked as if he took a swipe at the Admiral's nose with the glittering naval sword that he carried, but of course he was merely saluting with it and it was only the angle of sight giving the illusion. My poor old feet were killing me. All this naval ceremony seemed a dreadful waste of time and I would rather have been at sea doing something useful.

The Admiral then did his walkabout bit, passing along the ranks of sailors, each clad in his very tiddliest sailor suit. We had already been inspected at least three times by our own NCOs and officers and of course there was nothing for the C.-in-C. to find amiss. He finally came to me. I think that he suspected from the cut of my jib that I was one of those infernal national servicemen that one heard so much of and he met my glassy stare and carried on by.

It seemed an age before he got back into the Buick, tucking his black and gold sword in first and then tumbling in after it. We were ordered to cheer ship. Off came our caps three times: "Hip-Hip! ... Hurrah!" we roared, in relief that our inspector was going away, not having sentenced us to a kit muster or a rescrub of the ship's paintwork.

We sailed on the Monday morning. Daily Orders said: "The ship will take passage to Malta, executing manoeuvres en route" (whatever that meant!). We made a rendezvous with an aircraft and the bridge were quite excited that the plane actually found us at the rendezvous point planned, without having to search for us.

We lowered our boats on a man overboard exercise, which went very well until someone noticed the presence of several Portuguese Men-of-War jelly-fish in the water and the volunteer "men-overboard" were recovered from the water with genuine alacrity! I had volunteered to be a man in the water but I had been deemed too small again. Harder to see, perhaps?

Later that same day, a look-out reported a green turtle swimming a parallel course to our own and the Captain, who happened to be on the bridge just then, watched it for a while through his glasses and then sent for a rifle from the Armoury. He fired several shots at the beast, one of which definitely struck home, for the spent bullet ricocheted from its shell and sent the turtle into a dive. It surfaced in a different area altogether from the original point of diving and although I spotted it swimming strongly away, I did not report it. By the time it was rediscovered, the range had opened considerably and the following shots merely splashed the creature. The rifle was sent down for cleaning and we continued our journey across the sparkling blue waters.

The Mediterranean was not always the sparkling gentle sea that one sees in the travel brochures and it was rough and grey for the most of one morning, certainly sufficiently to make my feeble stomach aware of the fact. I survived without actually being sick and recovered in time for supper. By the time that I was due to stand my middle watch, the weather was serene again and I spent a long time gazing at the sky and observing the stars and shooting stars, which one could see with great clarity due to the cleanliness of the air. The stars were so bright that they could be seen to the very level of the horizon, which fooled the look-outs several times, for they were forever reporting: "Bridge: starboard look-out, masthead lights, bearing..." only to be told: "That is a star, clot!" by the Officer of the Watch.

We passed several large ships in the night. One was a cruise liner, ablaze from stem to stern with millions of glittering lights and even at a passing range of some miles, her orchestra could plainly be heard. I imagined the cosiness of the passengers, each with his or her own cabin and a personal steward, wonderfully exotic food, no watches to keep and no-one to tell them what to do or what not to do. I'll do that one day, I promised myself. I am still waiting!

I was off watch and sound asleep in the mess during the following afternoon when we came in sight of the entrance to Grand Harbour. The rattles and bangs of the mooring crew aloft and the shouts and commands of the Maltese dockyard workers failed to arouse me and it was only as the day's work came to an end and my messmates filtered back in for tea, that I became aware of the sudden quietness of the ship. Looking out of the port scuttle, I saw a sunbaked stone wall where the blue sea had previously been. Malta had not changed since I visited it in *Ocean*; the hot streets reflected the fierce sun and the dusty dockyard smelled the same.

Several of us descended on the town and ensconced ourselves in a bar that we had not visited before. The beer was warm and scented, and we traded English cigarettes for it for a while, until we realised just how exorbitant the exchange rate was!

A small boy had been wandering up and down the formica tables, hawking the favours of his slightly older sister. If his description was to be believed, she appeared to be a cross between Jane Russell and Brigit Bardot but we were not fooled and kept our seats. After he had gone out into the street, I looked down to the table to find that both my lighter and cigarettes were missing. I made a mental note of what he looked like, but neither small boy nor smoking implements were seen again.

The following day, the ship was scheduled to sail but I enjoyed a stroke of luck, for I was detailed, along with the "Jack Dusty", a nickname for a storesman, to remain at the dockside to receive and care for some naval stores that were due to be brought in by lorry. I smuggled my camera ashore with me and took some photographs of *Savage* from the far side of the basin as she reversed out of the dockyard and made out to sea past the forts.

The day was spent loafing in the sunshine and taking it in turns to sneak off to a small bar adjacent to the dockyard gate. We could not wander further as we were out of the rig of the day in our No. 8 working rig. The wretched stores failed to turn up and in fact delayed our departure to sea on the following morning.

There seemed no real reason for our visit to the island. In the week that we spent patrolling the waters offshore, nothing of interest or particular note occurred. We returned to the dockyard each evening and so we had the chance to get ashore fairly regularly but we had little to spend and apart from a few small "rabbits", and a new lighter, the shopkeepers and barmen of the Gut made little profit from our visit.

We finally left on another blistering day, to the accompaniment of the "Still" piped from each ship in the harbour as we passed. Daily Orders had us bound for home, by way of Alexandria and Gibraltar, but for some unexplained reason Alexandria passed down the port side without a visit from *Savage* and we put on steam for a very fast passage to Gibraltar. Once more in the shadow of the Rock, we stagnated against the dockyard wall and wondered what it was all about.

A naval photographer came aboard late one morning. He was a Petty Officer, burdened down by all sorts of leather satchels, containers and several unwieldy cameras. He was taken to the First Lieutenant by the quartermaster and I set a rumour going that we were about to have our photographs taken.

It was amazing to me how easily my "buzzes" took hold, for I was well known as a notorious "buzz-spreader". I actually saw people combing their hair in the washroom mirror and sorting out a clean white front! However, shortly afterward, we put to sea and steamed slowly round to the south-eastern face of the Rock where the great wartime concrete block was plainly visible. The order was piped to "Clear lower decks, hands to man the falls to port!" This meant that all off-watch NCOs and ratings had to leave what they were doing and fall in on the upper deck to man the powerful ropes called "falls" which operated the raising and lowering of the ship's boats.

The ship's motorboat, powered by a Dorman four-cylinder diesel engine, was far heavier than the twenty-seven foot whaler swung on davits to starboard, but by clearing the lower deck there was always sufficient muscle-power to easily handle the weight of either boat and the task of taking up the falls, taking the strain, marrying the falls (joining the fore and after davit lines together) and hauling away or alternatively, lowering away, was always an excuse for a bit of a skylark and never a chore. On this occasion, since my duty station upon entering or leaving harbour was with whichever of the boats were to be used, I found myself in the motorboat, together with the Engineer, the Coxswain and the Photographer.

Once lowered jerkily toward the water, we slipped and motored away from *Savage*, which then proceeded for the next hour or so to steam up and down off Gibraltar, sometimes at speed and sometimes in a more leisurely fashion, whilst the photographer took many pictures of her. The normally calm sea, however, was soon churned up sufficiently to spoil the artist's shots, so instead of lying heaved-to with the engine in neutral, we moved about to minimise the effect of the wash from the *Savage* and proceeded with the filming exercise.

Finally, the P.O. decided that he had enough pictures and the Coxwain, Leading Seaman Chapman, stood up in the stern with his arms crossed over his head, indicating that we were ready for recovery. *Savage* came to a stop and as we nudged gently alongside, the lower deck was cleared to haul us up again.

Once safely on board and on our blocks with the gripes lashed about our outboard side to secure us to the davits, we were free to disperse and I returned to my mess to have a cup of tea.

"What was all that about?" I queried. Our stores tiffy, Leading hand "Stoney" Mason answered.

"I've seen this before. Those photographs are the first step to selling the old ship off. I'll bet you anything you like that they will be given to some overseas Navy, such as the Omani's or the South Africans and they will buy the *Savage* from under our feet!"

I was quite horrified at this suggestion. Surely the Admiralty would not consider parting with such a famous, working example of second-world-war technology as the dear old *Savage*? What an ignominious end for such a fine old character. She would lose her name and her history in such a sale and I could not believe that Stoney could be right in what he said. Events were to prove him right, although the end result was not quite the same.

As September drew into the end of its second week, we sailed for home and after a fast passage through the Bay of Biscay and up the Channel, we finally docked at Chatham. I was due a short weekend leave and duly arrived home at Hainault late on a Saturday afternoon. I had travelled up the line with a chap in my mess, who lived at nearby Romford. "Ollie" Hyde was one of the ship's Asdic operators. As neither of us had a current girlfriend, we decided to meet up at the Ilford end of Valentine's Park and do "a bit of scouting about" on the Sunday to see what we could find.

Nobody took our fancy in the park and what is more to the point, nobody took a fancy to us, so we sauntered along the high street prior to Ollie getting his bus back to Romford. A girl came toward us, leading a rather scruffy mongrel on a leash. "What a nice little dog!" I quipped cheekily, and stopped to pat it. It was all part of a plan to get to talk to young ladies with dogs and on this occasion, it worked.

The dog-walker's name was Pearl. It was not her dog but her next door neighbour's; I did not catch his name. I tried palming Pearl off on Ollie but he was too slow to make an impression on her, and as you have to be quick in these matters, we saw him off on his bus and I walked Pearl all the way home to her house on the Woodford Avenue at the Redbridge roundabout. There we exchanged addresses and she said that she would write.

The ship sailed early on the Monday forenoon and we slipped out to sea, past Sheerness and Garrison point, the sand bars and shoals, into the grey waters of the North Sea. We were not to sail far, however, for an hour or so later found us anchoring off Mersea Stone at the entrance to the river Colne.

That evening we took the libertyboat to Brightlingsea but this proved to be a rather boring run ashore, as Brightlingsea was just a small fishing town with a ship repairing dock, a small wharf for coal ships and a dying sprat fishing industry. We failed to find the cinema that was allegedly in the town somewhere but enjoyed a good walk about and a "half" in The Anchor on the Hard, before returning to the ship.

To my delight, I received a letter from Pearl the following day. Our meeting had been rather brief and I had not really expected to hear from her. She wrote a very nice letter telling me about her life at college in Walthamstow and a bit about her family. Her father, P.O. "Wally" Norris, had been an Engine Room Artificer in submarines during the war and had been lost in *HMS Tetrach* out of Malta in 1941. She had an uncle and aunt living in Queenborough, at the back of the Isle of Sheppey and only a few miles from Sheerness. I enjoyed her letters and as the weeks turned eventually to months, our correspondence became something to look forward to.

The summer nights began to lengthen and a chill mist enveloped the Colne in wreaths of damp, grey wisps which the sun took longer and longer each day to dispel. As motorboat's crew, I was called upon to man the boat as it lay at the ship's boom at five o'clock one morning, as the officers had it in mind to do a little duck-shooting before breakfast.

Once alongside the officer's gangway, they boarded with such a selection of artillery that I began to doubt that anything shot by them would prove edible anyway, there being one shotgun to three .22 target rifles! We motored slowly up the river, sticking mainly to the navigation channel since we had no echo sounder. The saltings and small strips of land to either side of us were full of geese, duck and gulls, all busily feeding in the grey light of dawn.

I manned a lead and line to plumb the depth of water as we crept closer toward the unsuspecting birds but the range remained too extreme to be sure of a good kill and so a gun was fired to startle the birds which, it was hoped, would then fly into range overhead. To my delight and the officer's chagrin, the birds flew the opposite way and no-one got a shot in. I could not understand why they could not be satisfied with just seeing the wild fowl. The Officer's Chef later said that he did not know how to prepare and cook a fowl if they had bagged one in any case!

We reached the end of the marked channel and as the tide was on the ebb, turned about just short of the James Cook shipyard at Wivenhoe and ran back around the wooded bend in the river, on our way back to Brightlingsea. As we passed the woods, someone spotted a bedraggled pigeon roosting in the branches of an oak and as one, the intrepid hunters raised their guns. It seemed that they all fired at once; amid a shower of oak leaves, the mangled remains of the pigeon fluttered to the ground and the gunshots echoed about the peace of the surrounding countryside. We did not go ashore to recover our trophy as the water was too shallow and there would have been little of the mangled victim to retrieve in any case. The boat picked up speed and we arrived at *Savage* just as "Call the Hands" was being piped.

However, our services as boatmen were booked for the following morning at the same time, as the officers were sending for a brace of proper guns from London and were determined to bag a duck if they possibly could. I took it upon myself to be the champion of the wildfowl on the river and when we assembled once more at the gangway at the crack of dawn, I had tucked my shaving mirror inside my shirt. I then spent the next few hours presumably standing in the bow, "scouting" when in reality, I was trying to pick up the watery rays of the sun with my mirror and flashing it to scare the victims away. The Coxswain did his bit by putting the boat on the mud a few times and we all had to shift forward or aft in order that we could reverse off. This, coupled with the fact that the guns had not arrived from London, led to the score "Hunters nil, Birds one!" Having failed twice, the Big Game Hunters looked at the fast ebbing tide and decided that they would not sally forth again the following day as there would not be enough water. So the wildfowl survived for another day.

We left our quiet anchorage the following morning and steamed northeast along the coast to Harwich, where we picked up a buoy in the river Orwell. Our task on this occasion was to take the Boy seamen from the shore establishment *HMS Ganges* at Shotley Point to sea for a day's gunnery practice. Each day we put to sea with perhaps forty of these youngsters and once out in the open sea, we would teach them how to throw a hand grenade and to fire a rifle and man one of the 4.5" guns.

This was all pretty routine stuff. However, one afternoon just after dinner, I was detailed to assist the Gunner, a Warrant Officer of the Royal Australian Navy, in instructing the Boys on the arming and throwing of the Mills 32 Hand Grenade. A fat lot of good I thought I would be, as I had never even seen a Mills 32 Hand Grenade before, let alone instruct in the use of it, and so I paid very close attention to the Gunner's instructions on its use!

We stood in the feeble sunshine on the quarterdeck as *Savage* dashed along at some eighteen knots. Garth and I came up on the deck with two brown boxes of grenades and proceeded to open them up. The grey grenades sat comfortably inside, like so many fresh-laid eggs; I did not like to disturb them but the Gunner took one from the box and played catch with it, throwing it from one sweating boy to another. No-one dropped it.

Eventually, having explained how it was intended to work, he demonstrated its use and, drawing the pin with his left index finger and thumb, threw the pin over the side! We stood momentarily open-mouthed at this and then as one, dived for cover. The Gunner stood alone with a big grin on his face.

"It won't go off!" he roared. "I am still squeezing the clip to the side. It is only when I let it go... like this," and he opened his fingers sufficiently wide to let the clip spring off, whereupon he lobbed the offensive thing over the side, "that it will go bang!" His "Bang" and the grenade going off were simultaneous.

We all crept out from under our cover which, I am sorry to relate, consisted of whomsoever you could pull in front of you to act as a shield! We all gathered round again, trying to look as if we had not really been scared at all. I wedged my boot against the "egg-box", full minus one, to stop it wandering away with the vibration and roll of the ship. The Gunner was talking again.

"Called the Mills 32 because it was invented by someone called Mills and it breaks into thirty-two pieces as it explodes. Most of the damage done by a grenade is when used in confined spaces or among a concentration of men." Like us now, I thought and slowly shuffled to the outer limits of the group. Gunner took another "egg" from the basket.

"Out pin...draw back right arm...lob". The clip went "ping" and the "egg" sailed through the air and fell into the water with a soft "plop". The grenade went off with a muffled "pop" five seconds or so after the clip came off and it was all over. Not much to that then, I thought.

We were lined up in a queue which stretched from the after guard rail back toward "Y" Gun. As Garth and I were only "helping", we were not expected to throw these infernal grenades and so we were sent along the queue with a nice safe grenade to show the Boys to get them used to the weight and feel of them, whilst the Gunner got the person at the head of the queue to actually throw one over the stern.

I noticed that the "tail end charlie" of the queue was pushing the ones that had just thrown their grenades to the front of him when in fact, they had been sent to go to the end, which meant that the lad at the back of the rank was always the same one. Obviously, he did not wish to play grenadiers and who could blame him. Gunner spotted that.

"Come here lad," he smiled, beckoning the cowering lad to the head of the queue. "Nothing to be afraid of..." and he went through the out-pin, lob, "bang" routine. The pimply-faced lad was too scared to listen. He took his grenade nervously and fumbled with the pin. What happened next seemed to do so in slow motion.

He crouched over the grenade in the attempt to pull out the pin, which may have been a little stiff. The pin fell to the deck, followed by the clip, making its distinctive "pinging" sound as it came off. The grenade fell from his nervous fingers and began a slow roll toward the scuppers.

The queue of observers, for the second time that day, dived left, right and backwards, desperately seeking space and protection away from the grey steel object of destruction.

Through all that chaos came the slim figure of the Gunner. The single thin gold ring on the sleeve of his jacket gleamed in the sunlight as his arm flashed confidently after the rolling grenade. There was only time for one try at it. His fingers closed on the steel grenade and with a quick flip, he tipped it over the scuppers and it slowly arced from sight over the side.

"Down!" he shouted. The grenade exploded perhaps a foot above the surface of the sea and splattered the ship's side with shrapnel. The lad on top of me slowly got off, rubbing a lacerated shin. A cotton ball of smoke billowed lazily astern.

The Gunner picked himself up and started to dust his uniform down. All I could think to do was to applaud and the others joined in, some sitting where they had fallen and the luckier ones coming from behind the "Y" Gun shield.

"Well held, sir!" I said in true cricketing parlance. The Gunner grabbed the grenade thrower by the sleeve.

"That's how not to do it, lad!" he said. "Now show us how it is done properly!" The grenade instruction was back in full swing by the time the First Lieutenant came along to see what all the commotion was about. He merely gripped the guardrail, looked quizzically over the starboard quarter and muttered: "That side will require repainting, Guns!" and returned to the bridge.

I shall always remember, one early October morning, seeing the tall mast of *HMS Ganges* rearing up out of the fog that cloaked the lower regions of the river Orwell and hearing the regular beat of a single drum, and then, slowly, rhythmically and in time to the beat, seeing the Boys of *Ganges* man the mast, reaching the top just as "Colours" were piped and all the naval ships in the river hauled down their "prep" flags and ran up their distinctive White Ensigns. We all stopped what we were doing, not only to salute our own Ensign but also to marvel at the courage of the small figure representing the "button-boy" at the very top of the mast.

In all, I suppose we spent some seven or eight days steaming about the East Coast, shooting at targets towed by a harbour launch or rolling depth charges over the side and generally making a lot of noise and fuss. We even laid a smoke screen from our smoke machine on the quarterdeck and our little ship dashed in and out of it like a child through the smoke of a bonfire on Guy Fawkes Night. The *Ganges* boys seemed to like it anyway.

Finally, we left, again with no idea of where we were bound but as we had turned southeast on leaving the Orwell, we guessed correctly on Sheerness and tied up comfortably to the usual buoy. It happened that I was duty watch and as the ship was Duty Guardship, I was detailed off to be part of the ship's shore patrol.

We proceeded ashore after supper, dressed in our second-best uniform and wearing white gaiters and belt, an arm band that bore the letters "NP", standing for Naval Police or Naval Patrol, I know not which, and swinging a vicious-looking pickaxe handle, known as a helve. The Petty Officer in charge of us got us to patrol the high street in Sheerness in twos. I met several members of my mess and they delighted in taking the general piss out of my exalted position. I countered by telling them to "move along there" in my most authoritative voice, all of this taken in good part.

We met up by prior arrangement with the Petty Officer, who had taken charge of a section of the public bar of a pub in the high street which he said he had requisitioned as his "command post".

"Might as well sit in here, lads," he said, when we had reported that all was quiet on the streets. "Nothing much will happen until the pubs turn out." And there we sat, chatting over a half-pint of mild until the landlord rang a bell and called: "Teem, genelemein hif you plearse!" Straightening our caps and belts to comply with regulations, we again split into pairs and sauntered off on patrol, peering into shop doorways and up the alleyways leading off the main street.

I was on patrol with "Soapy" Hughes, an ME2 from the Stoker's mess. We had hardly spoken before, although we had been on the same ship for nine months together. It was simply that our paths never crossed because of our very different jobs on the ship. Soapy's idea of shore patrol was to hide in a shop doorway until it was time to go back to the assembly point for debriefing, and then back to the ship and bed, so we made along the brighter part of the well-lit street and made a bee-line for a fairly dark shop front where we could hide and have a fag in peace and quiet. However, as we passed the entrance to an alley, a movement caught his eye and he shone his torch into the darkness to reveal a rating from *HMS Diamond*, having his wicked way with a local lass up against the adjacent wall. Soapy tapped his helve on the wall.

"Oy, oy, matie," he said. "That will be enough hov that there! You are creatin' a public disturbance; sod off somewhere else where you can't be seen!"

It seemed a very reasonable demand under the circumstances, but the lady concerned thought otherwise. Despite her tulle rock and roll skirts and petticoats tucked under her armpits and her knickers around one ankle, she seemed far from embarrassed. "Piss off, Jack!" she hissed. "Go and rattle yer stick elsewhere!"

The sailor remained locked to her stomach like a captured fly to a spider, his fishy eyes all glassy and his mouth opening and shutting but saying nothing. It was obvious that he was very drunk. Even so, he knew better than to argue with the Naval Patrol but there seemed little that he was able to do as his brassy companion had stated their intent. I caught Soapy's arm.

"Leave them to it," I advised. "They'll be on their way in a minute or two." I doubted the sailor would even last that long. Soapy grunted: "Saucy bloody cow!" and we wandered on and took station in a shop doorway a little further along the way. Sure enough, the girl came out a few minutes later and strode past our hiding place, hissing some obscenity as she passed. The sailor must have left by the other end of the alley, possibly minus his paybook and money.

Raised, intoxicated voices grew louder from the far end of the high street and we guessed that the rest of the Patrol were having a more illuminating evening. A police car sped past our refuge in the direction of the noise and a little later we heard the sound of breaking glass. I rather wanted to join in but Soapy was in charge and so I followed his lead and did nothing. The row started to quieten down but a woman's voice was raised in protest, punctuated with messdeck adjectives. Soapy finally stood on his fourth fag-end.

"OK, Pete," he said. "Now's the time to join in at the double. It should all be over when we get there!" We sprinted up the street, the sound of our heavy boots rattling back at us from the darkened shopfronts. We were in time to see a rather stout lady, clutching a policeman's helmet and swinging hammerlike blows at all about her, being forcibly thrust into the interior of a Wolseley police car. A line of rather sullen matelots stood at the side of the road, having their names taken by a police sergeant and our Petty Officer. He sported a cut on the cheek and his tie had taken up residence under his left ear. His eyes burned with the exhilaration of recent combat.

"Where the bloody hell have you two been?" he rasped. "Didn't you hear my whistle?" Of course we hadn't, and we busied ourselves in prodding the prisoners into the interior of the Naval Patrol van that had just drawn up, thus avoiding further criticism.

It had been another boozy brawl; no-one knew how it had started or what it had all been over, but all were determined to protest their innocence long and loud and at great length, even as the van doors were closed to muffle their protests. The casualties on our side amounted to the P.O.'s cut cheek and two buttons lost from his jacket, a black eye on one of the Stokers and a patch of hair removed from another, who had got too close to the angry fat lady. Soapy said that it served them right for getting close to the source of the trouble too quickly. "Always let 'em knock seven bells out of each other first before you gets in with yer stick." It sounded good advice to me.

It was closer to midnight before we reboarded *Savage* and I was unexpectedly very tired, so much so that slinging my hammock was a monumental task. I felt little better the following day, which was brightened by the ship making up to Chatham in time for me to pack my suitcase and steam home for a short weekend.

I arrived home feeling exhausted but I still did not think that anything was amiss until I left home on my bike on the Sunday morning to cycle over to Pearl's house to pay a surprise visit. Even that short distance took my every effort to cover; it seemed that all the blood had drained from me and all I wanted was to sleep. Parking my machine in the front garden, I knocked for the first time on the door of the house in Woodford Avenue, which was answered by Pearl's mother who, when I had introduced myself, told me that Pearl was still in bed! I was, however, ushered in to await her rising and was sat in the front room, apparently a great honour, with a cup of tea.

I was quickly joined by Pearl, who explained that she was in the habit of doing her homework from college in bed on a Sunday morning and I put the matter right by apologising for the unexpectedness of my visit. We sat and chatted, with more tea to keep us company. Her granny came in several times to collect the cups and finally, I was invited to lunch, an offer that I gracefully declined and took my leave, saying that my dinner would shortly be ready at home.

Pearl saw me to the garden gate. We touched hands briefly, knowing that her mother would be peeking from behind the curtains. I promised to write a letter as soon as I returned aboard and with a final wave, cycled off home. So hot and sweaty was I by the time I reached the foot of the hill leading to my street, that I was forced to get off the bike and walk. Mother took one look at my pale face and obvious distress and sent me to my bed where I fell into a deep sleep.

The Navy insisted on implementing peculiar rules for people falling "sick on shore". Apparently, the word of the patient's GP would not do, for the Navy promulgated a list of Navy doctors whom one had to consult if you reported sick when on leave.

I awoke on the Monday afternoon to the ministrations of our family GP who finally bought me round. He had been sent for since no-one could arouse me. Apart from an obvious exhausted condition and a rather slow heart-beat, little could be found wrong with me and it would appear that I was suffering from the earlier virus that had confined me to the RN Hospital at Gillingham.

It was agreed that a few days in bed would soon put me on my feet again and he would send the authorities aboard *Savage* a medical certificate. That should have been the end of the matter but I knew that it could not be done that way; the certificate had to come from a Navy-designated doctor. Since this gentleman practised in rooms at Chadwell Heath and we had no telephone, it was apparent that somehow, the "corpus dilecti" would have to get to him.

After our own doctor had gone and I had been sick a few times, I dressed in my warmest cycling gear, retrieved my cycle from the shed in the garden and wobbled off to Chadwell Heath. I do not remember much of the journey. Even pedalling slowly, the sweat trickled from my chin and by the time I chained the bike to the railings outside the Navy doctor's surgery, I must have looked like death warmed up. I sat down heavily in the waiting room, having told the receptionist who I was and what I wanted. She looked at me anxiously from her desk with a worried frown. Perhaps she thought that this sick matelot, seeking a naval Sick-on-Shore chit, had some fearsome tropical virus that would wipe out the victims of the Sprains and Coughs and Colds fraternity that so patiently awaited their turn at the doctor's stethoscope, for suddenly she approached me and from a respectful distance announced that "Doctor will see you next, Ordinary Seaman".

I had become aware that the persons sitting both to left and right had found excuses to move away and that I sat bathed in sweat, in a corner on my own. No-one helped me when I found difficulty in getting to my feet. There was not a Samaritan amongst them. Had I not been feeling so very faint and numb, I would have had great delight in breathing on them all but I finally wobbled to my feet. "Are you alright, dear?" asked the receptionist, standing back a pace. Perhaps she was giving me room to pitch headlong at her feet. I could not answer but shakily pushed open the door to the doctor's consultancy room.

I suspect that Doctor Smith had seen them all in his time. All those who wanted an extra week or so tucked up at home with the cosy old lady, away

214

from the privation and degradation of the Armed Services and I afterward wondered if he was elected to the job of diagnosing Sick-on-Shore men because of an inclination to believe their illness as nothing other than a desire to dodge the column.

I stood at the end of his red-brown mahogany desk, my colouring exactly matching the beige wallpaper of his surgery. The sweat trickled through my hair and gathered in large droplets on my chin before plopping off the end. I did not sit down because he had not invited me to.

"And what seems the matter with you, my boy?" he asked, as if I had merely stubbed my toe on a pavement. I was having difficulty with all my normal functions by now and talking was another of them.

"I'm not well," I answered. He stared at me in silence for a second or two. Suddenly it dawned on him that he had a genuinely sick sailor in front of him and not the usual "chit seeker".

"Good God lad, sit yourself down. How long have you been in this state?" I briefly told him my symptoms and added that my own GP had been called and had diagnosed exhaustion. All the while, he was taking my temperature and listening with his cold stethoscope.

"You're not at all well, are you?" he said. I could have told him that. He scribbled out the precious chit. "Go home and get into bed," he said. "Don't let yourself get cold and come and see me in a week".

Obviously made of sterner stuff than his receptionist, he helped me from my seat and assisted me to put my jacket on. "You lads in the Navy, you know, always going somewhere and getting these little viruses that we doctors have never seen and probably never will again...". He continued the theme as he ushered me to the door and out into the waiting room beyond. "Hope to see you livelier next week... NEXT!" and I tottered out into the street, past the cringeing receptionist whose frantic glare told me that I was passing too close to her.

How I got home, I shall never know but I slipped into a hot bath and then fell sound asleep once more beneath the sheets. I was vaguely aware of people coming and going, as if passers-by in a dream but it was Thursday before I awoke to mother trying to get me to swallow a tablet and some tea. Whether or not it was that tablet or the tea that did the trick but I found myself awake at a little after two in the morning, feeling ravenously hungry and dying of thirst. Within another few hours, I was as fit as a fiddle and trying to find an excuse to get out for an hour or two on my bike!

In truth, I suppose it did take the week to properly recover but at least I was not suffering on the ship or in the RNH. Pearl and I went to the pictures a few times and I once went to Walthamstow to meet her from her college on the bus. I was quite sorry when the Tuesday evening came round and I sat once more in Dr Smith's surgery under the scrutiny of the receptionist. Dr Smith pronounced me fit and well and able to travel back to Chatham and gave me a signing-off certificate to take back with me on the following day.

I packed my case reluctantly that evening but made no frantic effort to join the early morning scramble back to Chatham. I left home in a more leisurely fashion and I arrived back to find *Savage* where I had last left her but under orders to sail the following day on NATO Exercises. I was designated "light duties" by the barrack doctor to whom I was sent but no indication of what had been the matter with me was ever given, as was usual. We called this the mushroom syndrome; we were kept in the dark and shovelled shit!

Savage set off once more out into the darkness of the closing nights of autumn, on darken ship routine and with doubled watches. The weather was deteriorating, with sheets of rain and blackened skies with no stars or moon, a falling glass and a rising sea. Our destination was given as HM Dockyard, Portsmouth.

CHAPTER
TWELVE

The foul weather continued unabated and I, for one, was relieved to see the Nab Towers standing guard at the entrance to Portsmouth dockyard. We tied up alongside in the basin, by which time it was time for bed. The following day had us entering the dry dock. The sides of the ship were propped up with great lengths of wooden shoring and the water was slowly pumped out of the dock, leaving us securely wedged upright in the middle of the basin. Needless to say, hardly had the water tricked down the last sluice before the usual gang of dockyard maties appeared.

Although there appeared to be no welding to do on this occasion, the welding gear was nevertheless dumped in the place most likely to cause an obstruction and as usual, we spent a long time treading over and around it, unable to shift it to a better site for fear of causing a strike. When eventually they did set to work, they slowly began to clean off the ship's bottom and to apply a thick maroon antifouling, the stench of which was so strong that we could taste it!

They banged loud and long underneath the hull and investigation revealed that our propellers were being removed. Rumour had it that the welding gear was for welding in rowlocks on the upper deck and that the ship was in future to be rowed everywhere, but a lorry arrived at the dockside and a new set of propellers were unloaded and craned down into the puddles in the bottom of the dry dock beneath the ship. These were later refitted with as much noisy enthusiasm as there was when their predecessors were removed and soon the end of these labours was announced by the gradual flooding of the basin.

Our morning tea was disturbed by the quartermaster, who burst into the mess with the news that a group of Indian naval officers had arrived aboard and were, even then, in conference with the Captain and other officers. Able Seaman "Burl" Ives had seen this before. "She's up for sale!" he announced. It was the second time that we had heard a rumour of our ship being sold off.

After "Stand Easy", we assisted the dockyard maties in vacating our position in the dry dock and the ship put to sea on speed trials in the Channel. The sea state was very calm and the old girl really hitched up her skirts and flew over the short swell. Nature ordered me to pay a "seating" visit to the heads and when the ship was at full speed, the dividing steel bulkhead

217

between the heads and the bathroom, somewhat rusty at the bottom where it joined the door post, split away and the whole panel rattled alarmingly. The ship was falling apart, I concluded.

Which would last the longer, my term of service in the Navy or the ancient hull which now threatened to split in twain? A visit to the heads when the ship was travelling at high speed was certainly a hazardous necessity. The constant thumping and vibration was bad enough whilst perched in this precarious sitting position but this was made worse by the ship executing a number of high-speed turns to port and starboard. I did not linger long!

It was dark when we returned to the dockside at Portsmouth but judging by the smiles of the officers on the bridge, *Savage* must have acquitted herself favourably. We later heard that she had reached a speed of over thirty-eight knots, a feat for her size and class, matched and beaten only by *HMS Manxman*, a fast minelayer of the Laytona Class.

We were joined aboard by the same crew of boffins as previously. I helped them aboard with their gear and one recognised me and said:

"Hello."

"How come that chap knows you?" asked Burl Ives.

"He's my uncle," I said with a straight face.

"Never!"

"It's true, but don't tell anyone because scientists on secret projects such as ours are not supposed to be on the same ships as their relatives." Burl was hooked.

"What secret project?" he asked.

I could not think of anything good enough on the spur of the moment and so I touched my finger to my nose, whispered, "Must go!" and left him guessing. I had ample time during the period before "Stand Easy" to think up some plot and I wove a tale about taking the ship to India and blowing air into the oxygen-starved areas of the Indian Ocean through the tubes leading from the "Fish and Chip Shop" but it did not get a very good reception in the mess and I was booed out of order. Something, however, was quite definitely "up".

This trip to Scotland proved to be our last. With the boffins once more ensconced in the Boy seamen's messdeck, there began the usual patrolling offshore, sometimes along the measured mile off the Isle of Arran, or else further out into the North Atlantic. The mysterious "Fish and Chip Shop" amidships would wheeze and puff alarmingly and the water fairly seethed alongside. At last the boffins seemed satisfied.

They shut the shop up and spent several days in fairly calm weather, loafing about the upper deck or leaning on the ship's rails, dirtying up our freshly scrubbed passageways and decks with their shoes. They engaged each other in heated arguments, waving their arms about and tapping long sheets of graph paper with the stems of their pipes but they never spoke to us. Perhaps they thought that we might ask awkward questions about their projects but in fact, we would not have done so since their work was of little concern to us.

Suddenly, a very unusual notice appeared on the Daily Orders. We were to return to Loch Long, where our baggage, hammocks and personal effects would be taken into store at the Torpedo Research Establishment there and the ship would be returning to complete "certain experiments in the Loch, which would necessitate conning her from the upper deck only". We utterly failed to find out what this was to be about. I even had the temerity to ask the First Lieutenant what these orders meant but he just winked and said, "Wait and see, my son!"

Our kitbags came out of retirement from the depths of our lockers and were filled with our kit, apart from the clothes that we wore and our cigarettes and lighters. The kitbags were then handed into the care of our Coxwain and disappeared to be locked away ashore somewhere. Meanwhile, the engineering staff had been busily welding and screwing a complicated system of levers and rods leading from the upper deck into the bowels of the ship and so, at last, when the ship left the dockside at Greenock, she was capable of being controlled entirely from the upper deck.

At one point during the journey to Loch Long, the theory was put to the test and apart from one or two minor hiccups, was found to work. We entered the Loch full of intrepidation. Suddenly, the Tannoy broke into life with, "Do you hear that!" The Captain came on the air. *Savage*, he told us, had been experimenting for some time with a system for countering the acoustic mine. The "Fish and Chip Shop" was the result. The homing torpedo could also be affected by the system but as yet, the likely results could only be guessed at and it was proposed to actually test the effects that very day. There was a likelihood that *Savage* may be struck and holed, in which case it was intended to beach her in the Loch and repair her later. Even though the torpedoes being fired at her would not contain a warhead and could therefore not explode, some risk was attached to the exercise. Hence the need to put our gear ashore and to find it desirable to conn the ship from the upper deck.

Our attention was then drawn to the sight of several harbour launches and a motor torpedo boat which came along the Loch to join us. We were allocated a boat station in a launch should the ship be in danger of sinking and these vessels were detailed to attend us closely following the firing of the homing torpedoes, ready to pick up "survivors" should this be necessary. Our own boats were swung out ready for use and the Falls were manned for the lowering of the ship's motorboat. Since my station for entering harbour was to close up at the motorboat, I was already aboard and ready to go; in fact, I would be the first to "Abandon Ship", should the order be given!

It was a cold day and no-one wanted to end up in the water, so it was with some pessimism and with icy fingers running up and down our spines that we saw the MTB turn fast at the end of the Loch and chase hard after us on her first run in. Suddenly, when she was some half-a-mile dead astern of us, we saw twin puffs of compressed air spurt from her port and starboard torpedo tubes and watched with our hearts in our mouths as the two long black cylinders of death plunged from her bows, to fall with a splash and a hiss into the oily, calm surface of the Loch. We held our breath for the few seconds that it would take the torpedoes to run, expecting their arrival to be heralded with a thud astern and the immediate loss of either propellers or steering gear. A ragged cheer from the bridge told us that the weapons had miraculously missed and this was confirmed by the sight of one of them surfacing to port and coming to rest with her nose poking out of the water towards the empty sky.

The second torpedo ran wildly in a semi-circle, having run the length of our starboard side at just a few inches below the surface. The charging MTB almost ran over her prodigy and there followed a little chase by one of the recovery launches until the erring torpedo gave in and floated to the surface.

However, to our great consternation, that was not to be the end of the proceedings, for after loading the MTB's torpedo tubes again and then again, we were subjected to several torpedo runs from different angles, the final one of which was from about three hundred yards astern. The closest we came to disaster was when we caught a glancing blow from a "wild" tinfish which strayed into our path. Had we had more searoom, even this minor collision could have been avoided and the frowns on the bridge turned to outright beams of delight. The Boffins emerged, hot and grimy from their "Fish and Chip Shop", the acknowledged heroes of the day.

It was dark by the time that we returned to our jetty, where our kit was handed back, the messdecks opened once more and life began to get back to normal.

Life is never "normal" for long. We stayed at a buoy on the Green Bank opposite Greenock and it was there one night that the duty Quartermaster was awoken at a little after two in the morning by a dull explosion which was followed by a spout of flame rushing into the cold night air from a ship moored alongside the dockyard at Greenock. The QM watched the vessel burn for a while and then thought that perhaps the duty officer would be interested in the conflagration, so he made his way to the officer's cabin and woke him. The sleepy Subby nearly fell over his braces on hearing the news.

"Clear lower deck," he squeaked. "Away motorboats crew, away life-boats crew! Fire Parties to muster abreast the gangway! Oh, why did this have to happen when I was Duty Dog?"

The cold frost of the night was punctuated by the strident ringing of the shore-based Fire Brigade engines and we stood around in groups on the frozen deck, watching the scene ashore. Little could actually be seen over the glare of the flames but the heat of the fire reached far out into the waters of the Clyde and we saw the surface steaming.

Our own motorboat was lowered and the ERAs loaded a portable water-pump aboard, powered by a Coventry-Climax 10hp petrol engine and with this heavy item, we made across the river toward the rosy glow of the burning coaster. The ERAs worked to load the pump's nozzle into the water and to make a firm base upon which to mount the pump. They seemed amazed when the pump motor started up on the first swing.

Our close proximity to the water made it impossible to direct a jet onto the deck of the ship but we did sterling work in cooling the hull plates of the ship, which hissed and steamed under the strong cold jet of river water. No evidence of the flames could be seen by now and a Fire Brigade officer eventually came to the deck and waved us away, as the fire was now thought to be well under control. We returned to the ship and were directed round to the boom aft to effect a recovery of pump and equipment in daylight, as the ship's company had been stood down and the decks were empty of men. However, we were made to struggle with the weight of the water-pump, which the ERAs insisted must be returned to the store from whence it had come. Perhaps they thought that someone may steal their little "baby" during the remaining hours of darkness?

We thought that this may have been the end of the saga and yet another piece of life's brilliant tapestry completed but late in the afternoon of the following day, we were startled to hear a loud boom from across the water, again coming from the coaster, and heard later from that venerable bearer of information, our postman, that two men had gone into the ship's hold to assess the fire damage. One of them had struck a match, thus igniting fumes and gases in the smouldering hold and blowing out two plates from the ship's side. One man had been blown up the ladder and landed on the upper deck whilst the other was killed in the hold. Obviously neither had attended a fire-fighting school such as our school at *HMS Phoenix*.

Life must go on. We shifted from our mooring at Greenock to come alongside Prince's Pier but as we had orders to sail to Chatham, I did not go ashore. The following day we singled up, slipped our berth and put to sea. I was glad to see the coast slip astern and the mass of the Isle of Arran gradually disappear.

Little was I to know that although I was fated to return many times to that lovely part of Scotland, the dear old *Savage* never would, for her days to paying-off, or in layman's terms, to go to the breaker's yard, had already been decided. We headed south at a good pace and had a very uncomfortable time off the Isle of Man and in the St George's Channel, which persisted until we rounded Land's End and headed up Channel. Daily Orders said that we would be carrying out exercises whilst in the Channel and gave no indication of our destination.

We quickly lost any idea of the ship's direction as night fell. When I came up on deck for the morning watch at 0400, the Plough lay well down slightly to the east of us and I guessed that we were heading roughly east-north-east. The ship was in total darkness as usual with neither navigation lights or deck lights lit and the radar watch was doubled together with the watch on deck. We changed course several times before daylight and at one stage, put on a spurt of speed that made one think that something was about to happen. We strained our eyes into the darkness, expecting the "enemy" to loom up ahead at any time, but the first faint glimmers of light appeared in the eastern sky and gradually, the feeble winter sun rose to an empty sea all about us. I came off watch at 0800 when my relief came to the bridge and I went below for a warming cup of tea, a wash and a fag.

Later, we stood balancing against *Savage*'s peculiar twisting roll on the quarterdeck awaiting instructions for the day. Now that winter was fast approaching, life at sea was becoming more spartan by the day. The air at sea was always warmer, or so it seemed to me, providing that it was not driven by any sort of northerly airstream, when it could, and most times did, prove bitingly cold.

We dressed in our usual No. 8 working rig but were allowed to wear a sea-jersey underneath. That was our only concession to the cold of winter. We were even forbidden to put our hands in our pockets to keep them warm. To discourage this practice, we were given scrubbing brushes and paint scrapers to occupy our cold hands and fingers. The best thing to do was to work with a will with these tools and look forward to when "Stand Easy" was piped, or better still "Secure", and the end of our working day.

The "buzz" came to our messdeck a little after supper that evening: we were joining a NATO exercise shortly and would be creeping around the North Sea and the Skaggerat, hunting out submarines, illuminating targets and joining in group attacks against other surface vessels. For once, the "buzzes" were right and these orders were confirmed by the Skipper over the Tannoy the following day. Determined to give a good account of ourselves, we settled into our shipboard routines with enthusiasm.

There followed several days of hyperactivity. We seemed, most of the time, to be chasing around like chickens without heads, first racing off in one direction, and then going through high-speed one hundred and eighty degree turns to chase back along our original track. Perhaps it was all designed to keep out of sight of the "enemy"; if so, it worked, for we saw no-one for days!

I had just swung into my hammock at 0410 one morning when the Tannoy squawked: "Do you hear that, Gun's Crews close up, Damage Control State One! Clear lower deck, spare hands to muster in the starboard passage". This was accompanied by the "Action Stations" klaxon. All around me, men were tumbling out of their sleep and struggling into their clothes by the light of the red police lamps, their eyes heavy with sleep and their tempers reflected in their language.

In just two minutes, the messdeck was an empty warm steel box, filled only with ranks of swinging empty hammocks, their bedding streaming down to the deck. This charade was to happen quite often over the next few days. One of the most irritating things that I found about it was when I wanted to enter the watertight door into the messdeck and some jolly wag on the inside whacked the clips back on as fast as I knocked them off. It was meant to be in good fun of course but it never ceased to annoy me, especially when I devised another route and they anticipated me and reclipped the door on that one too.

Our wanderings took us well up to the edge of the northern ice-fields. One afternoon a little before dusk, we were treated to the thunder of heavy artillery somewhere south of us and our little bridge became instantly filled with officers; we went again to Action Stations and tore off in the direction of the gunfire. There was nothing but empty, blue-grey sea when we got there but the Asdics people reported a strange echo and we dashed around in circles trying to locate what it was.

I don't remember the actual outcome of all this activity but we did not sight a submarine. The weather remained bright but very cold and most of our time off duty was spent asleep on the cushions over the lockers in the mess. It was a strange time of constant alertness, with little time to relax and forget where we were and what we were supposed to be doing. Not that we had much idea of our mission; I wonder if the officers did either?

Word eventually came that our function in the exercise was complete and we were free to stand down and return to Port. I had predicted that we would have done just that within the next twenty-four hours or so, but my calculations were only roughly based on what fuel we carried and largely depended on whether or not we refuelled from a tanker.

It was a relief to see the navigation lights on after dark, as I had a horror of the ship running someone down should they also be steaming without lights. We were heading south in the North Sea, with the coast of Norway to port, and a general air of relaxation prevailed after the routines of Darkened Ship, constant Action Stations and Damage Control Stations.

I had recently been to see an "oppo" in the radar room and he had pointed out to me, on the Plot, a large Dutch cruiser, steering a parallel course to our own and overhauling us on the starboard quarter bound for her own home port of Den Helder. I returned to the mess and said to the assembled bodies that if they wanted to see a big ship, one was due to come in sight on the starboard side. No-one took any notice from their crib board or from the card school but a little later the penny must have dropped, because a chappie took a look aft from one of the scuttles and said that he could just see the ship lying low down to the north-west.

"What ship is she, Cobby?" he asked. The Devil took me.

"The Russian heavy cruiser, *Marshall Bulganin.*" I answered. "The officers were talking about her on the bridge. She's been shadowing the NATO exercise and has now broken off to shadow us." Everyone took interest at this point and all took turns to peer sideways out of the scuttle to see the grey shape on the horizon, her navigation lights bright in the dusk of evening.

During the course of the evening, I fed in all sorts of little theories as to why such a vessel should be following us and interest continued to flow from my colleagues, to the extent that some went aft to the galley flat and looked out over the calm sea at the huge craft. Rounds were conducted at 2100 and several men rigged up their hammocks and prepared to turn in. I took up my towel and repaired to the bathroom for a luke-warm shower.

It was a mild, close evening with a black, heavy sky that threatened rain. As I came back to the mess, and just as I was about to enter through the watertight doorway, there was a great white flash of lightning followed by an immediate peal of thunder. The percussion made the ship shudder. I jumped through the door. "Action Stations!" I shouted. "She's firing at us!" To my unspeakable horror, my shipmates leapt to their feet as one and fell over each other in their haste to don steel helmets, anti-flash gear and clothing. Despite my pleas of "Not really, I'm joking!" they were so tensed that as a man, they clattered along the port passage bound for their Action Stations at the tubes and guns. Fortunately, halfway there, someone realised that he hadn't heard the Action Stations bell and they stopped. A further clap of thunder and a deluge of cold rain confirmed that they had been hoodwinked and they returned to lash me up in my hammock for the night where I could do no more damage!

I happened to be cook of the mess on the following day and, having scrubbed out the mess and peeled the potatoes for dinner, I was on my way aft to empty the peelings down the gash-chute, a large galvanised chute which was lashed on the stern rail, down which we dumped all of our rubbish when at sea. As I sauntered lazily along, I was astounded to see an officer dressed as a Naval Commander coming along the upper deck towards me. As he approached, I recognised our Engineering Officer, Mr Moss. Obviously, his promotion had come through overnight, for the last time I had seen him, he was wearing his usual white overalls with the shoulder straps of an Engineering Lieutenant Commander. I saluted smartly as we passed: "Good morning, sir," I said.

The new Commander Moss returned my salute with a half smile. He was well known as being a bit of an introvert, his life revolving around his engines and a tank of guppies that he kept in his cabin. Every time that I ever saw him, he would be clad in his white overalls, with a wad of cotton-waste in his hand.

Just as he passed me by, I heard him gasp and I looked back to see him clutching thin air as his brand new Commander's cap was whisked from his head by a sudden gust of wind, to be spun over the side into the sea. He ran to the rail and stood looking helplessly after it as it rose and fell on the cold grey water. However, his loss had been spotted from the bridge and the ship slowed down and started a hard turn to port, the look-outs pointing all the while at the distant headgear as if they were marking a man overboard.

I stowed my gash bucket behind a torpedo-tube, for I knew that the ship's boat would be called away and I was already at the davits and clearing away the gripes by the time the pipe, "Clear lower deck, away motorboat's crew!" was made. Leading Seaman Wiltshire was the Coxswain. Soapy Hughes was engineer and I was bowman.

Clad in our life-jackets, we boarded the motor boat and she was swung out on the davits. When we had taken the turns off the lifelines, the mass of men on deck lowered us away toward the rolling sea beneath. They were in a buoyant mood. Lowering the boat to recover the new Commander's cap was a laugh that they would make quite some mileage out of in the messdecks that night and we in the boat shared their infectious spirit.

Our keel kissed the top of a wave and we slipped into the trough and, passing the heavy falls and blocks clear over the side, we motored powerfully away from *Savage*'s side. Our Coxswain, following instructions from the bridge, headed off on a course and I took station in the bow of the boat, looking for the first sign of the lost cap. I quickly saw it and pointed the way for us to go and in a moment or two, we drew alongside the precious cap which floated white top uppermost. There was quite a sea running and I may well have missed the cap with my first stab with my boathook but I leaned out over the side to make a perfect recovery.

"Got it, Hookey!" I shouted above the hiss and roar of the sea but before I could haul it safely aboard, the Coxswain shouted, grinning from ear to ear:

"Give it a good dunking first, Cobby!" and so I returned the waterlogged cap to the sea and we went round again. We did this a second time but as we pulled away to make a third turn, to my horror I saw the cap tip over and slowly begin to sink in a stream of bubbles. I had time for only one frantic swipe with the boathook. The heavy galvanised end of the boathook flashed down as far as I could reach and I caught the cap on an upward stroke. The cap, by then full of water and weighing several pounds, whipped straight up out of the sea and cartwheeled over the top of the 'midships cabin of the boat and slid gracefully over the starboard side. Above the hysterical laughter of the motorboat's engineer, the Coxswain blew three sharp blasts on his whistle and shouted "Hard astern!"

The old Dorman diesel stopped our headway instantly and we slowly began to make way astern. There was no sign whatsoever of the brand new cap by now and I desperately clambered onto the highest point of the short forward cabin top to command the best sighting point of the foaming white sea ahead. The cap appeared briefly once more, washed up by the urgent reverse thrust of our screw. It was just within range and I lunged madly at it again. The thrust of the boathook completely unbalanced me and I began a dive straight over the side of the boat, which I only managed to stop by clutching on frantically with my left hand.

My right side hit the sea as the boat rolled upright but I dare not let go of the boathook, which, to my absolute amazement, emerged from the water with the new Commander's cap firmly impaled on the end. The violent contact with the boathook had opened up a seam and the end of the boathook protruded through it. Suddenly, it was not funny any more and it was a rather apprehensive crew that returned the boat to the ship's side. The suppressed humour of the ship's company in hauling the boat back up to her davits was plain to see; after all it was not they that were to run the risk of the Commander's wrath.

Once aboard, I handed the damaged cap to the Coxswain, pleased to be rid of the infernal thing, and he slunk off to the bridge to reunite cap and owner. We awaited his return, or alternatively, our summons to the bridge, with some trepidation, but Hookey came back in good spirits. Apparently, the Commander was impressed at our efforts to recover the wayward cap from such a wild sea and he had taken the cap from the Leading seaman, inspected it briefly and said that it could easily be stitched up at the seam.

It was a good thing that the dunking of the expensive cap had been done on the side away from the line of sight on the ship and our skylarking had not been seen. Needless to say, the matter was an object of much humorous discussion in the mess that night.

The sea must have known that this was to be *Savage's* very last voyage on her surface of many moods, as just for a change the wind dropped and the water became as still as the proverbial village pond. The Captain had us assembled aft and addressed us concerning the future of the ship. It was hoped, he said, that she may yet be sold rather than be broken up but in the meantime, we were to decommission her at Chatham and those not sent on draft elsewhere would work under the First Lieutenant and his staff on stripping all her contents and preparing her to be cocooned for storage. Cocooning was a process whereby all the guns, radar and most external working equipment were encased in a large silver-coloured sheet which would be drawn tightly about the article, whereupon all the air would be sealed out, to preserve it. We were the last crew that *Savage* was to see.

He spoke at some length about how impressed he had been at the happiness that had been a feature of life aboard during his time on the ship, due to our keenness at our work and our good behaviour. He wished us luck wherever we went and said that he hoped to serve with us again sometime.

We responded lustily to the Coxswain's call for three cheers for the Skipper and the Captain looked really moved by it all. When we were dismissed, I stood at the rail for a long time, looking down at the sea that hissed and gurgled, bubbled and popped mysteriously in the underwater holes leading from the "Fish and Chip Shop", which terminated just beneath the bootcapping. The old girl had spent many years at sea and I wondered what she thought about it all. Had we done her justice? Had we been the best crew that she had ever known, as our Captain had implied?

A lonely gull hung effortlessly above our stern, crying plaintively in the gathering mist that swirled coldly about the surface of the limpid sea. I suddenly shuddered as a chill came over me, more from the depth of nostalgia than from the cold, and I made my way to the mess for tea. Sadly we rounded the North Foreland and Daily Orders confirmed our fears. Savage was to make passage to Chatham to "pay-off". These words meant the end of the ship's commission.

She had been a faithful old servant and had spent nearly fourteen years at sea, in the early days as a submarine chaser, convoy escort and a hunter of surface German raiders, and she had landed British spies on the Norwegian coast. Her name constantly cropped up in books about the last war. Her post-war years had been spent in the usual destroyer tasks: showing the flag, fishery protection, training men to become efficient destroyermen, Asdic operators, Gunners and Torpedomen. Yet she had done more than just these training tasks; she had brought us together as a family of sailors and integrated us as a team.

She had most certainly made a man out of at least one in my mess — me! Age had caught up with her and there was also the need to release her from the serving lists in order that she could be replaced by the newer, more sophisticated frigates and destroyers which the Navy needed to move into the requirements of the 1960s and the '70s.

We stopped briefly at Sheerness but only long enough to rig her tripod mast with her Paying-Off Pendant, a foot long for each year of her commission. It fluttered behind her like a great white bird in the cold bright air of the November morning and suddenly, I felt sad that the ship and I were to part. Joe Gregory said that it was because I was becoming "anchor-faced", meaning that I was beginning to enjoy the Navy and was "all for it!" He was close to the truth.

A little before lunch-time we entered the first of the locks into the inner basin of Chatham dockyard, where we were greeted by a cacophony of ship's sirens and hooters, each adding her own tribute to our retiring destroyer. The dockside was thronged with well wishers at our berthing point, each coming to pay their final respects to the old girl and I took care to keep clear of the gangway, lest the influx of so many visitors found me a job to do!

My calendar told me it was the 8th of November and later that day, I marked off the usual square with a green-ink pen, since it was a special occasion. Whilst we were having tea, a group of officers came in, waving at us to remain seated as they walked through and round and then out through the port passage. Perhaps they were on some sort of sentimental journey of their own and their brief promenade around the messdecks and flats, the upper deck and the superstructures, was their nostalgic farewell to what had perhaps once been home to them at one time too.

The real effect of *Savage*'s redundancy came the next morning for the Tannoy was in constant use, calling all manner of ratings to report to the ship's office for their drafting papers and it became evident that at the end of the week, the mess would be decimated to just the working party clearing up the ship and removing the stores ashore. Since none of the national servicemen in the mess received the summons to the ship's office, it was clear that we were to be that working party. One by one, *Savage*'s sailors left her:

Leading Seaman Wiltshire, Leading Seaman Chapman, the Store's Tiffy, Leading Storesman Stony Mason, Able Seaman Ray Bean, Able Seaman Cowie, Able Seaman Spike Jones. Soon they would be gone; we shook their hands, said that we would keep an eye out for them in the future and wished them luck.

With just five months left to serve in the Navy, I was naturally concerned about what may be my next step. Authority gave no indication and the next day started a pattern of hard labour, when our small skeleton crew worked on removing the stores and equipment which *Savage* would no longer require.

The foodstores were the first to be emptied. In so doing, we came across a box which, when opened, revealed a row of tins of beans in tomato sauce, bearing the date 1944. Several tins were taken into the mess for "analysis" and proved to be the best Pusser's beans that I had ever tasted. However, once our food stores were emptied, we could no longer eat on the ship and so we were officially taken onto the books at the barracks, allotted a berth to sling our hammocks and issued with the necessary paperwork to be also victualled in there.

Each morning we fell in outside Nelson Block and were marched into the dockyard to *Savage* to begin our day's toil immediately after Divisions. The comforts of RNB were much appreciated but it was strange to think that we should no longer sling our hammocks in the stuffy, crowded messdeck beneath the heaving fo'c'sle.

The messdeck on the ship, stripped of its men and its fittings, was a bare cold place. No longer did we scrub the decks or polish the scuttles, and the rexine cushions and the collapsible pine tables had disappeared on a lorry to some lonely store somewhere. We perched on the empty lockers in the steel emptiness at "Stand Easy" and quietly supped our tea. At night the ship was left to the cockroaches and the ghosts of the past.

One morning, Garth and I were detailed to empty the Spirit Store of all the empty wooden barrels that had once contained our rum rations. The barrels stood silently, stacked neatly in the store, smelling strongly of the spirit that they had once contained. I have always thought that rum smelled better than it tasted and I drank in the pleasant fumes as we parbuckled the barrels up the steep ladder to the deck above, where we rolled them onto the upper deck for collection by a lorry. Some of the barrels had been in the store for quite some time and suddenly, as we moved one toward the base of the ladder, it made a very attractive slopping sound. It was not quite empty. Had we found gold in the hills of Dakota, we could not have been more elated and I nipped away to the messdeck to find a suitable container into which we might syphon our precious find.

I was lucky that the upper deck seemed devoid of officers or NCOs, who may have asked what I was up to with two Pusser's tea cups and I slid quickly down the ladder to the spirit store. Garth had the barrel on its side and was poking his fingers into the hole and sucking his fingers, rather like a bear stealing honey from a hive. Gently we manoeuvered the cups under the barrel and rolled the hole undermost. Our efforts were rewarded by the sound of liquid trickling out and we drained the barrel completely, filling the two cups to the brim. Our concentration on this ticklish task relaxed our look-out and we nearly jumped out of our skins as something white fell with a soft "flop" onto the deck behind us.

We turned in horror to see the First Lieutenant's cap lying on the deck, where it had fallen from its owner's head as he peered upside-down from the hatch opening above us.

"What's going on here, my son?" he asked. Even upside-down, we could see the suspicious look on his face.

"Er, just checking the barrels, sir!" stammered Garth. Shiny shoes took the place of the red face and Number One came down the ladder to retrieve his cap and to investigate further.

The two guilty cups of rum stood hid behind the by now empty barrel and I contrived to place myself between the inquisitive officer and them. Jimmy was confused; a dexterity born of long practice told him that these two toe-rags were up to something but he could not quite see what it was. He watched us apply a lashing to another innocent barrel and looked for something to criticize but found nothing.

"Carry on," he said finally. "I want this store emptied by "Secure" this afternoon if possible!" and he ascended the ladder and we heard his shoes tapping off along the flat above.

We breathed again and having found a more secure hiding place for our illicit booze, spent the rest of the afternoon, sipping and lashing, hoisting and sipping, rolling and lashing, sipping and hoisting and giggling until there were just two empty cups and we were well and truly pissed! "Secure" was piped as, in a fit of laughter, we rolled the last barrel out onto the upper deck and leaned on it for support. The First Lieutenant's nostrils twitched. I am sure that he suspected something was up but he merely narrowed his eyes in our direction and we fought to control ourselves as we were fallen in to return to barracks.

On the upper deck, the dockyard maties had been unusually busy in putting the ship into "mothballs": the radar equipment, the guns, the "Fish and Chip Shop", and the various engine and ventilation intakes were all sealed with silver-coated canvas which radically changed the shape and lines of the old ship.

Eventually, after about two weeks or so of constant labour, the work on *Savage* came to an end. After "Secure" one afternoon, we were assembled on the quarterdeck and addressed by the First Lieutenant. Our work on *Savage* was complete, he told us, and he thanked us all for coping with what was essentially a very sad and mundane task in the manner that we had. It had not been easy to live on a ship and then to see her stripped and ready for the executioner at the last and it had not been a task that he had any joy in.

"Now it is finished and we are all about to go our different ways," he said. "I wish you all good luck and look forward to serving with you again perhaps in the future. Tomorrow morning, *Savage* goes out onto the trot off Gillingham until her future is finally decided. P.O. Bull with Able Seamen Cobbold, Downer and Williams will be the towing party and will assemble at the dockside at 0930 ready for the tug." Our First Lieutenant shook our hands one by one as we stepped over the brow for the last time and wished us every success. "Goodbye, my son!" he said to me. "Behave yourself and go easy with the paintbrushes!"

We marched off into the barracks, leaving *Savage* a dead, empty thing lying in the putrid dockyard water, stripped now of life and content. It was a very sad occasion and most of us had a lump in the throat that took some swallowing. My "lump" was extended to the following day when our small work party put the destroyer to the buoy in the Medway and then came ashore leaving her to float alone in the river. I remember looking over my shoulder from the deck of the tug at the pennant number, "D27", painted in black on her stern and that was to be the last I saw of her. I later heard that she was finally taken to Portsmouth and laid up a trot there for some time until she was towed to the breakers in South Wales in 1962.

Our only consolation was that we were now in the comfort of the Barracks, with good food, a regulated daily job and with a reasonable prospect for leave in hand. I had a bunk in Nelson Block alongside Garth, Jim and Seabag and many other old "Savages" and so we were not among strangers. It was not to last long. My diary shows that we remained in the barracks complex for just two days.

Our principle task was chasing fallen leaves about the various roads and pavements around the barracks and the only fun it gave me was the eventual bonfire at the end of the day. On reporting for the morning work muster on the 10th November, we were told to report to the drafting office in small batches. We queued apprehensively. Where would we be going next, we

231

wondered? The weatherbeaten old Chief sought my name on a list and ran a pencil down the list several times, missing my name on each occasion. This gave me enough opportunity to read the list upside down and to see that Garth, Jim and Seabag were also on it.

"What's yer name again, lad?" asked the Chief. I said "Cobbold" several times until he got the gist of what the word looked like and he finally found it. He beamed from ear to ear at that, as if it had been a hard task to perform and he had solved it alone and unaided.

"Cobbold!" he said, as if hearing the name for the first time. "Got it... Cobbold of this!" and he made an obscene gesture. He made himself laugh at his own joke.

"I've heard that one before," I muttered and waited for him to say where I was to be drafted.

"You're in *Obdurate* from today. Pack your gear and give your work party P.O. this chit releasing you..." and he went on to tell me about my leaving routine, and that the *Obdurate* lay at so-and-so basin in the dockyard. I had seen my new ship several times during my service and there was very little to tell her apart from *Savage*, except that *Obdurate*'s armoury was a little different and she still had her torpedo tubes amidships.

I packed my kitbag and had just finished when Garth and Jim came into the block to pack theirs also. I generally helped out in order that we may walk through the dockyard to our new posting together. We were all a bit disappointed in not having the chance to stay longer in barracks, have a bit of leave and enjoy barracks luxury a little longer, but with only some six months left to serve, perhaps it was just as well to get on another ship and hope that the time passed as well as it had on *Savage*.

It was dark as we approached *Obdurate*'s gangway and we rattled up the wooden slope and presented ourselves to the duty Quartermaster, who in turn, called out the duty P.O. He ticked our names off a list and asked the QM to pipe for one of the duty watch to conduct us to our new messdeck. Between decks, *Obdurate* was the twin of *Savage* in many respects and our journey along the port passage leading for'ard, was quite like being back on our old ship again.

As we stepped into the light and warmth of another mess, the Leading hand rose to greet us and then introduced us to the other members of the mess. Apparently we were expected, and in fact had been victualled in for supper. We were shown a hammock space and allocated lockers, and after supper, stowed our gear away and made friends with our new shipmates. Sailors are an easy-going bunch and our settling-in period was easy and without any undue hitch. I turned in after rounds and lay in my hammock writing to Pearl, giving her the details of my new address and situation.

The ship was in the dockyard for a few days, long enough to get a weekend leave in, as my new watch allocation was not the duty one, and I joined in part-of-ship working, happy in the thought that I would be off on the Friday evening on a "Friday while". Again I found myself detailed to motorboat's crew as my main task on the ship and my new Coxswain and I worked together on the motorboat most of the next day and got to know one another.

Friday and freedom finally came. I hitch-hiked home in record time from the bridge at Chatham and went straight to Pearl's house to make arrangements for the weekend. We went to the pictures on the Saturday and visited her aunt's house in Ilford on the Sunday. I had no time for cycling. The time tore past in a blur and in no time at all it was Monday morning, a quarter to five, and my struggle back to the dockyard began again. I arrived aboard to find that we were sailing that very day and we moved out of the dockyard into the cold waters of the Medway, bound for Holland and Amsterdam.

CHAPTER
THIRTEEN

Although *Obdurate* bore many similarities to *Savage*, she was a different design and was built to perform a separate function for the wartime Navy. She had been launched in early 1942 and commissioned that September, her principle task being convoy escort duties and mine-laying. Her armament was lighter than *Savage*'s; she was armed with small 4-inch guns, her mast was the new latticed design and she lacked the top speed that *Savage* had so often displayed. However, she was a force to be reckoned with. This she had demonstrated when involved in the fracas with Sherbrooke's destroyer squadron, which successfully beat off *Lutzow*, *Hipper* and six other German destroyers in defence of a convoy bound for Russia in the early days of the Second World War.

Here I was again, at sea in a Second World War destroyer, in surroundings somewhat familiar but annoyingly different in small ways and with a new band of messmates to get to know. We steamed slowly into the sheltered waters of Den Helder, entered the canal and cruised past the fishing village of Vollendam, up to Amsterdam itself. Once alongside the harbour wall, we could not wait to go ashore to sample the delights of the wonderful city. The Dutch people were very pleased to see us. If one went into a bar, there was always a smile of "welkom" and folk stopped you in the street to touch your collar for luck and to regale you with greetings in Dutch, to which we poor ignorant linguists would nod and say: "Thank you, thank you!"
We swapped our English cigarettes at the Tabac shops for boxes of Dutch cigars. The exchange rate was very much in our favour, I seem to recall, and the ship fairly reeked with cigar smoke.

Visitors came aboard and were conducted around the ship; we spent some time in making sure that all was bright and clean to impress these fastidious people. The Dutch Navy laid on a coach and took us on a tour of the dykes and villages of the country. It was here that the only sour note of our visit to Holland was struck.

It was arranged for the coach to stop at a wayside restaurant for a meal and coffee. This facility was all free and part of Dutch hospitality to us. The coffee was served in tiny, delicate china cups and a stainless steel coffee spoon adorned the saucer. These spoons bore either a daffodil or a tulip motif on them and I am ashamed to say that they were mercilessly filched as souvenirs, to such an extent that the Petty Officer in charge of the coach read us the riot act, turned all the lights out on the vehicle and arranged for his cap to be passed around in an effort to recover the missing spoons. Most were thus recovered but I don't think the incident went down well either with the Dutch Navy representative or our own ship's officers.

For we simple sailor folk, there was one great disadvantage in visiting Holland. In spite of the relatively few miles separating our two countries, we were quite unable to speak their language and in the main, they were unable to understand ours. I first drifted ashore with Garth on the Thursday evening and we made for the centre of the town, through the streams of cyclists. We found ourselves outside the imposing front of Centraal Station and then turned left down some of the side streets. Our wanderings bought us to Canal Street.

We met a gaggle of our stokers coming towards us from sampling the delights of this notorious area, where prostitutes sat in the uncurtained windows of their flats overlooking the street in various stages of undress, encouraging men to knock on their doors for sex. Apparently, the stoker's mess had contained a young lad who had, as one dour salt delicately put it, "never dipped his wick" and the mess had had a whip-round to put the twenty guilders or so together to purchase the short-time services of one of these delightful ladies.

The lad had been patrolled along the street to take his pick of the goods on display but his companions had raised all sorts of objections when he showed any interest in an even remotely attractive girl, and had finally pitched him through the portals of a house toward the eastern end of the parade. The door had slammed shut behind him with an air of finality and then, some three minutes later, according to his companion's watches, he had been ejected back into the street again, fully clothed and minus his innocence, twenty guilders and perhaps his pride. The curtains to the lady's boudour were drawn to reveal a large red-headed overweight courtesan, once more ready for trade. They had picked him the hoariest wench on the street! The tale had us in stitches but some of my laughter was tinged with a little sympathy for the slight blonde lad, who stood throughout this tale, studying the caps of his boots with glowing ears.

Our interest fired by this tale of debauchery, we started a slow reconnaissance of Canal Street. The girls sat in full view, framed in their lighted windows and dressed only in the flimsiest of undergarments. It was like a free strip-show. They either read a book or smoked a cigarette and gazed lazily out at us looking in. When a customer had made his selection, he merely approached the side door.

Usually, before he had time to knock, the door would open and only then would the girl leave her position at the window to draw the curtains, thus indicating that she was "engaged". We watched this spectacle for some time and took turns in timing the event, from the time that the curtain was drawn until the time that the client emerged back onto the street, and I believe the average time was only eight minutes. However, even this peep-show became repetitious after a while and we split into smaller groups and wandered on further.

Garth and I, fancying a drink and a sit down, slipped into a small bar bearing the legend "The Old Nickel", in one of the streets away from the main concourse and there we sat at a large round table which occupied the greater part of the interior and ordered two beers. Several Dutchmen sat at the bar and they nodded in a friendly fashion as we settled ourselves down to a well-earned rest. Garth fell into conversation with one chap and so they vacated their station at the bar and joined us at the round table. The evening began to develop into a very jolly one indeed.

We bought them a drink and they in turn bought one for us. In no time at all, the large round table was covered in empty Pilsner bottles and used glasses. No attempt was made by the barman to take away the empties and as there lurked quite a few full bottles of beer among them, we needed to drink up the existing supply before this could be done. Somehow, he did not get around to it.

We were later joined by two Merchant Navy Officers who were from a ship in the docks at Rotterdam and by this time, the table was so full of bottles that empties constantly fell off onto the floor. There was not even space for an ashtray and our cigarette ends were dropped into the empties. I became rather drunk.

My recollections of that evening cease at about ten thirty but apparently, I continued drinking and joined in with the nautical sing-song that was in progress. I became aware of travelling in a motor car later in the evening and I finally came into the land of the living aboard a merchant vessel in the docks at Rotterdam, whence I had been conveyed with Garth and our two Merchant Navy friends. A cold buffet had been prepared and we were given glasses of whisky. There was a lot of chat and laughter and, according to my friends, I joined in as enthusiastically as any and looked perfectly alright. Garth flopped back in his chair and looked extremely fragile and it seemed the right time to call it a day.

Our host, 2nd Engineer Harry Green, called a taxi for us and we all piled into the car, having thanked our friends for their hospitality and promising to call on them again whenever the opportunity to do so arose. Today I can remember the officer's name but not that of his ship! We arrived back to *Obdurate* a little after 0400 and slept soundly in our uniforms until "Call the Hands" was piped.

When I reflected that, prior to joining the Navy, my only incursion into a public house had been for an orange squash when out cycling with my club mates, I was forced to observe that my new mode of life was having a very unhealthy effect upon me and some time during the course of the very long forenoon, I again resolved to abandon the Demon Drink and to avoid contact with the interior of public houses before real harm befell me.

My resolution was severely tested over the next few days. Garth and Jim paid a return visit to the ship at Rotterdam and I chanced to meet them returning to the ship late one night. Jim had been having trouble for some time with his wife and he chose that particular evening to take the easy way out and lie down in front of an Amsterdam tram! Garth and I snatched him out of its path in good time but he was at a very low ebb and we had quite a time convincing him life was great, wife or no wife. He ended up resolving to "give her the push" next time he wrote.

It was a problem all too familiar in the Service in those days. I called it the Married Man's Syndrome. It was very hard to get a wife or girlfriend to wait for you, visits home were neither often enough nor long enough, which led to tension on both sides. This was reflected in the very high rate of divorce, separations and infidelities on both sides, and our freedom of movement and the sailors' love of sexual adventure made it no easier. The sort of temptations which came the sailor's way did little to alleviate the problem. There were all sorts of illicit affairs going on and these were not only confined to the lower deck. It was very much a Service disease and I dare say that the Army and Air Force carried the same failure rate among the married personnel.

We had one more run ashore in Amsterdam, during the Feast of St Nicholas on the 21st November. I had decided to buy Pearl a cute little bracelet made up of small, oval, enamelled shapes depicting traditional Dutch scenes in blue and white, linked together with a silver chain for her birthday on the 25th. I had spotted this object in a little jeweller's shop in the town but had to wait for another payday before venturing forth to buy it. However, with the purchase price at last in my pocket, I went ashore with some of my messmates and eventually bought the bracelet and stowed it safely away in my money-belt. The streets of Amsterdam were filled with not only the local populace but those from the provinces too. They had flocked into the city for the annual parade of St Nicholas: a local dignitary, dressed in the red robes of the historic King and led by a group of his blackamoors and several brass bands, together with other important persons and townspeople, paraded through the streets of the beautiful city, observing the old ritual of distributing sweets to the children that lined the route.

The pavements were packed to overflowing and it was a difficult task to make any progress along the streets at all, so having watched the parade pass by, we took to the side streets where the going was easier and in so doing, became utterly lost. Every turn that we made seemed to bury us even deeper in the back streets of the town and nowhere did we see any familiar landmark that might put us back on route. There were few people about and those that we saw, we feared to ask directions from, since there remained this awful language barrier but finally, after yet another false turn, we were reduced to having to ask directions.

I saw a lady approaching. She seemed to be in her middle forties and my logical thinking was that she would likely to have been in Holland during the Occupation and therefore may have some command of German.

"I'll ask this lady for the high street," I told my companions. I crossed the street toward her, aware that every eye was upon me. "Guten abend, Frau," I said for openers. The lady stopped and looked expectantly at me over the top of her bifocals. "Bitter schon, wie ist der Hoch Strasse?" I enquired. My colleagues looked from one to the other, nodding their approval. They were mightily impressed so far.

The lady took off her glasses and looked first one way and then the other up the street and in a perfect Oxford accent replied: "You go straight up there, turn to your left, take the second on your right..." Apparently, she was an English schoolteacher on holiday! The rest was lost in the bellows of laughter from my shipmates, who found the situation extremely funny. I thanked a rather bemused lady and we quickly retraced our steps back to civilisation.

The time came to leave Amsterdam and we did so with great regret. Our bows turned once more into the grey, salt waters of the North Sea and we set off at a spanking rate, heading for home. I turned in a little after midnight, having stood the evening watch as lifebuoy sentry, a miserable task if ever there was one. One stood for four hours facing aft, looking into the ship's wake astern. The idea was that should anyone fall over the side, the lifebuoy sentry would be the last person to observe his plight and would throw him a lifebelt fitted with a phosphorous flare and would then raise the alarm by sounding a klaxon nearby. Long blasts indicated that the man overboard was to starboard and short ones meant he was to port. The ship would turn hard to whichever side the man had fallen and prepare for lowering her sea boat to find the man and rescue him.

In reality, even if a man was seen to go over the side and the appropriate signal raised, either he would be lost in the vastness of the water or he would be dead from exposure to the bitter cold water by the time he was picked up. The chances of even seeing him in the dark or hearing him above the sounds of wind, sea and ship, were somewhat remote.

I remember doing an experiment on the subject one evening with Seabag. He threw a large cardboard box over the port side amidships. I did not know just when he would throw it and waited some time to see the box. I never did. The speed of the ship and the relatively small circle of illuminated water about the stern meant that the box slipped astern and out of sight in less than forty seconds from when it was thrown overboard amidships. A man falling over the side would hardly have time to break surface in that time and all he would see would be the ships stern-light roaring away into the distance, leaving him to a lonely, cold, panic-stricken death.

However, I always took the job very seriously, afraid that I might have it on my conscience should such a dreadful thing occur during my watch. My eyes suffered badly from straining into the salt-laden darkness looking for the slightest object. I do remember once spotting something in the dark but just as I was about to hurl the lifebelt and press the alarm button, a roosting seagull, glowing faintly white in the darkness, took off from the sea. It was a frightening moment that I never forgot.

We awoke to a cold, rough sea and it was immediately obvious that we were no longer heading for the east coast. Land lay at about eight miles off to the port quarter; we were going north. Daily Orders, however, stated that we would pick up our buoy at Sheerness at 1600 and so we did not panic over much but as the day drew on and there was no change of course, serious doubts crept in as to our destination. We finally turned one hundred and eighty degrees just after tea-time and then our speed fell considerably. It was unlikely that we should see Sheerness that evening. It was another irritation that we had to suffer.

Tired as I was, I could not turn in for the night as there was to be a film show on my messdeck. I slunk off to the Boy's messdeck aft and sat playing cards and "uckers", a nautical version of Ludo, until after Rounds at 2100 and then returned to witness the closing scenes of an atrocious Abbott and Costello film before finally slinging my hammock in the fo'c'sle.

Sheerness and Garrison Point were reached just before "Stand Easy" the following morning. A long low fog surrounded the coast line and we crept in on a sea as calm as a mill-pond, using our radar. It bought us unerringly to our buoy, the whaler was slipped with the buoy-jumping crew and they pulled the heavy anchor cable to the ring of the buoy by means of a steel hawser. The massive shackle was attached and the telephone socket on the buoy was connected by means of a jack-plug to the ship's telephone cable. This, we always maintained, was so that the officers could telephone their tailors or girlfriends in London. We were never allowed to use the facility.

Our boats were then lowered and these circled the ship until the quarter-deckmen had run out the boats boom aft. This boom was merely a large varnished pole that protruded from the starboard after quarter and it carried a lot of wires and Jacob's ladders, which were used as a means for the duty boat's crews to man their boats from the ship's deck.

As my "part of ship duties" were as bowman to the motorboat, I would work all day on the boat, scrubbing it out in the morning to the Coxswain's satisfaction, polishing what brass fittings she was equipped with and acting as the bowman whenever she set off on a trip and came back alongside again. It was drummed into me that a ship is often judged by the standard of her boat and her boat's crew. We wore No. 2s and plimsoles and executed our boat drills and manoeuvres to the highest standard, aware that the eyes of other ships in the anchorage were upon us at all times.

Any errors were zealously reported to our Officer of the Day by his counterpart officers of other vessels who chanced to spot them. It was often with great delight, and at great length that these small errors would be reported. It was said that some young "snotties", a slang word for young trainee Midshipmen, spent the majority of their watch observing the actions of other ship's boats. The Aldis lamps winked constantly, transmitting morse-code messages from ship to ship and we always worried that the messages may refer to us when out on a trip.

The air was cold, damp and still and a rose-red sun tried its best to make something of the day, to no avail. Just before dusk at 1600, great banks of fog rolled in up the river Medway and the duty watch posted double the normal look-outs and the usual fog warnings were put into effect. This involved siting the ship's bell up on the fo'c'sle, where it was rung vigorously for a period of time, between which the look-outs would strain their ears for any sounds of an approaching vessel.

In those days, quite a number of vessels used the river for commercial purposes and these would steam slowly down the fairway, announcing their presence with long mournful blasts of their sirens. Our bell-ringing declared that we were a vessel at anchor off the fairway and their sirens indicated that they were a steamship under way but I was always apprehensive in thick fog, fearing that a ship would wander out of the navigation channel and run into us in the grey darkness.

At that time of the year, fog often hung about the coastline for days on end, which it now chose to do and we became virtual prisoners on the ship. The postman could neither get ashore with our mail nor recover mail for us from the Post Office ashore and, of course, nor could our itchy feet get ashore either.

There was no time to sit about loafing; the First Lieutenant saw to that. Frost or no frost, ice or no ice, there were plenty of steel ship's plates to scrub and miles of brass rails and instruments to polish on the bridge. Often I would start polishing the brass at the port side of the bridge and having got to the starboard side, be called upon to start again on the fog-dampened brass on the port side again! It was a good time to have an extra careful scrub out down in the messdecks and we worked under the supervision of our Leading hands on scrubbing and polishing, until all the decks were squeaky clean and the scuttles shone like gold by the lights of the messdeck lamps. New Turk's heads would be spliced to adorn the stanchions supporting the deck-heads and our pine tables would be burnished white. It was after all, our home for more than five days of the week on average and it is fair to say that we were very proud of keeping it clean and tidy, not only because it was our duty so to do, but because we had a pride in the mess.

It was also a good time to thoroughly overhaul our washing and ironing and to get our uniforms into tip-top order, a task somewhat neglected at sea. Sometimes of an afternoon, a pipe would be made, "Secure, hands to go to make and mend, stand fast duty watch!" All men not on duty were then, in effect, given the afternoon off to attend to their outstanding darning, sewing and ironing and the men on duty usually got time off when their watch was finished. Such privileges were, however, quite rare!

I looked out of the scuttle on the fourth day and still saw no shore lights where shore lights should have been. The fog swirled thick and damp as before. Our ship's boats hung from their painters as if on a sheet of grey glass and had even a feather touched the surface of the river, it would have sent out a ripple. We were full of hope that a "Make and mend" may be piped for the afternoon.

My kit was by now in first class condition and I intended a good "kip" on the cushions for the afternoon. It was not to be. During the mid-morning, our Captain and Engineering Officer suddenly appeared on the quarterdeck, dressed in their very best uniforms and looking very "tiddly". To our surprise, a harbour launch from the dockyard suddenly loomed up through the grey curtain surrounding us.

"Ahoy, *Obdurate*?" called the bowman.

"Aye, *Obdurate!*" I answered. I was in the motorboat, pumping out and cleaning.

The launch tucked quickly under our officer's gangway, as if the Coxswain of the vessel thought that he may lose sight of us if he had to make another run in. Our two officers boarded her and she set of with them into the fog. I listened to the sound of her twin Gardener engines for what seemed like ages through the fog and then they were gone. This event had an air of mystery about it and several "buzzes" started. However, we all returned to our daily tasks and no "Make and mend" was piped.

I was glad to leave the upper deck at "Secure" at 1600 but I had the Last Dogwatch on the fo'c'sle as a look-out on fog watch, which further employed me from 1800 to 2000. I came down with the ringing of the ship's large brass bell repeating in my ears, to find that my enthusiastic ringing of this instrument of warning to other vessels made me quite hard of hearing for the next few hours! I amused myself with a count-up of the remaining unmarked squares on my graph. I slapped Garth on the back: "Only one hundred and thirty-one days to go before you and I hit civvy street, mate!"

A strong breeze sprang up during the night and upon looking out of the scuttle first thing next morning, I was treated to a perfect view of the cranes and buildings that constituted *HMS Wildfire* at Sheerness.

"Don't know what you're cheerful about, Cobby," said Jim. "No fog means that we are bound to steam off somewhere without getting any leave!"

Daily Orders did not say that we were going anywhere, and perhaps it was as well that we did not, for a force nine gale ripped down the river and the water was rough enough for the ship's boats to be hauled up on their davits, although not swung in. The movement below was only slight, thank goodness, and I only pretended to be seasick for the amusement of my colleagues.

The Captain returned with the Engineering Officer the following day. We sailed in the afternoon, our destination being Portsmouth and we duly arrived after punching a head sea that failed to make me sick for a change. It was bitterly cold on deck as we stood in line for entering harbour and a real comfort to get below to the stuffy warmth of the messdeck.

We slowly steamed up the Solent on a miserable, damp, chill morning. The Needles and the coastline of the Isle of Wight were glimpsed, but briefly, through the cold mist that wreathed itself, phantomlike over the surface of the sea. We tied up alongside in Portsmouth once more.

Garth, Joe, Gregory and I went to the pictures in the evening and tried half-heartedly to chat up two girls in the row behind. I quickly gave up; one girl was wearing a wedding ring — trouble! In any case, my courtship with Pearl was going quite well; she wrote frequently and her letters were interesting. Her family were very friendly and we seemed to be getting along very well. I really had no need to spoil things by any further involvements. I was looking forward to a nice weekend at home, with possibly a bit of warm sunshine, the opportunity to get the bike out and go for a bit of a ride and an evening or two out with Pearl.

We came out of the cinema and met a group of our shipmates, a little the worse for wear. They were on their way to a tattoo parlour that was still open in the town and so we fell in with them. We found ourselves outside a converted shop, the front window plastered with photographs of the designs that one may choose from. The interior was likewise papered with brilliantly coloured pictures of various tattoos. The tattooist, a greasy-looking Teddy-boy, blew the ash from the cigarette between his lips and looked at us from under his eyebrows.

"Take a seat, be with you in a minute". He was colouring in a dragon on the back of a Royal Marine who, stripped to the waist, was too drunk to care. I sat gazing up at the transfers and the photographs of people actually under the needle of the tattooist; they all looked drunk to me. There was a plump, redheaded girl in one photograph, naked to the waist except for a rather soiled-looking towel draped over one fat breast, while the other was in the process of being tattooed. The design was a black panther and the outline was being inked in with a needle that dribbled black ink over the end of her nipple. It all looked very painful.

"Are you going to have one, Cobby?" I was asked.

"No, thanks!" was my immediate reply.

The tattooist looked up from his work on the Marine's bloodstained back. His lip curled back over his yellow teeth in a sort of friendly grin which managed to look more like a snarl.

"Yer don't know what yer missin'," he said. "It don't 'urt, do it?" he asked the Marine.

"Nah!" was all the reply he got. I suspect that some of the effect of his customer's Dutch courage may have been wearing off.

The portrait completed and covered with a sheet of tissue paper, the rather pale Bootneck vacated the chair and one of our crew took his place, baring his upper arm. The artist rooted among the selection of needles scattered about the top of a small table littered with bottles of ink, tissue paper, drawings of tattoos, coffee cups and an overflowing ashtray, until he found the needle colour that he required, flipped the old one from the vibrating head of the tattooing machine and dug straight into the living flesh. I winced. The victim winced and someone said: "F*** that!"

The tattooist grin-snarled again. "It don't 'urt, do it?" he asked. Between clenched teeth our shipmate hissed: "Nah!" That was the closest I ever came to being tattooed.

We left the tattoo parlour and hung about a mobile coffee stall, reluctant to return to the ship. We stood drinking what passed for coffee until the clock on the Guildhall boomed one and the stall owner passed among us pushing a large stiff broom, sweeping the discarded cigarette ends into a metal dust pan. A Naval Patrol strolled authoritatively past. We all avoided their gaze and when they had finally disappeared from sight, returned our plastic mugs to the tea-stained counter and made our way back to the dockyard.

Wednesday dawned cold and misty and it tried to snow, but all that would fall from the heavens were the occasional bursts of sleet. The paintwork of the superstructure required scrubbing, or so the "Jimmy" said. It looked alright to me. I was issued with a scrubber, a bucket of Teepol, and crystals. I set about trying to make the paint look brighter.

The ship's butcher set up his wooden chopping block and tools, using the Seaboat locker as a table as he always did, and hung a fresh carcass up at the port davit, ready for the daily meat issues to the cooks of the messes. "Meat issues are now being made on the upper deck Port side," announced the Tannoy.

Our butcher was a qualified man; he had been on a butchery course and was very proud of his ability to cut and weigh the meat issues to the cooks of the mess. You told him how many men you had to victual for and he could cut off their ration with the flick of a sharp knife or one blow of a meat cleaver. When the cut was put into the scales for weighing, he was seldom more than an ounce or two out.

The "Jimmy" chanced along on his constant tour of the upper decks and working parties. He stopped to watch the performance. I did not actually hear what was said but it was apparent that he made some remark to the butcher about the way in which he performed his duties. I heard raised voices.

"'Ave you done a butchery course, then?" demanded the butcher.

"Well no..." began the First Lieutenant.

"Well piss off and stop interfering!" growled a very red-faced butcher. There was a pregnant pause. There was about to be a big confrontation, which the butcher would regrettably get the worst of; demonstrating a hot temper was not the right thing to do to an officer. I felt that I should help him out of the situation if at all possible. There was hardly a second to think, but what was needed was a diversion and so I kicked over my bucket of lukewarm scrubbing water in the direction of the aggravated parties. The butcher avoided the approaching tide of water very easily by swinging his rump up on the Seaboat locker and pulling his legs out of the way. The First Lieutenant had no room to move, so he faced the sloshing grey water and rocked back to the heels of his shoes, thus avoiding getting a bootful.

The cooks of the mess, queueing for their meat issues, fared worst of all. There were too many people standing in a confined space and they trod on each other's toes in their efforts to avoid getting their feet wet. The language was not nice but I sprang forward with profuse apologies and began mopping up the mess. In that brief minute or two, our hot-tempered butcher had time to recant. He turned to the First Lieutenant.

"Well, sir," he muttered. "When I was on my butchery course, the Chief said that we were to ..." The fresh tone of respect in his voice gave the "Jimmy" time to reconsider his action. He listened to the point that the butcher made and then argued a point or two of his own. Our butcher stuck to his point, but with respect this time, and the "Jimmy" ended the conversation by adding that he should pick his words carefully when taking issue with a senior officer, to which the butcher mumbled: "Yes, sir, sorry, sir!"

Thus did peace return to the upper deck and when I had finished listening to the tirade of "silly sods" directed at me for my tricks with the bucket, I went for a refill of Teepol and continued my tasks. Later, someone poked me in the back and I turned to see the "Jimmy" glaring at me in mock anger.

"I don't need you to play diplomat, either!" he said.

"No, sir," I answered with a grin.

Christmas week was fast approaching and the Admiralty did not let us down. Their Lordships knew how important it was that we poor sailors got home for Christmas leave and they accordingly ordered us round to our home port of Chatham. Celebrations began with the hoisting of the traditional Christmas tree to the masthead, where the electricians clambered aloft to wind a festoon of coloured lights amid the branches of the small tree.

Again, I was lucky; I had first leave and would be home for Christmas Eve and the seven days of Christmas, but back aboard for the New Year. Even the grumpiest man cheered up and passed his fags around when leave was announced! With travel warrant, pay and leave pass safely stowed away, I left the ship and made my way home casually. The London tube trains were filled with office workers also on their merry way home to start the festivities, and my collar was constantly tugged by "luck-seekers", who believed my story that the luck did not work unless you also kissed the owner of the collar! It worked every time but I did not always claim the kiss; it rather depended on the desirability of the lady!

I spent Christmas Eve at Pearl's house, where her family celebrated right royally. We had Christmas Day at my home, having to walk both ways from her house to mine, since there was no transport available. It was, I recall, a jolly good time in spite of the cold weather.

We went to a dance at the Ilford Palais and rode home to Redbridge in style in a taxi through a snowstorm that I hoped would prevent my returning to my ship by a day or two. But the promising piles of snow quickly turned to slush in a warm, westerly breeze and I had to get up, bloated with turkey and Christmas cheer, at a quarter to five one morning, my leave having expired, and trudge back to the ship for the New Year.

I arrived at the end of the first part of my journey at the entrance to the Tilbury ferry at about a quarter to six. The ferry had just left the Gravesend side of the river and was making a slow, crab-like passage across the fast current of the Thames towards us. My attention was taken by a young chap struggling with the weight of a large motorcycle on the rather slippery, frosty surface and I offered to give him a hand. We man-handled the large machine up the ramp and aboard the ferry and fell into conversation as the boat retraced its way across the cold river. The motorcyclist was a Royal Marine, stationed in Chatham at the Kitchener Barracks and the powerful bike was his mode of transport from his Dagenham home to the barracks. However, he told me, he was shortly to be posted to Malaya and the bike would have to be sold.

I was offered a lift into Chatham and, cold or not, the chance to ride on such an interesting motorbike was one that I found impossible to refuse. The fact that the bike had no kick-start and that I was needed to give it a push to start it (possibly being the reason leading to the offer of the lift), did not escape my notice but I was happy to assist. The bike fired up with a throaty roar that threw a strange thrill through me and I clambered onto the tiny pillion seat and clung on for dear life as the machine shot off up the road as if it were rocket-powered.

The road about me, and the light traffic for that time of the morning, became a tear-filled blur as we threaded our way out of the streets of Gravesend and onto the A2, heading toward the Medway Towns. I got my breath back as the large speedometer showed that we had slowed from nearly seventy miles per hour to a seemingly sedentary thirty as we thundered across the Rochester bridge and I was, by then, thoroughly in love with that machine.

Cold and stiff, I dismounted outside the Marine barracks and enquired of my new friend just how much he had in mind to ask for the motor cycle. "Twenty pounds," was his reply. Twenty pounds was a lot of money. I took his name and mess number and said that I would think about it. Think about it I did; all I could see in my mind's eye was the 1921 650cc single cylinder AJS, with me in the saddle, roaring swiftly to and from Chatham, cutting my travelling time in half, while I enjoyed the speed and thrill of the ride to boot.

By the end of the first week, I had raided my Post Office book and withdrawn the twenty pounds and a further six pounds for the insurance, grateful that the bike was already road-taxed, as otherwise I would have been unable to buy it on my limited funds. I took the money into the Marine Barracks, fearful that such a beautiful machine had already been snatched up by someone else but it was not sold and I was delighted to hand over my money.

After giving me the documents and taking my cash, my Marine friend pushed from behind and I thundered off up the road, largely out of control until I had become used to the weight and balance of my new steed. I drove it at a moderate speed home to Hainault and left it in the garden shed with strict instructions that my brothers were not to interfere with it. Since my immediate younger brother was, by now, in the Royal Air Force doing his spell of national service, I had little to fear from that quarter but my smallest brother was renowned as an inveterate machine diddler and severe threats had to be made to ensure the safety of my new acquisition.

I looked forward to a weekend at home, when I could get the feel of the new machine and do some improvements on it. Her Majesty's Navy had other plans, however, and when the second leave had returned by the opening week of January 1957, our Daily Orders had us instructed to sea.

We left the large dockyard buildings astern on our way down the Medway on the first leg of our journey and Chatham disappeared in a light screen of white snowflakes. Once clear of Garrison Point and out into the Thames Estuary, the snow did not seem too heavy; visibility was about two to three miles, but as we rounded the North Foreland, the darkening sky burst into heavy snow showers. They came in great swirls, for all the world like a child bursting a feather pillow.

As darkness came, the snow came in earnest and swept in devilish whirls along the upper deck. It became so dense that all that could be seen of the after superstructure deck-lights was a faint yellow glow. The ship slowed to about eight knots or so. The "clutter" on the radar screens made reading that vital instrument impossible; all look-outs were doubled and the ship began sounding her siren, as she would in thick fog. Just for once, fortune smiled on me. I was on duty during the Evening Watch and at midnight, I was free to turn in for the night and to let someone else worry about the ship. The look-outs complained of being totally blinded by the falling snow and the ship slowed again.

Obdurate had an open bridge configuration as had the old *Savage*, with a canvas screen mounted in the front to deflect the wind. The snow was so heavy that it was impossible to see from one side of the bridge to the other and as I left to come off watch, I could not help but feel really sorry for the Navigator and the bridge staff, who would now be responsible for our safety as they steered the ship onward into the kaleidoscope of wildly swirling snowflakes. Nevertheless, I slept like a pig and awoke to a freezing morning and an orange sun trying hard to penetrate the falling snow. The ship pitched fore and aft in the long rollers of the Channel and our speed of some five or six knots was not enough to iron out our discomfort.

"Hands to fall in for work" was not piped that day; instead, we all turned to relieving the watches to enable them to stand down at regular intervals to get a hot drink or a meal and to warm their frozen hands and faces. The wind, although not strong in nautical terms, was very cold with a vicious bite to it and a half-hour spell at look-out was enough for anyone. The mess was filled with people trying to get warm and the teapot hardly ever got cold.

Since the sea breaking over the upper deck amidships was freezing into great ice slabs, a party was detailed to chip these away and the area was designated out of bounds; all trips aft were made via the catwalks between superstructures. Towards late afternoon, our position according to Able Seaman "Tug" Wilson was given as somewhere eight miles off the eastern end of the Isle of Wight, but the snow again obliterated any visual objects. We were really guessing our position by a sextant shot at noon and our estimated course and last position.

The radar plot looked like an early television set without the aerial plugged in and no targets could be seen, although one ship was reported by a very experienced operator and we felt proud of him when a small coaster, blowing her siren, passed down our starboard side at half a mile.

Supper was a very crowded affair; the sea had abated somewhat and everyone from the off duty watches seemed to pick our mess to sit in. It was the least that we could do to ask them to bring their suppers with them and some eighty men sat listening to our radio with their dinners on their laps in a messdeck normally occupied by eighteen.

The news had just filtered from the bridge that we were about to make a turn at the Needles and steam up to Southampton until the weather cleared when, as if by magic, it stopped snowing and a brilliant moon burst out of a dark velvet sky. All was activity on the bridge; our position was immediately checked and confirmed, the radar set came back to life and we began to pick up speed, quickly working up to our twenty-two knots cruising speed. It was rough in the Atlantic but at least we were able to see where we were and more importantly, were able to be seen ourselves.

The huge hump of the Isle of Arran was never more welcome a sight and as we approached the entrance to the Clyde on a cold bright Sunday morning, we sang lustily the words of the "Sailor's Hymn" at our Church Parade. "For those in peril on the sea..." It was not only a rough sea that the sailor had to fear; the thought of steering blind in so congested a waterway as the English Channel still fills me with dread.

We came alongside at Greenock. Having settled the ship down, we secured from the upper deck and Sunday continued as normal. Sunday was the strangest day of the week in the Navy. We were allowed just half an hour's lie-in; "Call the Hands" was piped at 0730. Most of the morning would be spent initially in clearing up the messdecks and scrubbing out the passage-ways, heads and washroom and then we would be piped to Sunday Divisions, which were followed by "Stand Easy" and then "Secure". This was a very prim and proper parade, the officers in their best and we in ours. On special Sundays, medals would be worn.

After devotions on the quarterdeck (usually a very simple affair where the lesson would be read by the Captain and the service led by the Jimmy, since we did not carry a Padre), we would return to the messdecks and almost immediately afterwards, "Up Spirits" would be piped. The ritual of issuing the "grog" would then occupy the next half hour or so, during which time great preparations would be in hand for dinner. The cook of the mess, assisted by many hungry volunteers, would appear from the galley, bearing the various metal fannies containing the dinner.

Sunday lunch was possibly the best meal of the week, consisting, as it did, of a joint of beef or lamb and all the vegetables needed to give the plate colour. Our mess Leading hand usually cut the joint and put it out on the plates and the cook of the mess and his volunteers would add the potatoes, gravy, tinned peas, cabbage or green beans as necessary. Silence would rein whilst eighteen pairs of jaws consumed that veritable feast but there would be more to follow.

The sweet was usually a surprise which the cook of the mess, who was responsible for it, would reveal to no-one. Sometimes it would turn out to be a humble offering of tinned fruit topped by evaporated milk but sometimes a really smashing jam roly-poly or, heaven help us, a spotted dick would grace our table. You could never tell, but if one of the older hands was cook of the mess for a Sunday, the chances of such a delight were higher than most. I always did my humble best to turn on a good sweet sticky pudding to round off Sunday lunch.

We would finish with a hot mug of tea and after the table was cleared and all the crockery stowed away in the messtrap, out would come the cigarettes and the occasional cigar and we would be at peace with the world. From Franklin Ingleman and "Family Favourites", we would slowly slip into the haze of a bloated sleep. You were entitled to sling your hammock and sleep the rest of Sunday afternoon away if you so desired and a majority did just that, unless we were in sunny climes, when the upper deck and superstructures would be littered with inert forms. As you could imagine, this peaceful routine could well be spoiled if we were at sea by the fact that there were still watches to be conducted and many a good meal, when collected from standing on the hotplate in the galley for some time, was not quite the same. Then again, there were the days when the sea was so rough that the last thing one wanted was a Sunday roast!

Come tea-time, the tea would be wetted and cook of the mess would make everyone a mug of tea. This would be a general signal for all rested bodies to arise and join the human race again and most did. Those that did not were in peril from the messdeck wags who delighted in playing pranks on their sleeping shipmates. One little trick was to see how long it took to make a chappie wake up with a desire to "spend a penny". The "prompters" stationed themselves under the victim's hammock and tried one of two well-tried and tested methods. If the sleepers hand hung over the side of his hammock, his hand would be carefully plunged into a jug of cold water to the wrist. This had to be done very carefully so as not to touch the sleeper with the sides of the jug and perhaps cause him to wake.

Having dunked the hand in cold water, the process would be repeated with a jug of luke-warm water, which often stirred the sleeper into thinking that a good pee would not come amiss and he would swing out of his hammock and make for the heads, puzzling as to how his hand had suddenly become so wet! The second method, and by far the more successful, would be the pouring of water from one jug into another in close proximity to the sleeper's ear. It was never known to fail.

Another jolly jape was to unlash a messmate's hammock very carefully and without waking the occupant, carry it and its occupant from the mess and relash it somewhere far away from its place of origin — the further the better. The bewilderment on the sleeper's face when waking up, perhaps on the upper deck or in an entirely different messdeck, always led to fits of laughter.

Sunday tea would be a toast and butter affair, if that, but the cook of the mess would start preparing supper. It was a good chance for us beginners to learn culinary skills and I always liked to assist in these functions. Supper was also a cooked meal. It usually consisted of fried foods, chips being the principle ingredient. The disappointment of not being at home on a Sunday was somewhat assuaged by this repast.

The evenings were very convivial affairs. There would be the radio to listen to, letters to write and the messdeck wags to entertain us. Usually, one of the chaps would have a mouth-organ and during my time in *Obdurate* a guitar, sporting only two strings, lay about the messdeck and I taught myself to play a few primitive tunes on it. No-one knew who owned it; it was just always there.

If there was a jolly thigh-slapping tune on the radio, someone would hop up and give an exhibition of "stanchion dancing". Stanchion dancing was performed by holding, with one hand, one of the stanchions supporting the deckhead and then doing a sort of tap-dance, where one kept at least one foot permanently on the deck, and rocked the foot back and forth to produce a tapping sound. Some men were very proficient at it.

Sometimes we were lucky enough to have a film show on one of the messdecks and we took it in turns to be host-mess for the projector and screen. "Pipe down" would usually be made at 2230 but the lights often stayed on longer with card schools and "uckers" championships going on, and it would be midnight before the ship went to sleep.

CHAPTER
FOURTEEN

The Febuary of 1957 found us in the dockyard at Chatham and I enjoyed a long weekend leave at home. That particular weekend threw every conceivable mixture of weather at me, if I remember correctly. I arrived home like a drowned rat on the Friday evening and then got thoroughly soaked again on my journey to Pearl's house, which, since the motorbike would not start, had to be done on the bus. The Saturday was little better, not so wet but windy, damp and cold and I had to squat outside the garden shed as there was no room inside to move around the motorbike in my quest for the reason for its non-starting.

A wire disconnected from the coil was the answer and she bumped into life in the first few yards on the hill outside the house. I roared off along the road, throwing my leg over the saddle in the manner of Geoff Duke at the start of the Isle of Man TT Races. It was too cold and slippery to go far, however, and so the bike went back into the shed to await sunnier days.

I went to the pictures that evening and then walked Pearl home for a coffee and a snog! We arranged to meet the following day for a walk about the shops in Ilford. The dusting of snow that greeted our efforts chased us into an ice cream parlour where we drank coffee to keep warm. We then went to my house for tea and I walked Pearl home in the evening, through streets covered in a thin layer of snow which turned quickly to a slippery slush.

My intentions to return to Chatham on the motorbike wavered but when, at five o'clock the next morning, I looked out to test the lie of the land, I found that the snow had gone. I decided to take a chance. My one problem was whether we might sail with insufficient notice for me to return the motorbike home and I would have to leave it in the dockyard. I did not relish leaving it alone and unattended there until my return, which could be a considerable time.

It started instantly and thundered effortlessly along the road to Romford. My route was the familiar one: through Romford and the back of Dagenham, along the A13 to Tilbury, across the ferry to Gravesend and then down the A2 to Chatham. It was very cold. My face froze, my eyes watered endlessly and I needed all my concentration to master the machine, since it was really much too big for someone of my slight stature.

I approached a roundabout at Dagenham too quickly and before I knew where I was, the machine went one way and I the other. Too frozen to be hurt, I picked myself up, glad that there was no-one about to witness my predicament, and hauled the great machine upright. My next difficulty would be in starting it by pushing the infernal thing but to my delight, it fired immediately and I hauled in the clutch, revved it up to keep it alive and climbed stiffly back onto the saddle. It was then that I noticed my knee protruding through the front of my best uniform! I reached the ferry, cold and damp and not a little cheesed off.

As I waited for the boat to come in, I met my old English teacher from my time at Gearies Secondary Modern School. Mr Last was now the headmaster of a school in Gravesend. He recognised me straight away and my delight in meeting him and having the chance to chat as we crossed the river together took the anxiety out of my situation, for I was rather apprehensive at what authority may say when they saw my ruined uniform trousers. I bade Mr Last farewell at Gravesend, where several matelots gave me an enthusiastic shove to start me and I snaked off up the hill with a wave of my gloved hand. The heavy machine had a mind of its own and I was hard put to control its tendency to slide sideways at the slightest touch of the rear brake. It was an excellent way to put on muscles in the shoulders, hips and forearms and I was quite exhausted by the time I entered the downward slope of the Khyber Pass.

I throttled back and raced down through the gears, hoping that the weight of the bike would be centralised when I finally came to stop or I would surely fall off, no doubt to the amusement of the sailors streaming through the dockyard gate and the adjacent barrack entrance. I was lucky. I effected an excellent stop at the dockyard gate, where I offered my paybook for inspection.

The dockyard policeman looked briefly at my "mug-shot", my torn trousers and dishevelled appearance and decided that I had trouble enough without him adding to it by asking for an entry permit for the machine. He waved me through. I parked the bike on the jetty alongside *Obdurate*. It was just ten minutes to eight. I was battered, frozen solid and quite weary.

The Petty Officer of the watch greeted me at the top of the gangway. He looked me up and down and to my absolute surprise, handed me my station card without comment. I was free to go for'ard and shift into the rig of the day. However, as I made my way to the mess, I met the Quarterdeck P.O. and as he asked how I came to be in such a state, I told him the tale from start to finish.

"Well," he said in conclusion. "You had best get changed and then get along to the sick bay and get those scratches seen to." I needed no second bidding and they kept me hanging about until "Stand Easy" was piped, having given me a letter for the M.O. in the barracks. I finally returned a little before lunch-time with my gravel-rash and grazes neatly patched up.

Obviously, I would have to replace the damaged uniform and so I awaited the next visit from Gieves, the naval tailors. There were various Naval Tailoring Companies that employed salesmen who used to call on all the ships in the principle ports, selling anything from a new sailor suit to a present for the wife and I was measured up and paid my first instalment by naval allotment for a "tiddly" suit of No. 1s, complete with a zip down the front of the jumper. I had this uniform within three days and very good it was too, much better fitting and more comfortable than the old Pusser's issue.

I roared home the following weekend in beautiful sunshine, wearing my No. 2s in case of accidents, and once home, the bike stayed where it was until I could be sure of more clement weather!

I failed to read Daily Orders upon my return but went to the mess to change into No. 8s, ready for work. It was there that I heard that we were to visit Amsterdam again and that we would sail the following morning. I liked Amsterdam and was quite excited at the prospect.

Our day passed slowly enough. We chatted about our weekend leave, chipped rust, applied paint and enjoyed the usual corned beef hash. Since finances were at an all-time low, I decided not to go ashore, but helped prepare supper and tidy up the mess, turning in before rounds at 2100 to read the latest letter from Pearl.

It snowed overnight on the 17th February and the bridge staff had to sweep the white overcoat from the binnacle and other bridge equipment before we could be ready to sail.

With the boilers steamed up to pressure, the instruction to cast off our springs came and I was employed on the quarterdeck in the hauling in and stowing away of the thick, cold, stiff wire ropes that secured us to the dockside. Regulations stated that all ropes and wires were to be worked with the bare hands but one of our team wore an old pair of industrial gloves on this occasion as protection against the bitter cold and the ice in the "lay" of the wires. We started the process of hauling in the spring, hand over hand; all went well at first until suddenly a wire snag caught in our comrade's glove.

His hand was hot inside the glove; he struggled to remove it, to no avail, and as the glove was firmly impaled on the wire snag, he was eventually dragged along with the wire toward the fairlead through which the former was to pass. His initial mumbled curses gave way to panic as it became apparent that unless he broke free shortly, he was about to lose a set of fingers, a hand or even an arm and he suddenly thrashed about in an effort to escape the ensnaring wire. The bridge were meanwhile shouting for the spring to be cast off, as the weight of the ship would soon be upon it. Wire ropes go with an awful crack and can whiplash a man in half should he be in the way.

I rushed forward, pulling out my sailor's knife, to attempt to cut the glove from the wire, since the victim was unable to do more than struggle single-handed but as I did so, the glove tore open with a loud rip and the man went one way and the crew straining on the now "loaded" wire, let go and fell the other. The dockyard matie on shore swiftly cast the eye of the spring from the bollard and the crisis was over. We meekly hauled in the wire and marked the place where the snag was, where the wire would eventually be replaced.

Our colleague nursed a rather bruised hand and wrist and suffered a verbal earbashing from the Quarterdeck P.O. but the bridge were none the wiser and there were no repercussions from the incident.

We waved at the small audience of friends and relatives that lined the pier at Gillingham as we steamed slowly down the Medway to Sheerness and the open sea. The North Sea greeted us with a cold easterly wind and a short chop which we took on our starboard side relentlessly. We seemed to steam irritatingly slowly across the swell, which caused a sickening roll. I managed to hang on to my stomach, however, but I was mightily glad when the following morning the coastline came closer and we could see the cranes and derricks of the waterway leading to the port of Amsterdam.

The bright lights of the city took us ashore in the evening and we had a tour of the by now familiar bars and cafés that we had discovered during our earlier visit in November of the previous year. In spite of being almost flat broke, I somehow succeeded in getting fairly well sloshed and had to take a seat outside Centraal Station until I had sobered up enough to return to the ship, which I did in the early hours of the next morning. So much for my earlier resolution concerning the demon drink!

Since my pockets were now completely empty, I had to curtail my trips ashore to what was provided free and fortunately, there was reasonable provision for ratings in my condition. Payday was expected the next Friday and we were scheduled to remain in Amsterdam until the Monday morning, so I planned a trip into Canal Street on the Saturday to see the sights, followed by "big eats" and a few beers.

I went ashore with a coach party and played football against a Dutch side from some unpronounceable town outside Amsterdam. I went on a tour of the museums and art galleries, gazing in critical manner at works by van Gogh and other Dutch artists as a guest of some obscure religious organisation and went to a tea party laid on by a local "Save a Soul a Day" outfit. That was the nickname that we applied to this kindly organisation, since it also had a long name in Dutch, with lots of gutteral sounds which we could never get to pronounce. I also booked a seat on a free tour organised for us by the Dutch Navy, in spite of our disgraceful performance as their guests on the previous occasion. Thus was I fully employed until payday would allow me to make my own tour arrangements.

There was quite a list of bodies wishing to go on the coach tour and in fact, it was so popular that there had to be two separate tours. I was put on the one for the Saturday. I did not mind too much, as it was generally thought that the coach would return by the early evening in any case and I would then have time for supper before going ashore.

We piled into the coach in our best suits. Our first stop was at a small museum on a dyke somewhere, where we were shown how the Dutch had managed to reclaim so much of Holland from the sea. From there, we motored through a village where the inhabitants wore their national costume all the time and we stopped to have the reasons for the style of dress explained to us. One of the Stokers put a bit of blight on the proceedings by asking the Dutch guide if he might see what the young ladies wore under their national costumes but, fortunately, the Dutchman's English was fairly limited and we were able to save his embarrassment by rephrasing the question to make it a different one entirely.

Once back on the coach, we drove for some miles across the flat, frosty countryside, dotted here and there by tiny hamlets of pretty, blunt-roofed houses. We seemed to be approaching a large complex ahead looking rather like a large Kew Gardens greenhouse. I overheard the chaps in front of me discussing it. It was the Bovenkarspel Flower Festival but it was not just an exhibition of bulbs and flowers. There were all sorts of products and produces on display and free samplings of cheeses, beers, breads and cakes to be had. But of greater interest to us sailor folk was a floorshow organised by fashion designers, with hundreds of young mannequins and female designers present to keep our eyes busy. All this had been gleaned from a messmate who had been on the previous day's tour. I resolved to keep an eye on these two passengers in front and follow their lead.

The interior of the building was enormous. Rows and rows of flowers stretched as far as the eye could see, many in early bloom and ready for other European markets on this cold February day. The very sight of such brilliance distracted me from my original intention and I let my guides disappear on their hunt for the ladies as I walked enchanted among the riot of colour and fragrance before me. Only when I had seen it all, did I make a beeline for the cheese section, where I was given several types of cheese to taste. I bought a small round wax-coated cheese for mother but it was such a nuisance to walk about with that I went outside to the coach and put it on my seat.

A shipmate called to me from the beer-tasting section on my return and I sat with my companions, studiously tasting and discussing various beers with a Dutch beer representative. When it was obvious that we had sampled the full range of his wares, we bade him farewell and vacated that section without a single purchase! Anyway, it was illegal to bring alcohol on board HM ships!

The strains of modern music took us to another part of the huge hall and there we found a fashion parade in full swing. We took a seat at the perimeter of the catwalk and spent an hour or so crunching peanuts and ogling the girls that paraded past in the latest French and Dutch fashions, until an announcement over the public address system, demanded our presence aboard the coach again.

It was already dark when we returned to the car park and, since we could no longer sit and watch the countryside go by, our journey back to Amsterdam was accompanied by a good old naval sing-song!

Supper was just about to be dished up. I sat in my best suit enjoying a good hot meal and listening to a messmate who had just spent eleven minutes and the equivalent of half a week's pay in the arms of a Canal Street floozie. Later, Garth, Jim, Ollie and I went ashore to view the scene of the crime. The "scenery" was very decorative, we thought, but not worth the risk and after a few promenades up and down Canal Street, we retired to something that we all preferred in the warmth and comfort of a well-lit tavern, where we stayed until late. A small souvenir shop was still open when we came out and we wandered in. I bought a table lamp in the guise of a ship in sail, her hull fashioned from a wooden clog.

I traded cigarettes for cigars as before, with a little man who permanently hung around the gangway. He sold all sorts of odds and ends and what he did not have in stock (that is to say in the pockets of his gaberdine raincoat), he was able to scuttle away and fetch within just a few minutes.

I loved Amsterdam. I liked the architecture, the cleanliness, the chiming clocks, the quaint cobbled streets and the bridges over the waterways. I liked the simple, unhurried attitude of the people going about their daily work, and the friendliness that they always extended to us, in spite of us being sailors. I was very sorry when it came time for us to go.

We had paid a visit to Canal Street on our last night there. The naughty girls had news of our departure and their pimps were out in force, offering all kinds of sexual pleasures at half-price as we were leaving. We did not take them up on the kind offers!

As we moved off towards the North Sea, I stood at the rail gazing across the fields on either side, thick with frost and edged by deep drainage dykes full of frozen water, and wondered how long it would be before I had the chance to return.

Leaving the coast of Holland astern, I reported to the bridge as look-out for the evening watch. It was bitterly cold but I would rather have been nowhere else as a huge full moon scudded in and out of the clouds, lighting the sea in great patches of silver light. These patches reminded me of the spotlights on a stage. All about them was total darkness; they lit up the water and it danced and sparkled with the purest silver light. The black clouds above glowed at their edges with white fire from the light of the moon and beyond a star or two twinkled through.

Our Divisional Officer sent for several of us on the following day and advised us to prepare for the examination to be rated Able Seaman. By now we had served eighteen months in the Navy and our only opportunity for promotion was now available to us. I took a rather cavalier attitude to it all, as it mattered little to me if I passed or failed, because apart from a slight increase in pay, there was no badge or other mark of distinction to show for it other than the title.

We mustered on the upper deck and spent the whole of the forenoon and most of the afternoon in examinations on bends and hitches, flags and signals, damage control, firefighting, parts of ship, naval routines, ranks and badges and in demonstrating our many skills in steering the ship and mooring procedures. Just before tea-time we were piped to muster in the after flat, to hear that we had all passed bar one.

The one exception was one that I shall call "John", to save him any embarrassment. He was failed on some aspect of his firefighting, but was quite unruffled about it, as I think he expected it. Somewhere along the way, I had collected one month's accelerated advancement, which meant that my pay as an AB would be back-dated to January, which I was quite pleased about.

That night, I was on duty during the middle watch as Bo'sun's Mate. A little after one in the morning, the Officer of the Watch told me to make a jug of "kye" for the bridge staff as usual and I laid aft to put the urn on in the after officer's galley, stopping on the way to give John a cigarette. He was on lifebuoy sentry duty, huddled up in his large duffel coat and gazing out across the ship's stern. We had exchanged a few pleasantries when, suddenly, I noticed a thin wisp of black smoke creeping up the hatch leading to the after officer's quarters. I grabbed John's arm.

"Good God, something's on fire!" I said, and hurried to the hatchway, which was rapidly filling with thick, choking smoke. John grabbed a breathing apparatus mask and clamped it on his face, while I punched the fire alarm bells and telephoned the bridge to tell the Officer of the Watch the location of the fire. I then returned to help John's rescue attempt by holding the end of the breathing tube in the fresh air.

John disappeared down the hatch as I fed the air tube after him and shortly afterwards, just as the first of the duty watch and fire parties arrived to assist us, he came up the ladder, having hauled the two Sub-lieutenants from their burning cabin below into the relative safety of the cabin flat.

After resuscitation in the open air, they began to recover and the fire parties, aided by the mass of the ship's company, who had been dragged from their beds by the fire alarms, quickly put the fire out.

The fire had been caused by a wet oilskin rolling against an electric fire with the motion of the ship and the actual damage was more in the way of smoke than flame. With the mess eventually cleared up, the men off watch drifted back to bed and the duty watch began the task of stripping the cabin and tidying up. The following day, John was rated AB.

We returned to a warmer British coastline and moored in the river Orwell, in sight of Harwich. The shore establishment, *HMS Ganges* and her tall training mast, stood on the other side of the river. We were also in sight of Parkeston Quay, from whence all sorts of shipping came and went. Cargo ships discharged there, troop ships took soldiers to and from duty in Germany and Scandinavia and the waterway in those days was a very busy one. My duty in the motorboat involved some rather perilous journeys in the crowded river and it took no little skill to pilot the boat. Many was the time that we ran for cover as a ship bore down on our small, poorly-lit motorboat in the darkness, and one really needed to be alert on our regular journeys into Harwich or Shotley with our cargoes of merry libertymen.

I went ashore to Shotley one evening with several of my new shipmates and we ventured into the pub on the foreshore. It was a wet and windy evening and my sole purpose for coming ashore was to telephone Pearl at her friend's home, as previously arranged, to tell her that I hoped to be home on the coming weekend.

The warmth and light inside the pub was a welcome sight since the world outside was a most inhospitable one, with a strong west wind rising and raining the proverbial stair-rods. I joined my mates at the bar and someone pointed out that my name was the same as that of the local brew. The name

"Cobbold" is on most Suffolk pubs and my mother had often told me that we were distantly related to the famous brewers.

"Do you get a free pint?" asked one of my friends. The landlord heard the question and answered that no-one got a free pint in his house, to which my friend replied that I was one of the actual Cobbolds advertised on the front of his pub. The man paused in drawing a pint.

"Can you prove that?" he asked.

"Well, I can prove I'm a Cobbold," I replied and showed him my paybook identity. "But how I fit into the brewing family, I cannot say." Mine host beamed at me.

"Have this on the house, Mr Cobbold!" he said and passed over a pint of Cobbold's Mild. "And what would your friends like?" Such an occurrence has not happened since, I might add, but it certainly put me up a peg or two in my shipmates' estimation.

Obdurate spent some time over the course of the next few weeks steaming up and down the east coast on fishery protection, keeping an eye out for illegal fishing vessels and seeing that the correct size of net was used by the many trawlers at sea during the cold and stormy months of that bitter winter.

The weather eased with the approach of March and the lighter nights and extra sunshine broke the spell of winter at last. We began to get the odd sunny day that made life worth living again. *Obdurate* was detailed to return to Chatham and we ploughed slowly through the last of the winter snowstorms toward Sheerness and the Medway. I had the evening watch until midnight and stood in the cold, staring at the wet snowflakes which effectively made nonsense of my look-out's job.

For some time now, I had become the object of a certain Petty Officer's most unwanted attention. I am not so sure that he was actually homosexual but he did enjoy irritating me by pawing me and making a general nuisance of himself, embarrassing me in front of my shipmates. I had even considered reporting him, but the retribution he would suffer as a consequence could have ruined his Service record and put him ashore. Besides which, he had not actually done anything other than behave in a very indiscreet manner for a person of his rank and status. I felt that I was able to cope with the situation but as I stood on the port signals bridge on this particular night, staring fruitlessly at the darkness and snowflakes, the Petty Officer in question appeared behind me.

"I've bought you some nutty, lad," he whispered and tried to thrust several bars of chocolate into the pocket of my duffel coat. I protested, pushed back his offering and took shelter behind the searchlight mounting, but he began chasing me around it, whispering that he wanted to talk with me "about something".

I easily avoided him, but by now with genuine concern I felt that I needed to do something positive to stop all further advances from this odious man. I stopped him in his tracks with an upheld hand.

"Just one minute, P.O!" I said quietly. "If you don't leave me alone, I shall have to report this matter to my father. He is a Lieutenant Commander in this Navy and he will know how to deal with the likes of you!"

The Petty Officer stopped and blinked. He did not know quite what to make of this statement but eventually he thought better of it, returned the chocolate to his pocket and turned and left me. I saw him no more that night. We met again on the deck in the morning and I made a point of deliberately stopping him and repeating the threat to report him. He was quite confused and left me alone for ages.

Obdurate finally made her berth in the dockyard at Chatham and we started a spring-clean of the upper deck and superstructure in readiness for the forthcoming summer programme. The ship's hull was first to receive our earnest attention and we hung over the side on "stages" for several days, scraping off the old loose paint, chipping at the rust, then undercoating and repainting with the traditional grey Pusser's "crabfat", a nickname for grey Navy paint.

The hull work completed, we moved on to the upper decks and superstructures. I was engaged on painting the mast black. *Obdurate*'s mast was of the later latticed type, whereas *Savage*'s had merely been a simple tripod one, so there was a larger area to cover and lots of nooks and crannies to fill. We painted the funnel and the boat davits and one afternoon, I was just beginning to paint the superstructure amidships, when along came the P.O. again and began to make a pest of himself. I was playing "tag" with him in my efforts to escape his attentions, when I heard a Pipe: "Stand by port side to receive mooring lines amidships".

I looked over the side to see a minesweeper approaching our port side with the crew at the rail, ready with their heaving lines and warps to raft alongside us. Leaning on the rail of the bridge, and now Captain of his own ship, was our old First Lieutenant from *Savage*, Lt.-Commander Gilbert. He saw me and grinned.

"Hello, son!" he said. "Still using a one inch paintbrush I see!"

"Yes, dad!" I saucily replied. "But now that I'm an AB, I hope to move on to a larger one!"

We continued our banter for some moments until with a wave of the hand he left his bridge. I turned to see my aggressor, with staring eyes and lowered jaw.

"There's my father!" I snarled. "Do you still want to play about now?" Convinced that my father actually was the Officer commanding the minesweeper, he went blood-red and scuttled for'ard at full speed.

I was not content to leave the matter there and when next I saw him, it was my turn to terrorise him.

"I was thinking of having a word with my father," I told him.

"You wouldn't do that, lad, would you?" he whined. "All in good fun you know".

"I'm not so sure!" said I with a frown. "It's my duty to report incidents of this nature to the correct authority and I should at least ask Dad's opinion on the matter."

My tormentor of the last few weeks suddenly crumpled into a blob of whingeing jelly and whispered urgently, promising all sorts of favours if I would reconsider. I actually got several plum jobs from him over the course of the next few weeks, and several bars of chocolate, this time with no strings attached! My messmates loved every moment of it and in many respects joined in on the leg-pull, talking loudly when in the P.O.'s presence about the way the Service winkled out "queers" and punished them in the naval prison at Portsmouth, before throwing them out with ignominy and no pension. I was never bothered again and after a while, we stopped our tormenting but treated the P.O. with little respect.

This situation was not to last very long, for on the 21st March, I received a draft chit appointing me to *HMS Neptune*, the Reserve Fleet in Chatham dockyard and that very day I began packing my gear ready to go on the 23rd.

The following day, Garth received the same draft and it became apparent that we would part company with all the souls that we had known before and that the original class of thirty-two that had joined in 1955 was now whittled down to just two. I went through the routine of trying to get all my dhobying washed and dried and stowed away. It was made more difficult by the fact that *Obdurate* was in the dockyard and that the engine room and boilers were shut down. As a result, I had to try to get my washing dry without the benefit of the searing heat of the boilers and it became all very inconvenient.

My time aboard *Obdurate* had flown by and I seemed hardly to have settled in before I was off again. I had made some good friends and we had had some good laughs. I said goodbye with regret and promised to come over to visit if the opportunity arose in the near future.

I was now left with only four months service to do, only one hundred and one days according to the graph, and it looked as though these would be spent ashore in the Reserve Fleet. One of my messmates advised me that the centre for the Reserve Fleet was the old depot ship *HMS Duncansby Head* and that men on the Reserve Fleet had a pretty easy time with local dockyard jobs and odd jobs about the various visiting ships. Although I dreaded spending the rest of my time wielding a paintbrush, at least I would be able to get regular weekend leave and that was something to look forward to.

I strode ashore down the gangway with my kitbag, hammock and suitcase, and, along with Garth and another chap going on draft elsewhere, loaded it all onto a handcart. We rumbled noisily through the side gate into RN barracks, en route to the draft office to get instructions for our final destinations.

The P.O. in the draft office shuffled through our draft papers. "That's right," he said. "Reserve Fleet, *Duncansby Head*. Through the side gate into the dockyard, bear right and you will see the *Duncansby Head* tied up alongside the north wall of the basin." It was back to the handcart and back through the gate into the dockyard but this time it was only Garth and I that made the journey. It all seemed a dreadful waste of time to me; why had we not been sent direct to *Duncansby Head*, I wondered?

Trundling the cart along the dockyard roads was quite good fun and so we made no haste to get there. The problem with wasting time in such a manner was that it became quite hard work pushing the heavy vehicle. We passed *Obdurate* twice and the Duty P.O. opened his mouth to ask what we were playing at, but did not and so we thought that the skylark had gone on enough. By now it was half-way through the afternoon; we made our way to the large depot ship that was to be our new hall of residence for the next few months.

We were met at the gangway by a Marine Sergeant. He took our draft chits without comment and calling a rating over from the Quartermaster's desk, had us shown to our mess. This AB showed us around the ship and told us of the daily routine that we should expect. We sat at the mess table, smoking and discussing life on the *Duncansby Head* until "Secure" was suddenly piped and the AB leapt to his feet like a scalded cat, rushing off to get cleaned for going ashore.

It seemed a nice easy-going routine. We began congratulating ourselves on finding a cushy berth at last, and having stowed our gear into our allocated lockers, shifted out of our No. 8s and into our tiddly suits for a run ashore.

We fell-in on our first morning for work. The routine was always the same. We lined up on the upper deck and a Leading hand or a Petty Officer came along with a clipboard. Some ratings were sent into the dockyard to work; others were given the name of a ship to report to. Usually we were sent in a group and this meant that we marched though the dockyard until we reached our appointed destinations. A lot of the time was spent hanging about waiting to begin work and usually, nothing much was accomplished before "Stand Easy". Eventually we would get going after this small quarter of an hour break. Sometimes we waited to receive the mooring lines of an incoming ship and would stand in a small hut, out of the wind and rain, or stand "sunbathing" if it were fine, swapping yarns and smoking out of sight of the stream of officers and other personnel going about their daily business. I felt like the great forgotten. I felt like the Navy no longer needed my services.

We were fed and watered in the barracks canteen and made sure to get over to the dockyard gate at 1130, just as "Up Spirits" was piped. At 1330 we turned back to work, having loafed away the best part of an hour and a half in the snooker room and in one of the television rooms. By the time that we arrived back at our work station, we were already thinking of skating off ashore for the evening, and the day dragged by on the leaden wings of boredom. "Secure" at 1600hrs was our welcome release.

Sometimes our duties took us but a few minutes to complete, yet all day to wait for them. We often spent hours awaiting the arrival of a designated ship. When she finally arrived in the basin, we took her heaving lines ashore, hauled in on her bowlines and springs and merely dropped them over the mooring bollards. The ship's company did the rest and with a wave of our hands, we were off to waste the rest of the day in some quiet nook out of sight and mind.

Upon our return to *Duncansby Head*, no-one asked any questions as to how we had got on and we were free to proceed ashore unless we were on duty or on the special duty roster for "Subsmash". It would be from this special list that seamen and engineers would be called in the event of a submarine disaster in our area and although I was often on this list, I am very glad to say that we were never mustered. Not that we had any specialised training in any case!

We slept aboard *Duncansby Head* in our hammocks. The ship was like a furnace but I managed to find a berth beneath a hatchway leading to the upper deck which, although drafty on occasions, was at least a little cooler.

Washing and toilet stations were all to be found on the quayside and at certain times of the day, the ship resembled an anthill with a constant stream of small ants, each with a towel over his arm, streaming up and down the gangways bound for the damp and dingy washrooms and shore heads. One small bonus was that if one was prepared to get up a little earlier, one could troop over to the barracks washrooms and also have a proper cooked break-fast in the messhall at the same time.

It was whilst doing exactly that one morning that I was caught by the barrack's morning flag hoisting ceremony and was late returning as a result. I rushed up the gangway of my depot ship, expecting to be hauled up in front of the Officer of the Day for missing my work muster but I had in fact not been missed. This led me to the obvious conclusion that we were not listed, and all one had to do was to have the nerve to miss the muster and one would be free all day to do as one pleased!

The difficult bit was in finding somewhere quiet enough to hide away. Any senior hand, upon asking what you were supposed to be doing, would quickly rumble that you were loafing and would set you to some horrible task by way of punishment. So it was of no use trying to hide about the messdecks or passageways.

One morning I was detailed to join in on painting the ship's side. It was the 27th March and my twentieth birthday. I drew a set of overalls and in company of another equally "motivated" rating, started slowly assembling the wooden plank and ropes that were known as a "stage" and which would form a seat as we swung over the side of the great, grey, steel expanse which we were expected to cover with paint by means of a paint-roller.

It took until "Stand Easy" to draw our paint and rollers from the paintshop and to assemble the stage. We sat in an empty messdeck, drinking a mug of tea each and listening to the radio until "Out Pipes" and with the words of Harry Belafonte's "Banana Boat Song" in our ears, we mustered on the upper deck to make a reluctant start on the acres of paintwork to be covered. My colleague tended the ropes above me and I slid down on to the stage to begin the first strip.

The sun shone hotly on my back when it appeared from behind the banks of black cloud that had threatened to drench us with a shower and, Heaven forbid, bring our painting expedition to a halt! I was in a happy mood. It was Thursday; I was due a long weekend on the following day and I was going home.

"Day-oh, day-ay-ay-oh! Daylight come and me wanna go home!" I sang, in my best Harry Belafonte voice. "Day, is-a-day, is-a-day, is a day-ay-ay-oh! Daylight come and me wanna go home!" My voice echoed this primitive dirge across the granite quaysides and off the old Victorian brick buildings. "Come mister tallyman, tally me banana, daylight come and me wanna go home..."

My colleague, up aloft, tapped a chipping hammer against the scuppers in time to my singing. This was the life; we were really having fun! Suddenly, a scuttle was opened and a head popped out, the owner's eyes protruding from his head in the effort to strain up and back at us.

"Pack up that bloody racket, can't you?" he bellowed. I airily waved my roller at him.

"What de matter wid youse man?" I asked in traditional West Indian. "Don't you know de words?" The face by now looked like a red tomato stuck to the ship's side.

"When I tell you to shut up, I mean shut up!" he roared. "I don't expect to be answered back. Get on with your work and not another peep out of either of you!"

It was apparent that this man was serious and I was a little crestfallen that our happy approach to our menial task was thus to be curtailed. As the head withdrew into the ship's interior, I muttered loudly:

"You should try doing a day's work out here on this pissing stage instead of spoiling other people's fun!" The head, redder than before, shot out from the scuttle opening.

"What did you say?" The voice had gone up an octave. Without awaiting my reply, the head shot back inside again and the scuttle banged shut, hard enough to raise an echo from the other side of the basin. My workmate said: "Sod that!" and disappeared from the upper deck.

Frantically, I climbed up the ropes, the stage swinging wildly at my speedy ascent and smearing the freshly painted surface, but I was in no mood to stop and bewail my spoiled handiwork. I clawed my way over the upper rail and imitated my partner's hasty retreat.

As I dashed aft to find somewhere to hide, I saw a very red Commander striding angrily towards me along the upper deck and so I ducked quickly towards a large locker, hoping to conceal myself behind it. It was a forlorn hope. The locker abutted the superstructure with no space to hide and so I wrenched open the lid and dived in head first. My shins took a scraping and I hit the bottom of my refuge with a bone-jarring thud as the lid dropped shut after me. I heard the Commander's angry footsteps march purposefully by.

From one of several holes in the side of my new hiding place, I saw him standing at the abandoned stage, his hands on his hips and obviously in a great temper. A Chief Petty Officer happened along.

"Chief," I heard the Commander say. "Where are the party manning this side?" The Chief did not know; he was an Engineering Room Artificer and painting ships was nothing to do with him.

I heard the Commander complaining that he had been at an important meeting below decks when this "awful African singing" had disturbed his train of thought, and when he had ordered the rating making the row to shut it up, he had been cheeked! The sweat dripped from my brow and down my nose. How was I to get out of this one?

"Nip along and find the man in charge of this lot, will you, Chief? Send him and that noisy bastard to me in my office!" The Commander swung on his heel and marched back the way he had come, his face knotted in anger.

"Aye, aye, Sir!" answered the Chief. He looked fore and aft along the ship's side. To my utter surprise, on seeing no-one apparently in charge, he made his way to the gangway and away across the dockyard! Clearly he was obviously not part of *Neptune*'s staff and sorting out their disciplinary problems was nothing to do with him!

I wandered about the empty messdeck seeking my fellow painter, whom I found hiding in a disused galley area. We hoisted up the stage from the ship's side and hid the gear in the locker, taking a chance on the P.O. in charge of the painting party not missing us before lunch. We repaired back to barracks at "Up Spirits!", for today was the day that I became eligible to draw my first official "tot". I queued in the flat of Nelson block where the rum-tub had been set up. My name was studiously ticked from the list and I was handed a glass of brown liquid, one part rum and one part water. I threw back my head and tried to swallow the lot in one go but it could not be done and it took several swallows before the ritual was complete. Dinner was taken in a rather pleasant haze and "Out Pipes!" was piped at last.

It was about mid-afternoon, as we continued our work at another part of the hull, that the angry Commander hove in sight. I was tending the ropes and my colleague was beneath with the roller, writing his wife's name on the ship's side in grey paint before filling in the spaces.

I stood up straight as the Commander bore down on me. One sailor in overalls looks much like another.

"Are you the lad that was here this morning?" he demanded. In broad Scots, I answered with a smart salute:

"Nay, Sir, they've away ta' the submarine pens!" He glared at me.

"Oh, I see. Carry on then," and he walked away. We saw him no more!

It had been a very close shave but I learned more than one thing from it. The locker which had so fortuitously come to my aid in the forenoon was an excellent hiding place to conceal oneself when avoiding the daily work muster! Subsequently, many a day was spent asleep inside or else reading the daily newspaper and watching the world go by through the peep-holes! I admit to loafing in my locker on several occasions without being detected. Getting in and out was difficult but on the odd instance when nature called, or my limbs became so stiff that I really had to emerge to limber up a little, my chances of being rumbled were increased and so I chose to use my refuge as a place to retire to when a really miserable task came up.

However, I enjoyed my fellow man's companionship more than the opportunity to loaf and I more or less attended each work muster, joining in on the daily life of *Neptune*. Thus, one morning at the end of April, I stood awaiting my labour's fate for the day when a P.O. came along.

"Anyone know much about gardening?" he asked. Such questions were usually trick ones. If you replied in the affirmative, you might wind up collecting leaves about the barracks or weeding the wall along the Khyber Pass, or something just as stupid. I kept silent; so did the rest of the assembled slaves.

"You'll do, then!" said the P.O., pointing directly at me. It was no good stepping back so that his outstretched finger pointed at the lad behind me; he had my number and that was that. "Report to Leading seaman Barratt in the gardens at the Wrennery," said the P.O. "And don't let me hear that you have got lost on the way!" Upon hearing the reference to the Wrennery, the assembled workers now wished that they had volunteered for the gardening vacancy and hooted derisively as I stepped out of line and made for the gangway on my way to the barracks and the Wrens' quarters at the far end of the main road.

It sounded like a cushy number. All I expected to do was to pull a few weeds. I would be that much closer to the canteen and, therefore, not constantly walking backwards and forwards between *Duncansby Head* and barracks several times a day for meals. Once through the dockyard gate into RNB, I doubled around the perimeter of the parade ground where some important parade training was being executed and strolled under the arch leading to the Wrens' quarters, an area strictly out of bounds to sailors!

A lone Leading hand, dressed in faded No. 8s, straightened up from hoeing a flower bed.

"Leading seaman Barratt?" I enquired. The Leading hand nodded.

"I'm your new assistant!" I declared cheerfully. His face hardly wrinkled. He reminded me of a garden gnome but on reflection, I felt that that was being unfair to gnomes everywhere, since most of those little chappies had more personality than he!

In the four weeks that I was destined to work with Leading seaman Barratt, it was fair to say that I never learned a single thing about him, not even his christian name.

I was put to work weeding a flower bed, picking up stones from the soil and making a pile of them in a corner of the garden next to a foul-smelling compost heap. I wondered if my new employer counted those stones each day to determine my work rate? "Stand Easy" was piped in the barracks and the Leading hand put down his hoe, and without a word or signal to me, wandered off in the direction of the Wrens' cookhouse. I decided to follow. We entered a blue wooden door at the end of the galley.

A cloud of hot steam greeted our entry into the inner sanctum and through the steam, I saw that the huge cooking vats and ovens were manned by several overalled Wrens. They looked very ordinary thus attired and nowhere as attractive as in their uniforms.

One large fat lady glanced across from pouring out a row of mugs of freshly brewed tea, swinging the teapot from left to right, and filling each to the brim. "Got a new assistant I see, Hookey," she observed. "Wait till Doris sees that one!" To me she said, over her shoulder, "Do you take sugar, dear?"

I sat nervously on the edge of a warm vat near the door, suddenly rather afraid for some unknown reason, perhaps of being the only accountable male in this bastion of feminine industry. My Leading seaman's lack-lustre attitude seemed to disqualify him. I felt that I was on show. All the Wrens seemed to take it in turns to come and see the "new bit of talent" and as I sat on the increasingly warm vat, I began to feel embarrassed and my neck and cheeks began to redden, a fact noticed by the audience, who said "Aaah!" to one another.

Hookey sat impassively on a stool, rolling a thin tickler cigarette which he lit with a taper, then tucking his tobacco tin inside the pocket of his shirt in a slow deliberate manner. It seemed the longest "Stand Easy" in memory but at last I heard, "Out Pipes" over the Tannoy and swung from my perch, eager to escape that place. I followed my new employer through the door into the cool of the garden outside, followed by several invitations to "come and see us soon, baby!" and a loud wolf-whistle.

Once in the safety of the outside world, I swiftly regained my composure. "There's a fruity little lot," I swaggered, in an attempt to recover my equilibrium as quickly as possible.

"Do you know anything about arranging rose arbours?" he asked. I didn't and he soon told me in very few words how to trail the prickly rose stems over the cherrywood arch. The cookhouse belles took every opportunity to wave at me during the course of the morning but I hoped to discourage them by not waving back. In any case, one never knew just whom may be looking. We secured to lunch.

"Be back here prompt at 1330," said Hookey, and left me to return the gardening tools to the tool-shed alongside the smelly compost heap. I thought about taking a dive into my locker on the *Duncansby Head* for the rest of the afternoon but the Leading seaman had written my name down on a piece of tickler paper and had put this inside his tobacco tin.

Back inside the barracks, I drank my "tot" and chewed my way thoughtfully through lunch. I would rather have been painting a ship today or tending mooring lines, I thought. The gardening bit was alright but the tea-breaks were a bit of a trial. Perhaps the novelty would have worn off by the afternoon break, I told myself and I returned to my duties among the flowers with renewed optimism.

Barratt only spoke when there was something to impart about the flowers or about my duties and I felt quite isolated in the garden. At afternoon "Stand Easy" I took a deep breath and followed Hookey into the cookhouse once more. I was greeted with "Hello, sweetheart!" and "Does your mother know you're out?" but I determined not to go red. I just smiled and found things to do, such as lighting a cigarette.

It was not too bad. I regained my perch and accepted a mug of fresh tea from the large Wren. I even found the courage to accept a freshly-baked jam tart from another, who was going around with a plate full of hot ones straight from the oven.

"He likes a hot tart!" one girl observed.

"Wait till Doris claps her minces on him!" giggled another and the whole crew laughed. Who the heck was Doris, I wondered, and made a mental note to ask the Killick when we got outside.

My first day in the rose gardens ended at last and Barratt left me to pack the gear away saying: "Don't be late in the morning". I had tea in the barracks and slowly made my way back to *Duncansby Head*. The mess was almost empty when I arrived; most off-duty hands had gone ashore on the first libertyboat and so I changed into the rig of the day and made my way after supper to the barrack cinema.

Garth was in his hammock reading a book when I came back and I stood telling him what a plum job I had landed until lights out. After a luke-warm shower I turned in, my back and arms aching pleasantly from the strenuous effort of my unaccustomed labours.

The next day, the same guard-drill was going on as I doubled across the corner of the parade ground in the barracks and a drill instructor glared at me for cutting across the corner of his hallowed ground on my way to the gardens. Barratt looked at his watch as I approached.

"Eight-thirty, I told you," he muttered.

"But I have to come all the way from *Neptune*," I protested, and he said no more about it.

271

I was put to work cutting the grass and adding the cuttings to the compost heap, and I pushed the ancient mower with a will, chopping the heads off daisies and dandelions alike until "Stand Easy" was piped once more. My heart gave a sickening lurch and I steeled myself for my entrance into the kitchens. We entered in absolute silence. Not one cat-call did I collect, a Wren said: "Hello, mate," passing me a mug of tea and a doughnut and I took my seat on a small stool alongside Hookey at the far end of the galley, closest to the door leading to the garden. The assembled Wrens sat smoking and drinking their tea and giving me but the briefest of glances from time to time. Had they been told off for their boisterous behaviour of the day before, I wondered?

Suddenly the gaggle of overalled girls turned their eyes to the door at the far end of the cookhouse and then respectfully stood to one side as a Petty Officer Wren, a gigantic specimen if ever I saw one, came striding through towards us. Hookey, in the act of lighting one of his thin tickler cigarettes, blinked nervously and completely missed the end of the fag with his lighter.

"Doris!" he muttered from the corner of his mouth. The Wrens closed in behind the approaching mountain of flesh, their eyes dancing with some sort of suppressed delight as the huge lady came to a halt in front of us.

"So this is your new bit of skin, is it?" she bellowed at Hookey. "Well he's a f****** sight better than the last one by the look of him!" I hated to hear women use foul language and I instinctively showed it. "Make you blush, did I dearey?" she asked, noticing my reaction. "You'll f****** well do more than that in my kitchen, darling!" The audience of assembled Wrens giggled in unison.

"What's yer name, sweetheart?"

"Cobbold," I replied, trying to appear quite unruffled.

"Cobbold?" she repeated. "Cobbold? Cob-hold of this, darling," and she made an obscene gesture with her ample bosom. Her minions roared their amusement. Suddenly, my "bottle" went.

"You will find me in the potting shed," I said to Barratt and without taking my eyes from Doris, I rose from my seat and walked out of the door.

"Oh, now then!" I heard Doris say to her cookhouse crew. "Bugger me if I haven't upset the poor little bastard!"

The floor of the potting shed was wet and stained dark brown with the liquid from the compost heap, which flowed downhill from the heap outside, through the shed and out the other side. I nervously smoked a cigarette, waiting for Hookey to return from his break. Two large black beetles scuttled across the floor, revelling in the rich brown sludge. I moved my feet to avoid them making contact with my shoes.

Leading seaman Barratt duly returned. He put on his wellingtons and a pair of gardening gloves.

"I want you to carry on with the grass cutting down the far end and when that is finished, come up and help me with turning the bit of land over up here." He made absolutely no reference to the conflict in the cookhouse. Perhaps he had seen it all before and did not want to get involved.

The grass was not completely cut come lunch-time and I was glad to escape from the quietness of the rose garden and get back into the barracks for my meal. I saw Hookey chewing into his lunch in the messhall but I chose to sit alone and eat; he was hardly what one could call a bosom pal and there was little point in discussing the matter of Doris and the cookhouse clan with him.

I returned to the grass and finished off the edges to the lawns. It all looked very clean and neat, with pretty contrasting green rows where the mower had formed a pattern. One of the Wrens at the galley window smiled briefly at me as I returned the heavy mower to the shed. I thought I detected a hint of sympathy in her eyes. I made up my mind then to return to the galley with the Leading hand for tea at "Stand Easy" as usual and face the music, but when the pipe came, my legs turned to jelly and I started towards the potting shed where I could hide for the next quarter of an hour before returning to work. A small arrogant voice inside asked me if I was going to be beaten by a brash, intimidating lump of lard like Doris, and I knew that it would be the moral end of me if I failed to stand up to her.

Hookey was already seated with a cup of tea as I entered the galley. I walked over to the tea-urn with every eye in the place on my small figure.

"One sugar, please," I said as calmly as I could to the Wren on the other side of the counter. A slight buzz went round as I took my mug and sat next to Barratt. His lighter had failed and I lit his cigarette and one of my own, aware that my hand had ever so slight a tremble to it. I shall never forgive the Wren at the far end of the galley, who called through the doorway to the hall beyond.

"Yer boyfriend's back again, P.O.!" I pretended not to hear and told Hookey that the grass was all done and the mower back in the shed.

"OK," he said, and started to tell me to join up with him after tea-break but neither of us concentrated on the spoken words. Our thoughts were on the doorway at the far end, through which I expected my tormentor to thunder at any moment. I did not have long to wait!

Doris barged in like the Royal Scotsman emerging from a railway tunnel. Charging straight up to me, like a galleon in full sail, she clasped me to her massive form.

"Give us a cuddle, my little man!" she boomed. "I'll give you this, you've more guts than the last lad!" I twisted one way and then the other to escaped her bear-like hug.

"Watch out for the tea, P.O.," I muttered. "It's going all over the floor."

"You can call me Doris," she announced. "I've really taken a fancy to you!"

I read somewhere that all sorts of awkward and serious dilemmas can be softened by a humorous word or two. Since to wriggle and whinge over the present situation would obviously be of no avail, I decided to give it a try.

"Put me down," I quipped. "You don't know where I've been!" Suddenly, she laughed and the audience laughed with her. Hookey looked at me out of the corner of his eye.

"I know where I would like you to be!" she countered.

"You'll have to join the queue!" I replied. She stepped back. Suddenly, I had succeeded. We fell into a succession of verbal exchanges and backchat which not only had the effect of keeping her ample hands off me but got her smiling and her Wrens laughing, and in no time at all, "Out Pipes" came to my rescue.

Replacing our mugs on the counter, Hookey and I returned to the cool sane world outside, leaving Doris waving and blowing me kisses through the window. "At least you didn't get de-bagged this time," was Hookey's sardonic remark, as we set to work on the job of turning over a flower-bed. So that's what I might expect! I made a mental note to ensure that my underwear was worthy of such exposure.

I felt elated at having stood my ground and keeping my dignity in front of all those Wrens and later that night, in the dark safety of my hammock aboard *Duncansby Head*, I resolved to handle Doris with humour and wit and perhaps take some of the battle into her camp, given the opportunity.

It worked. She began to look forward to our little battles of wit during tea-breaks and apart from a daily hug and the occasional big wet kiss, both her language and brashness abated and in fact, we had many interesting conversations in the heat and steam of that stainless steel galley.

The weeks slid by easily. I attended the gardens each day and helped my Leading seaman plan the arrival of the late spring and early summer flowers. Sometimes we sat in the potting shed, poring over seed catalogues and drawing plans of flower-beds and arches of roses, a strange sort of employment for a sailor one might think. Often the rain chased us into the cookhouse and we spent many an hour supping tea and eating biscuits or cakes hot from the ovens.

We had a daily responsibility to provide the wardrooms with a selection of whatever flowers were in season and we took to picking a bunch of flowers for the Wrens' galley as well. I even gave Doris a large bunch of somewhat redundant snapdragons and irises which, proffered with puckered lips, led to a slight rosiness about her cheeks. Even Hookey raised his eyebrows in something approaching admiration at that gesture! I had taken the battle into the enemy's camp with a vengeance.

The final days of May approached and the end of my time in the Navy drew ever closer. The graph paper was by now black with filled-in squares, the unfilled ones a tiny patch of white about to be overwhelmed by the tide of eager black biro. I began to wonder if that was what I really wanted.

CHAPTER
FIFTEEN

On the first day of June, I met George as he queued up for his "tot". He had arrived into the barracks on the previous day on draft from his last ship *HMS Tumult*. It appeared that we would now be serving out our remaining month of life as sailors in the relative comfort of the barracks.

He was pleased to see me and after work that evening, I went round to his dormitory in Duncan block and sat chatting about what had happened to us both since we last saw each other. I was able to tell him that Garth was also in the barracks somewhere.

Garth was working as part of the Barrack Guard, a job which entailed touring the roadways and parade ground area, dressed in his second best uniform with belt and gaiters, on the lookout for unauthorised goings-on or trespassers. Since these duties were conducted on a thirty-six hours on and thirty-six off basis, I had seen little of him, but on the one occasion that we had met, he had not arrested me when I had poked out my tongue at him!

The following day, Jim Baxter appeared and he had seen Jim Bouchier, Seabag and old Cookie from our very first days in Victoria Barracks. It became obvious that we were all assembling for our final discharge. I had often wondered if we would see each other again. According to my graph, we were due to leave in just a month's time, on the Fourth of July.

I was on my way to the Wrennery to perform my gardening chores one afternoon when my name boomed out over the Tannoy.

"Able Seaman Cobbold, report to the main gate!"

I remember wondering if they meant me or if there was another Able Seaman Cobbold floating about. I decided to respond anyway and made my way to the guardroom where the Tannoy calls were made. The Duty Chief and a Royal Marine bugler stood enjoying the afternoon sunshine, keeping a wary eye on the Khyber Pass for approaching taxis or staff cars. I patiently awaited their kind attention. The Chief finally turned to me and raised his eyebrows by way of interrogation.

"You had me piped, Chief?" I queried. "Able Seaman Cobbold?"

"Ah yes," said the Chief. "Come with me, lad," and we entered the inner sanctum of the guardroom. He sat heavily on a chair behind a large pine desk and took a typed list from a pile of papers on his desk.

"Cobbold, Peter Michael, C/J 953009?"

"That's right, Chief," I answered.

"Gardener, Wrennery?" he enquired.

"Yes," I replied. What was this all about, I wondered? I hoped that it was not a job change at this late stage. I was just beginning to get into the swing of gardens and flowers and grass-cutting.

"You're a lucky lad; you are going on your demobilisation leave on the fifth," he said. "You have all day tomorrow to pack your gear, do your leaving routine and tell your work party that you are finished!" He handed me a sheaf of coloured forms. "Muster here at the main gate at 1100 for dispersal on the fifth!" I took the offered papers with a shaking hand.

"You mean that I can go on Wednesday?" I asked rather stupidly. "I didn't know anything about demobilisation leave!" The Chief rocked back in his chair.

"Don't you want to go then?" he asked. "'Cos it can be arranged!" I stuffed the long-awaited papers down the front of my No. 8 shirt.

"I want to go alright!" said I with a broad smile. "But I did not know that we got a month's demob leave."

The Chief rose from his chair and stretched his weary limbs. It was time to stop prattling away with these part-time sailors and return to the duties at the main gate where, heaven forbid, an Admiral might just turn up to enter the sacred portals when the Chief was not ready to receive him.

"There you have it, lad!" he yawned. "I expect it is to give you time to look for a job outside. Off you go before I change my mind!"

I hurried across the perimeter of the parade ground towards the Wrennery, my feelings very mixed. One half of me had looked forward to this time for so long! The other half had developed a love for the Navy. I was free! It began to dawn on me, I was free! I was going "outside"; I had come though the system, done my time! I was free!

No longer need I dash up and down the "line", not knowing when I might get home again. I did not have to put up with the petty rules and regulations, that were part of service life, any longer! I would be free to start living again, to save some money, make long-term plans for the future, perhaps settle down with Pearl...

My head was in a whirl. I had known that a time would come for thinking these thoughts and making these plans but I had expected at least another month of service to complete, and one had learned never to think further in advance than the next weekend!

278

I wandered almost abstractly towards the entrance to the Wrennery and the Gunnery Instructor on the upper roadway found it necessary to shout "That man there!" twice before I heard him.

"Do you mean me?" I asked, pointing at the small of my chest. He caught me up.

"Yes, I bloody do mean you, cloth-ears!" He stood in front of me with his great hands on his hips, leaning backwards ever so slightly and frowning down his nose at me.

"What do you think you are on, a ruddy Sunday School ramble? This is the Royal Naval Barracks, Chatham, not Green Park at Easter! You move at the double in a smart and seamanlike manner at all times!"

"Yes, P.O.," I mumbled, but a small voice inside my head was mimicking his tirade and making comic remarks at his ill humour at the same time. I no longer took the authority of his uniform seriously; I was about to become a civilian again.

After checking my papers, he allowed me to proceed, but not before reminding me that although my papers said that I was about to become a civilian again, he had the power to cancel any thoughts of demob leave that I might have, and he could make me double round the barracks until the last day of my Service or until hell froze over, if he had a mind! He looked fierce enough to do just that and I doubled away to the Wrennery contenting myself with muttering "Silly bastard!" when out of ear-shot.

Leading seaman Barratt looked up from the compost heap as I approached, and pointedly consulted his watch. He looked older suddenly.

"I'm sorry I'm adrift, Hookey," I said, panting slightly from my exertions, and I told him about the result of my being called to the Regulating Office and of my approaching draft to civvy street. He rummaged through my handful of papers. Not a trace of emotion showed on his lined face; not delight for me nor envy on his own part.

"I don't expect that I shall get much help from you today," he muttered and as if to punctuate the statement, "Stand Easy" was piped. We strolled into the Wrens' galley, took our cups of tea and seated ourselves as usual. This was to be my last cup of tea in the Wrennery. Come to that, it was my last actual working day in the Navy! There were only a few hours of work left in that day in any case!

In came Doris. She no longer dashed up to embarrass me as before but stopped to ask something of one of the cooks and then came towards us.

"Where's the fags, then?" she asked. Barratt never gave her a cigarette and I'm sure she would have fainted in surprise should he even have offered one. I took a packet from my shirt pocket and shifted up along the stainless steel top of the cooker to make room for her ample rear. I considered whether or not I should say anything about my leaving. I decided not to, as the de-bagging referred to by Hookey may become a reality!

We spoke about the weekend leave and remarked on the smells from the compost heap, which the Wrens always said overpowered the odours of cooking and made their efforts smell worse than they really were. "Out Pipes" sounded. I slid off the cooker top, smacked Doris's ample rump and said: "Well, cheerio, see you around". I had said my first goodbye.

We returned to the garden and watched the efforts of a blackbird who tried to haul a great long worm from the lawn.

"I suppose I shall have to get across to the office and arrange a replacement for you," said Hookey, quietly. The last I saw of him was passing through the gate of the Wrennery into the barracks. When it became time to "Secure", he still had not returned and I was left to stow the gardening tools back in the shed and leave it unlocked but with the padlock in the hasp. I did not see him again.

Seabag and Garth were in the messhall having tea when I returned there from the washroom. They had heard the good news too. We sat excitedly going through the leaving routine papers until we were chased out by the messhall staff, who wanted to clear up the tables ready for supper. We retired to the peace of Garth's dormitory to sort out what we were going to tackle first on the morrow and arranged to meet at 0830, after breakfast, outside Duncan block. We would go about our final tour of this service establishment together.

I returned to *Duncansby Head* and called at the ship's office. I found it closed. I explained to the Duty P.O. that I would be off into RNB the following day for dispersal ashore and he suggested that I mustered at the ship's office first thing to tell them of my draft. He did not seem too interested in the suddenness of the proceedings and I made up my mind not to bother to do as he suggested, but meet Garth and Seabag as arranged.

After supper, I spent the earlier part of that evening stowing my kit into my kitbag and trying to organise just what I needed to leave out of it in order to keep me going over the next thirty-six hours. I went to the telephone box and telephoned my parents' neighbour, Mrs Heath, to ask her to let my folks know that I was coming home for good this time. We chatted for quite a while until I suddenly realised that I would have all the opportunity in the world to talk to Mrs Heath, if I wanted to, in just a few hours! I made out that I was out of coins and ended the conversation.

There was no way that I could let Pearl know about the news, so I decided that rather than write a hurried letter, I would wait for her outside her office and surprise her.

It was my last but one night in the Navy. How I slept through it, I really don't know, but the bugle blasting out Reveille caught me asleep nevertheless. Dressed in my second-best uniform, I scooted over to the barracks for breakfast. It was going to be a long day. This time tomorrow, I told myself, I will be putting on my tiddly suit and going out of that gate for the last time. Breakfast tasted of sawdust.

Armed with my precious papers, I arrived at the entrance to Duncan block. It was raining fitfully and as I dashed across the roadway, the door was held open for me by George. They were all there; George, Jim, Garth, Cookie, Cowie, Jim Bouchier and Seabag. It was as if I had died and the gates of Heaven were being opened to receive me by all the best friends that I had ever had in the world. Their delight registered in the smiles on their faces. "Come on Cobby; trust you to be late!" one said.

Our first stop was the barrack's equivalent of the ship's office and the first piece of paper was produced to the C.P.O. behind the desk. We leaned on the other side of the counter, awaiting his august judgement. He sensed our excitement.

"Going out tomorrow, eh lads?"

"Yes Chief," we chanted in unison.

"Right, although you are going out, my lads, you are not yet finished with the Service," he told us. "Under the National Service Acts, you are obliged to stay on the Reserves for the next five years and longer if so directed. At nine o'clock you will have a talk with an officer about that."

We sat impatiently in a classroom until the officer, a Lieutenant, appeared. A folder containing all sorts of information concerning our rights under the National Service Acts was given to each of us. We did not have time to go through and read this information at the time, but the officer gave us a résumé of the contents.

Apparently, we had about a fifty per cent chance of being called back for Annual Training, something none of our group had expected. Annual Training lasted for about two weeks a year and we would be paid regular rates whilst so employed. Therefore, our uniforms and equipment must be constantly maintained to a high standard. Would we be issued with a dhoby bucket, I wondered?

"I hope that you men have enjoyed your term of service with the Royal Navy," said the Lieutenant. "A lot of time and effort has been spent in training and equipping you to become good seamen. From your records, I can see that you all have an excellent conduct sheet. Have you ever considered the advantages of re-enlisting? The service has a good plan for re-enlisted national servicemen; you will qualify for two years back-pay to regular rates of pay and some of you have earned advancements to higher ranks that would be a pity to throw away. Then again, you may care to consider joining the Royal Naval Reserves and making, as it were, a weekend career with the Navy. The pay is good and there are good opportunities for advancement, which are more applicable to you, as ex-serving men."

Our faces remained impassive and perhaps the Lieutenant realised that he was preaching to the converted; "out" was what we had earned and "out" was what we wanted. No-one asked any questions or showed any interest in his kind offer!

"In any case," he concluded, "all the information you require is in your folder. You will receive your discharge papers before you go and you must always keep these papers in a safe place where they are readily to hand. If you should change your minds about re-enlisting, you may do so without any loss of seniority or pay by calling in at your nearest Royal Navy Recruiting Centre or reporting back here to the barracks. There is, however, a time limit on this offer! It remains for me to thank you for the service that you have so readily undertaken and to wish you good luck in whatever you do in the future. You may now carry on to begin returning what gear you do not have to take home with you and to start your rounds of the medical department and so on." To a chorus of "Thank you, sir," he wearily scooped up his papers and stuffed them into a briefcase. No new recruits this time.

We spilled out of the classroom to begin our leaving routine. Our hammocks and bedding were returned to the bedding store, where we were told that we would be bedded down that night, our final night as sailors, in Nelson block. We were to call and collect a temporary issue of bedding for the one night from this store before 1500hrs.

The medical department was next on the list. I was surprised to see that I had put on exactly a stone during my enforced term of service. I now weighed nine stone four pounds with the increased weight on my shoulders and arms. The doctors made no comments to any of us and we progressed to the dental section. "Stand Easy" gave us a break on our way and we repaired to the NAAFI to treat ourselves to a last binge of sticky buns and fizzy drinks.

"This time tomorrow, they will be piping for us to fall in for dispersal!" said Seabag and another jolt of excitement went through me.

Since none of us had been detailed a duty watch, we decided to go on a final run ashore, where we could have one last booze-up together. It was arranged that we would clear up our leaving routine as quickly as possible, return for our temporary bedding and loaf up in the dormitory in Nelson block to make our plans for the evening.

The dentists were as uninterested as the doctors and we sat around for ages in the corridor waiting to be seen. Nobody took any notice of us and we had ample opportunity to chat about what the future held for each of us. I was surprised to realise that no-one really knew what they intended to do once they arrived home and became civvies again. We were beginning our lives all over again.

Thoughts of returning to our old jobs seemed very tame after the Navy life of activity and regimentation. Somehow, I could not see myself back at the office in the Law Society, turning over sheets of printed figures, whilst outside the wind blew along the shores, the sun shone and the sea curled and hissed on the beaches.

The thought that I would no more see the wheeling gulls and feel the sun on my face as I worked on the upper deck, nor visit again those far-off places that held so much attraction for a young man, began to make me think about the alternatives. I decided to try and put my thoughts together at the earliest quiet moment but here and now, with my shipmates turning over their rather sketchy plans for the future, was neither place nor time.

The dentist did not discover anything to work on and we returned to the sunshine outside, in time for our last tot and then dinner.

On the railings outside the messhall where we went for our lunch, a number of ends of string were tied securely to the iron uprights, waving idly in the summer breeze. These were the "leads" to imaginary dogs that some people took to trailing around after them. Some of these people took the ownership of these "dogs" most seriously and should one stop to pass the time of day with such a person, one may well be asked to say "Hello" to their "dog"!

On this momentous day, we took the ends of string and plaited them together to confuse the ownership of the "dogs" and sure enough, as we piled out from dinner, a heated argument about whose "dog" was whose, was going on. That was another piece of loony humour I knew I was going to miss.

We drew our temporary bedding and wandered across to Nelson block where we were billetted in a most forlorn section of the building, on squeaky galvanised bedframes that had not seen an occupant in months or even longer. But we did not care. Seated upon the noisy iron frames, we lit our cigarettes and prepared to waste the rest of the afternoon until 1600, when we would be free to go to tea and then ashore for the long awaited "last night piss-up". I think we made a little too much noise at one stage of our elation and the double door at the far end swung suddenly back to reveal a tall, straight Petty Officer, dressed in the rig of the Barrack Guard.

"Oy," he bellowed. "What are you lot then?" Suddenly, I found myself saying, in a bold voice:

"Civvies!" There was a silence.

"Are you the lot going out tomorrow?" we were asked.

"Yes, P.O."

"Well bloody well keep the noise down then!" was the reply, and the P.O. withdrew. It just proved that it was not all shout and scream and that the Service was, after all, staffed by human beings.

The final tasks awaiting us the next day were simply to dress and attend the Pay Office, where we were to collect our final payment up to the fourth of July and our victualling allowance, travel documents and Service record documents. There would be nothing hard in that, we said.

"Secure" was sounded by bugle, signalling the end of the working day, and shortly afterward "Hands to tea" was piped. These familiar pipes were being heard for the last time.

We went to tea in ones and twos. George and I went together and Garth, Jim and Cowie joined us as we ate. I suddenly felt very tired and sat quietly, listening to the others chatting. I was all too aware that by this time tomorrow, I would be at home and would probably never see again these lads that had become such firm friends.

We splashed about the washroom and dressed into our very best uniform for our run ashore. Usually, we would rush ashore at the earliest opportunity and on the first libertyboat, especially if going "up the line" home or to the pictures. But as we were planning a pub crawl, it was considered prudent to attend supper at 1830 first, to strengthen the inner man for the assault on the strong ale to come, and so we took our time about our ablutions and relaxed in the dormitory until supper was announced over the Tannoy. We would miss that infernal Tannoy.

I wonder if someone on the catering staff was aware that there was a group of sailors aboard for their last supper on that particular evening. The supper was exceptionally fine and we left the tables and returned our eating irons in good spirits.

The rest of the evening, until we finally noisily returned to the darkness of the dormitory stifling with the heat of sleeping men, is all a bit vague in my memory. I was aware of us joining in a singsong in one pub and being applauded for our efforts, whereas in the next we visited, the air was thick with hostility. We therefore returned to the first pub and the night ticked slowly by. Since it was our last night in uniform, it was rather sad and desperately nostalgic. It was every bit as that first night in the Royal Navy had been, but for very different reasons.

I stood undressing at my open locker. The graph, the first thing that I always pinned up wherever I went, stared blackly back at me. Just thirty-two days remained on the white squares and only one of those needed to be coloured in black. The remainder were leave squares and warranted a red.

"Hey, gang!" I whispered loudly, and called them about me. I took out a black biro and with great ceremony, blacked in the very last square. George, Jim, Garth and Seabag, Cowie, Jim Bouchier and Cookie looked over my shoulder and when the deed was done, someone whispered: "About bloody time too!" and they turned and made back to their beds in the semi-darkness.

I think if someone had said that he would have signed on if we followed suit, the Navy may well have suddenly acquired eight new recruits the following day. But no-one did.

I lay in bed thinking of all the remaining members of the class of thirty-two at the other barracks at Pompey and at Guzz. Were they remembering us too? Wee Mac, Andy Gray, Ian Body and Jock from the Western Isles: how did they feel at that moment? I smiled in the darkness; Wee Mac was probably too pissed to care!

What had it all been about? What lessons had we learned from it all? It had most certainly made men of us. We could cope with looking after ourselves domestically. We had seen something of the world and had learned a bit of how the other half lived. It had not been all bad but of course, there were aspects of the life that I would not miss at all. There would be no more standing on the wing of an open bridge during the middle watch, straining my eyes into the darkness of a cold and hostile sea on the look-out for whatever might lurk there. There would be no more hours spent marching about a parade ground with the curses of the Gunnery Instructor ringing in my ears. No more would I suffer the miseries and indignity of wretched seasickness. Nor would I be kept from my home and family and the sport that had been so dear to me.

A bugle called a final "Reveille". In spite of the fact that the Tannoy was not operating in our block for some unknown reason, we all heard it and sat up.

"This is soddin' it, lads!" someone said. It was the last day. A group of submariners watched us in envy.

"Lucky bastards," muttered one from under his counterpane.

The sun blazed in through smoke-stained windows as we dressed in our No. 2s and went to breakfast. We were "caught" by morning Colours on our return across the roadway and stood silently at the salute, as the White Ensign was hoisted to the masthead on the parade ground. That was another thing that we would not have to witness again and yet another part of our daily lives as sailors was to pass into history.

Back in the dormitory, we packed away all of our belongings for the last time, leaving our best uniforms in the lockers ready to change into in just two hours time, when we would finally muster at the main gate for dismissal. We hurried to the bedding store to return our bedding.

I suddenly had a good idea. It had been agreed the night before that we would go out of the gate by taxi, rather than struggle with kitbags on the bus. "Why not put old steaming caps on top of our kitbags and pitch them into the air as we go out of the gate?" I suggested. My mates loved the idea. It would be a last rebellious act and a much better proposition than a two-finger salute to the Jaunty on the gate, as had been suggested the previous evening! We rummaged through our kitbags and retrieved our oldest, most battered caps and put them on the top of the neatly folded clothes within, where they could be easily reached.

We mustered outside the Pay Office. The Wrens inside glared at us through the windows and we decided that although they were by far the most miserable, ugly set of Wrens that we had ever encountered, nothing could dampen our spirits during our last few hours in the Navy. We were called inside, one at a time.

It came to my turn and I stepped into the office as the man before me came out. There was no "off caps, name and number" routine this time. A Lieutenant Commander looked up as I approached his desk.

"Cobbold?" he asked.

"Yes, sir." He smiled.

"Going ashore for the last time, eh?" he grinned. "How does it feel?"

"Very nice, sir!" I replied. He was counting pound notes while a Chief Writer made entries on what appeared to be a pay packet.

"Will you miss the Service, do you think? Have you enjoyed your time with the Navy?" asked the Lt.-Commander.

"To be honest, sir," I said, "I will miss the comradeship and I never thought that I would ever admit it, but I think that I have enjoyed the last year or so. I have been to places that, ordinarily, I would not have had the chance to visit, but I am glad to be going out."

"Well, you are free to change your mind but don't leave it too long, or you will lose your seniority for your next rate." He held out the pay packet. "Here is your pay to the end of your service, together with your discharge papers. Good luck, young man!"

The Chief looked at me, ready to pick me up should I not remember to salute the officer but I did not forget that one!

"Your folder contains quite a few handouts on what to do now that you have left the Service," he said in a broad Scots accent. "If you have any queries, sort them out before going ashore".

"Now that you have left the Service" - those important words that I had so long looked forward to hearing! Strangely, they sounded nowhere as sweet as I had imagined they would.

"Thank you, Chief," I said.

"Next!" he called, without looking up, and Garth entered as I marched out.

We stood out of sight behind some parked handcarts to the side of the Pay Office until the final member of our gang came out of the office with his papers and pay. We went over to the NAAFI to buy our tobacco allotment which was to last us until the beginning of July. My final pay and allowances amounted to £28 13s and it had been a long time since I had had so much money at one time.

"Stand Easy" was piped just as we entered the NAAFI. The usual crowd of loafers had got there before us, even though the NAAFI was not supposed to be open before the pipe was made, and we queued up for our final cigarette ration. In future, cigarettes would cost me 1s 8d for twenty, instead of the 2s 4d per hundred, the current rate for Blue Liners. I would give up smoking anyway, I had decided; it did not go with cycling.

We took a seat and bought a cake and a "goffer", a nickname for a fizzy drink supplied by NAAFI, taking the opportunity to open our packets of discharge papers. The folder, S1596, contained an Order for Release, a document stating that we had finished our service but that we were still on dispersal leave. Our nice crisp travel warrant came out next, and then an International Certificate of Vaccination against smallpox.

A smart blue booklet with a drawing of an anchor was next. It was entitled "For your Guidance", with a sub-title "What To Do On Leaving the Service and How To Do It". The latter part of the sub-title raised several good-humoured remarks. If there was something that we had all learned during our time in the Navy, it was most certainly "How To Do It!"

There was a National Insurance leaflet, NI53, concerning the contribution paid to the National Health Fund on our behalf during our term of service. I made a mental note that when I returned to civilian employment, my National Insurance stamp would cost me 6s 9d!

The next large form, S459, was our Certificate of Service. It listed our service conduct as "Very Good", a sombre judgement awarded to everyone. However, when it came to the Efficiency Assessment, not everyone was listed as being "Satisfactory" and there were four gradings to be allocated; Superior, Satisfactory, Moderate and Inferior.

We sat talking among ourselves, a little subdued by now. Names and addresses had been exchanged and Jim Bouchier, who lived at Southend, said that he intended holding a "coming-out party" as our first reunion.

"Out Pipes" echoed around the tarmac parade ground and we emerged into the bright sunshine to busily make our way to Nelson block. Only three-quarters of an hour remained for us to shift into our best uniform and report to the main gate for dispersal. I was both excited and saddened at once.

The dormitory was empty and sunlit. There was a slight odour of unwashed feet. Noisily, we opened our squeaky aluminium lockers and drew out our uniforms for the last time. There was much laughter and happy banter as we dressed and stowed away our used clothing into the great khaki kitbag, making sure to leave the old steaming cap on the top and within easy reach.

It was 1120. In the dockyard, the ship's crews would be looking at their watches, anticipating the pipe for "Up Spirits" and then "Hands to dinner." The ships at sea would be approaching the end of the forenoon watch and it was a beautiful day to be at sea, with hardly any wind and with a bright, refreshing sun. I could imagine a ship's bow cutting through a glassy sea, the odour of fuel oil and funnel smoke, the rattle of boots on steel ladders and the smell of dinner wafting from the galley where the duty chef leaned on the stable door of his domain, watching the activities of the crew on deck.

Elsewhere, new recruits would be smashing their way across a parade ground, their ears ringing to the exaltations of their "friendly" instructor: "Swing those arms, chest out, chin up! More punch in it, you're like a load of constipated fairies!" We had done all that; it was behind us now.

Two taxis waited at the gate, their drivers leaning on the wing of one car, enjoying the summer sun. I was a little surprised to see that the drivers had been allowed to bring their vehicles inside the gate.

The gate was manned by a large burly naval policeman, a Chief Gunnery Instructor. He glared at us from under the stiff peak of his cap and tucked his pacey stick tighter under his left armpit. Since we were burdened down with kitbag and suitcases, we were excused marching. It was very hot.

"Put your kitbags only in the cars," said the Chief, "and fall in over here with your suitcases." The drivers opened the car boots and we went four to a car, placing our kitbags inside and swiftly stowing the steaming caps inside on the passenger seats, an act made easier as the Chief had his back to us. Even our last instruction was executed too slowly for the Navy's satisfaction, for the Chief found it necessary to speed us on.

"Come on, come on!" he roared. "You'll be late for your own funerals!" We fell in outside the guardroom window with our suitcases. Our taller members stood on the flanks, and I took the centre with Seabag and Garth to either side. We came to attention, picked up our dressing and then stood easy, placing the suitcases alongside our left legs. The Officer of the Day came out of the guard room, tugging at his shirt cuffs.

"Attention!" bellowed the Jaunty. All eight of us snapped up straight. Out of the corner of my eye, I saw the Lieutenant return the Jaunty's regulation style salute.

"Men for Dispersal, ready and correct, sir!"

"Stand them at Ease, Chief," whispered the Officer. This Officer of the Day seemed to have a permanent smile on his face. He took station in front of us. "Stand Easy, men," he said.

He told us about our tobacco ration and reminded us that technically, we were on leave prior to our ultimate discharge on 3rd July, and therefore still subject to naval disciplines and regulations. However, we were free to return to our civilian occupations. I wondered if I should salute my office manager, were I to start work the following Monday?

"I hope that you have enjoyed your period of service with the Royal Navy," said the Lieutenant airily. "Do remember that should you wish to re-enlist, you should do so during this period of leave in order to ensure the continuity of your service. It only remains for me to wish you jolly good luck for the future." He tugged at his cuffs again and turned to the Jaunty. "Carry on ashore the Dispersal Men, Chief!"

We were called to attention again whilst the salutes were exchanged, and the Chief bellowed: "Turning right, dismiss!" I felt numb all over. I was thrilled to bits to be going, but at the same time suddenly full of a strange sort of insecurity, for although I was free to go, I still had no idea to where.

The Chief was actually smiling. I could tell by his manner that it was not something that he often did! The Officer of the Day shook hands with us and we all seemed to say "Thank you, sir!", as if our release was entirely his doing. With a final salute, we made for the cars.

We tumbled excitedly into the seats and wound down the windows. Both cars started up and moved slowly through the black iron gate. The Chief stood grinning grimly at the entrance to the guardroom as we accelerated away.

Once clear of the gate, eight arms shot out of the open car windows and eight old sailor caps arced into the air to a mighty cheer of freedom from their owners, which echoed back off the walls of the Khyber Pass as we sped away.

GENERAL INDEX

Index

INDEX OF SHIPS AND SHORE ESTABLISHMENTS

Index